D1598286

Torah MiEtzion
New Readings in Tanach
Shemot

ישיבת
הר עציון
YESHIVAT
HAR ETZION

מגיד

MAGGID

TORAH MIETZION
New Readings in Tanach

SHEMOT

EDITORS

Rav Ezra Bick &
Rav Yaakov Beasley

Maggid Books
Yeshivat Har Etzion

Torah MiEtzion
New Readings in Tanach
Shemot

First Edition, 2012

Maggid Books
A division of Koren Publishers Jerusalem Ltd.

POB 8531, New Milford, CT 06776-8531, USA
& POB 4044, Jerusalem 91040, Israel

www.korenpub.com

ISBN 978-161-329-0071, *hardcover original*

A CIP catalogue record for this title is
available from the British Library

Printed and bound in USA

כִּי יְדַעְתִּיו לְמַעַן אֲשֶׁר יְצַוֶּה אֶת בָּנָיו וְאֶת בֵּיתוֹ אַחֲרָיו
וְשָׁמְרוּ דֶּרֶךְ ה׳ לַעֲשׂוֹת צְדָקָה וּמִשְׁפָּט
(בראשית יח, יט)

Dedicated in loving memory of
Dr. William Major *z"l*
אברהם זאב בן יהודה ז"ל

A Holocaust survivor and devoted psychiatrist, Dr. Major was animated by a deep love of Torah, Israel and the Jewish People. Through his personal example of quiet dignity and deep commitment to ḥesed and Torah study, he conveyed these values to his family and made an indelible impression on those who were privileged to know him.

Dr. Major cherished Yeshivat Har Etzion, which in his eyes embodied his loves and commitments, and was deeply grateful for all that his children gained there. It is therefore a singularly fitting tribute that this series – which brings the profound and innovative Torah of Yeshivat Har Etzion to the broader public – is dedicated to his memory.

תהא נשמתו צרורה בצרור החיים

Contents

Editor's Preface

This is the second volume of the five-volume series on the Torah, comprising a selection of *shiurim* given on the *parasha* by different lecturers, all of whom are connected in one way or another with Yeshivat Har Etzion. Most of them originally appeared as part of the *parasha* series of the Israel Koschitzky Virtual Beit Midrash, which has been appearing for the last sixteen years and is disseminated over the internet. But the impetus for publication is not merely a desire to repackage a successful and interesting series of *shiurim*. The VBM series has managed to be itself the catalyst for the written expression of a body of work, from different authors, which represents a distinct approach to *parshanut HaTorah*, one which has been developing over the last forty years in the yeshiva and its affiliated Herzog Teacher's College, and which is today the most vibrant and influential school of modern biblical interpretation in the Torah world.

A criticism often raised concerning the approach typified in these volumes is that it ignores classical commentary, or, even worse, denigrates it. I think that even a cursory examination of this work should lay that charge to rest. It is true as I pointed out in the preface to the first volume on *Bereshit*, one of the major calls of this method is to read

Tanach with the assumption that it interprets itself, and I admit that this kind of reading requires one to approach the text initially free of preconceptions. This is how the major medieval commentators themselves read Tanach. Only a fool, however, would imagine that one could safely ignore the centuries of close reading, interpretation, analysis, and understanding granted us by the finest minds of Jewish learning. In fact, a fresh rereading of the text, as it is presented, is a prerequisite for comprehending the classical commentaries, for recognizing the basis of the claims and suggestions found therein. The assumption that one cannot understand Tanach without Rashi renders Rashi unintelligible. That all modern readers need to stand on the shoulders of giants is a given; to believe that one can stand there without the ability to read the holy text itself is absurd. The deeper understanding of the text – and in many cases, of the commentaries themselves – offered in these volumes, testifies to the creativity of this approach.

The importance of this series is not so much in introducing a new method, for I am sure that most readers have had some exposure to it, either directly through reading or hearing one of the authors, or through other similar authors. The importance is in its concentration in one place, demonstrating the power and consistency of reading the entire Tanach in such a manner. It is not a method of producing a *ḥiddush*, or of solving some particular hitherto unexplained problem, but of approaching Tanach as a whole. The book is a recommendation that everyone should read each *parasha* in this way – should read, or perhaps reread, and then reread again, and thereby understand the message and the meaning.

*   *   *

The majority of the essays in this book were originally published in the *parasha* series of the Israel Koschitzky Virtual Beit Midrash (*www.vbm-torah.org*), where tens of thousands of readers have already seen them. They have in some cases been shortened for publication in the book. The archives of the VBM have between ten and fifteen excellent articles on each *parasha*. The originals of the articles published here, as well as all the others, can be accessed on the VBM website.

The article of Rav Aharon Lichtenstein was adapted by Ari

Schwab from a *sicha* delivered to overseas students at Yeshivat Har Etzion on 18 Tevet 5769.

The article of Rav Breuer zt"l is translated from his book *Pirkei Moadot* (Tevunot 1999). The articles of Rav Yoel Bin-Nun and Rav Mordechai Sabato were translated from *Megadim*.

Many more studies in all aspects of Tanach can be found in the fifty volumes of *Megadim*, the Tanach journal of the Herzog College.

Those articles originally written in Hebrew were ably and elegantly translated by Kaeren Fish, David Silverberg, and David Strauss.

In the name of all of the authors, I invite the readers to comment and contribute to the ongoing endeavor *lehagdil Torah uleha'adira*. We hope and pray that these volumes will contribute to the continuous discovery of new and deeper interpretations of *Torat HaShem*.

Ezra Bick
Rosh Ḥodesh Ḥeshvan, 5772

VBM: *http://www.vbm-torah.org*
VBM *parasha* archives: *http://www.vbm-torah.org/parsha.htm*
Correspondence: office@etzion.org.il

Introduction

Individual and National Identity

Adapted from a lecture by
Rav Aharon Lichtenstein

Two questions bothered the commentators about the opening verses of Exodus. First, the *sefer* begins with the conjunctive *"vav"* – *"Ve'eileh Shemot – And these are the names of the children of Israel."* Why does the *sefer* begin with an apparent linkage to the preceding story? Second, what is the need for this list of names in the first place? The list has already been recorded, in greater detail, in *Parashat Vayigash*. Why is it repeated now, at the beginning of Exodus?

Let us focus on one midrash (*Shemot Rabba* 1:3) adapted by Rashi (1:1, s.v. *ve'eileh*):

> Although the Torah enumerated them by name while they were living, it enumerates them again when it tells us of their deaths, thus showing how dear they were [to God], that they are compared to the stars, which God brings out and brings in by number

and by name, as the verse states, "He brings out their host by number; He calls them all by name" [Isaiah 40:26].

Repeated enumeration is an expression of fondness. This is true on a personal or psychological plane, but it translates into a cosmic dimension as well.

This idea is also mentioned at the beginning of Numbers, a book in which *Benei Yisrael* are counted twice – in *Parashat Bemidbar* and in *Parashat Pinḥas*. There, the Midrash notes that if someone possesses something dear, he counts it again and again. I had a stamp collection as a child, and I would count those stamps over and over, even though I knew how many there were. In the beginning, those objects are not only counted – they are mentioned by name.

The Midrash (*Shemot Rabba* 1:2) also addresses our first question by contrasting the opening word, "*Ve'eileh*" with "*eileh*." The latter, the Midrash explains, refers to a break from the past. At the beginning of Creation, the Torah states, "אֵלֶּה תוֹלְדוֹת הַשָּׁמַיִם וְהָאָרֶץ" – "These are the generations of the heavens and the earth" (Gen. 2:4). The term "*eileh*" is employed because Creation marked a break from what came before. Creation signified the introduction of order as opposed to "תֹהוּ וָבֹהוּ" – "unformed and void" (Gen. 1:2), design as opposed to chaos. In our verse, however, the term used is "*ve'eileh*," indicating continuity; it lets us know that the seventy souls mentioned earlier were righteous, as were those who follow. Accordingly, there is nothing substantive added to our understanding, evaluation or appreciation of the twelve tribes simply by dint of relating to them, hovering over them as it were, numbering and naming them. It is simply an expression of affection.

Seforno (1:1, s.v. *eileh*) suggests a different answer. Each tribe needed to be named to single out each one's stature, status or virtue, as opposed to subsequent generations, who assimilated or lingered in passive spirituality. Rashbam (1:1, s.v. *ve'eileh*) says that the word "*ve'eileh*" is used to contrast the initial paucity of the group with the subsequent population explosion.

THE TRIBES OF GENESIS AND EXODUS

What is the difference between Genesis and Exodus? Broadly speaking, the first book is about individuals and families. The families are of two kinds. Some are mentioned in lists of fathers and sons, such as the descendants of Noaḥ, Esau and Ishmael. There is a paterfamilias and subsequently a family identity. The *avot* (patriarchs), however, are different. They are promised large families, but they are also individuals, and this individuality is emphasized by each one being mentioned separately, each with his own *berit* (covenant) and his own mode of *avodat HaShem* (divine service). This is why we mention all three individually in the first *berakha* of the *Shemoneh Esrei*. In composing that *tefilla*, Ḥazal took their cue from *Parashat Shemot*; at the burning bush, God identifies himself as both "God of your forefathers" generally and as "God of Abraham, God of Isaac, and God of Jacob," individually (Ex. 3:6). God did not wait for Moses to ask, "And they shall say to me, 'What is His name,' what shall I tell them?" (3:13). He offered His calling card, as it were, already in their first encounter, mentioning all three patriarchs separately. There is only one God and only one genealogy of the Jewish People, but mention is made of the *avot* on two planes; HaShem is God of each one separately as well as collectively.

Genesis, then, focuses on familial events, with tragedy, struggles and strife. We get to know each of the characters, certainly the primary ones, at one level or another.

Exodus, as Ramban says in his introduction, is about community, the forging of the entity of the Jewish nation. The promise of nationhood was given to the *avot* in Genesis, but Exodus is the story of how this was accomplished. Major components of this process are narrative, with each episode adding elements to the composite. One element of the book is the forging of national identity through the trials and tribulations in Egypt. Ḥazal describe in numerous places (e.g. Zohar, *Shir HaShirim* 25b) that "they went down to Egypt for catharsis, and emerged from the purging furnace complete," based on the reference to Egypt as "כּוּר הַבַּרְזֶל" – a furnace, a forge (Deut. 4:20). The exodus from Egypt added another dimension to this identity, and a further tier came with *Matan Torah*, when the Jewish People received the Torah. Then, as Ramban notes at the beginning of *Parashat Teruma* (25:2, s.v. *ka'asher*), the building of the *Mishkan*, the Tabernacle, brought the Presence of God into the collective.

Exodus is a book concerned with the forging of a collective identity. That being the case, it will not do to rely on the list of names from *Parashat Vayigash*. There, the children of Jacob are listed in terms of their personal identities, as individuals, as parts of a family unit – but nothing more. They are not the fountainheads of a community. Exodus does not list the individual children of Jacob, but the beginnings of the tribes. This is true not only in a practical or historical sense, as they were the ancestors of the Jewish People, but in a halakhic sense as well.

The Torah describes *Matan Torah* as "יוֹם הַקָּהָל" – "the day of the community" (Deut. 9:10, 10:4, 18:16). In some contexts, "*kahal*" refers to the whole of the Jewish People, embracing all the tribes. The entire nation participated in the revelation at Sinai. Yet there is also a sense that each tribe has a distinct identity.

Ramban notes at the beginning of *Parashat Shofetim* (Deut. 16:18, s.v. *veta'am*) that judges must be appointed "*bishe'arekha*," "in your gates," and "*lishevatekha*," "for your tribes." Based on the Gemara, Ramban explains that in addition to the local court required in every city, each tribe in the city must have its own court. This court has the same authority for that tribe as the high court has for all of Israel; it can establish edicts and decrees and the like. A tribe is a mini-nation. This arrangement is similar to the federal and state courts in the American judicial system.

Ramban connects this point to another discussion. The Torah states in *Parashat Vayikra* (Lev. 4:13–21) that if the court errs and most of the nation follows the erroneous ruling, the burden of guilt is not upon the individuals who listened, but on the court. The judges must therefore bring a sin offering. Although this is subject to a dispute between *Tannaim* (*Horayot* 5a), we rule that each tribe is considered a separate unit and must bring its own sin offering in such a case. Families, sub-units of the tribes, are not considered separately – they are simply part of their tribe.

By mentioning the tribes again at the beginning of Exodus, the Torah grants them a new capacity. Earlier, they were mentioned as individuals. Here, they are not individuals, the sons of Jacob, but rather fountainheads, founding fathers; they are the beginning of what Exodus is all about. This is a different role historically speaking; it is a different type of life.

The Midrash adds something that rounds out this point and simultaneously, seemingly, undermines it. Rashi quotes a verse in Isaiah (40:26) about stars: "He brings out their host by number; He calls them all by name." The Midrash itself cites a more familiar verse, which we recite daily in *Shaḥarit*: "מוֹנֶה מִסְפָּר לַכּוֹכָבִים לְכֻלָּם שֵׁמוֹת יִקְרָא" – "He counts the number of the stars; He calls them all by their names" (Psalms 147:4). According to both verses, the stars are first counted and then named. Rav Yehuda Amital often distinguished between these two aspects, between "*mispar*" and "*shemot*." A number is a quantitative assessment that relates to each element as part of a collective. In counting, the individual can get lost. Names, on the other hand, are about forging unique identities. If there are two people in the same town with the same name, some identity is lost. In fact, there are halakhic problems in such a case with regard to the giving of a *get* and with regard to loans (e.g. *Gittin* 24b and *Bava Batra* 167b).

We deal with stars as numbers, parts of a galaxy, supernovae, or whatever contexts they are involved in. But each star also has a personal identity. The juxtaposition of these two elements means that we need to speak of two identities – each person has a unique name, and each exists as a member of the Jewish People. Collective identity does not uproot personal identity, but adds to it. This is the meaning of the linking "*vav*" of "*ve'eileh*"; being a founding father does not uproot or substitute for the personal identity of the tribe, but adds on to it.

DUAL IDENTITY

This brings us back not only to the verses, but to ourselves. When and where are we better off – as part of the organic unity of *Benei Yisrael* or somewhere out there in the Diaspora? There are certain aspects of spiritual identity that can be developed in the Diaspora. Some aspects of one's personality can be developed without regard to the Jewish past or future. These, in and of themselves, should not be dismissed; we can obtain the status of a *ben Torah* in Johannesburg or New York, and this is important for the Jewish People and doubly important for the individual Jew.

Nevertheless, our fullness as Jews is obtained best, most richly and completely, in *Eretz Yisrael*, which lets us live lives as rich and full as possible in terms of *avodat HaShem*, our service of God.

The concept of dual identity is not limited to Jews. The question of division of identity concerns not only students of social history or philosophy, but those living in certain countries at certain times. In the Greco-Roman world, as compared to the modern world, collective identity occupied a very central place – are you a Greek or a barbarian, and if you are a Greek – from where? But the modern world – this is the heart of liberalism – does not like collective identity, favoring instead individual predilection, orientation, self-fulfillment, etc. The difference is partly that of outlook, but it is also existential.

Broadly speaking, there are two stages – the book of Genesis, before national identity is formed, and post facto, when we can put the national facet aside to focus on individual growth. In between is the book of Exodus, the time when we need to focus on collective identity.

Recent history in *Eretz Yisrael* demonstrates this process. Before the *Yishuv* was settled, each person was separate; there was little of cohesiveness. What nation existed here? Others, be they Ottoman or British, were in charge. So we could focus on individual development, as indeed those in Eastern Europe or North Africa did. As things came to a head, as we envisioned a collective community and state, collectivism became very dominant. The kibbutz was the fullest expression of this trend, but it was also expressed in other elements, such as education. As the country increasingly became perceived to be, if not self-sufficient, at least solvent, the focus on oneself at the expense of the country began its gradual ascent.

This issue faces us as *benei Torah*, as members of the nation, and, for many, as citizens of Israel. The important thing is to retain the linking "*vav*" – "*ve'eileh*." A Jew must recognize that the collective and the personal are intertwined, no matter which he chooses to superimpose on the other. We do not have purely individual or collective identities. This outlook is necessary to live as an *oved HaShem*, as a servant of God; it is important not only for socio-political but also for religious purposes.

The Ba'al HaTanya (*Likutei Torah, Parashat Re'eh*) notes that prayer must contain two elements – we must address God both as individuals and as a community. Similarly, we speak of *teshuva* (repentance) of the individual and *teshuva* of the community. One little "*vav*" makes all the difference.

Let us be certain that in our lives, this "*vav*" is not diminished further; it must be part of a context that, like the yeast in dough, helps forge and mold our total identity.

Parashat Shemot

The Double Birth of Moses

Rav Elchanan Samet

I. FROM ONE MOTHER TO ANOTHER

The Torah introduces the story of the birth of Moses at the beginning of chapter 2 of Exodus. Three stages of Moses' salvation in the story's second half form an inverse parallel to the three stages of increasing danger in the first half, nullifying them completely, as follows:

1. The concealment (v. 2):
   And she saw him, that he was good, and she concealed him for three months.
   2. Placing the ark in the river, under his sister's supervision (v. 3–4):
   She took for him an ark of gopher wood … and she placed the child inside it, and placed [it] in the reeds at the river bank. His sister stationed herself at a distance, to know what would become of him.
      3. Pharaoh's daughter finds the ark (v. 5–6):
      And Pharaoh's daughter went down to bathe upon the river … and she saw the ark … and she opened, and saw him – the child.
         3A. Pharaoh's daughter has mercy on the child (v. 6):

[A]nd behold – a child crying, and she had compassion for him and said: This is one of the Hebrew
children.

2A. The sister suggests that the child be given over to a wet-
nurse (v. 7–8):
And his sister said to Pharaoh's daughter, "should I go and
call on your behalf for a wet-nurse from the Hebrews"...
and she said... "Go."

1A. The child is openly returned to his mother (v. 8–9):
And the young girl went and called the mother of the child,
and Pharaoh's daughter said to her: "Take this child and nurse
him for me...." And the woman took the child and nursed him.

Does verse 10 fall outside the framework of the inverse parallel
upon which the story is built? Not necessarily. Verse 10 corresponds to
the story's introduction in verses 1–2:

And a man from the house of Levi went and took a daughter of
Levi; and the woman conceived and *bore a son.* (v. 1–2)

And the child grew up and she brought him to the daughter of
Pharaoh *and he became a son unto her,* and she called his name
Moses, and she said: "For I drew him (*meshitihu*) from the water."
(v. 10)

In an article in Megadim (#22, Tammuz 5754), Rav David Tee explains:

The story opens with the birth of this son, and concludes
with the adoption of the son. In a certain sense, these framing verses of the story conveys the essence of what happens,
while the plot that develops within the framing verses is simply an expansion of it.... The framing verses therefore express
the story's essence, the exchange of mothers. It would seem
appropriate for the pattern of "and she conceived... and she
bore... and she called him" to occur in succession, such as we
find in the case of many other mothers who give birth, but this

4

is not what happens here.... The child is transferred from the guardianship of one mother to that of a different one.... The calling of the name ... is done by Pharaoh's daughter, rather than by the natural mother. The plot describes the transition from the house of the mother to the house of Pharaoh's daughter, but the framing verses illuminate the way in which Pharaoh's daughter truly steps into the shoes of the mother, becoming the one who leaves her stamp upon him.

II. THE MEANING OF THE NAME "MOSHE"

Rabbi Tee correctly perceives that the crux of the "exchange of mothers" is expressed in the child's naming. The right to choose the child's name is often reserved for the mother in biblical stories describing a birth, while in our case this right is reserved for Pharaoh's daughter. Certainly, Moses had a name from Amram and Yokheved before he was weaned and returned to Pharaoh's daughter. But the text only records the name given to him by Pharaoh's daughter, thereby confirming and approving the legality of her status of motherhood.

The right to choose the name is not always given to the biological mother. For example, Rachel and Leah choose the names of the children of their maidservants; for they see themselves as the mothers of those sons. They gave the maidservants to Jacob in order that the children who would be born would be considered theirs.

What is it that makes Pharaoh's daughter – both in her own eyes and in the eyes of the narrative – Moses' mother? As we shall see, Pharaoh's daughter herself answers this question in the very name that she selects.

Is "Moshe" the original name that Pharaoh's daughter gives him? This creates two problems. First, she did not speak Hebrew; why give her adopted son a Hebrew name that would be out of place in his royal Egyptian environment? Second, if she gave him a Hebrew name that was meant to hint at the circumstances of the beginning of their relationship – "For I drew him out of the water" – then his name in Hebrew should be *"Mashui"* (literally, "drawn"), not "Moshe." Even if we were to conjecture that that "Moshe" is the Hebrew translation of the original name in Egyptian, this question remains pertinent.

Professor Umberto Cassuto addresses these questions in his commentary on Exodus:

> The naming is to be explained in a different way. First, it is stated that "he became her son"; and she called his name Moshe, that is, *son* in Egyptian.... Thereafter it is stated, in the manner of homiletical name-etymologies, that the sound of this Egyptian name recalled the Hebrew verb מָשָׁה ["draw out"], and it appeared as though the princess had this in mind ("for she said" = "for she thought"): "Because I drew him out of the water."[1]

"Moshe" is therefore an Egyptian name, meaning "son." Pharaoh's daughter declares that the child she is adopting is her legal son, and accordingly she is giving him his name: "And he became a son to her – and she called his name 'a son.'"

But how does the text attribute to Pharaoh's daughter a midrashic reason for the name based on the Hebrew, one completely different meaning from her original intention; a meaning that could not possibly have occurred to her?

The Netziv was familiar with this explanation for the name "Moshe," based on the ancient Egyptian, and accepted it. His explanation of verse 10 solves the problem above:

> "And he became a son unto her" – Since she saved him from death and also raised him, it was considered as though she had given birth to him, as she says: "And she called his name Moshe." And I have seen written in the name of Rabbi Shmuel of Bohemia, that in the Egyptian language, this word in this form means "son"... and this interpretation is correct.
>
> Thus she explains the reason why the child is hers: "for I drew him out of the water" – for it is as if he drowned in the river, and so his father and mother have no portion in him, and I am the mother of the child....
>
> Accordingly, the word "*meshitihu*" (I drew him out) is not

---

1. U. Cassuto, A Commentary on the Book of Exodus, Jerusalem, 1967, pp. 20–21.

related to the name Moshe, but rather explains why she called him ["son," i.e.] Moshe. (Ha'amek Davar, Exodus 2:10)

Pharaoh's daughter does explain the name that she gives the child ("Moshe," meaning in Egyptian "my son," or "my child") by the fact that she saved him from drowning in the river, thereby acquiring him for herself. When the Torah comes to translate her thought or her statement – which was formulated in Egyptian – into Hebrew, it does so through a play on words. Therefore there is no discrepancy between the name "Moshe" and its reason – "for I drew him out of water," for the reason pertains not to the etymology of the name (which is actually Egyptian), but rather to the legal basis for her being the one to give him his name.

III. BIBLICAL STORIES OF "REBIRTH"

The story of Moses' birth belongs to the series of biblical narratives whose subject is the "rebirth" of the main character. In a story of rebirth we find a baby, young child or youth, whose life is endangered to the point where he nearly dies. He is miraculously saved from that danger, and his life is returned to him as a gift. The Tanach relates to this miracle as a sort of rebirth of the child. Among the 'children' who experience rebirths are Ishmael in the wilderness of Be'er Sheva, Isaac after the *Akeda*, Joseph after being thrown into the pit, the episode of the resuscitation of the Shunamite woman's son by Elisha (II Kings 4) and Yoash, saved from the hands of Atalia by Yehosheva, his sister (II Kings 11:1–3).[2]

In each of these stories, the rebirth signifies the beginning of the child's existence on a different level – his existence is imbued with a new destiny. The nature and purpose of this destiny are always connected to the nature of the danger in which he found himself and the way in which he was saved, which themselves always hint at this difference in his future existence. In order to achieve this new level of existence or this new destiny, he had to be at death's door, and then merit the miracle of salvation. The miracle itself, and the special circumstances through which it comes about, create a change in the personality of the child,

---

2. See Rabbi Samet's shiur online at *http://www.vbm-torah.org/parsha.60/04vayera. htm* for an expansion of this idea.

making it clear to him and to all those around him that from now on a new chapter is starting in his life, in which his destiny will be realized.

A comparison of the above stories reveals several differences between them. They may be babies (Moses, Yoash), toddlers just weaned (Samuel), young children (Isaac and the son of the Shunamite), or youths (Ishmael, Joseph). The rebirth of the youths signifies their entry into a different adulthood than what awaited them had they remained within their families: Ishmael enters into a life of desert freedom as a "wild man"; while Joseph enters a life of slavery, preparing him for the rise to greatness in Egypt and for the role that he is destined to play in saving his family. The rebirth of the babies and the just-weaned toddler (Moses, Samuel, and Yoash) is meant to mold their childhood in a world very different from the one into which they were born naturally, in order that each of them will develop from childhood onwards to be suitable for a great and new national leadership role. The rebirth of the children (Isaac and the son of the Shunamite) is meant to mold the attitude of their parents towards them, such that they will relate to them on a different level than was the case before.

In the case of Moses, the metaphor of rebirth is closest to its original meaning. Moses emerges anew into the world from the sealed ark that was floating upon the water, and upon reemerging – with his life given back to him again, as it were – he acquires a new mother. Later on she will adopt him as her son, give him his name and mold his education and his environment from early childhood until maturity.

IV. MOSES' "REBIRTH" – HIS FUTURE ROLE

Why was it necessary for Moses – future savior of Israel – to be "reborn" in the unique circumstances described in our *parasha*? Why was it necessary for him to pass from his biological, Jewish mother to an adoptive Egyptian mother – and why did she have to be the daughter of Pharaoh?

Ibn Ezra provides an in-depth and detailed response to these questions in his long commentary (on verse 3), and hints at three answers:

First, Moses had to grow up specifically in the royal palace, "that his soul might be habituated to be on the highest level ... not lowly and accustomed to being in a house of slaves." Ibn Ezra is acutely conscious of the profound psychological significance of exile and enslavement on the collective psyche of *Benei Yisrael* and on each individual among them.[3]

Leading the nation of Israel in this generation, in which the battle for freedom will occur, there must be a leader who is himself free. Such a leader cannot arise from among the ranks of the oppressed, degraded masses of slaves. Prolonged oppression creates a lowly soul, and the nation accustoms itself to injustice and mistreatment as though it were a normal social arrangement. Moses encountered this slave mentality when one of the Israelites criticized him: "Do you mean to kill me as you killed the Egyptian?" But Moses had killed the Egyptian because he "struck a Hebrew man, of his brothers!" This same Israelite, it appears – or one of his friends – was the one who brought the killing of the Egyptian to Pharaoh's attention. Immediately, "Pharaoh heard this thing and sought to kill Moses, and Moses fled."

In order to cultivate a free leader whose soul has not been warped by chains, there was a need for him to be completely severed from the company of his fellow Jews from earliest childhood. He had to grow up in a social environment of free people – preferably, in the royal palace. This would give him the self-awareness of a prince, a member of the Egyptian royalty, allowing him later to stand before Pharaoh without fear, and to conduct the negotiations with him in the accepted way and using the mannerisms he had learned in childhood, in Pharaoh's own court.

Second, Moses' education in the Egyptian royal palace presented a danger from the opposite direction, the danger of identification with the oppressor and the social norms prevalent in Egypt, out of a sense of belonging to the royal family. This danger appears even more severe, and no less likely, than its predecessor.

It appears from the story that Pharaoh's daughter never tried to blur Moses' origins, the fact that he was "one of the Hebrew children," and therefore she agreed to give him to "a wet-nurse from among the Hebrews." From the fact that Moses later "went out to his brothers," we learn that he was aware of his ethnic origin. But the danger was that

---

3. See his long commentary on Exodus 14:13, discussing why the Jewish people did not attack the Egyptians by the Red Sea even though they enjoyed far superior numbers.

Moses himself, who had grown up in the Egyptian palace, would seek to deny his origin.

Here we must pay attention to the identity of Moses' "second mother," in whose home Moses was educated. She was the daughter of Pharaoh who, in the crucial moral test that she faced at the river, made her decision and acted against her father's decree, showing compassion to the Hebrew baby. According to her father's decree, he should have been cast into the river to die. By saving the Hebrew baby's life, and by adopting him as her son, Pharaoh's daughter gave wordless expression to her opposition to her father's policy of enslavement and murder.

Although Moses grows up in the Egyptian palace, his name and the circumstances that brought about his upbringing there – which had never been hidden from him by his adoptive mother – constantly reminded him of his origins and identity, and this sharpened the fundamental difference between himself – a refugee born of an oppressed nation – and his noble Egyptian surroundings.

Paradoxically, it was specifically Moses' upbringing in the very heart of evil – in Pharaoh's palace – that gave him the ability to negate completely the enslavement of his nation and to regard it as an injustice requiring correction.

Ibn Ezra perceives the continuation of our chapter as proof of Moses' moral character, formed in the home of Pharaoh's daughter: "Do we not find that he killed the Egyptian *because he had committed unjust violence*, and that he saved the daughters of Midian from the shepherds *because the latter performed unjust violence*?" Although the condition for engaging in such acts is that "his soul not be lowly and accustomed to being in a house of slaves," this condition is not sufficient. Even someone who grows up free does not necessarily object to every act of moral injustice, unless he has a moral personality. Moses had such a personality.

Finally, Ibn Ezra notes that it was not only the educational aspect that necessitated Moses' upbringing as a free person in the royal palace, but also the future social and political requirements of *Benei Yisrael*. In order to be accepted by his brethren as a respected leader, Moses had to approach them "from the outside." Here, too, we must add that the royal Egyptian background with which Moses presents himself to his people must have increased his importance in their eyes, and their identification with someone who had chosen to return to his oppressed people in order to redeem them from servitude.

V. EXCHANGE OF MOTHERS TO FOIL PHARAOH'S DECREE

Our story serves a dual purpose; it is not only the "story of Moses' birth," the birth of the person destined to save Israel from Egyptian bondage, but also the continuation of the narrative in chapter 1, a story illustrating how Pharaoh's decrees against the growth of *Benei Yisrael* were foiled.

The motif of Moses'"rebirth" at the hands of Pharaoh's daughter is meant to serve this second purpose, too. Attention should be paid to the wondrous turnabout that takes place in our story. Pharaoh decrees, "Every son that is born shall be cast into the river," and in this instance it is the child's own mother who places him in the river. She certainly does not "cast" him there, heaven forbid, but rather places him lovingly in an ark, in an effort to do whatever she can to protect his young life. Nevertheless, in this act the mother is somehow fulfilling – against her will – the decree of Pharaoh. The child's life is indeed in grave danger.

Who saves the life of this child, drawing him from the river and thereby nullifying Pharaoh's decree? None other than Pharaoh's own daughter! This illustrates a wonderful victory over that decree. Even at the moment when his decree seemed to be attaining its objective – to the point where *Benei Yisrael* themselves seem to be partially collaborating with it – we find the divine agent coming to cancel the decree from within Pharaoh's own royal palace.

From this point of view, Pharaoh's daughter continues the work of the midwives (who, according to a literal reading of the text, were themselves Egyptian women), who not only refused to cooperate with Pharaoh's secret instruction, but actively "gave life to the children." Likewise, Pharaoh's daughter not only fails to cast one of the Israelite children into the river, but actually draws him out from there and gives him life. But in light of the circumstances of Pharaoh's new decree "to all his nation," it is not enough to draw him out of the water; she must be ready to bring him up under her guardianship and in her home in order that the child will live.

With the completion of Moses' "rebirth," when he enters Pharaoh's daughter's home and receives his new name, "Moses," it becomes clear to him and his parents, as well as to readers of the narrative, that a great change has taken place in his life. A great new destiny has been added to his existence – a destiny for which he must grow up in this new and surprising environment, Pharaoh's palace. The child drawn from the water by divine grace and through the good heart of a God-fearing Egyptian woman is destined to devote his life to drawing his brethren from the waters of Egypt – the troubled waters in which they are trapped, and the waters of the Red Sea through which they will pass as a redeemed people.

From Egyptian Prince to Israelite Redeemer

Rav Ezra Bick

It is a commonplace of rabbinic commentary that Genesis is the story of individuals – the forefathers, and Exodus is the story of a people. For instance, this is one explanation given for the repetition of the verse "And these are the names of the Israelites who came to Egypt" (Gen. 46:8 and Ex. 1:1). Our *parasha* repeats this census in order to introduce "And the Israelites reproduced and swarmed and multiplied and were strengthened greatly, and the land was filled with them" (Ex. 1:7) – in other words, the individuals became a people.

Obviously, there is one outstanding individual personality in Exodus; however, it would not be correct to say that the central theme of Exodus is the life-story of Moses. Nonetheless, there can be no question that his personality is an important focus of the story of the exodus, at least to the extent that it is an important factor in the development of the people of Israel. As Moses plays a crucial role in the formation of the people, the Torah tells his personal story and highlights his character traits in order to help us understand how a motley gang of slaves becomes the chosen people. This is most clearly true in Moses' personal history before God's revelation to him at the burning bush. I therefore wish to examine four linked incidents: the Egyptian striking the Hebrew, the two fighting Hebrews, Pharaoh's attempt on Moses' life, and the rescue of the daughters of the priest of Midian. These incidents are recounted in nearly telegraphic brevity, with only about two verses each. Therefore, we will have to read them very closely to pick up the hints and meanings in each episode.

I. FIRST DAY OUT

> And it came about in those days, and Moses grew and went out to his brethren and saw their suffering; and he saw an Egyptian striking a Hebrew of his brethren. (Ex. 2:11)

The opening is very puzzling. "In those days" – what days? Surely not the days described in the previous verse: "And the child grew and she brought him to the daughter of Pharaoh and he became her child; and she called his name Moses, for I drew him from the water" (v. 10). This describes the age when he was weaned, and was big enough to be separated from his nurse-mother. In fact, using a stylistic form, which will be repeated several times in this *parasha*, the Torah distinguishes between Moses' age in these two verses by using the same phrase twice. Twice, in two consecutive verses, the Torah states that "Moses grew." Clearly the verb must mean different things, or else it would not have been repeated. Rashi suggests "the first (growing) is size, and the second is position, as Pharaoh appointed him over his house." This interpretation grants different meanings to the two instances of the verb "grew." Ramban comments simply, "He grew and became a man...in the previous instance it says the 'child grew' until he no longer needed to be weaned... and afterwards he grew and became a man of intelligence." The verb's meaning is the same, but refers to two different and distinct stages, one in infancy and one much later. Since it is clear that Moses has grown a great deal, this makes the phrase "in those days" difficult to understand.

Continuing the verse, we note that twice the Torah refers to the Jews as "his brethren." Moses goes out "to his brethren," and he sees an Egyptian striking a Hebrew "of his brethren." The Torah reveals what lies behind Moses' actions – not curiosity, not only a protest against injustice, not merely a desire to help the persecuted and the weak, but a deep identification with his brethren, with his brothers. Moses, in this story, is not being held up as a paradigm of universal justice, but as a champion of his own people. This is made clear by the second instance of a polysemic twin, the double-but-different verb case. Moses "*sees* their suffering" and he "*sees* an Egyptian striking a Hebrew." Rashi, on the first "seeing," comments: "He prepared his eyes and heart to feel sorry for them." The two instances of "seeing" in the verse do not have the same meaning. The second means to see in the normal sense. The first however does not refer to mere perception. This is clear by the grammatical form of the Hebrew – "vayar *besivlotam*." The suffering is not the direct object of his seeing ("vayar *et* sivlotam"). He "saw" *into* their suffering. Rashi explains that "vayar *be-*" means to understand, to delve into, including identification, to open not only one's eyes but one's heart as well, as opposed to "vayar *et*" which is mere sense-perception.

This takes place because Moses is not facing slaves or foreigners, but, from the onset, "his brethren." Even before he saw them, he had gone out "to his brethren." He is searching for his brothers, and therefore he "commiserates with their suffering" upon seeing it. Therefore, when he sees, in the normal sense, an Egyptian (not a brother) striking a Hebrew "*of his brethren*," he reacts not by writing a letter to the editor of the Nile Times, but by striking the Egyptian dead. Moses is not a judge or superior, but one with the suffering slave. He is a protagonist in this conflict, not a referee.

This explains the opening of the verse. We have learnt that Moses is being brought up in Pharaoh's house as a son of Pharaoh's daughter. In that house, the Egyptians are his brethren. And then, "in those days," i.e., from within that social framework; Moses "went out" to his real brethren, to those in whom he discovered his brotherhood and identity. The Torah emphasizes, in the words "in those days," that Moses' heart beats with a Jewish identity – not as a natural result of a good Jewish upbringing – but rather in spite of his upbringing, because he had chosen to identify in such, because, in Rashi's words, "he has prepared his eyes and his heart." The Torah is emphasizing the opposition of "those days" with "his brethren," with the passage from one to the other indicated by the verb "went out."

The protagonists in this story have no names – there is "the Egyptian" and there is "the Hebrew." Even Moses loses his name after the initial "going out." He simply joins his brethren and becomes one of them. The stirring in Moses' soul is national identification, not personal ethics and not justice.

II. THE SECOND DAY

> He went out on the second day, and behold, two Hebrew persons were fighting; and he said to the evil one, "why do you strike your fellow?" (v. 13)

We already know that "to go out" for Moses means leaving the Egyptian household where he still lives in order to join his Israelite brethren. Imagine then the chagrin and disappointment the idealistic Moses, just beginning to be swept up in his new-found identification with his suffering brothers, so soon after he put his life on the line for the national ideal, must feel when the sight that meets his eyes on the second day is two Hebrews, two of his brothers, fighting between themselves. Notice that here the verb is missing, the Torah does not say "and he *saw* two Hebrew persons." This verb has been set aside for the eyes of Moses that have been "prepared to feel sorry for them." The sight of the second day cannot be grasped by the eyes and heart of Moses who is "going out" to his brethren. How does Moses, the Jewish patriot, react?

Moses remonstrates, "why do you strike your *fellow* (*re'akha*)?" He does not call one the "*brother*" of the other, and the Torah does not remind us here that they are his brothers. Moses does not see them now as brothers of his, and surely not as brothers of each other. The word "*ehav*," brethren, in the previous story, does not designate a familial relationship, nor an ethical one (as in "all men are brothers"), but the heartfelt bond of identification and shared destiny that Moses has discovered the previous day. On this, the second day, it is not present between them, and Moses does not react on the basis of his feelings from yesterday. Rather, here is Moses as the ethical personality. Perhaps Moses' willingness to assume the role of the ethical teacher derives from his feelings of responsibility as a "brother," but the reaction itself is very different from the leap of commitment from the day before. Moses' rebuke assumes a measure of objectivity, of distancing, which is quite the opposite of the spontaneous identification of yesterday.

The "evil one" immediately senses this:

And he said: "Who has made you *a ruler and judge* over us; are you planning to kill me, as you killed the Egyptian?" (v. 14)

He accuses Moses of being, not his brother, but a judge. All of a sudden Moses has, in a manner not explicated in the text, identified the guilty party (two Hebrews are fighting, but Moses speaks to "the evil one"). He is discriminating (in the sense of distinguishing), rather than embracing any Jew simply because he is a Jew. That is exactly what the "evil one," this early Jewish patriot, is angry about. Are you going to treat me, your brother, as you treated the Egyptian, a stranger to you?

This, I think, is what Moses fears. "And Moses feared and said: Indeed, the matter is known." The deliberately enigmatic phrase, "the matter (*hadavar*) is known," elicits many midrashic interpretations. I would suggest that it includes not merely the fact of the killing of the Egyptian, but the attitude that lay behind it – that Moses no longer identified as an Egyptian himself but had joined, in heart and soul, the Jews. This made him a rebel, an Israelite who had risen and killed an Egyptian, and not merely a royal delinquent, who presumably would not have been punished too severely by his foster-grandfather in despotic Egypt.

We have seen two sides of Moses, Moses the Jewish patriot, and Moses the ethical judge. In both cases, Moses had to "go out"; that is, leave his Egyptian background, in order to come to grips with these two new and dialectical sides of his personality. This "going out," transcending of one's childhood training and natural personality, now becomes even more extreme, as Moses has to flee Egypt.

III. EXODUS

The third incident is the most concise of all, completely described in one packed verse:

Pharaoh heard about this matter, and sought to kill Moses, and Moses fled from Pharaoh; and he *sat* in the land of Midian, and he sat by the well. (v. 15)

Most English translations state that Moses did not *sit* in the land of Midian, he *settled* there. That is quite correct. This highlights the third example of our polysemic twins – in both cases and in very close proximity the Torah uses the verb "*yashav*." But of course "*yashav*" in a country means to dwell or to settle, whereas when Moses came to the well, he sat down by its side. This merely highlights the real question – the order of the verse is clearly backwards! Moses is fleeing Pharaoh, arrives in Midian, and comes to the well. First he sits down, and only later could he be said to settle. In fact, any mention of settling should be postponed until after the story of Reuel's daughters, since Moses presumably has no home at all in Midian until he is brought to their house. Why does the Torah say immediately after "Moses fled" that he settled in Midian, and only afterwards begin the story of the well and the seven daughters?

This story, as opposed to the first two (and the fourth), does not describe an act of might or bravery. Moses flees from the danger into which he has been placed. I would suggest, though, that this is not merely a bridge to the next story, Moses' confrontation with the shepherds of Midian. The verse is so detailed that it seems impossible to view it only as an explanation how Moses happened to be in Midian. The Netziv points out that the expression "Moses fled from Pharaoh" is unnecessary and the verse would have read just as well had it said, "Pharaoh sought to kill Moses and Moses fled to Midian." I think the answer is that the Torah wishes to stress not just the geographical movement, but the completion of the cultural break. Moses is fleeing *from Pharaoh*, is completely breaking his connection to the Egyptian royal house. Possibly, even though Moses identifies with his brethren and feels their suffering, he might still seek to help them from a position of power within the Egyptian system. Pharaoh forces him to flee for his life, and it is not important only that Moses flee *to* Midian, but even more that he is fleeing *from* Pharaoh.

As such, Moses is in a difficult and strange position now. Cut off from his Egyptian roots, he has not found himself welcomed by the Jews either. His one encounter has in fact led to his banishment. Moses, forced to flee from Pharaoh, is (perhaps subconsciously) heading to *settle* in Midian. This is the meaning of the juxtaposition of "Moses fled from Pharaoh" and "he settled in the land of Midian." He has not actually done any action that could be construed as settling – on the contrary, he has no place of his own and therefore sits, a homeless stranger, by the well, outside the city – but the movement from Egypt to Midian is equally described as "fleeing from Pharaoh" and as "settling in Midian." This part of the verse does not describe what happens *after* he travels – that is the content of "he sat by the well" – but is an alternative description of the movement itself. Moses is replacing his childhood milieu, going to settle in a strange place.

We now understand the importance of this verse and the incident it tells. Moses is overcoming his natural cultural identity. He is leaving Egypt and searching for his brethren. But divine providence decrees that he can only come home to the Jewish people by first being completely divorced from the hope of any natural belonging. Moses will not join the Jews simply because he has discovered that he is more comfortable with their cultural ways. The path from Egyptian to Hebrew is not a simple one. First he will find himself with no home at all, a stranger settling in a strange land to which he has no natural connections, as he expresses it in naming his first son – "I am a stranger in a strange land" (v. 22). Only afterwards, after hearing the voice of God who sends him back, will he make the voyage to join the Jews.

IV. RESCUING THE MAIDENS

This brings us to the last incident of Moses' pre-prophetic life. The part that concerns us, that which deals with Moses' character and its development (rather than with his marriage), is, like the previous three incidents, told in a terse and concise manner. One verse describes the characters (v. 16), and one verse describes the situation before Moses and his reaction:

> The shepherds came and chased them away, and Moses rose and saved them, and watered their sheep. (v. 17)

Moses' reaction here is fundamentally different than in the first two cases. In the first, Moses acted patriotically out of identification with "his brethren." The root of his action was group identity. In the second he acted ethically as a judge, in rebuking the evil perpetrator of an evil act. The root of his action was justice. In this case, Moses has no identification with the daughters of the priest of Midian, and he is not interested in justice. The verb the Torah uses is *"vayoshiyan"* – he saved them. Moses is acting heroically, and the root of his action is nobility and bravery. He sees the strong oppressing the weak, and "rises up" to rescue the weak. The Torah stresses that he subsequently waters the sheep for them, an action not necessary from the perspective of the conflict which precede it. Moses is helping those who need help, rather than helping his brethren or admonishing the wicked. He neither punishes the shepherds nor admonishes them – he simply rescues the girls.

This personality trait, while admirable, seems very distant from what we expect as necessary from the future deliverer of Israel. Obviously, to be the leader of the Jews, Moses needs to be their champion and feel their sorrow and oppression. He needs to have a fine sense of justice and ethics, for the leader of Israel in Exodus is also the one who will bring down the Torah and teach them the ways of God. But why is a necessary condition of Moses' education that he be a wandering hero-knight, a sort of Hercules who without any personal interest rises up to help the helpless? The answer, of course, is that Moses' leadership of Israel, if in part based on his love of his brethren, also requires an innate sense of help for anyone who needs assistance, without the element of patriotic identification. For this to come out, Moses, unlike any other Jew of his time, had to be divorced from the Jews totally, to be a stranger in a strange land, in order to face seven strange maidens struggling with the local bullies and to instinctively rise and rescue them. With that personality, he will be sent back to rejoin the people he never knew and be both one of them and their leader.

V. EPILOGUE – MARRIAGE

Moses marries Tzipora, one of the seven daughters he has rescued. It surely is ironic, in light of how I interpreted the meaning of Moses' fleeing Egypt, that the daughters describe him as "an Egyptian man." The Torah says, "Moses agreed to dwell (*lashevet*) with the man, and he gave his daughter Tzipora to Moses." There is an air of passivity in this statement. Moses did not settle down in Midian after all; he *agreed* to dwell with the man. We have the impression of his being persuaded and agreeing with no great enthusiasm. (This is the third "*lashevet*" in this section, and the meaning is neither to settle, as in "*vayeshev be-eretz Midian*," nor to sit, as in "*vayeshev al habe'er*," but means to join a family – "*lashevet et ha'ish*," to move in with the man). If we did not know better, we might think that the Moses saga is over, the promise of his great deeds of youth buried in domesticity and shepherding, a stranger, dependent on a local dignitary. Moses, who went out to "see" his people's suffering, and saw an Egyptian striking a Hebrew of his brethren – what does he see now? The next "seeing" will be God's: "And God saw the Israelites, and God knew" (v. 25). Soon afterwards, Moses will "see and behold the bush is burning in fire and the bush is not consumed" (3:2). But that is already a different chapter.

Moses' Crisis

Rav Mosheh Lichtenstein

And Moses agreed to dwell with the man, and he gave Tzipora, his daughter, to Moses. And she bore a son and he called him Gershom, for he said: "I have been a stranger in a strange land." And it came to pass during those many days that the king of Egypt died, and the children of Israel sighed from the labor and they cried.... And Moses shepherded the flock of Yitro his father-in-law, priest of Midian, and he led the flock far into the desert. (Ex. 2:21–3:1)

With these few verses the Torah recounts the story of Moshe Rabbenu's (Moses') adult life; from the time he matures and goes out as a young man to see his brethren, to the time he returns to Egypt – at the age of eighty – to present himself and God's demands before Pharaoh. Several decades are squeezed into these three verses. Years go by between his frightened flight from Pharaoh's police and his return to his brethren, yet the Torah reveals nothing about his activities during this time. All the spiritual development and character-building that take place during these years is hidden from us. We know nothing of his spiritual trials and tribulations and their effects on his inner stature. Who is the Moses who flees from Pharaoh and who is he who is called upon at the burning bush to deliver the nation of Israel; what are the changes that occur in him through his efforts to strive continually upwards in the building of his exalted personality? Obviously, we would be eager to learn what happens to him during this time, but the verses, as we have seen, leave out a large portion of his life, jumping from his youth to his fully mature status as God's elected emissary.

We shall focus on this period, attempting to understand what happens to Moses during those "many days" and the meaning of the Torah's strange silence in this regard. However, before examining this *parasha* itself, let us first turn our attention to a similar situation regarding another exalted biblical personality – *Avraham Avinu* (Abraham).

Abraham, too, appears on the biblical scene in all his adult, full-blown spiritual glory, after he has already become *Avraham HaIvri*, God's chosen. Our first meeting with him occurs after he has accepted the Creator of heaven and earth, firm in his belief, calling out in God's name as he relentlessly lays the foundation of *Am Yisrael*.

Obviously, we are extremely interested in the process by which the father of our nation arrives at his faith and by the factors and events which influenced him. But here, too, the verses reveal nothing. However, if the verses do not distinguish in this regard between Moses and Abraham, and the path which leads both of them to prophecy is obscure and unknown, the approach of the Midrash in these two instances is completely different. In the case of Moses, the Midrash continues the Torah's policy of obscurity, while, when it comes to Abraham, the rabbis expound at length on his actions and adventures in Ḥaran and Ur Kasdim, in an attempt to complete the sketchy picture which arises from the biblical verses.

Why is this so? Why does the Midrash build such a detailed spiritual profile for the young Avraham ben Teraḥ while refraining from doing the same for Moshe ben Amram? The answer lies in a basic difference between these two personalities with regard to the nature of the "unknown period" in their respective lives, as is clear from a reading of the Torah narrative itself.

In fact, the Torah's silence with regard to Abraham prior to the command of *"lekh lekha"* is not at all similar to its silence in the case of Moses. Before Abraham's appearance in the Torah as a fully integrated personality confident in his path, we know nothing at all about him.

However, from the moment he is introduced to us, there is a continuous and complete description of his deeds and actions. From his departure from Ur Kasdim until his burial in Ḥevron, from the construction of his first altar when he calls out in God's name until he binds his son on the altar on Mount Moriah, there is no break in the continuity of the story. There are no periods of obscurity and secrecy in the story of Abraham's life; there is only a division of periods: the period prior to his appearance before us, and the period thereafter. The first period is not a "black hole" in the story of his life; it is rather the period prior to the story's beginning – it is pre-history. For reasons of its own the Torah chooses this division and leaves Abraham's early life out of the narrative. And, as is so often the case, that which the written Torah leaves out, the oral Torah fills in – expounding at length in the Midrash on those episodes where the verses chose brevity.

The same cannot be said of the story of Moses, however. Here the Torah is silent not prior to his appearance in the verses but rather thereafter. From the time of his birth until his burial, the Torah is with him, from cradle to grave. The period enveloped by the Torah's silence is not before or after the time framework of the story, but rather in its very midst. We hear of the birth of the young Levite, we read of his childhood in Pharaoh's palace, and we follow closely his actions as a young man when he goes out to his brothers. This early period is laid out before us in great detail until he suddenly disappears and all there is in the Torah is a long silence, not broken until he reappears several decades later.

This is not a period prior to the narrative framework, but a disappearance in mid-narrative. This disappearance is an integral part of the story itself. Moses' flight to Midian and the textual silence regarding his doings during that time are located in the midst of the story's time-frame, since they are part of the story. The lack of noteworthy events is itself an event – one of withdrawal and seclusion. Moses' disappearance and silence following his escape to Midian tell us that he secluded himself and changed the course of his life. The silence of the text is an expression of the hermetic life of seclusion and isolation which Moses lives in the desert during these years.

The non-story here *is* the story, and it is for this reason that the Midrash makes no effort to expound the narrative as it did in the case of Abraham: The story isn't lacking a chapter; it is told in full, but here the technique used is that of silence, expressing Moses' concealment and seclusion – the essence of his existence during this period.

A close examination of the text reveals that this self-imposed isolation came in the wake of a crisis. Moses underwent a profound crisis, as a result of which he took off to the desert and enveloped himself in silence. What was this crisis? What caused it and what were its consequences? In order to answer this question, we must review what happened to Moses just prior to his departure from Egypt, and his spiritual character at the time, as revealed to us by the text.

The Torah recounts two stories about Moses prior to his departure for Midian. The first describes his encounter with the Egyptian who is beating a Jew, while the second records what happens to him when he sees two Jews striking each other. If we were to sketch a picture of Moses' personality based on the description offered in these episodes, we would be faced with a youth (or young man) with a very high level of moral sensitivity, who cannot tolerate any expression of moral injustice. Moses' spiritual refinement causes him to rise against any act of suppression or effort to trample the rights of others by use of force. A deep-seated moral flame burns deep within him when he sees the Egyptian beating the Jew, and a strong sense of injustice fills him as he watches the two Jews fighting.

However, there is an additional quality which his sensitive nature possesses. Moses will not be satisfied with the expression of moral indignation alone; he must act. Therefore, he reacts by attempting to correct the situation, unwilling to accept the existence of evil as such. He doesn't merely sit and bemoan the situation; he translates his feelings into actions. He is not the type to restrain himself in such a situation. He strikes the Egyptian and he harshly rebukes his brethren. If there is justice – it must be immediately manifested!

The background, relating to Moses' action, is worth pointing out. He has spent his life, until now, in Pharaoh's palace, lacking nothing. He has received all his needs throughout life and has never encountered deprivation, discrimination or injustice directed against either himself or his immediate surroundings. The helplessness of the innocent in the face of the tyrant and the sense of cruel Fate are completely foreign to him. He is unfamiliar with the experience of trying to cope with a cruel and unjust regime, or the encounter with the neighborhood bully who strikes fear into the heart of his neighbors. Undoubtedly he knows that *Benei Yisrael* were enslaved and forced into hard labor, but only the first-hand encounter with such reality makes him experience and realize the suffering of his brethren.

This encounter between a noble and sensitive soul, inexperienced in the tribulations of life outside of the palace walls, and the obtuse reality of the world, is what gives rise to Moses' inner crisis. Actually, it is a double crisis: First, the very existence of such a harsh reality gives him no rest; in addition, he cannot grasp how *Benei Yisrael* have come to terms with their bitter fate and are not rebelling against it.

On the first day, upon encountering the Egyptian, whip in hand, Moses immediately reacts to the injustice. "And he struck the Egyptian and buried him in the sand." No questions are asked, no discussion need be had and no second thoughts ensue. He acts on the spot, burning with zealousness for justice and morality. All his feelings of justice and truth are aroused and find immediate expression.

However, the situation is not so simple and straight-forward. Coupled with the description of Moses' action, the Torah sees fit to point out that before striking, Moses takes one preliminary precaution: "And he turned this way and that and saw that there was no-one." By taking this necessary precaution, Moses is already addressing a harsh historical and moral reality. He cannot, as an individual, solve the problem that he has encountered without first ascertaining that no agents of the secret police are in the vicinity. He is thereby forced to recognize the existence of an obtuse reality in which justice and righteousness are powerless to act without first ensuring that the long arm of the tyrant isn't around the corner.

The very recognition of this reality bears the seed of crisis. However, Moses still believes at this stage, as he deals the Egyptian his due share of punishment, that the situation can be corrected. The full impact of the crisis hits him only the next day. It is only then that he understands the full extent of the problem facing him, and the difficulty of establishing justice upon earth. Prior to his departure from the palace to visit his brethren he had never imagined a reality in which one nation could be so oppressed and humiliated at the hands of cruel enemies. When he becomes aware of this reality, he assumes as self-evident that the oppressed nation will do everything in its power to rise up against its oppressors and fight against its bitter fate. However, upon encountering this socio-historical reality of *Benei Yisrael*, he realizes that they have no will or inclination to rise against the situation. Rather he finds apathy and further injustice; apathy in the face of their situation, and injustice in their dealings amongst themselves. Historical reality is not perceived by them as something to be changed; they do not imagine such a possibility. From their point of view, the tyrant and the slave-driver are fixed and unchanging facts of life. History includes injustice, and a strong regime – like a strong animal in nature – will persecute and trample. If Moses expected that his action on the first day would awaken his brothers to refuse to accept such a situation and arouse them to act, the second day causes him bitter disappointment. The cruel reality reveals itself to him as being more deeply rooted than he had realized.

The reaction of *Benei Yisrael* to his actions, the disdain and scorn which they exhibited towards him, and his own consequent feeling of helplessness, coupled with a sense of the long arm of the tyrannical regime seeking to crush him, all come together to cause a great crisis in his sensitive soul. His despair of possibly influencing the historical sphere and his disappointment in *Benei Yisrael*, who – were it not for their weakness – could effect a change, bring him to the brink of depression. He turns his back on the historical effort in general and those pertaining to the Jews in Egypt in particular. The *Midrash Rabba* (at the beginning of *Parashat Va'ethanan*) points out the profound significance of the words uttered by Yitro's daughters: "An *Egyptian man* saved us from the shepherds," explaining that Moses is identified in Midian as an Egyptian and not as a Jewish fugitive. This points to Moses' feeling of detachment from the historical fate of those who feel no compulsion to act in their own interests.

Moses is still a youth. If his initial reaction was one of immediate and sharp protest, accompanied by attempts to save the persecuted, the other side of the coin is the crisis and despair he experiences when his efforts meet no success. If justice is not achieved immediately then despair and frustration set in at the inability of historical fulfillment, especially in relation to those who do nothing to help themselves. Moses lacks the character which recognizes the existence of a harsh reality but does not despair of correcting it by means of a stubborn and drawn-out battle which offers no overnight victories. He also is incapable of sensing empathy for the weak and downtrodden, broken in spirit. The same profound moral fervor leads him, in his early years, to a feeling of crisis, despair and detachment, which transforms his flight to Midian from a journey forced upon him by historical circumstances into a self-imposed seclusion.

However, the story does not end here. Reaching Midian, Moses once again reveals kind-heartedness and moral sensitivity in saving Yitro's helpless daughters from the hands of the bullying shepherds. This incident, though, only serves to exacerbate his dejection. When he left Egypt his frustration and despair were directed towards the historical reality on the national level, but he did not harbor the same feelings regarding human society on its elemental social level. He believed that human fraternity still had its place in society, and he meant to seclude himself only from the historical effort, not from life in human society altogether. "And he dwelt in the land of Midian and he sat by the well." He chooses the well, the local meeting place, as his dwelling place. However, additional disappointment awaits him. Here, too, the strong oppress the weak, and here too in the social microcosm, morality and justice have no place, devoid though it may be of the pressures which existed in Egypt. The law of survival of the fittest prevails at all levels.

From the depths of his aching soul, Moses decides to opt for a solipsistic existence. He leaves even the well and focuses on the limited family unit. Ultimately, as time goes on, we find him in an advanced stage of removal from involvement in human society and from any effort to correct the social historical reality of the world – "And he shepherded the sheep far into the desert."

"And he came to the mountain of the Lord, to Ḥorev." His attempt at seclusion in the desert is undertaken in an attempt to find God. Not in the corrupt and aggressive human society will he find God, but in the desert. There will he be able to seek wisdom and spiritual fulfillment, as he directs his attention to communion with God far from the corruption of human society.

Thus time rolls on. Moses is engaged in seeking the God of truth and serving Him in the desert, as he attempts to scale the peaks of spiritual elevation. Yet, throughout these "many days" *Benei Yisrael* are sighing and groaning because of the Egyptian oppression. "And it came to pass during those many days [i.e. during the time that Moses dwelt in the desert of Midian – see Rashi and Ramban], the king of Egypt died, and *Benei Yisrael* sighed because of the labor, and they cried out, and their plea reached God because of the labor." Moses is involved in serving his Creator and in delving into the fundamentals of wisdom; the suffering of his brethren has disappeared from his mind. Throughout these years, in response to the crisis he has undergone, he suppresses the feelings of pity and humane-moral indignation hidden in the depths of his soul.

Moses though will be commanded to set aside his personal existential concerns and spiritual development in order to plunge into the depths of historical selflessness, with a firm belief in man's ability to change the harsh reality in which he finds himself. God Himself addresses him and calls upon him to act in order to redeem the oppressed nation; even if the nation is powerless to fight against those who enslave it. The whole purpose of the episode of the burning bush is to extract the future master-prophet from his solitary existence in the desert and to return him to the sphere of action on the historical-national level. God's words to him teach him that his personal quest for God is not sufficient so long as it is not accompanied by a recognition of the secret of the transformation from God's name as He is known (the Tetragrammaton) to "*Ehyeh*" – meaning the God who descends and is active in the midst of the human historical reality (see Rashi). From the heights of God's mountain, man is ordered to descend to the depths of the bush, and just as the God of Abraham, Isaac and Jacob sees fit to remove His *Shekhina*, as it were, from His Throne of Glory in order to save His nation, because He hears their cries and is aware of their suffering, so is it incumbent on His servant of flesh and blood to act likewise.

"Israel Is My Son, My Firstborn"

Rav Zev Weitman

Upon setting out for Egypt, God commands Moses to say to Pharaoh,

> Thus says the Lord, Israel is My firstborn son: and I say to you, Let My son go, that he may serve Me. But if you refuse to let him go, behold, I will slay your firstborn son. (Ex. 4:22–23)

This is at first glance puzzling. What is the point of a warning about the slaying of the Egyptian firstborn before Moses' first encounter with Pharaoh? Why does God command Moses to say to Pharaoh, "And you refused to let him go," when Pharaoh has not yet refused, nor even been asked, even once, to let Israel go?

Secondly, we must ask what does the Torah wish to tell us through the juxtaposition of the threat directed at Pharaoh – "Behold, I will slay your firstborn son," and the surprising incident that occurred that night when Moses and his family sought to rest from the journey – "The Lord met him, and sought to kill him"?

Is there any connection between the declaration to be made before Pharaoh, "Israel is My firstborn son," and the corresponding threat against *his* firstborn son," and the subsequent "And she [Tzipora] cut off the foreskin of *her son*," referring to the son of Moses, saving his life because God "sought *to kill him.*"

Finally, why does God seek to kill Moses? There seems to be no mention of any prior warning or sin. In summary – why does the Torah begin with an unintelligible warning directed against Pharaoh, and then immediately proceed to report about an incomprehensible punishment meted out against Moses who was sent to stand before Pharaoh?

In order to understand the meaning of this story, we must first explain the Torah's intentions in the verse, "The Lord met him, and sought to kill him." Who did God seek to kill, for what reason, and what exactly caused God to relent at the end?

Among the commentators we find three main approaches:

1. Rashi and the first explanation in Ibn Ezra: God sought to kill Moses for having been negligent about circumcising his son Eliezer,[1] and Tzipora in her resourcefulness circumcised her son, thus rescuing Moses.
2. The second explanation in Ibn Ezra: God sought to kill Moses' son, Eliezer, because he had not been circumcised by Moses.[2]
3. Rashbam: God sought to kill Moses, because he had tarried and delayed carrying out of his mission, and the circumcision of his son served as an atonement-offering that saved Moses from God's anger.

The first two approaches agree that the reason that God sought to kill somebody was Moses' neglect of his son's circumcision, and they differ only on the question of whether God sought to kill Moses or his

---

1. Prior to this point, we were told about one son of Moses – Gershom (Ex. 2:22). In this passage (4:20), the Torah alludes that Moses has more than one son, and only at the beginning of *Parashat Yitro* do we learn that "his sons" mentioned here number two and no more, and that the name of the second son is Eliezer (18:3–4).
2. As opposed to Rashi and Ibn Ezra, who assume that the uncircumcised son is Eliezer, Moses' younger son, the *Targum Yerushalmi* suggests that the younger son, Eliezer, had been circumcised, whereas the firstborn son, Gershom, is the one who was uncircumcised.

uncircumcised son. These explanations are based on the story's continuation, where Tzipora's circumcising her son causes God to not kill either Moses or his son. It follows that God's anger was apparently caused by Moses' failure to circumcise his son.

The primary difficulty with these explanations is that the essence is missing from the text: Scripture gives no reason for God's anger, and it must be inferred from the act that led to the rescue. Nowhere else in the Torah do we find that God seeks to kill somebody without first explaining that person's sin and transgression.

In contrast to Rashi and Ibn Ezra, Rashbam suggests that God is angry due to Moses' negligence in carrying out his mission – "because he was slow in his going, and he brought his wife and sons along." He thereby resolves the difficulty that we do not find a hint to Moses' sin. This story is a direct continuation of the previous stories, which dealt at length with Moses' reluctance to carry out God's mission and God's anger with Moses about that.[3] According to Rashbam, the circumcision and blood that saved Moses from death did not repair the sin, but served as an atonement that saved Moses from punishment for his sluggishness and tarrying.

Expanding upon Rashbam's position that the story of God's seeking to kill Moses should be connected to the previous stories which tell of Moses' refusals and evasions, it is possible that the intervening passage – "Israel is My firstborn son" – also deals with the same issue. In light of the view that God sought to kill Moses because of his slothfulness in carrying out his mission, as described previously, we can suggest that

3. "And the anger of the Lord burned against Moses" (ibid. 4:14). Already Rashi (ad loc.) cites Rabbi Yehoshua ben Korha's puzzlement cited in *Zevaḥim* 102a: "A [lasting] effect is recorded of every fierce anger in the Torah, but no [lasting] effect is recorded in this instance," and the view of Rabbi Yossi that a lasting effect is recorded in this instance as well, for the consequence was that the priesthood which had been designated for Moses was now handed over to Aaron. The difficulty is easily resolved according to Rashbam, for "And He sought to kill him" and "And the anger of the Lord burned against him" were both connected to Moses' hesitations and his attempt to avoid fulfilling God's mission to redeem Israel. Thus Rashbam writes in his commentary (ad loc.): "And [God's] fierce anger had a [lasting] effect, according to the plain sense of the text, as stated: 'That the Lord met him, and sought to kill him.'"

the section of "Israel is My firstborn son," apparently a threat directed against Pharaoh, also contains an allusion and threat to Moses about the calamity that is liable to befall him in the wake of his evasion of the mission that God had cast upon him.

God, angered by Moses' tarrying and by his evasion of the mission cast upon him, repeats here what had already earlier been told to Moses, that He plans to harden Pharaoh's heart. He also mentions the plague of the slaying of the firstborn which Pharaoh will eventually suffer, and he commands Moses about things that he is to say in the distant future, when Pharaoh will have indeed hardened his heart, and time after time failed to let the people of Israel go.

God says these things in advance, in order to convey a message to Moses that can be understood in two different ways, and that intimates to Moses that he too is being warned here against his continued avoidance of carrying out God's mission (the allusions to Moses are set off in brackets):

> And you shall say to Pharaoh [but you too, Moses, should know], Thus says the Lord, *Israel is My firstborn son*: and I say to you [to Pharaoh, but also to you – Moses], Let My son go, that he may serve Me: and if you refuse to let him go [you Pharaoh, but you too, Moses, who constantly refuse to carry out My agency], *behold, I will slay your firstborn son* [the son of Pharaoh who refuses to let Israel go, but yours too, Moses, who refuse to fulfill My agency].

God tells Moses that he should say to Pharaoh that his refusal to release the people of Israel – God's firstborn son – will bring about the killing of his own firstborn son. But the message is formulated ambiguously, alluding also to what may befall Moses, who also refuses, evades and delays carrying out God's mission. Through the words that are directed towards Pharaoh, God alludes also to a threat directed towards Moses – that he too is liable to lose his firstborn son, as he too is included among those who refuse to act on behalf of the release of God's firstborn son from Egypt. These words are conveyed to Moses after he took with him his wife and children – an act that Rashbam defines as slothfulness in carrying out his mission, "because he brought his wife and sons along."

Based on this approach, I would suggest that when it says in the next story, "And it came…that the Lord met him, and sought to kill him," this does not mean that God wished to kill Moses (as proposed by Rashbam), or even Eliezer (as proposed by Ibn Ezra in his second explanation), but rather Moses' firstborn son, Gershom, for it was precisely about this that God had warned him. When Moses continues delaying, and tarries in his lodging place, the threat is immediately carried out. First, Moses is given a warning – "Behold, I will slay your son, your firstborn," and in the next section the threat is carried out – "The Lord met him, and sought to kill him," i.e., Moses' firstborn.[4]

The rescue of Moses' firstborn is achieved, as explained by Rashbam, in the wake of the circumcision of his younger son, Eliezer, an act of atonement, similar to a sacrifice (only that according to Rashbam, it was Moses who was saved in the wake of the circumcision, whereas

---

4. S.D. Luzzatto already suggested this, after asking about the verse: "Behold, I will slay your son, your firstborn": "There is a difficulty, for this is the last of the plagues, and Moses only mentioned it to Pharaoh at the end; why then is it mentioned here?" He explains that God wanted to hint to Moses that should he fail to carry out God's mission and thus delay Israel's exodus from Egypt, he too would be punished with the death of his firstborn. According to him, God was angry because Moses brought his wife and children to Egypt without informing them of his mission, and there was concern that they would dissuade him from fulfilling his mission, so that he should not put himself in the dangerous position where Pharaoh might kill him. The incident at the lodging place was meant, according to Luzzatto, to force Tzipora to part from Moses because of the circumcision of her younger son, and Moses would then continue to Egypt on his own, to fulfill his mission without disturbance. A similar approach is suggested by Y. Blau (*Hatan Damim, Tarbitz* 26 [5717], pp. 1–3). According to Blau, the threat against Moses' firstborn was meant to coerce Moses into accepting his mission, and he is hard-pressed to explain why this coercion takes place only after Moses accepts the mission upon himself. He also explains that the threat is connected to the Destroyer threatening Pharaoh's firstborn son, in the sense of "Once permission is granted to the Destroyer, he no longer distinguishes between righteous and wicked." Here too he is hard-pressed to explain why the Destroyer threatens Moses even before it destroys Pharaoh. Rav Yoel Bin-Nun ("*Hametz uMatza bePesah, biShavuot ubeKorbanot haLehem,*" *Megadim* 13 [5751], p. 40, note 31) says that he accepts Blau's interpretation, but that the true explanation is that the incident is a sign and symbol of what would happen to the people of Israel at the time of the slaying of the Egyptian firstborns, and the way in which they would be saved – by way of the Paschal blood.

according to the explanation offered here, it was Gershom whose life was then in danger).

Like the saving of the firstborns of Israel at the time of the tenth plague, the saving of Moses' firstborn also depended on the letting and displaying of blood. At the time of the slaying of the firstborns, the blood of the Paschal sacrifice is displayed on the doorposts of the houses of Israel. In the case of Moses, the foreskin and the blood attached to it are displayed at the feet of the firstborn who was about to die, and they bring about his rescue. In the case of Moses – *"And she cast it [vataga]* at his feet"; in the case of the blood of the Paschal sacrifice – *"And touch [vehigatem;* same Hebrew root as *vataga]* with it the lintel and the two side posts" (12:22).[5]

This resolves all the difficulties we raised at the beginning. It is clear why the warning, "Behold, I will slay your son, your firstborn," is given not in its proper place, for it is essentially directed at Moses who refuses and evades carrying out God's mission. This also explains the past tense in the expression, "and if you refuse to let him go" (*vatema'en leshalḥo;* literally, "and you have refused to let him go"), because these words were meant to be understood in two ways – directed not only at Pharaoh in the future, but also, and perhaps primarily, at Moses.[6] We can also understand now whom God seeks to kill and why, and also the connection between the matter of "Behold, I will slay your son, your firstborn," and the adjacent story of "And He sought to kill him."

Support for the explanation that the threat, "Behold, I will slay your son, your firstborn," refers not only to Pharaoh, but also to Moses, may be brought from the fact that the threat to slay the firstborns was told to Moses after his ninth refusal, and is realized immediately following his tenth delay. This is similar to the slaying of the Egyptian firstborns,

---

5. This correspondence was also noted by Luzzatto and the *Da'at Mikra* commentary. *Da'at Mikra* brings two explanations for the blood's power against the Destroyer: as a barrier which the Destroyer is not permitted to cross, or as atonement for and redemption of the blood that was to be spilt.

6. Since these words are directed primarily at Moses and not at Pharaoh, they are formulated in past and present terms ("And I say to you … and you refused to let him go…. Behold, I slay your son").

which immediately follows Pharaoh's tenth refusal to fulfill God's command to let the people of Israel go from Egypt.

Moses' ten refusals and evasions can be counted as follows. There are five clear and manifest evasions:

1. And Moses said to God, "Who am I, that I should go to Pharaoh, and that I should bring the children of Israel out of Egypt." (3:11)
2. And Moses said to God, "Behold, when I come to the children of Israel, and shall say to them, 'The God of your fathers has sent me to you;' and they shall say to me, 'What is His name?' what shall I say to them." (ibid. v. 13)
3. And Moses answered and said, "But, behold they will not believe me, nor hearken to my voice: for they will say, 'The Lord has not appeared to you.'" (4:1)
4. And Moses said to the Lord, "O my Lord, I am not an eloquent man, neither yesterday nor the day before, nor since You have spoken to Your servant: but I am slow of speech, and of a slow tongue." (ibid. v. 10)
5. And he said, "O my Lord, send, please, by the hand of him whom You will send." (ibid. v. 13)

Afterwards, there is another evasion on Moses' part:

6. And Moses went and returned to Yeter [Yitro] his father-in-law, and said to him, "Let me go, I pray you, and return to my brethren who are in Egypt, and see whether they are still alive." (4:18)

God commands Moses to appear before Pharaoh in Egypt, but instead of leaving immediately, Moses goes to Yitro and asks for his permission. The proof that this is yet another evasion is that afterwards God must turn once again to Moses in Midian and repeat the command to return to Egypt: "And the Lord said to Moses in Midian, 'Go return to Egypt'" (4:19).

If the repetition of a command implies that Moses did not obey the first command, making the second command necessary, then the Scriptural text alludes to two more refusals and evasions on the part of

Moses. Following the second refusal, listed above, we find a twofold statement of God:

> 7. And He said, "Thus shall you say to the children of Israel, '*I Shall Be* has sent me to you.'" And God said *moreover* to Moses, "Thus shall you say to the children of Israel, 'The Lord God of your fathers, the God of Abraham, the God of Isaac, and the God of Jacob, has sent me to you.'" (3:14–15)

The emphasis in the verse, "And God said *moreover* to Moses," teaches that we are dealing here with a new and additional statement, which is not a continuation of the previous statement. This additional statement teaches that Moses was not satisfied with and did not accept what was stated earlier, and therefore God had to turn to him a second time. The twofold statement might even allude that Moses responded with refusal and with an argument that Scripture chose to omit. This was the understanding of Rashi, who fills in what is missing in the words of Moses:

> Moses said to him: "Master of the Universe! Why should I mention to them other sorrows? They have enough with this sorrow!" God replied to him: "You have spoken rightly: Thus shall you say to the children of Israel."

We find a similar redundancy and an additional emphasis in the continuation of the narrative (following the third refusal listed above):

> 8. And the Lord said to him, "What is that in your hand? . . . . That they may believe that the Lord God of their fathers, the God of Abraham, the God of Isaac, and the God of Jacob, has appeared to you." And the Lord said *furthermore* to him, "Put now your hand into your bosom." And he put his hand into his bosom; and when he took it out, behold, his hand was diseased, as white as snow. . . . "And it shall come to pass, if they will not believe you, nor hearken to the voice of the first sign, that they will believe the voice of the latter sign." (4:2–8)

Here again, the emphasis of "furthermore" alludes that Moses was not satisfied with the first sign and that he was not persuaded to go out and execute his mission, and therefore God gave him an additional sign.

Another delay alluded to in Scripture is the delay noted by Rashbam – Moses' taking his wife and sons with him to Egypt (which occurs after the sixth delay listed above):

9. And the Lord said to Moses in Midian, "Go return to Egypt: for all the men are dead who sought your life." And Moses took his wife and his sons, and set them upon an ass, and he returned to the land of Egypt. (4:19–20)

Instead of returning immediately as commanded, Moses first takes his wife and children. Even though it would seem that Moses fulfills God's command and returns to Egypt, taking his wife and sons constitutes a delay and hindrance in carrying out God's mission. Again, the proof that God's command was not properly executed is that immediately afterwards God addresses Moses a second time, including in His words the threat of "Behold, I will slay your son, your firstborn":

And the Lord said to Moses, "When you go to return to Egypt, see that you do before Pharaoh all those wonders which I have put in your hand.... And you shall say to Pharaoh: Thus says the Lord, Israel is My firstborn son, and I say to you, Let My son go, that he may serve Me: and if you refuse to let him go, behold, I will slay your firstborn son." (4:21–23)

The next and final delay is the one in the wake of which God seeks to kill Moses' firstborn son – the delay at the lodging place where they stopped to spend the night:

10. And it came to pass on the way, in the place where they spent the night, that the Lord met him, and sought to kill him. (4:24)

Moses heads toward his lodging place rather than towards Egypt, as God had commanded. In the words of Rashi: "Why then was he threatened with punishment? Because he busied himself with the affairs of his lodging place first" (according to Rashi, this "busying himself" made him liable for mortal punishment because it involved neglecting the mitzva of circumcision. We propose that this "busying himself" made him liable for the death penalty because it brought about a delay in the fulfillment of God's word and his mission to take the people of Israel out of Egypt).

If this is correct, then just as the plague of the slaying of the Egyptian firstborns followed Pharaoh's tenth refusal to fulfill God's command,[7] so too Moses' firstborn was in mortal jeopardy owing to Moses' tenth delay and hesitation with respect to fulfilling God's command and executing His mission. Following Pharaoh's tenth refusal, God kills his firstborn, and this is precisely what almost happened to Moses the tenth time he refused or delayed carrying out God's command. Only the blood of circumcision saved him, just as the blood of the Paschal sacrifice saved the firstborns of Israel at the time of the slaying of the Egyptian firstborns.

The lesson to be learned from this is that a heavy responsibility to fulfill God's command and carry out His mission falls upon the shoulders of the leaders of Israel. God tells Moses that the time has arrived to redeem the people of Israel, to take them out of Egypt, to bring them to *Eretz Yisrael*, and to plant them in its midst. And God issues a warning that all those who hinder and delay the execution of His plan to redeem "Israel, My son, My firstborn," put themselves at risk of paying

---

7. Did the slaying of the Egyptian firstborns come upon Pharaoh in the wake of his tenth refusal? After all, three of the plagues are not preceded by any warning or demand to let the people go. However, before the plagues began Pharaoh had been asked to let the people of Israel go, and three times he refused to do this:

"And Pharaoh said, Who is the Lord, that I should obey His voice to let Israel go? I know not the Lord, nor will I let Israel go." (Ex. 5:2)
   "And the king of Egypt said to them, Why do you, Moses and Aaron, distract the people from their works? Get you to your burdens." (ibid. v. 4)
   "And the heart of Pharaoh was hardened, that he did not hearken to them; as the Lord had said." (ibid. 7:13)

Accordingly, even if we count only seven refusals during the period of the plagues, we still reach a total of ten refusals on the part of Pharaoh.

the heavy price of the death of their own firstborns – whether they are Israel's external enemies, like Pharaoh who refuses to send the people of Israel out of his land, or they are Israel's leaders. Both of them are leaders designated by God to redeem the people of Israel and take them out of Egypt. And if they refuse, avoid, or delay cooperating with God's plan to redeem the people of Israel, if they offer all kinds of excuses for their refusal, neither will be spared, and both will suffer punishment at the hand of God who wishes to redeem His people. This is true even if he is a celebrated leader like Moses, there being none more faithful or humble than he, and there having arisen no other prophet like him whom the Lord knew face to face.

Moses' Jewish Identity: Who Is the Uncircumcised Child?

Rav Yoel Bin-Nun

I. THE QUESTION OF MOSES' IDENTITY

Upon studying the opening chapters of Exodus, the reader is struck by a fundamental question. Who is Moses, during the first part of his life? How does he view himself, how is he viewed by his environment (in Egypt and in the desert), by the people, and by the Torah itself?

The possibilities are manifold. Is Moses the son of Yokheved, Levi's daughter, or is he the son of Pharaoh's daughter? Is he the son of Amram, of the house of Levi, the brother of Aaron and Miriam, or is he Yitro's son-in-law, husband of Tzipora? When does he become Moses, man of God, divine servant, or in other words, Moshe Rabbenu.

The first half of chapter 2 states:

> And a *man of the house of Levi* went and took a *woman of the house of Levi*. And the woman conceived, and she bore a son…. And she took for him an ark of bulrushes…. And *his sister* stood far off…. And the daughter of Pharaoh came down to bathe in the Nile…. And she said: "This is one of the Hebrews' children." And his sister said to Pharaoh's daughter: "Shall I go and call you

a nurse of the Hebrew women, that she may nurse the child for you?" And Pharaoh's daughter said to her: "Go." And the lass went and called the child's mother…. And the woman took the child, and she nursed him. And the child grew, and she brought him to Pharaoh's daughter, and he became her son. And she named him Moses, and she said: "For I drew him (*meshitihu*) out of the water." (v. 1–10)

Why does the Torah describe Moses as an anonymous personality? Why not begin with the name of his father and his mother, like every character in Genesis? Why not mention the name of his sister? They are all known to us from other places in the Torah.

The Torah apparently wants to leave the reader in the dark when it comes to Moses' identity. It is enough to compare these introductory verses to the family tree in *Parashat Va'era*, "And Amram took Yokheved his aunt as a wife, and she bore him Aaron and Moses" (6:20); or to the second census in the book of Numbers: "And the name of Amram's wife was Yokheved, daughter of Levi, whom she bore to Levi in Egypt; and to Amram she bore Aaron and Moses, and their sister Miriam" (26:59).

In light of the middle and the end of the chapter, which talk about Moses' life in Pharaoh's house and Reuel's house, in Egypt and in the desert, it appears that the Torah's main aim in this chapter is to open the question of the identity of Moses, who is born and grows up in such an unusual way.

It is ironic to find the absence of names in Exodus – "*Shemot*" – the Book of Names – in all places! Exodus also contains strong (yet nameless) women throughout the book. There is a clear distinction between Genesis and Exodus when it comes to the gender divide. Genesis is consistently dominated by males throughout, and genealogical passages listing the transitions from fathers to sons form its superstructure. Genesis defines its participants' identity. Exodus, on the other hand, is characterized by strong women – the Hebrew midwives, Shifra and Pua; Yokheved, Moses' mother and his sister Miriam the prophetess (who leads the Song of the Sea for all of the women), Pharaoh's daughter (who names Moses), Tzipora, who circumcises his son and saves his life, and the women "who thronged at the entrance to the Tent of Meeting"

(38:8). Fittingly, according to the sages, women did not participate in the Sin of the golden calf, Exodus' most serious transgression.[1]

Chapter two's second half introduces Moses' wrestling with his identity: "And he went out to his brothers, and he saw [them] in their burdens; and he saw an Egyptian man beating a Hebrew man from his brothers." (v. 11) The Torah repeats and emphasizes the term "his brothers." Pharaoh's desire to execute Moses is understood only because Moses remains a "Hebrew" in his consciousness. He knows very well who "his brothers" are and what is happening to them. Moses is identified as a Hebrew by the entire environment, even when confronting the two fighting Hebrews. In killing the Egyptian, he puts himself in opposition to Pharaoh's decree and his rule.

The Torah does not reveal how Moses remained a Hebrew in Pharaoh's house. The biblical narrative bears the character of a skeletal novel, full of verbs which describe events in the form of a tight summary, without description of background and scenery, without ruminations or prolonged explanations. Midrashic literature fills in the lacunae; generally, these narrative explorations maintain the concision of the original text. Three possibilities occur to me: (1) Pharaoh's daughter revealed to Moses his identity, perhaps even maintaining communication with his mother secretly; (2) Egyptian aristocrats, perhaps even with Pharaoh's collaboration, ensured that Moses would know who he was not, so that he would not even consider competing for the throne; (3) Moses discovered this by himself over the years, from different clues (emerging from the two prior explanations). This is the first stage of Moses' struggle with his identity – while Moses grows up in Pharaoh's palace, he does not become an "Egyptian."

Strikingly, however, this is precisely how Reuel's daughters describe him: "And they said, 'An Egyptian man rescued us from the hands of the shepherds'" (v. 19). How did this occur? A simple answer is that they made their assumption based on his dress. However, a simple answer does not suffice here. The description of Moses as "an Egyptian man" by the daughters totally negates his reason for coming to Midian, as this is the result of his flight (his exodus!) from Egypt after he saved

1. See *Bemidbar Rabba* 21:11.

"a *Hebrew* man from his brothers" by slaying the "*Egyptian* man beating" him. It is difficult to escape the two opposite meanings of the phrase "an Egyptian man" in this story.

II. MOSES – "THE EGYPTIAN MAN"?

Midrashic sources analyze this expression and undermine Moses' title of "an Egyptian man":

> Was Moses an Egyptian? Rather, his dress was Egyptian, while he was a Hebrew.
>
> Alternatively… this is what Yitro's daughters said to Moses: "More power to you for rescuing us from the hands of the shepherds!"
>
> Moses replied to them: "That Egyptian whom I killed – he saved you."
>
> Therefore they said to their father, "*An Egyptian man*" – that is to say – who brought this about? It was the Egyptian man whom he killed. (*Shemot Rabba* 1:32)

Another well-known Midrash has Rabbi Levi describing the dialogue when Moses petitions God to be allowed to cross the Jordan at the end of his life:

> "Master of the Universe, Joseph's bones may enter the land, but I may not enter the land?"
>
> God said to him: "He who acknowledges his land may be buried in his land, but he who does not acknowledge his land may not buried in his land."
>
> From where do we know that Joseph acknowledged his land? His master's wife says [Genesis 39:14]: "See, he has brought a Hebrew man to us" and he does not deny it; rather, he says "For I was certainly stolen away from the land of the Hebrews" [Genesis 40:15]. Therefore, he will be buried in his land….
>
> "You, who did not acknowledge your land, you may not be buried in your land."
>
> How so? Yitro's daughters said "An Egyptian man rescued

us from the hands of the shepherds".... And he hears this and remains silent; therefore, he may not be buried in his land: "For you shall not cross this Jordan" [Deut. 3:27]. (*Devarim Rabba* 2:8)

This Midrash understands Moses' identity issue completely differently, holding him accountable for Yitro's daughters' misconceptions. This is perplexing, however, as it is explicitly stated that Moses is not present when the daughters say to their father, "An Egyptian man rescued us." In my opinion, the midrash of Rabbi Levi relates to the words of Moses himself at the end of the passage:

And Moses agreed to dwell with the man, and he gave Tzipora his daughter to Moses. And she bore a son, and he named him Gershom because he said, "I have been a sojourner (*ger*) in a foreign land." (Ex. 2:21–22)

Unlike the land of Egypt, the land of Midian is foreign to Moses, implying that the land of Egypt had not been foreign. This is the converse of Joseph's position; he maintains the connection to the land of his origin.

This is the heart of the matter. Even though Moses departs Egypt as a fugitive, his conscious identity remains in Egypt, together with his enslaved brethren.[2] In Pharaoh's palace, Moses contends with the royal family to identify with his brothers "in their burdens," but in the land of Midian he is distanced from his brethren and from his land, so that his identity undergoes an extremely difficult crisis.

Just as Pharaoh's daughter rescued Moses from the waters of the Nile, making Pharaoh's house a refuge, so too the Midianite priest's house serves as a refuge when Moses is a penniless, condemned fugitive. Moses builds his family in his father-in-law's home just as Laban's house served as a refuge for Jacob when he fled, marrying his wives and building his household. However, Laban swaps Jacob's beloved for her older sister and alters his wages ten times (Gen. 31:7, 41), to the point of

---

2. Moses departs Egypt before the nation does, and he also sees God upon Sinai well before the people do. It appears that this is the justification for the idea of rebuilding the Jewish nation from Moses when the people sin.

almost destroying Jacob; while the Midianite priest and his household receive Moses with honor and love, and Moses repays them with honor and love. Eventually, they will return and join the nation of Israel – in Midian, however, no inkling of this destiny had occurred to them, or to Moses. Presently, Moses' assimilation seems inevitable. What could have been more natural "in those many days" (2:23)[3] than the full integration of Moses into his father-in-law's house, until he and his family are fully incorporated and blended with the Midianites?

However, Moses announces unequivocally his determination to maintain his identity by naming his firstborn son "Gershom, because he said, 'I have been a sojourner in a foreign land.'" [4] Furthermore, at the time that he finally receives his mission from God, he says "to Yeter his father-in-law…. 'Please let me go, and I will return to my brothers who are in Egypt and I will see if they are still alive'" (4:18). Moses remained anchored among his brothers in Egypt and not any other environment. Even his second son, born in Midian, Moses named "Eliezer: 'for…the God (*Elokei*) of my father was my help (*ezri*), and He rescued me from the sword of Pharaoh'" (18:4). This second declaration confirms that Moses' identity remained inextricably linked to his father's God and His salvation. No other mindset was acceptable to Moses.

Thus, the midrash of Rabbi Levi is turned on its head; it is Joseph who abandons his identity, and Moses who maintains it in the face of all obstacles. When Joseph rises to greatness in the house of Pharaoh, finding the comfort of home and hearth, he declares at the birth of his firstborn, Menashe, "God has made me forget (*nashani*) all of my toil and my father's entire house" (Gen. 41:51), thus completing his excision of his childhood home from his memory. Moses, on the other hand, maintains his identity as one of the brethren who reside in Egypt and emphasizes his connection to them, despite his forced separation from them in another land, despite the fact that one of his brothers had handed him over to Pharaoh (specifically after he had endangered him-

---

3. Moses stands before Pharaoh at age eighty, but he is relatively young when he flees; see *Shemot Rabba* 1:27.
4. See Yechiel Bin-Nun, *Eretz HaMoria* (Tevunot Press, Alon Shvut, 2006), pp. 12–26, 61–62, 102–105.

self and saved another of his brothers) and despite the warm embrace of his father-in-law's home.

Joseph is born in the land of the Hebrews and is kidnapped from it due to his brothers' hatred; therefore, he treats them as foreigners (*vayitnaker*; Genesis 42:7) once he has risen to greatness in Pharaoh's house, eventually becoming viceroy. Moses is raised in Pharaoh's home but is not integrated into it; he even maintains his identity and acts like a foreigner toward the rule of Pharaoh by killing an Egyptian to save his beaten brother. He must flee and leave the land of Egypt, but even the land of Midian becomes "foreign" to him because of the strength of his identification with his brothers in Egypt, his suffering brethren.

Moses is Joseph's polar opposite.[5] Therefore, if Joseph merited being buried in the tribal lands of his descendants, why not Moses? Moses made an unmistakable declaration of identity through naming his sons: In Pharaoh's house I did not become an Egyptian man, and I maintained my identity and my identification with my suffering Hebrew brothers; in Midian, I have not become a Midianite! Not for my dear father-in-law, who has given me a house and a daughter and a family, and not for my wife, who has spent all of her days in the land of Midian. My firstborn son, also the firstborn of his mother Tzipora, will be named after his distant brothers, whom he and his mother do not know at all, and he will bear in his name the awareness of our temporary sojourning in the land of Midian, which has been a welcoming land of refuge but nevertheless remains a foreign land. My second son will bear in his name the appellation of my father's God and my memory of being saved from Pharaoh's sword.

How do Yitro, Tzipora, the other family members and the Midianites in general react to these declarations by Moses? Once again, the

---

5. Both Moses and Joseph are special children within their families; each is honored in Pharaoh's house and ends up in a foreign land where he marries the priest's daughter and has two sons. At the same time, there are many differences: Joseph is an older brother, while Moses is a younger brother; Joseph is raised in his father's house, while Moses is not; Joseph is a master of dreams, while Moses is a prophet. Furthermore, the Tetragrammaton disappears from the Torah during Joseph's story and reappears when it is revealed to Moses. Most importantly, Joseph brings the Israelites down to Egypt, while Moses leads them out.

Torah does not tell us. It is possible that they are enraged; it is possible that they peacefully and respectfully accept the man Moses, the foreigner. Perhaps Moses goes off to take care of "the sheep of Yitro his father-in-law, the priest of Midian…beyond the desert" in order to avoid this tension. In the meantime Yitro and Tzipora raise the boy as Gershom, accepting the name which contradicts everything that is precious and known to them, with all of the anticipated difficulties for a child who is raised in such an environment.

III. THE ENCOUNTER "ON THE ROAD, AT THE LODGING"

We turn to Moses' journey to Egypt at the end of chapter 4, after his long discussion with God at the Burning Bush. At this point, we must ask a vitally important question – has Gershom been circumcised? Most of the Midrashic literature and commentators assume that Gershom has been circumcised, and they believe that the uncircumcised son is Eliezer, the second child, who had been born just before the journey to Egypt. This is possibly alluded to in the verse: "Moses took his wife and his *sons*, and he had them ride upon the donkey, and he returned to the land of Egypt" (Ex. 4:20) – this is the first verse to indicate that Moses has two sons. Even according to this approach, however, there is a difficult conflict between the covenant of the Patriarchs and the exodus, as is clear in the talmudic analysis of this episode:

> Rabbi Yehoshua ben Korḥa says: "Great is circumcision, for all of the merits that Moshe Rabbenu had acquired did not suffice for him when he neglected circumcision, as it says [v. 24]: 'God met him and sought to kill him.'"
> Rabbi says: "God forbid that Moshe Rabbenu neglected circumcision; rather, this is what he said: 'If I circumcise and then depart, this is dangerous…. If I circumcise and tarry three days – God has told me [v. 19] "Go, return to Egypt."' So why was Moses punished? It was because he saw to the lodging first, as it says [v. 21] 'And it was on the road, at the lodging.'"
> Rabban Shimon ben Gamliel says: "It was not Moshe Rabbenu that Satan wanted to kill, but rather that infant, as it says

'For you are a blood-groom for me' [v. 25] – let us see: who is called a groom? I would say that this is the [circumcised] infant." Rabbi Yehuda bar Bizna expounded: "At the time that Moshe Rabbenu neglected circumcision, Wrath and Fury came and swallowed him, and nothing was left of him but his legs. Immediately, 'And Tzipora took a flint, and she cut off her son's foreskin' [ibid.]; right away [v. 26], 'And he released him.' At that time, Moshe Rabbenu sought to kill them [the Wrath and the Fury]." (*Nedarim* 31b–32a)

According to Rabbi and Rabban Shimon ben Gamliel, there is a clash between the commandment of circumcising the newborn infant and the mission to deliver Israel from Egypt; between the covenant of the Patriarchs and the exodus from Egypt. Moses decides to set out on his mission, and he pushes off the circumcision because of the health risk of travelling with a newly-circumcised infant.[6] However, this delay puts a life in danger regardless, because Moses makes circumcision an issue secondary not only to the mission itself but even to the sleeping arrangements. Only Tzipora understands this and circumcises the infant.

According to Rabbi Yehoshua ben Korha (Rabbi Yehuda bar Bizna follows in his footsteps), Moses neglected the circumcision in a flagrant way, and awesome Godly forces (personified as angels, "Wrath and Fury") "swallow" him for this reason. Nevertheless, Moses does not surrender; he fights against these, akin to what he says himself (about the Sin of the golden calf, Deut. 9:19): "For I was in dread of the wrath and the fury with which God raged against you to exterminate you."

It is hard to penetrate the logic of these midrashim.

All the people that were born in the desert, on the road as they left Egypt, were not circumcised. For forty years the Israelites went through the desert. (Joshua 5:5–6)

---

6. Rashbam and Ḥizkuni argue that Moses should have left his family in Midian; see also *Mekhilta DeRabbi Yishmael* ibid. about Aaron's words.

Joshua has to remove "the shame of Egypt" from them as they enter the land (ibid. 2–9). Thus, hundreds of thousands of Israelites remain uncircumcised under Moses' leadership, but this "neglect" is reasonable and requires no punishment, as it is dangerous to circumcise on the road, in the desert. Nevertheless, for not circumcising his son, before Sinai, Moses is punished "because he saw to the lodging first"? What source did Rabbi Yehoshua ben Korḥa and Rabbi Yehuda bar Bizna find that Moses fights against powerful forces and does not want to circumcise his son? The sages all struggle with Moses' apparent tense relationship with the commandment of circumcision, but where do they see any indication of this?

Other midrashim (*Targum Yerushalmi* 4:25; *Yalkut Shimoni Shemot*, chapter 167) interpret the uncircumcised boy as Gershom, the firstborn,[7] as the result of a pre-nuptial agreement with Yitro. Moses and Yitro agreed that the firstborn son would be raised according to Yitro's ideology, while the second child would be Moses' to raise.[8] Therefore, Gershom had not been circumcised when they left Midian. According to this view, Moses neglected the commandment for years, abandoning his firstborn son to an idolatrous education.[9]

However, this is difficult to accept literally. The Midianites are descended from Ketura and Abraham, as is explicit in Genesis (25:1–4), and they are even more committed to circumcision than the Ishmaelites. The text clearly states that Tzipora knows how to circumcise her son, and she saves her son by doing so. Were Gershom handed over to the education of Yitro and Tzipora, he would have been already circumcised many years earlier. Why, therefore, wasn't Gershom circumcised?

We can answer this question if we realize that the Midianites circumcised their sons by virtue of belonging to the seed of Abraham

---

7. This is Shadal's explanation (34:24); see Y. Blau, "Ḥatan Damim", *Tarbitz* 26, 5717, pp. 1–3; my "*Ḥametz Umatza*," *Megadim* 13 (5751), n. 31; Z. Weitman, "*Beni Vekhori Yisrael*," *Megadim* 48, 5768, n. 5.

8. This seems to be an attempt to explain the historical split among Moses' descendants: Gershom's failure (Judges 18:30) vs. Eliezer's success (1 Chron. 23:15–17).

9. Rabbi Elazar HaModai says this explicitly in the *Mekhilta DeRabbi Yishmael*, ibid.; but other midrashic sources claim that Yitro had already abandoned paganism before Moses' arrival; see *Shemot Rabba* 1:32.

by way of Ketura.[10] Consequently, circumcising Moses' firstborn son in the house of the priest of Midian would have turned the parents and child into a Midianite family; exactly what Moses struggled against as expressed in the children's namings. Moses cannot fulfill the covenant of the Patriarchs in Midian because, in that environment, the act would signify throwing in his lot with the Midianites; it would have been impossible to circumcise him there as an expression of becoming part of the Jewish people!

Accordingly, it is specifically Moses' struggle to maintain his identity which prevents him from circumcising his son "in a foreign land," while his wife and his father-in-law want to circumcise the child with all of their might. Only the name of the child prevents them from doing so, as this name constitutes a declaration of Moses' struggle against circumcision as an expression of Midianite identity.

This allows us to explain the issue of "the Wrath and the Fury" mentioned above. According to the Gemara, Moses fights them with all of his strength, and it may be that the meaning of this war of his is that Moses withstands all the pressure and does not let them circumcise his son – as a Midianite – even though the covenant of the Patriarchs is also set aside. For this decision, the various sages of the land of Israel criticize Moses for neglecting the covenant of the circumcision. Possibly, they believe that Moses would have been obligated to circumcise his son in any case, relying on the God of his fathers to save him from Midian as He saved him from Egypt, and even if all of the family were circumcised for the sake of forging their Midianite identity – at the end of the day, his Israelite identity would return and resurface.

---

10. Circumcision served two purposes in the ancient world, as a social act signifying adulthood and as a protective act to ward off destructive angels. The first appears in Egyptian sources; see *ANET*, Princeton 1955, p. 326. The latter appears in Phoenician sources; see Eusebius, *Praeparatio Evangelica* I, 10. The Torah propounds a different type of circumcision, that of a family covenant and determining one's identity; this is appropriate at the age of eight days. This appears to be the Midianite conception. Therefore, I reject Shadal's contention that Tzipora wanted Moses to delay the circumcision until the age of thirteen years. It was Moses who wanted to delay the circumcision.

IV. WHEN DID GOD WARN PHARAOH?

Now we can read the difficult passage of Tzipora's circumcising her son in full:

> And Moses went and returned to Yeter his father-in-law, and he said to him, "Please let me go, and I will return to my brothers who are in Egypt and I will see if they are still alive." And Yitro said to Moses: "Go in peace."
>
> And God said to Moses in Midian: "Go, return to Egypt; for all the men who sought your life have died." Moses took his wife and his sons, and he had them ride upon the donkey, and he returned to the land of Egypt; and Moses took the staff of God in his hand.
>
> And God said to Moses: "When you go back to Egypt, see all the miracles (*mofetim*) which I have placed in your hand and perform them before Pharaoh; but I will strengthen his heart, and he will not send the people out. And you shall say to Pharaoh: 'Thus says God: Israel is My firstborn son. And I say to you: Let My son go, that he may serve Me; and you have refused to send him out. Behold, I will kill your firstborn son.'"
>
> And it was on the road, at the lodging, that God met him, and He sought to kill him. Then Tzipora took a flint and cut off the foreskin of her son, and she cast it at his feet; and she said: "For a blood-groom are you to me." And He released him; and she said: "A blood-groom for circumcision." (Ex. 4:18–26)

The greatest difficulty of this obscure passage is not the identity of the uncircumcised son, nor is it whom God seeks to kill (Moses or the infant). The great difficulty are the two verses which mention the warning about *Makkat Bekhorot* (the Plague of the Firstborn), which lead straight into "And it was on the road, at the lodging."

Is it not obvious that these verses should have appeared in *Parashat Bo*, where they are missing? In that chapter, Moses says to Pharaoh (Ex. 11:4–5): "So says God: 'At midnight, I will go out in the midst of Egypt. And every firstborn in the land of Egypt will die.'" However, we do not see God communicate any of this to Moses beforehand. This statement is specifically in our passage: "And you shall say to Pharaoh: 'Thus says God: Israel is My firstborn son. And I say to you: Let My son go, that he may serve Me; and you have refused to send him out. Behold, I will kill your firstborn son.'" This statement completes God's word to Moses about *Makkat Bekhorot* and its special significance. It is missing in chapter 11, and it is written in chapter 4, without any evident context – Moses has not yet met Pharaoh even once, and Pharaoh has not yet refused to do anything. What reason is there for these verses to be in chapter 4, without any section break before the circumcision "on the road, at the lodging"?

The statement here is not comparable to what God told Moses at the Burning Bush:

> But I know that the king of Egypt will not let you go…and I will send forth my hand and strike Egypt with all of my wonders which I will do in its midst, and afterward he will send the people out. (3:19–20)

In our passage there is a notification that, "I will strengthen his heart, and he will not send the people out" (v. 21); however the language of the following verses is different: "And I say to you: Let My son go, that he may serve Me; and you have refused to send him out. Behold, I will kill your firstborn son." (v. 23) God is not notifying Moses of what is going to come about in the future, but is directing Moses what to say in the debate with Pharaoh after the plagues and before the final defeat.

There is not one scintilla of doubt that these verses are part of the warning about *Makkat Bekhorot*, leaving the following question: Are the verses said to Moses when he leaves Midian, or are they actually said to Moses before *Makkat Bekhorot* and only moved up in the text of the Torah? In my view, they are told in practice to Moses before *Makkat Bekhorot*, but they are moved up in the text and inserted immediately before the passage of the circumcision "on the road, at the lodging," in order to teach us the meaning of the circumcision. It is a condition for the paschal service and the redemption from the land of Egypt – this is the circumcision of "Israel is My firstborn son" as opposed to the smiting of Pharaoh's firstborn son. This foreshadowing may be understood if the uncircumcised son is the firstborn Gershom and not the younger brother. Pharaoh's firstborn son stands in parallel to God's "firstborn son," as well as Moses' uncircumcised firstborn son.

This is not a punishment for Moses; no sin is mentioned here. This is a sign of the circumcision which will stand in the way of the exodus from Egypt because "Israel is my firstborn son," just as it keeps Moses from fulfilling his mission. This symbolism is given by way of the firstborn son of Moses specifically, because his brothers in Egypt have already been circumcised, so that their identity is clear. This sign is conveyed by [the angel of] God to Moses ("and He sought to kill him") via the circumcision blood of the 'blood-groom.' This evidently parallels the destroyer who will not smite the Israelites in the merit of the blood on the lintel and the two doorposts in *Makkat Bekhorot*. This idea is famously expressed through the dictum "Through your blood, you shall live" (Ezek. 16:6, in preparation for the covenant with God) – as the sages put it: "by the paschal blood and by circumcision blood."

Apparently, the Israelites in Egypt kept (for the most part) the tradition of circumcision due to the covenant of the Patriarchs, and only a few needed to be circumcised before the paschal service. Therefore, the obligation of circumcision appears in the framework of the laws of the *Korban Pesaḥ* (the Paschal Lamb, Ex. 12:43–48), clarifying that the *Korban Pesaḥ* is dependent on the circumcision – "and no one uncircumcised may eat of it." Not only is the uncircumcised man himself forbidden to eat of the *Korban Pesaḥ*, because he is not a part of the community of Israel in practice, but the circumcision of all the members of the household, including the slaves, prevents the masters of the household from eating the Passover, as the sages teach (*Mekhilta DeRabbi Yishmael, Pisḥa Bo*, 16).

Thus, the Torah moves the warning of *Makkat Bekhorot* up due to its relevance to the passage of the circumcision of Moses' firstborn son; only there does the link between the redemptive blood of the covenant of the Patriarchs and the redemptive blood of the *Korban Pesaḥ* in Egypt become clear. The Torah presents this specifically through the prism of one who was separated from his nation and his brothers to such an extent that he could not circumcise his firstborn son, because he was "a sojourner in a foreign land"; in this circumcision, he returns to the covenant of his forebears. Therefore, God does not confront him about the issue of the circumcision in the land of Midian, but only at the time that he leaves it – "And it was on the road, at the lodging"; nor does He do so in the land of Egypt, where Moses is planning to circumcise his son according to his own view. Moses is sent to bring them out of Egypt, not to reaffirm his identification with the Israelite community, "my brothers who are in Egypt."

V. BETWEEN MOSES AND TZIPORA

However, another serious question arises – how does Moses not comprehend this? Had he not been told anything about this from the beginning? Does only Tzipora understand? Why does this passage stop abruptly with "A blood-groom of circumcision"?

It appears that Moses intends to circumcise his son among "my brothers who are in Egypt," surely not in Midian and not on the road. The roadside circumcision is compelled upon him by way of a sign which Tzipora understood. According to the view that God wanted to kill Moses, it is more understandable why he cannot do anything, but even if it is the infant who is in danger, Moses cannot act. Moses does not want to circumcise his son, despite the danger, because he plans to do so among his brothers, as part of affirming his Israelite identity. On the other hand, Tzipora understands, because she has always wanted to circumcise her son, and Moses' entire struggle about his identity has been difficult for her, as all males in her family are circumcised.

Let us consider the closing verses: "'For a blood-groom are you to me.' And He released him; and she said: 'A blood-groom for circumcision.'" In the standard interpretation, she is declaring to the angel: If you have come now to kill my son, take this blood of circumcision, and let the child-groom go. When he releases him, she says: Indeed, the child-groom has been saved by the blood circumcision.

However, in my view, she is also alluding to Moses, that he should have circumcised the boy long ago. In our language, she would have said: I told you to circumcise the boy, and you, Moses, did not listen. You were stubborn, and lo and behold, witness the danger you have brought on us, particularly on the boy. It was only his circumcision which saved him!

Only Tzipora, who has wanted to circumcise their son all these years, and knows how to circumcise, is able to conceive, at the moment of truth, that this could be the path to salvation. Only she is capable of acting with speed and decisiveness at the time that Moses cannot do anything to oppose the angel of God.

Now we understand why Moses sends his wife back to Midian after this event. There is no need to propose that Tzipora remained in the inn because of the danger and later returned to her home. The Torah spells out what happens explicitly in *Parashat Yitro* (18:2–4):

> And Yitro, Moses' father-in-law, took Tzipora, Moses' wife, *after he sent her away*. And her two sons; the name of one was Gershom, because he said, "I have been a sojourner in a foreign land." And the name of one was Eliezer: "for the God of my father was my help, and He rescued me from the sword of Pharaoh."

The first verse refers to Tzipora's *shiluḥim* – her being sent away, her banishment – the term is one generally used for divorce. Moses sends his wife back with their sons because she has undermined the meaning of the names that he had given them. Moses thought that Tzipora circumcised her son like a Midianite and for the sake of their Midianite identity, an act which he was prepared to fight, and concerning which he was prepared to confront "the wrath and the fury." The result is the painful *shiluḥim* of Tzipora, along with her two sons, to her father's house; the tragic loss of Moses' family is outweighed only by the great mission of saving Israel.

However, Yitro cannot make peace with his daughter's *shiluḥim*. It is only his obstinacy which brings about the family's return to the bosom of the nation in the desert "where he was encamped, God's mountain" (18:5), and in Yitro's words, "I, your father-in-law Yitro, have come to you, along with your wife, and her two sons are with her." Thus it is clear why Tzipora is sent off and why Yitro comes to Moses in the desert. This redefines the famous midrashic question about the opening of chapter 18, "'And Yitro heard': What news did he hear and come?" The news of the exodus was the opportunity for Yitro to come, but his main impetus is clear in his words about Moses' wife and two sons, as the sages expounded: "If you will not do it for me, do it for your wife; and if not, do it for her sons." This effort also brings about, in the end, the joining of the entire family of Yitro to the Jewish nation.

If so, one may also explain Moses' total disregard of his wife and her sons, who are his sons. All of his words and his actions in the rest of the chapter are directed to Yitro. The Torah does not record even one word that Moses says to his wife or her sons, who are his sons. Even if some dialogue between them occurs, the Torah does not cite it.

There are two possibilities to explain this. The first is that Moses cannot bridge the abyss which gapes between him and his wife, and he builds everything on the character and status of Yitro his father-in-law. Perhaps even if he agrees to accept the return of his wife and her sons, who are his sons, it is only because of the honor and status of Yitro his father-in-law.

Another possibility, which seems more feasible to me, is that the Torah does not want to discuss the discord and crisis in Moses' family, since any discussion of this topic would bring along with it an inevitably difficult and unjustified attack on Moses. Therefore, the Torah mentions Tzipora's *shiluhim* only offhandedly, and does not describe their reuniting.

However, Miriam and Aaron (and certainly many of the people) cannot be silent. This is why Miriam is punished (Num. 12) – and according to Rabbi Akiva, Aaron as well (*Shabbat* 97a) – as God in his glory defends Moses, who, being "very humble, more so than any man on the face of the earth" (ibid. v. 3), cannot and does not know how to defend himself. The incident of "the Kushite woman," however we might explain her identity, is a clear proof of the Torah's desire to hide the crisis in Moses' family life and to purify him from the murmurings against him, specifically those coming from within his family.

Thus, Moses' struggle with his identity is the key to understanding obscure passages in the Torah, such as the circumcisions of the firstborn son who had remained uncircumcised in the "foreign land." Moreover, the foreshadowing of the warning of *Makkat Bekhorot* and its juxtaposition with the circumcision of Moses' firstborn son, as well as the *shiluhim* of Tzipora, her return to her father, and her return to Moses in the place of the cloud and the manifestation of God's glory, at the foot of God's mountain, are now understood.

Parashat Va'era

The Two Consecrations of Moses

Rav Yonatan Grossman

I. INTRODUCTION

At the beginning of our *parasha* (6:2–12), we read of Moses' appointment as God's agent to secure the release of the Hebrew slaves from Egypt. All the elements that we would expect to find in such a consecration are present: the problem of slavery, Moses' task, and the ultimate goal – redemption. However, this entire section seems superfluous – Moses was already appointed as God's messenger at the burning bush! What need is there for a second consecration?

To properly identify the need for both prophecies, we must turn back a few pages and carefully examine the cryptic yet critical depiction of the bondage, presented by the Torah immediately preceding the vision of the burning bush. The Torah describes God's "thoughts and emotions," so to speak, prior to choosing Moses as the savior of His people:

> After many days, the king of Egypt died, and the Israelites were groaning under the bondage and cried out; and their cry for help from the bondage rose up to God.
>   God *heard* their moaning,
>   And God *remembered* His covenant with Abraham, with Isaac and with Jacob.

> God *saw* the Israelites
> And God *took notice* (*vayeda*). (2:23–25)

I divide the verse this way in order to associate more clearly each verb with its subject. The verse focuses on *four* actions undertaken by God: He hears, remembers, sees and takes notice. The following verses, where God appears to Moses at the burning bush and informs him of the impending redemption, parallel the previous ones – but only *three* of these verbs are mentioned:

> God said:
>> "I have surely *seen* the plight of My people in Egypt
>> And have *heard* their outcry because of their taskmasters;
>> Yes, I have *taken notice* of their sufferings." (3:7–8)

Strikingly, in the latter description, God's "remembering" has been omitted! When the Torah informs us, the readers, of God's reaction to the enslavement of the Jews, it mentions that "God remembered His covenant"; but at the burning bush, God does not mention this to Moses. The divine promise to our Patriarchs remains concealed from the father of all prophets.

II. THE CHOICE OF MOSES

In order to understand God's omission of the patriarchal covenant as He speaks to Moses, we will analyze God's choice of Moses to lead His people out of slavery. While the Torah gives us no clue as to why God chose Abraham to father God's nation, the Torah does tell us much about Moses' background before he is chosen as God's messenger. Over the course of *Parashat Shemot*, we read about several of Moses' experiences, which can be seen as preparation for God's revelation at the burning bush. We may reasonably assume that the Torah presents to us those stories which are relevant to our understanding of Moses, and thus critical for understanding the rest of the story.

We encounter three episodes involving the young adult Moses:

1. When Moses had grown up, he went out to his kinsfolk and

witnessed their labors. He saw an Egyptian beating a Hebrew, one of his kinsmen. (2:11)

2. When he went out the next day, he found two Hebrews fighting. (2:13)

3. Now the priest of Midian had seven daughters. They came to draw water, and filled the troughs to water their father's flock. But shepherds came and drove them off. Moses rose to their defense and he watered their flock. When they came to their father, Reu'el...and said..."He even drew water for us and watered the flock." (2:16–19)

The motif of these three stories is Moses' aggressive commitment to helping the oppressed. Apparently, the Torah, in its treatment of Moses' character, emphasizes his resolute moral conviction. Many commentators have already dealt with the evident progression throughout these episodes: in the first incident, a conflict exists between an Israelite and an Egyptian; Moses instinctively intervenes on behalf of the suffering Jew. In the following incident, the element of the suffering at the hands of the oppressor is less obvious; here, the two combatants are both from Moses' nation – "two Hebrews." Finally, in the third encounter, the oppressed bear no relationship to Moses whatsoever; they come from a foreign nation (Midian). Yet, Moses rescues them as well, as one who naturally seeks to assist those in need, regardless of their heritage or ancestry. Indeed, Moses identifies with those who suffer, regardless of which nation they are from.

This is the Torah's presentation of Moses, a man of robust moral fabric.

After this preparation, Moses chances upon the burning bush, where God informs him of the imminent release of *Benei Yisrael* from bondage. As noted, God employs only three of the four aforementioned expressions. Conspicuously, He omits the fourth element, that of remembering His covenant to the Patriarchs.

In analyzing the various actions attributed to the Almighty in this context (hearing, remembering, seeing, and taking notice), our first step involves an obvious division into two distinct categories. The "seeing," "hearing" and "taking notice" relate to God's reaction to the suffering of the slaves, the pain and misery which He now plans to bring to an end.

These three verbs must be understood in this light: "I have surely seen the plight of My people in Egypt and have heard their outcry because of their taskmasters; yes, I have taken notice of their sufferings." God sees the oppression that has overcome His nation, He hears their cries resulting from the bitter bondage and He knows and recognizes their pain. Thus, these three actions involve the actual enslavement of *Benei Yisrael* and their consequent suffering.

In contrast to these three verbs, the "remembering" clearly relates to an entirely different dimension. Regardless of the suffering experienced by the nation, God recalls the covenant with the Patriarchs (referring, most likely, to the *"Berit Bein HaBetarim"* with Abraham, in Genesis 15).

In other words, the Torah presents two reasons for which God has decided to redeem His nation:

A. The moral reason – God wishes to end the unjust oppression to which *Benei Yisrael* have been subjected. Regardless of any previous promises to, or future destiny of, the people in question, the suffering itself (i.e., the torture, the cries and the pain, as specified in the verse) demand divine intervention.

B. The historical/national reason – God, Who keeps His word, must fulfill His promise to Abraham, Isaac and Jacob that their progeny would inherit and settle in the Land of Canaan.

Upon revealing Himself to Moses at the burning bush, God informs Moses of only three of the four divine "reactions" to the slavery, namely, the three relating to the moral necessity of redemption. Nowhere throughout the entire dialogue with Moses at the bush does God make even a subtle reference to His promise to the national forefathers.

This omission of such a critical and relevant ingredient of redemption becomes all the more glaring in light of God's introduction to Moses at the burning bush: "I am the God of your father, the God of Abraham, the God of Isaac and the God of Jacob" (3:6). In other words, God introduces Himself as, primarily, the God of the three national Patriarchs. We should have expected, after such an introduction, some reference – if only an allusion – to the covenant. However, despite the fact that the

Torah had presented this element of God's reaction just a moment earlier, God omits the covenant from His opening prophecy to Moses.

Strange as it may seem, as Moses leaves the bush and heads towards Egypt to carry out the divine plan of redemption, he is unaware of the second reason behind this redemption – the national, historical element. He was never told of God's "remembering" the covenant, which led Him to save His people from bondage.

This feature of redemption, which had disappeared at the burning bush, resurfaces at the beginning of our *parasha*, during the second consecration of Moses: "I have now *heard* the moaning of the Israelites because the Egyptians are holding them in bondage, and I have *remembered My covenant*" (6:5). In addition to the action of "hearing," of which Moses was told at the bush, God introduces a new factor: "and I have remembered My covenant."

Thus, Moses undergoes a second formal inauguration, which informs him of an additional motivation behind God's intervention in Egypt – the divine covenant with the Patriarchs. This prophecy is laden with expressions regarding the destiny of the Nation of Israel and its national calling ("I will take you to be My people, and I will be your God"). These expressions are adopted mostly from the two covenants which God had struck with Abraham – "*Berit Bein HaBetarim*" (Gen. 15) and "*Berit Mila*" (Gen. 17).

Upon his initial consecration, Moses is charged with the responsibility of saving *Benei Yisrael* from their foreign oppressor. He is chosen as God's moral agent, if you will, ordered to perform the work of the Almighty as the moral ruler of the world. In this context, then, we understand the significance of the three prior incidents – they underscore Moses' firm stand on behalf of the weak and oppressed. This commitment to justice renders him worthy of assuming the role of the Almighty's moral agent, saving the oppressed (*Am Yisrael*) from their oppressor (Egypt).

Although in our *parasha* Moses undergoes the process of consecration for a second time, this process differs drastically from his initial inauguration at the burning bush. Now God orders him to redeem the progeny of the Patriarchs, the three national forefathers with whom God had made a treaty and given a historical promise whose fulfillment has now become imminent.

III. WHY TWO CONSECRATIONS?

Obviously, one difficulty remains unresolved: why does God distinguish so sharply between the two motivations behind His saving *Am Yisrael*? Why does He reveal them to Moses over the course of two distinct prophecies? To resolve this issue, we must carefully examine two earlier narratives: the story of Moses' escape to Midian, and his encounter with the officers after his failed first presentation to Pharaoh.

Chapter 2 of Exodus describes how Moses is born to a Hebrew woman but raised by an adoptive Egyptian mother – none other than the Egyptian princess herself. Presumably, questions of national identity occupied Moses' consciousness for some time. Nevertheless, upon leaving the confines of the palace and observing the oppression of the Hebrew slaves, the text emphasizes that Moses related to them as "his brethren." Later, when Moses witnesses the disturbing confrontation between two slaves and censures the perpetrator, the latter responds angrily, "Who made you ruler and judge over us? Do you mean to kill me as you killed the Egyptian?" The delinquent is not content with merely criticizing Moses' efforts, but, apparently, he quickly reports Moses to the Egyptian authorities. As a result of this informer, Moses must flee his homeland and abandon his nation.

We can reasonably speculate what Moses felt. He endangered his stature in Pharaoh's government for the sake of assisting his suffering brethren. In turn, these beneficiaries of his sacrifice betray Moses, turning him over to the officials who have now issued his death warrant.

Moses, left with no alternative, abandons his ungrateful brethren and heads towards Midian. Whereas earlier we read of "A *Hebrew man* from his [Moses'] kinsmen," now Yitro's daughters refer to him as "an *Egyptian man* saved us." It would seem that even in his own mind, Moses undergoes a deep-rooted, emotional crisis of sorts. Back in Egypt, he may have seen himself as a "Hebrew," even though he was raised as an Egyptian. Confusion and doubt regarding his self-definition are now implanted within the innermost recesses of his being. It stands to reason that on account of his people's betrayal, Moses has stripped himself of his Hebrew identity. This may help clarify his baffling decision not to circumcise his son. Even after his assumption of responsibility as the redeemer of Israel, he neglects his son's circumcision, perhaps reflecting his ongoing ambivalence surrounding his identity. Only when his life is threatened does his wife (a Midianite!) perform the ritual.

Indeed, Moses' task as redeemer of Israel does not automatically translate into the renewal of his identification with the Hebrew slaves. Moses could easily identify with the moral underpinnings of the redemption with no connection whatsoever to his personal identity. Morality itself requires his involvement, and his work on behalf of the suffering stems from his firm opposition to injustice. National identity is of no relevance or consequence. Moses is chosen on the basis of his moral determination; therefore, God informs him only of the moral background behind the imminent redemption.

IV. MOSES AND THE OFFICIALS

Then, towards the end of *Parashat Shemot*, we read of the encounter between Moses and Aaron and the "officials of *Am Yisrael*." The latter emerge crestfallen from their audience with Pharaoh, who has refused their request that his decree that the Israelites must now gather straw on their own be rescinded. As they exit the palace, they meet people who are "standing facing them" (5:20) – Moses and Aaron.[1]

Why are the claims of the officials against Moses and Aaron significant? In the Torah's description of the meeting, we already detect covert criticism of Moses and Aaron (from the officials' perspective): "And they came upon Moses and Aaron standing facing them, *as they emerged from before Pharaoh.*" In contrast with the usual formulation in the Torah, the indication of time ("as they emerged from before Pharaoh") is mentioned only at the end of the verse, after the description of the meeting itself. The change seems to hint at the mood and the psychological state of the officials at the time of the meeting. The indication of time, postponed until the end of the verse, creates a sense of the meeting taking place in the midst of the audience with Pharaoh, or

---

1. Rashi maintains that "men of Israel" met Moses and Aaron, rather than the officials, but this interpretation is very difficult to understand. The end of the verse describing the encounter states: "when they emerged from before Pharaoh," creating the impression that these people are the same ones who previously stood before Pharaoh – i.e., the officials. Indeed, most commentators disagree with Rashi.

at least against the background of that audience. Clearly the officials have already left Pharaoh's presence, but this fact is delayed in order to make the reader party to the feelings of the officials. Their meeting with Moses and Aaron is an extension of their preceding audience with Pharaoh, and their words to Moses and Aaron should be read in light of Pharaoh's words to them.

This explains the officials' attack. They had come to Pharaoh hoping to lighten *Benei Yisrael's* suffering, but because of Moses and Aaron's request that Pharaoh allow *Benei Yisrael* to leave Egypt, he now refuses their request. Far from making life easier, Pharaoh explains that the reason for his new, stricter edict is the request by Moses and Aaron, "Let us sacrifice to the Lord our God." The Torah wants the reader of the story to understand the mood of the officials and not judge them too severely.

Even the word for "meeting" mentioned in the introduction contains a few important hints about the encounter. The verb employed by the text for the encounter is "they met" – "*vayifge'u*" (from the Hebrew root *p-g-a* – פ.ג.ע). This verb (in simple case) has two different meanings in Tanach. Sometimes it describes a meeting which we could call "neutral," with no accompanying emotion of love or anger. For example, the description of Jacob as he heads for Ḥaran: "He came upon (*vayifga*) the place and he lodged there, for the sun was setting" (Gen. 28:11). Similarly, we read about his return to Canaan: "And Jacob went on his way, and angels of God met him (*vayifge'u bo*)" (Gen. 32:2).

At other times, however, this verb has negative connotations, even to the point of physical "*pegi'a*" (assault), as in the law pertaining to a murderer: "when he meets/assaults (*befig'o*) him he shall kill him" (Num. 35:19). Similarly, when Doeg slays the *kohanim* (priests) of Nov, we read: "The king said to Doeg, 'Turn and attack (*ufega*) the *kohanim*,' and Doeg the Edomite turned and attacked (*vayifga*) the *kohanim*" (1 Sam. 22:18).

The meaning of the verb in the introduction to the meeting in our case seems to fall into the first category, for it describes an "incidental" meeting between the officials and Moses and Aaron. However, it seems that the choice of this specific verb for the meeting is no accident.[2] The

---

2. It should be noted that the more common term for the description of an encounter in Tanach is the root *p-g-sh* (פ.ג.ש). This verb is used in two ways. It can refer to a

same verb has already appeared in our story, seventeen verses previously, in Moses' request that Pharaoh allow *Benei Yisrael* to go:

> And they said: "The Lord of the Hebrews has spoken to us; let us then go on a three-day journey in the desert, that we may sacrifice to the Lord our God, lest He *attack us* (*yifga'enu*) with pestilence or with the sword." (5:3)

Here, the verb clearly is to be interpreted in its more sinister sense ("with pestilence or with the sword"). The Torah, prior to the "meeting" between the officials and Moses and Aaron, mentions this request by means of Pharaoh's words ("Idle, you are idle, *therefore you say, let us go and sacrifice to our God*"). Therefore, in its repeated use of the same verb, the text may be hinting at this meaning as intended by Moses – "lest He attack us" (*yifga'enu*).

It is not only through the use of the verb "*p-g-a*" that the Torah hints at a link between these two images (Moses standing before Pharaoh, and Moses standing before the officials of *Am Yisrael*). There is also the fear of the "sword" that is directed at the speaker in each instance. Corresponding to Moses' words, "lest He attack us with pestilence or *with the sword*," the officials complain to Moses and Aaron that through their actions they have provided "*A sword* in their hand to kill us." We detect a note of irony – while you Moses are concerning yourself with the possibility of God's sword, we are actually bearing the brunt of Pharaoh's sword.

In any event, through the connection between the two images the

---

pre-planned meeting, such as that of Moses and Aaron in our *parasha*, following the burning bush episode: "And God said to Aaron: Go towards Moses, to the desert; and he went and met him (*vayifgeshehu*) at the mountain of God, and he kissed him" (4:27). It is also used for a chance encounter, such as that of Abigail and David, formulated in the text – from David's point of view – as a chance meeting: "And behold, David and his men were coming down towards her, and she met (*vatifgosh*) them" (Ex. 25:20), or "Yoav ben Tzeruya and the servants of David went out and met them (*vayifgeshum*) at the pool of Givon, together" (II Sam. 2:13).

Torah seems to want us to attribute to the verb *"vayifge'u,"* as it appears in the introduction to the meeting, the negative association as well.[3]

Similarly, the expression that is juxtaposed with the verb – "standing facing them" (*nitzavim likratam*) – adds to the sense of anger and confrontation that is about to take place. This combination appears only twice more in Tanach:

1. In Moses' warning to Pharaoh just prior to the plague of blood: "Go to Pharaoh in the morning; behold, he goes out to the river, and *stand before him* upon the bank of the river, and the staff which turned into a snake shall you take in your hand" (Ex. 7:15);
2. When the angel stands before Bil'am and his donkey: "I have sinned, for I did not know that you were *standing before me* on the way" (Num. 22:34).

In both of these cases, there is a clear confrontation between the person who is "standing" and the one whom he "faces" (Moses facing Pharaoh; the angel facing Bil'am). Moreover, in every instance where this expression is used, the person who is "standing" mentions, or is holding, an object used for striking. The officials of *Benei Yisrael* tell Moses and Aaron that they have given "a sword into the hand" of Pharaoh and his servants to kill them; Moses presents himself before Pharaoh and warns him, staff in hand (and with this staff he will strike the water); and the angel who stands before Bil'am holds a sword in his hand.

The officials accuse Moses and hold him responsible for the increasing burden of work, even implying that his activities could lead to their death. They downplay their anger at Pharaoh, to the point where it almost disappears. From their initial position as agents of Pharaoh, who had "gone out and said to the people, thus spoke Pharaoh" (Ex. 5, 10), they now become the voice of the oppressed people, directing their anger not at Pharaoh, but at Moses and Aaron. This accusation may

---

3. In general, the various translations have rightly rendered the verb *"vayifge'u"* as "they met." However, the covert implication here finds expression in Durham's translation of the verse: "Thus they hurried to confront Moses and Aaron" (J.I. Durham, Exodus, World Biblical Commentary, Texas 1987, p. 66).

be unjust, but it clearly reflects the identification of the officials with their people and not with the oppressors.[4] From their perspective, it is Moses and Aaron who have "given the sword" into Pharaoh's hand; it is they who have made Israel "odious" to Pharaoh. The responsibility for the increasing severity of the royal decrees rests with them (and not even with Pharaoh himself, who is simply reacting to the Israelite uprising). Moses accepts the angry accusation and even adopts it. He turns to God and passes on the accusation, including the accusatory tone, to God himself:

> Lord, why have You *done evil to this nation*, why have You sent me? For since I came to Pharaoh to speak in Your name, *he has done evil to this nation*; and You have not saved Your people at all! (Ex. 5, 22–23)

Moses tells God that "this people" to whom he has been sent, "this people" are suffering, and then he pointedly reminds God that they are "Your people." It is not only that they, an anonymous people, are suffering, and morally You should help them – they are *Your people*; in other words, they are the descendants of the forefathers with whom You struck a covenant.

He speaks two sentences, each ending in a similar way – evil has been done to this nation. But there is a difference between the two statements concerning the responsibility for the deterioration of the situation. In the second sentence, it is difficult to discern who stands behind the verb *"hera"* ("evil has been done"). It may be a general description of the situation with no specific identity being defined as its cause. But it seems more likely – as Rashi and Ibn Ezra understand it – that Pharaoh, mentioned in the first part of the verse, is the cause – for it is he who has done evil to the nation through his decrees. Accordingly, it is Pharaoh who is responsible for the deterioration of their situation. However, it is not Pharaoh whom Moses blames – *just as the officials did not blame*

---

4.   Understanding this chapter primarily in light of the role of the officials is developed in Yonatan Grossman, "The Officers of The Israelites: From Beaters to Beaten," *Studies in Bible and Exegesis*, 11 (forthcoming, hebrew).

Pharaoh. Prior to this statement, in the first sentence, Moses says explicitly: "Why have *You* done evil to this nation?" It is clear that Moses is presenting God as the responsible party.

Our *parasha* concludes with God's response to Moses, and in the next *parasha* the wheel of salvation begins to turn. What is the significance of the encounter between Moses and the officials for the rest of the story?

The words of the officials hint at a different episode in his life that we alluded to previously. They echo the words of the Hebrew man who struck his fellow Hebrew, and who was reprimanded by Moses many years previously (2:13–14). The parallel between the two images is, first and foremost, linguistic:

Moses and the Hebrews	The Officials of *Am Yisrael*
"Who has made you a prince *and judge upon us*; Do you mean *to kill me?*" *And Moses fled* from before Pharaoh.	"May God look upon you *and judge* …to put a sword in their hand *to kill us.*" *And Moses returned* to God.

This linguistic parallel serves to hint at the real connection between these two episodes. In both cases, Moses seeks to help his brethren and to save them from their persecutors. Chapter 2 presents the incident concerning a single Egyptian who strikes a Hebrew, and Moses comes to his aid. Now the Torah is describing an attempt to come to the aid of the entire nation, suffering at the hands of their Egyptian tormentors. Again, just as in the first incident, Moses' brethren turn their backs to him: "Do you mean to kill me, as you killed the Egyptian?" said the Hebrew many years ago, and now the officials of *Benei Yisrael* tell Moses that they actually have no desire for his favors or his involvement in their lives.

While the officials hurl their accusations, Moses is surely remembering the previous occasion when he tried to help his Israelite brethren, and received a similar response. The words of the officials arouse the old memory of his betrayal by his people, of their reporting him to the Egyptian ruler.

Now, Moses faces a similar reality, and he must decide how to act. The plan for saving the nation does not seem to be working out as planned, and Pharaoh has suddenly intensified his decrees. Now, Moses could escape once again to Midian, returning to Yitro and to his family and resigning from the assignment. But this is not what Moses does. It is not to Yitro that he returns, but to God: "And Moses returned to God," with a prayer and a demand that He save His people.

An accusation like that of the Hebrew or the officials can be met in three ways. It can lead one to abandon the mission, as Moses did sixty years earlier. It can be haughtily rejected, simply denied, as often occurs in such situations. Or it can be accepted, accepted so deeply that the accused identifies with the accusation and the sentiment that underlies it, which is what Moses does now. Just as the officials undergo a transformation and become spokesmen for their people, Moses now becomes a spokesman for Israel, emotionally expressing his identification with their pain and suffering, reflecting the original accusation against him onto God Himself.

Moses undergoes an important development in the wake of the harsh accusations of the officials. He decides here that the option of severing himself from his nation no longer exists. Moses' "corrective experience" does not take place because of any change in the behavior of the nation. On the contrary, his Israelite brethren still show no desire for his presence or his help. But Moses himself has changed. This time he does not escape to Midian; rather, he stands before God and pleads on behalf of the nation.

Moses' renewed identification with his nation, and his ability to overcome their earlier rejection of him, had already begun to show itself at the circumcision of his son, which took place at the lodge on the way to Egypt (4:24–26). There he declared his identification with the family of Abraham, against his will, because of the threat of the sword that hung over him. A second stage was hinted at when the Torah described his emotional meeting with his brother Aaron, his return to his family, symbolically his return to the embrace of the Jewish people. Now, the process of Moses' identification with his nation is complete. Of his own free will he returns to God and demands that the nation be saved from the yoke of Egyptian servitude.

Just as the officials' words to Moses and Aaron remind us of an earlier image in Moses' life, so they also foretell the rest of his life. When Moses stands before Pharaoh and warns him of the impending plague of blood, we are once again reminded of the officials' words:

Between the Officials and Moses	Plague of Blood (chapter 7)
And they met Moses and Aaron *standing facing them* as they *came out* from Pharaoh…	Behold, he *goes out* to the water, and you shall *stand facing* him…
to give a sword *into their hand* to kill us…	Behold, I shall strike with the staff which is *in my hand*
You have *made us odious*…	and the Nile shall *become odious.*

The Torah seems to want to teach us that the outcry of the officials, in their distress over the suffering of the people, is the basis upon which Moses rests when he comes to speak to Pharaoh. Out of the officials' identification with the suffering of the nation, Moses also identifies with them, and thereby draws strength to stand before Pharaoh.

Moses now reaffirms his identification as part of the people and, as such, he experiences their pain together with them. Their critique does not undermine his sense of leadership; on the contrary, it evokes his impassioned plea to the Almighty and his request for the promised deliverance of his own nation.

Immediately following his petition to God, Moses undergoes a second inauguration, a process that opens *Parashat Va'era*. Only now can God disclose to His chosen messenger the second factor of the redemption, the national-historical element. After Moses senses and identifies totally with the plight of *Am Yisrael*, he is prepared to learn about the national redemption, the redemption that sets this nation apart from the rest of the world.

From this point on, Moses leads the nation as God's agent, with two concurrent responsibilities facing him – moral and national. The new leader now faces both the moral responsibility of saving a downtrodden people from the unjust oppression and cruelty of a foreign ruler, and the national duty of bringing about the fulfillment of the promise to his forefathers. He will lead his people to the land where they can both live in freedom and independence and realize their potential as God's chosen people.

The Lineage Interruption

Rav Yair Kahn

Parashat Va'era is rich with topics which are profound as well as fascinating. Beginning with the Divine Attributes and culminating with the age-old problem of free choice and foreknowledge, we are confronted by an array of basic problems in Jewish philosophy. Nevertheless, my point of departure is what at first glance appears to be a mere textual problem:

> Behold *Benei Yisrael* have not listened to me, how then shall Pharaoh listen, and I am of uncircumcised lips. (6:12)

This statement, where Moses describes his hesitations after HaShem outlines the five-step process of redemption at our *parasha's* beginning, is repeated almost verbatim in verse 30. In between, we find what appears to be an artificial insertion, a partial listing of the lineage of the Jewish people. Rashi even comments: "This statement [v. 30] is the same statement mentioned above [v. 12]...it was repeated at this point because of the interruption."

This "interruption" has always troubled me. Why was it necessary to insert the lineage of the Jewish people at this point? Are there no locations more fitting for this survey? For instance, chapter 4, when

Moses returns to *Benei Yisrael* from Midian, seems suitable. Alternately, it could have been placed in chapter 7, following Moses' dialogue with God right before the beginning of the plagues.

Rashi (on 6:14) already notes that the survey is incomplete. Apparently, the Torah was interested not in the lineage of the entire Jewish people, but in the family background of Moses and Aaron. Therefore, although beginning with a brief account of the tribes of Reuben and Simeon, there is a detailed discussion of the household of Levi, culminating with a comprehensive account of Moses and Aaron's lineage.

This observation, however, does not solve our problem, but merely redirects it. Why was it crucial to trace the *yiḥus* (lineage) of Moses and Aaron at this specific point? Why not inform us of Moses' *yiḥus* at the beginning of chapter 2? Why is Moses first introduced to us anonymously as the child of a mysterious *"ish mibeit Levi* – a man from the house of Levi" (2:1)? Why reveal Moses' full identity to us only in mid-dialogue with God?

The interruption in mid-discussion, which forced the Torah to repeat Moses' statement in order to pick up the story thread, is so odd and out of place, that it bears witness to the absolute necessity of noting Moses' family background at this particular juncture. The Torah is transmitting a subtle message to us that we are obligated to decipher.

I believe that a close examination of the verses in question will reveal a sharp difference regarding the role of Moshe Rabbenu as described at the beginning and the end of the chapter. Furthermore, I will try to show that Moses' lineage is critical specifically for the role described at the end.

God's command to Moses which generated the first statement (v. 12) differs slightly from the demand which precedes the repetition. Initially, God orders Moses to speak to Pharaoh "to allow *Benei Yisrael* to leave his land" (v. 11). However, in verse 29 Moses is commanded to "speak to Pharaoh all that I say to you." It is interesting that while in verse 11 the content of Moses' assignment is explicitly emphasized – to free *Benei Yisrael*, in verse 29 the purpose is entirely absent. All that is mentioned is the general demand to speak whatever God will command.

At first glance, this might be taken as support for the thesis that verse 30 is merely a repetition of verse 12, so that an abridged version of the command suffices. However, a sensitive reading of verse 29 clearly reveals that not only brevity is at work here. "God spoke to Moses, saying: 'I am HaShem, speak to Pharaoh king of Egypt all that I speak to you.'" There are additions which were introduced, not found in verse 11. The demand of HaShem, as described in verse 29, is followed by the superfluous clause "all that I say to you." More strikingly, it is preceded by the declaration "I am HaShem." These elaborations seem to indicate a basic difference between the two verses. The initial command is pragmatic in nature. Moses, functioning as a political leader of *Benei Yisrael*, is charged with a defined task, freeing the people from bondage. In contrast, the significance of the second command is unrelated to any practical outcome *vis-à-vis Benei Yisrael*. "I am HaShem! Speak to Pharaoh in My name. Tell him all that I say to you." Moses is ordered to be the mouthpiece of HaShem, to deliver to Pharaoh a divine message, to represent, as it were, God Himself. To speak in the name of God is not merely a hollow abbreviation of the previous task. Rather it is the essence of a distinctly different role that was thrust upon Moses. The disregard of the pragmatic agenda highlights the religious nature of his mission.

Moshe Rabbenu's twofold response corresponds to his dual role. Verse 12 comprises a logical proof: Just as *Benei Yisrael* didn't listen to me, so will Pharaoh ignore me. In verse 30, the logical argument is absent. Within the pragmatic context, the issue is one of results. Will Moses be successful in his political assignment or not? However, the demand placed upon Moses in verse 29 raises an entirely different issue. How can a frail finite human being possibly be a representative of HaShem? "Behold, I am uncircumcised of lips; how will Pharaoh listen to me?" How can one with uncircumcised lips possibly speak in the name of Pure Holiness? The issue is not whether or not Pharaoh will agree to free *Benei Yisrael*. The problem is the absurdity inherent in the role itself.

As a matter of fact, the second account of Moses' argument is followed by an explicit description of the divine nature of Moses' task: "Behold I have made you a 'god' (*elohim*) to Pharaoh and your brother Aaron shall be your prophet" (7:1). Furthermore, it should be noted that up until this point Moses and Aaron have not performed any signs or miracles in Pharaoh's presence. They merely demanded the temporary release of *Benei Yisrael*. It is only from this point on that they begin to perform miracles (see 7:8–13.)

For the task with which Moses was initially charged there was no necessity to delve into his family background. Even the son of the anonymous *"ish mibeit Levi"* is capable, with extraordinary personal abilities, of assuming a role of political leadership. His unique qualities, coupled with the singular circumstances he experienced as a child, were sufficient reason to choose him to lead *Benei Yisrael* out of bondage.

However, the role of divine representation cannot be accomplished by any human being, no matter how great. It is impossible for any finite individual to fulfill such a role. The mandate to represent HaShem was not and could not be given to anyone on the personal level. Rather this divine role was reserved for an entire nation, chosen to be a "kingdom of priests and a sanctified nation." Therefore, prior to introducing the second aspect of his argument, there is a prerequisite of rooting Moses firmly within the context of *Knesset Yisrael*. Moses, the talented son of the anonymous *"ish mibeit Levi,"* is charged with the task of leading *Benei Yisrael* out of Egypt. However, it is only Moses the son of Amram, the grandson of Levi, who is appointed by HaShem as a divine representative to speak to Pharaoh in the name of HaShem.

At the end of the genealogical listing, Moses and Aaron are introduced twice. "These are Aaron and Moses who were told by HaShem 'take *Benei Yisrael* out of Egypt'" (6:26). This verse refers to the political role, as leaders charged with the task of practically freeing *Benei Yisrael*. At this level Aaron and Moses are equals, and Aaron the elder is mentioned first. However, when referring to the representative role, of speaking to Pharaoh, Moses is primary. "They are the ones who spoke to Pharaoh the king of Egypt…they are Moses and Aaron…. Behold I have made you a god to Pharaoh, and your brother Aaron shall be your prophet" (6:27, 7:1).

Moshe Rabbenu was chosen both as political leader of *Benei Yisrael* and as a messenger of HaShem. His leadership expresses itself in clearly defined political categories; together with Aaron, he is charged with leading *Benei Yisrael* out of bondage. He is unsure how he can possibly convince Pharaoh to fulfill this task, since even *Benei Yisrael* ignore him. Furthermore, Moses, as a manifestation of *Knesset Yisrael*, is the messenger of HaShem, charged to speak to Pharaoh in His holy name. He alone is given the impossible role of divine representation. Hence, he questions the paradoxical nature of this task thrust upon him.

Nevertheless, the inscrutable will of HaShem prevails. Moses as leader, rooted in his unique individual qualities, successfully leads *Benei Yisrael* to freedom, while Moses as a manifestation of *Knesset Yisrael* speaks to Pharaoh in the name of HaShem.

This understanding of the complex role with which Moses was charged casts an illuminating light on the purpose of the ten plagues. From the pragmatic perspective, which fulfills itself in achieving the result of freedom, the comprehensive constellation of the ten *makkot* seems superfluous, if not absurd. Is it necessary for the Almighty to batter Pharaoh with ten separate *makkot* in order to emerge victorious? Was the Omnipotent unable to overpower Egypt immediately? "For now if I would stretch out My hand, I could smite you and your people with pestilence, and you would perish from the earth" (9:15). Evidently, the *makkot* had an additional purpose. "However for this have I sustained you, in order to show you My power, and so that My name shall be proclaimed throughout the earth" (9:16).

The dramatic battle between Pharaoh and Moses was waged on two fronts. One front concerned itself with political sovereignty over *Benei Yisrael*. The issue of freedom or slavery hung in the balance. On the second front, *Benei Yisrael* were only incidentally involved. The subject was of a cosmic-religious nature: who controlled the fate of *Benei Yisrael*. In the *haftara* we read: "And the land of Egypt shall be desolate and waste, and they shall know that I am HaShem, because he (Pharaoh) has said: the river is mine and I have made it" (Ezek. 29:9). Pharaoh deified himself. He considered himself not only master of the Israelite slaves, but their lord as well. He demanded their worship along with their labor. The phrase "Thus spoke Pharaoh" (5:10) in response to "Thus spoke HaShem" is both striking and instructive.

Until chapter 6, the main focus was the issue of slavery. Moses and Aaron, the leaders of the people, demand a limited form of freedom. They are met with scorn and abuse, both by Pharaoh as well as *Benei Yisrael*. In the following chapter, a new front is opened in the Moses-Pharaoh confrontation. *Benei Yisrael* are demoted to a secondary role, as HaShem begins to smite Pharaoh and Egypt. Moses is charged with speaking to Pharaoh in His name.

At this point the *makkot* begin. They were not to overpower Pharaoh or to conquer Egypt. Rather, the purpose was to prove beyond doubt the absolute existence, omnipotence and omniscience of HaShem. "Thus says HaShem: with this you will know that I am the Lord" (7:17). "So that you should know that I am HaShem in the midst of the earth" (8:18). "So that you should know that there is none like me in all the earth" (9:14).

Moses' subsequent career should be viewed from this dual perspective. We find that Korah's attack on the authority of Moses is automatically translated as a rejection of HaShem: "Therefore you and your company are gathered against HaShem" (Num. 16:11). Moses did not serve only as the political leader – "And he was a king in Yeshurun" (Deut. 33:5) – Moses was a prophet as well, who delivered the transcendent word of HaShem to *Benei Yisrael*. His unique level of prophecy was rooted in Moses' special status as divine representative.

And there never arose in Israel a prophet like Moses, whom HaShem knew face to face, in all the signs and the wonders, which HaShem sent him to do in the land of Egypt, to Pharaoh and to all his servants, and in all the mighty hand and great awe that Moses performed in the sight of all Israel. (Deut. 34:10–12)

A Sign of Faith?

Rabbanit Sharon Rimon

I n our *parasha*, Moses and Aaron confront the Egyptian magicians in the challenge of turning a staff into a serpent. What is the meaning of this test? What is its purpose? Let us review, briefly, the various commands pertaining to the signs, both in relation to *Benei Yisrael* and in relation to the Egyptians.

In *Parashat Shemot*, Moses was commanded to perform signs before *Benei Yisrael*; to turn the staff into a serpent, to make his hand leprous, and to turn the water into blood. The purpose of these signs is explained there as follows:

> In that they will believe that the Lord God of their forefathers –
> the God of Abraham, the God of Isaac and the God of Jacob –
> appeared to you. (4:5)

The signs are supposed to bring the nation to faith in God's revelation to Moses.[1] But do these signs represent any proof of prophecy?

---

1. The Rishonim are divided on the question of whether the sign is also meant for Moses, or only for the nation. In Ramban's view, the reinforcement of faith is meant

In Rambam's view, faith that comes about through signs is not complete and wholehearted, but rather defective, since it is possible that the sign was performed through witchcraft. *Benei Yisrael* believed in Moses not because of the signs, but because of their experience at Mount Sinai:

> *Benei Yisrael* did not believe in Moshe Rabbenu because of the signs that he performed, for one who believes on the basis of signs has a deficiency in his heart, since a sign may be performed through enchantment or sorcery. Rather, all the signs that Moses performed in the wilderness were done out of necessity – not to bring proof of his prophecy. It was necessary to drown the Egyptians ... and likewise all the other signs. On what basis, then, did they believe in him? Because of the revelation at Sinai, where our eyes saw and not those of a stranger, and our ears heard, and no other. (Rambam, *Yesodei HaTorah*, 8:1)

Why did Moses then request the signs? Rambam explains:

> When the Holy One, blessed be He, said to him at the beginning of his prophecy, at the time when He gave him the signs to perform in Egypt and told him, "That they may listen to you," Moshe Rabbenu knew that one who believes on the basis of signs has a deficiency in his heart; so he considered and thought and was not ready to go [to Egypt], and he said, "But they will not believe me" – until the Holy One told him, "These signs are meant only for until they leave Egypt. After they leave and stand at this mountain [Ḥorev], the doubts that they entertain about you will depart." (ibid.)

In other words, Moses himself knew that faith that is based on signs is not serious faith. But God told him that the faith in his signs

---

for the nation and not for Moses, and the signs are merely an indication that he is destined to perform original acts (or some other sign of punishment). However, it is possible that the signs are meant to strengthen Moses' faith that God is indeed giving him the power to carry out his mission (see Abarbanel).

was to be only a temporary state of affairs, so long as the nation was still in Egypt.

Indeed, Aaron performs the signs before the nation, and the signs are effective and the people believe: "The people believed, and they accepted that the Lord had remembered *Benei Yisrael* and that He had seen their misery, and they bowed down and prostrated themselves" (Ex. 4:31).

However, this faith does not last long – "They did not listen to Moses, out of anguish of spirit and hard labor" (6:9).

Even if the signs were meant to provide an initial reinforcement of faith amongst *Benei Yisrael*, what was their purpose for Pharaoh and his magicians? Was the purpose the same for them? Did the signs lead to faith in God or in Moses as a prophet in their eyes?

WHY WERE THE SIGNS NOT PERFORMED
AT THE FIRST ENCOUNTER?

Initially, Moses is told about the signs in relation to *Benei Yisrael*, but not in relation to Pharaoh. Only during Moses' journey to Egypt does God appear to him and tell him to perform the wonders before Pharaoh:

> The Lord said to Moses: When you are going back to Egypt, see all the wonders which I have placed in your hand, and do them before Pharaoh. And I shall strengthen his heart, so that he will not let the people go. (Ex. 4:21)

Here the purpose of the signs is not made clear, and Moses is also told that Pharaoh will not change his stance in their wake.

In the first encounter with Pharaoh, Moses and Aaron tell him to let *Benei Yisrael* go – but they do not perform signs for Pharaoh. Pharaoh rejects their request, and declines to acknowledge God: "Who is the Lord, that I should listen to Him?" He then makes the slavery of *Benei Yisrael* even more unbearable.

Why do Moses and Aaron not perform their signs for Pharaoh? To answer, we shall examine their second mission to Pharaoh. At first, God reminds them once again of the signs and the wonders: "I shall harden Pharaoh's heart, that I may multiply My signs and My wonders in the land of Egypt" (7:3). In other words, the signs and wonders are important in and of themselves – "That I might multiply My signs." God then goes on to foretell that the Egyptians will recognize God: "The Egyptians shall know that I am the Lord, when I spread My hand over Egypt." But is this going to happen as a result of the signs? Seemingly, the verse is telling us that the knowledge of God will come about in the wake of the plagues – "When I stretch out My hand over Egypt" – rather than as a result of the signs.

Let us now review the rest of the mission, and try to answer our question.

IS AARON A BETTER "MAGICIAN"?

In chapter 7, we encounter for the first time an explicit command to perform a sign for Pharaoh, turning the staff into a serpent. However, the performance of the sign will come not at Moses and Aaron's initiative, but at Pharaoh's demand: "When Pharaoh speaks to you, saying, 'Give a sign for yourselves,' then you shall say to Aaron" (7:9).[2]

Why does Pharaoh request a sign? What is the significance of the signs that are given in response? Are they aimed at causing the Egyptians to believe in God's prophet or God? It is difficult to propose that either is the case, since in reality the signs fail to convince Pharaoh. On the contrary – the magicians succeed in doing exactly the same, using their magic arts!

But Aaron manages to do something that they are unable to do, and his staff swallows theirs. Moreover, his staff swallows their staffs after it has returned to being a staff: "Aaron's staff swallowed" (Rashi, ad loc.), and this is a "miracle within a miracle" (*Shabbat* 97a). However, is this sufficient reason for faith? Is the fact that Aaron is a somewhat more talented and successful "magician" reason enough to believe in God and in Moses, His servant? It may be that the signs were intentionally not

---

2. While the Torah does not tell us that Pharaoh indeed requested such a sign, it seems that the Torah simply omits mentioning it. It seems clear that the demonstration of the sign did take place, in light of God's words to Moses. Ramban argues that the Torah will occasionally omit details in a story, where it is clear that it must have taken place, for instance, in the story of Shekhem (Ramban, Gen. 42:34; Nechama Leibowitz, Exodus p. 120, note 4).

impressive. The Torah tells us, at the end of this episode (7:13): "Pharaoh's heart was hardened, and he did not listen to them." What is the significance of this hardening of the heart? Perhaps it was a miracle, with God acting directly to harden his heart. However, it is possible that God caused his heart to be hardened as a result of seeing that his magicians were able to perform the same signs. This gave Pharaoh the sense that he could handle Moses and Aaron, and even take on God, as it were. It may be for this reason that even the subsequent plagues did not deter him.

But why does Pharaoh demand signs? Seemingly, Pharaoh is not trying to find reinforcement for his faith. He is certain that their words are worthless. He tries to find some pretext by means of which to turn them away. By demanding signs Pharaoh is certain that he will prove that Moses and Aaron are worthless, inferior even to the magicians.

In light of this, it is possible that although the signs only equate Moses and Aaron with the magicians (with a slight advantage to the former), this is sufficient, for the objective is not to establish faith. Rather, it is a response to Pharaoh's demand, so that their status *vis-à-vis* Pharaoh will not be weakened (and perhaps will even be strengthened).

However, the entire process may also be understood differently. For this purpose, let us recall the other encounters with the magicians.

MAGICIANS FOR DREAMS AND MAGICIANS FOR SERPENTS

Egyptian magicians appear for the first time in the story of Joseph and Pharaoh's dreams. Comparing the two narratives, we discover surprising similarities. In both cases, the magicians compete against Hebrews – Joseph or Aaron. Both times, the situation comes about as a result of Pharaoh's fears. In the first instance, Pharaoh is anxious about his dreams: "And it was, in the morning, that his spirit was uneasy" (Gen. 41:8); in the second instance, Pharaoh is worried about *Benei Yisrael*: "He said to his people, Behold, the nation of the children of Israel is greater and more numerous than we…they shall fight against us and go up from the land" (Ex. 1:9–10).

Despite the seeming similarities, the ending is different. In Joseph's case, the confrontation leads to an acknowledgement of God: "Pharaoh said to his servants: Can there be found a man such as this, with *God's spirit in him*?" (Gen. 41:38–39). Here, however, Pharaoh does not believe, and his magicians are similarly unimpressed: "He did not listen to them."

Nevertheless, if we pursue our chapter further, we discover that the conclusion is indeed the same. Pharaoh, admittedly, does not believe – but the magicians, ultimately (in the plague of lice) come to recognize that "it is the finger of God"; they even tell this to Pharaoh (Ex. 8:15). Let us consider the comparisons:

	GENESIS – Joseph and the magicians	EXODUS – Aaron and the magicians
Pharaoh's concern:	"And it was in the morning that his spirit was uneasy" (41:8) – anxiety because of the dreams	"The nation of the children of Israel is mightier and more numerous than we...they shall fight against us and go up from the land" (1:9–10) – fear of *Benei Yisrael*
Subject of the confrontation:	Pharaoh's dreams	The staff and the serpent
Personalities involved:	The magicians and Joseph: "He called for all the magicians of Egypt" (41:8). "Pharaoh said to Joseph: I have dreamed a dream" (41:15).	Aaron and the magicians: "Aaron cast the staff" (7:10). "The magicians of Egypt, they too, did the same, with their magic arts" (7:11).
Advantage of the Hebrews over the Magicians:	"I have told it to the magicians, but none can explain it to me" (41:25). "And Joseph said...and the matter was good in Pharaoh's eyes and in the eyes of all of his servants" (41:37).	"Aaron's staff swallowed their staffs" (7:12).
Swallowing:	"The thin sheaves swallowed the seven healthy sheaves" (7).	"Aaron's staff swallowed their staffs" (ibid.).
Recognition of God:	"Pharaoh said to his servants: 'Can there be found a man such as this, with God's spirit in him.' And Pharaoh said to Joseph: 'After God has made all of this known to you'" (41:38–39).	"The magicians said to Pharaoh: 'It is the finger of God'" (8:15).

What is the meaning of the parallel between these two narratives? From the parallel, we can suggest the following – the dreams parallel the signs! The signs were not meant to establish faith. They came, just like the dreams had come previously, to convey a message, to present a vision. The signs would teach the Egyptians the meaning of the struggle against *Am Yisrael*!

To grasp this concept more firmly, let us try to understand the significance of a staff that turns into a serpent. Ezekiel records seven prophecies about the destruction of Egypt. His first prophecy, which is also read as the *Haftara* for *Parashat Va'era*, opens with a description of Pharaoh's pride, and the attendant punishment:

> In the tenth year, in the tenth month, on the twelfth day of the month, the Lord's word came to me, saying: Son of man – set your face against Pharaoh, king of Egypt, and prophesy about him…. So says the Lord God: Behold, I am against you, Pharaoh, king of Egypt – *the great serpent that crouches in the midst of its rivers,* and who said: My river is mine; I formed it for myself. I shall put hooks in your cheeks, and make the fish of your rivers stick to your scales, and I shall bring you up from the midst of your rivers, and all the fish of your rivers will be stuck to your scales. And I shall forsake you…. And all the inhabitants of Egypt shall know that I am the Lord, because they were a reed staff to the house of Israel. (29:1–6)

The prophet calls Pharaoh "the great serpent."[3] The serpent seeks to swallow up the weakened, downtrodden *Am Yisrael*: "And *Benei Yisrael* groaned from the labor, and they cried out" (Ex. 2:23).

Now the signs come into play. They show and clarify the true power of the serpent. First, they show that *Am Yisrael*, appearing like a

---

3. In historical sources, too, Pharaoh is portrayed as a serpent. Augustus' memorial coins show a crocodile (which presumably was the serpent) as the symbol of Egypt (see Y.Z. Mowshowitz, *Da'at Mikra, Yeḥezkel* 29, note 12). The Greek historian Plutarch likewise writes about the special admiration that the Egyptians showed towards the serpent, and the special qualities that they perceived it as possessing (see S.H. Bodenheimer, "HeḤai BeArtzot HaMikra" vol. 1, p. 102).

dried-out and pitiful stick, is destined to become a living being – and one capable of confronting Pharaoh, the serpent. Just as the staff is able to turn into a serpent, so *Am Yisrael* is destined to be revived.

The next stage sees Aaron's staff swallowing the staffs of the Egyptians. The arrogance of the serpent will be broken, and it will be *Am Yisrael* who will break it. The Midrash provides the following beautiful description:

> "Take your staff and cast it before Pharaoh" – the Holy One, blessed be He, said: "This wicked one, in his arrogance, calls himself a serpent, as it is written, 'The great serpent.' Go and tell him: See this staff – it is dried-out wood, and it becomes a serpent, with a life-force and a spirit; it swallows all the [other] staffs and ultimately returns to being dried wood. Likewise you – I created you from a putrid drop, and gave you kingship, but you have become arrogant and you say, 'My river is mine; I formed it for me.' Behold, I shall return you to nothingness! You have swallowed all the staffs of the tribes of Israel – now I shall remove what you have swallowed from your mouth." (*Yalkut Shimoni, Parashat Va'era, remez* 181)

Am Yisrael will be revived and arise, while the great serpent will return to chaos and nothingness.

As we have seen, there is a parallel between the story of the magicians here, and their appearance in the story of Pharaoh's dreams. The latter may contribute to and enhance our understanding of the former. The message is not merely about dry wood that turns into a living being, and not only about the victory of one nation over another.

In Pharaoh's dreams, we saw that the thin sheaves swallowed the healthy sheaves, and the thin cows swallowed the fat cows. The same message comes through here: Aaron's staff – a single staff stands alone against the many staffs of the magicians. *Am Yisrael* is a weak nation (perhaps great in number, but weak and downtrodden) against the strong Egyptians. But the staff of *Am Yisrael* is destined to swallow that of the Egyptians.

The clear, powerful sense of security in the present (satiation, rule, dignity, power, etc.) can be overturned in a moment; it can be swallowed up and disappear.

When Pharaoh sees the staffs of the magicians being swallowed up by Aaron's staff, he is meant to remember the dream of the previous Pharaoh, in which the king was made to understand that the abundance and contentment would come to an end. He is meant to understand that the situation of "satiety" in Egypt in his own times, with its rule of power, may similarly come to an end.

In light of the above, we might say that there was no attempt to prove or inculcate faith by means of the signs. The signs did apparently strengthen the status of Moses and Aaron, but did not lead to faith in God or in Moses. The main function of the signs was their message.

KINGS AND DREAMS

Let us examine the third place in Tanach were there is mention of magicians:

> In the second year of the reign of Nebuchadnezzar, Nebuchadnezzar dreamed dreams, and his spirit was uneasy, and his sleep evaded him. So the king commanded that the magicians, conjurers and sorcerers be called, to tell the king his dreams. And they came and stood before the king. And the king said to them, I have dreamed a dream, and my spirit is uneasy to know the dream. (Dan. 2:1–3)

In the book of Daniel, Nebuchadnezzar dreams a dream and does not know its meaning: "His spirit was uneasy and his sleep evaded him" – just like Pharaoh, "And it was, in the morning, that his spirit was uneasy." The magicians try to interpret the dream but are unsuccessful, until Daniel comes and manages to interpret it. Here, too, we are explicitly told of a contest between Daniel and the magicians, and of Daniel's superiority:

> The king spoke with them, and among all of them there was none like Daniel, Hanania, Mishael and Azaria, so they stood before

the king. And in any matter of wisdom and understanding that the king asked of them, he found them ten times better than all the magicians and conjurers who were in his entire kingdom. (Dan. 1:19–20)

In Daniel's case, too, the dream concerns four kingdoms, with the last of them being the Kingdom of Heaven (Dan. 2:44) that will reign forever.

Of the three places in Tanach where representatives of *Am Yisrael* confront magicians, two deal with interpretation of dreams, explaining how the future is going to look. In light of our discussion above, it seems that the middle case – the confrontation between Moses and Aaron and the Egyptian magicians – also deals with a vision of how the future will look with regard to the relationship between Israel and Egypt.

SUMMARY

Getting back to the magicians and Moses and Aaron: realistically, *Am Yisrael* appears to be approaching extinction, heaven forefend. The Egyptian empire rules everywhere; Pharaoh is the serpent over the whole world. *Am Yisrael* is a nation of slaves, despised and downtrodden. But the divine view is different. It becomes apparent that there are things that lie beyond the regular forces of nature; that divine rule extends even over things that appear all-powerful. Even the great serpent himself is transient; he, too, is destined to be swallowed up.

The Ran, in his *Derashot* (#3, "*Vehateshuva al zeh*") writes the following with regard to the magicians:

Because this was the land of magicians and enchanters, and what was going to be put to the test was one of the aspects of natural wisdom, therefore it was proper that it be believed that it was done by divine power, with no doubt, and that that which is impossible in nature is not impossible for the blessed God.

The magicians tried to achieve wonders using "scientific" means (as they understood them), using "natural wisdom" – which they believed only they possessed, over and above the regular knowledge of all the nation.[4] What they did not understand was that there are forces beyond the forces of nature; they did not understand that there is a divine view of reality.

The magicians were indeed good at what they did. They knew how to predict the future, in accordance with the reality at any given moment. But there were things that they were not able to foretell. They could not foretell the revolutions that God would generate in reality. Therefore, they failed to interpret Pharaoh's dream. Only God's hand could turn the good years into bad years, contrary to all forecasts.

Similarly, only God's hand could overturn the reality of Pharaoh's reign over all the world, to weaken Pharaoh and to free Israel from Egypt.

The issue at stake was a religious one, and therefore the challenge takes place between the magicians and Moses and Aaron. Ultimately, it is the magicians who understand and declare, "It is the finger of God" – the magicians, and not Pharaoh. This may be the result of the special hardening of Pharaoh's heart. But there may also be a different reason. Pharaoh knew that the magicians were capable of performing various special feats through their scientific powers, therefore he was able to attribute such "magical" powers to Moses and Aaron, too. But the magicians were conscious of the limits of scientific powers, and at a certain stage were forced to admit, "It is the finger of God."

It is possible that for *Benei Yisrael*, too, the signs were not a test of faith. This was not an attempt to prove that Moses was a genuine prophet of God. The signs did provide a certain degree of reinforcement of faith, but this was not their purpose. For *Am Yisrael*, too, the signs were symbols of strength and encouragement: a sign that the inanimate staff was going to come alive, a sign that even a leprous hand could heal, a sign that the Egyptians were going to be punished through having their water turn to blood. These signs, along with God's encouraging promise, "I

4. The Rishonim are divided as to whether the magicians actually succeeded in performing any real feat. Rambam (*Moreh Nevukhim*, part III, chapter 37), insists that witchcraft has no substance, and some of the commentators adopt this view. However, Ramban (commenting on our chapter) and other commentators seem to suggest that there was some substance to the actions of the magicians. From the Ran it appears that their words did contain something real, based on real, scientific knowledge (but see also *derasha* #5 of the Ran; we shall not elaborate further here).

have surely remembered you," gave *Am Yisrael* hope, and strengthened their faith that God was going to save them.

> And the people believed, and they accepted that the Lord had remembered *Benei Yisrael*, and that He had seen their suffering, and they bowed down and prostrated themselves. (Ex. 4:31)

"Measure for Measure": Keywords in the Story of the Exodus

Rav Nathaniel Helfgot

I t is well-known that the stories of the exodus contain many examples of *"mida keneged mida"* (literally – measure for measure), where we find the Egyptians suffering the same fate that they imposed – or planned to impose – on *Benei Yisrael*.[1] Sometimes, such parallels are emphasized by means of similar wording or other literary devices. In this article, we shall concentrate on the repeated use of the two Hebrew roots *k-b-d* (כ.ב.ד. – "heavy," "hard") and *ḥ-z-k* (ח.ז.ק. – "strong") in the first part of Exodus.

It is interesting to note that the saga's two great adversaries, Moses and Pharaoh, are both presented in these terms. Moses describes himself as *"khevad peh ukhevad lashon"* (Ex. 4:10 – heavy of speech and of a heavy tongue), and consequently claims that he is unworthy of appearing before Pharaoh in order to bring *Benei Yisrael* out of Egypt. Pharaoh, on the other hand, is described throughout as *"khevad lev,"* hard-hearted (8:11, 8:28, 9:7). This hard-hearted king, in response to Moses' demand

---

1. See, for example, Amos Ḥakham, *Da'at Mikra* on *Sefer Shemot*, vol. 1, p. 282, note 58.

to "Let my people go," decrees: "Let heavier work (*tikhbad ha'avoda*) be laid on the men, so that they may labor in it; and let them not regard vain words" (5:9). In the end, it is the *"khevad peh ukhevad lashon"* himself who prevails over the *"khevad lev."*

Parallel to the root *k-b-d*, we also find the word root *ḥ-z-k* being used throughout the story – specifically in the description of the ten plagues. In the chapters dealing with the plagues we find that the strengthening or hardening of Pharaoh's heart is mentioned ten times. In the plagues of blood, lice, boils, locusts and darkness, the Torah speaks of the *strengthening* of Pharaoh's heart (either by his own doing or by God's intervention), while in the plagues of frogs, gnats and pestilence the Torah speaks of the *hardening* of his heart. The plague of hail is unique in that both actions are mentioned: "and he hardened (*vayakhbed*) his heart, he and his servants. And the heart of Pharaoh was strengthened (*vayeḥezak*), and he would not let *Benei Yisrael* go" (9:34–35).

Within the cycle of the plagues we already find the foundation of *"mida keneged mida,"* as pointed out by the commentaries, for during the first five plagues Pharaoh acts autonomously ("He hardened his heart"), while from the sixth plague (boils) onwards, "God strengthened Pharaoh's heart" (9:12), "For I have hardened his heart" (10:1). God punishes Pharaoh for hardening his heart and causes his heart to be strengthened (independently of his will) in order that the entire weight of divine anger can be brought down upon him. But beyond this internal cycle, we find further evidence of verses and events which counter the "hardness" and "strength" of Pharaoh.

Pharaoh "hardens" (*meḥazek*) his heart over and over again for the purposes of holding on to *Am Yisrael* and perpetuating their slavery, but when the time comes for the exodus, the Egyptians try to hurry them: "The Egyptians urged (*vateḥezak*) the people, that they might send them out of the land in haste" (12:33). *Benei Yisrael* are commanded to remember that on the day of the exodus, "God took you out by strength of hand (*beḥozek yad*)," and when laying *tefillin* each day we are commanded to remember that, "with a strong hand (*beyad ḥazaka*) God brought you out of Egypt" (13:9).

Keeping this emphasis in mind, the first sign shown to Moshe Rabbenu takes on particular significance. His staff turns into a snake, and God commands him, "Stretch out your hand and take (*ve'eḥoz*) its tail" (4:4). But when Moses obeys the command, the Torah says, "And he stretched out his hand and grasped (*vayaḥazek*) it." As becomes clear from *peshat* (as understood by the author of the *Midrash Rabba*),[2] the snake is symbolic of Pharaoh or of Egypt, and Moses is destined not only to hold it (*le'eḥoz*) but to grasp it with strength (*lehaḥazik*), thus turning it into dry wood devoid of any power or life. We may even see this as a continuation of the hint mentioned to Moshe Rabbenu in the previous chapter: "But I know that the king of Egypt will not let you go, unless it be with a strong hand (*beyad ḥazaka*)" (3:19).

The climax of the exodus story is the splitting of the sea, and here the pattern we have traced also reaches its climax. God tells Moshe Rabbenu, "I shall strengthen (*veḥizakti*) Pharaoh's heart and he will pursue after them" (14:4), and then God uses a new expression for the first time: "And I shall gain honor (*ve'ikavda*) by Pharaoh and by all his host." After all the hardening of Pharaoh's heart, the story progresses towards its culmination: God will be honored through the Egyptians. The backdrop is ready for an extraordinary and miraculous event.

After the internal arguments within the Israelite camp have ceased and the nation is ready to enter the sea, the Torah once again repeats and emphasizes: "And I will strengthen (*meḥazek*) the heart of Egypt (not only Pharaoh's heart!) and they shall follow them, and I will gain honor (*ve'ikavda*) by Pharaoh and by all his host, his chariots and his horsemen. And Egypt shall know that I am the Lord, when I have gained honor (*behikavdi*) by Pharaoh, by his chariot and his horsemen" (14:17–18). Now the miracle takes place – the sea opens, the nation proceeds and the Egyptians pursue them, but:

2. "Rabbi Eliezer said: The reason why the staff turned into a snake was to represent Pharaoh, who is called a snake, as it is written: 'So says the Lord God, Behold, I am above you, Pharaoh king of Egypt, the great serpent.' And He called the leviathan a 'piercing serpent,' for it bit Israel. God said to him: 'You have seen Pharaoh, and how he is like a snake; in the future you will strike him with your staff, and in the end he will be like wood. Just as the staff does not bite, so will he not bite'" (*Shemot Rabba* 3, 12). See also Ibn Ezra, as well as Nachum Sarna, *Exploring Exodus* (New York, 1986), pp. 57–60.

God looked to the Egyptian camp through the pillar of fire and cloud, and brought confusion into the Egyptian camp. And He took off their chariot wheels, that they drove heavily (*bikhvedut*). (14:24–25)

It is specifically now,[3] at this point of heaviness (*khvedut*), that the Egyptians sense that the battle is lost: "And the Egyptians said, Let us flee from Israel, for God fights for them against Egypt" (14:25).[4]

In light of this perspective on the story of the exodus, the significance of the conflict between *Benei Yisrael* and *Benei Edom* in the book of Numbers (chapter 20) is to be noted. This encounter is the first instance of conflict between the new generation of *Benei Yisrael* and another nation. The majority of these Jews were never in Egypt, at least not as adults. Moshe Rabbenu takes this opportunity of reminding them of the exodus:

Thus says your brother Israel: You know all the travail that has befallen us, how our fathers went down to Egypt, and how we dwelt in Egypt for a long time, and how Egypt troubled us and our fathers. And we cried to God and He heard our voice, and sent an angel and took us out of Egypt. And here we are in Kadesh, a city on the outskirts of your border. (Num. 20:15–16)

---

3. Here the providence of "*mida keneged mida*" reaches its climax, as Ḥazal commented in the *Mekhilta* on this verse: "Rabbi Yehuda says: The same way that they meted out, You meted out to them. They said, 'Let heavier work (*tikhbad ha'avoda*) be laid on them,' and You paid them back in the same way; therefore it is written: 'And they drove heavily (*bikhvedut*).'"

    It may also be that Ḥazal saw as the basis for the famous explanations of the multiplicity of plagues which Egypt suffered at the Yam Suf (as we recite in the Haggada: "In Egypt they suffered ten plagues, and at the sea they suffered fifty plagues," etc.) the special terminology of "I shall gain honor (*ve'ikhabda*) by Egypt." This is the only instance of God expressing Himself thus – describing the punishment which He will bring upon the Egyptians. On this point see Amos Ḥakham, *Da'at Mikra* on *Sefer Shemot*, vol. 1, p. 244.

4. Perhaps this is really the conclusion of a circle which began with the story of the snake, symbolic of Pharaoh, when Moses fled (*nas*) from it, and here, ultimately, Egypt flees (*anusa*) from before *Benei Yisrael* and their leader, Moshe Rabbenu!

Moses' intention in mentioning the history of *Am Yisrael* is not clear: is he trying to emphasize their suffering in order to arouse compassion and kindness on the part of Edom, or is he conveying a veiled threat – "Look what happened to the Egyptians, who tortured the first generation of *Benei Yisrael!*"?[5] Either way, Edom's message is clear: "'You shall not pass.' And Edom came out against him with many people and with a strong hand (*be'am kaved uveyad ḥazaka*)." Here, too, the parallel with the story of the exodus is inescapable. Edom is saying, as it were, to Israel: "The 'hardness and strength' are now in my hands and not in yours; the second generation of Israelites will not benefit from the path of 'strength and hardness!'" *Benei Edom* have not learned the lesson of what God did to Pharaoh and the Egyptians, which we commemorate every Pesaḥ.

---

5. The Torah's use of the parallel words, "He sent an angel (*malakh*) and took us out of Egypt," and then, at the beginning of this *parasha*, "Moses sent messengers (*malakhim*) from Kadesh to the king of Edom," emphasizes this possibility.

Between Va'era and Bo

Rav Mosheh Lichtenstein[1]

I. INTRODUCTION

The first seven plagues appear in *Parashat Va'era* and the last three in *Parashat Bo*. This division is not accidental; rather it reflects a very significant aspect of the meaning of Exodus. In *Parashat Va'era*, the struggle between Moses and Pharaoh relates to the recognition of God, and it is toward this objective that the plagues are directed. In *Parashat Bo*, on the other hand, the goal of the plagues is to take Israel out of Egypt. The moment that Pharaoh declares at the end of *Parashat Va'era*, "The Lord is righteous, and I and my people are wicked," the first objective is achieved and the plot advances to the next stage, i.e., bringing Pharaoh to send Israel out of his land.

In light of this development, the very nature of the plagues changes in accordance with the new objective. Thus, the plagues in *Parashat Bo* are utterly different from those in *Parashat Va'era*. The plagues in *Parashat Va'era* are characterized by the following:

1. Plagues whose purpose was to harass, rather than to destroy;

---

1. See the discussion by Rav Ezra Bick in *parashat Bo* for a different approach to the same question.

2. Removal of the plague, in the wake of Pharaoh's request, only on the next day;

3. The magicians' serving as Pharaoh's aides.

All this changes in *Parashat Bo*. From the very beginning of the *parasha*, we encounter harsh plagues that are meant to destroy the Egyptian economy. The locusts do not merely vex Egypt, but rather they destroy the Egyptian food stocks. In their wake, there is no food left from vegetable sources. As opposed to the aftermath of the plague of blood when the grain became repulsive, here it disappears; as opposed to what happened with the plague of hail, there is no surviving remnant, but rather the entire crop is destroyed. It is not by chance that Pharaoh describes the plague of locusts as "this death." The plague of darkness brings life to an absolute standstill, and is like temporary death. As for the killing of the firstborns and the destruction that it wreaks, nothing needs to be added. To summarize, we are talking about the threat of total destruction of the country and plagues that involve death.

The reason for this is simple. In *Parashat Va'era*, it was necessary to bring Pharaoh to inner recognition, and therefore it was impossible to exert excessive force that would have broken him immediately. In *Parashat Bo*, God wishes to cause Pharaoh to send Israel out, and for that purpose great force is used to subdue Pharaoh and break him immediately.

II. SERVANTS INSTEAD OF MAGICIANS

In light of this, we can discern a number of changes that take place in *Bo* in contrast to *Va'era*.

First of all, the *magicians* leave the picture, and in their stead we encounter Pharaoh's *servants*. Pharaoh's servants constitute the civil administration that runs the country and worries about Egypt's day-to-day functioning. They do not concern themselves with theological questions, but rather with the welfare of the kingdom and its resources. Thus, as long as the debate concerned only theological matters and did not threaten the welfare of the state, they did not intervene. But as soon as the state began to suffer harm, and the center of the plagues' gravity shifted to the attempt to destroy the economic and human foundations of Egypt, they entered into the thick of things, and their words reflect the efficacy of the plagues. Already at the time of the plague of hail – which begins the process of the vanquishing of Egypt, in addition to the struggle over the recognition of God – Pharaoh's servants make their appearance and begin to reflect the concern about the price extracted by the plagues. In the plague of locusts, with which *Parashat Bo* opens, their presence assumes critical importance, reflecting the new objective of the latter plagues:

> And Pharaoh's servants said to him, "How long shall this man be a snare to us? Let the men go, that they may serve the Lord their God: know you not yet that *Egypt is lost?*" (Ex. 10:7)

In their eyes, the theological struggle is not worth the destruction of Egypt. Their non-intervention in the proceedings until that point stemmed from the fact that the previous plagues did not threaten to destroy Egypt, whereas the plagues of *Parashat Bo*, which were meant to bring about the exodus of Israel from Egypt, extracted a very heavy cost.

III. IMMEDIATE REMOVAL

The very same reason underlies another change in comparison to *Parashat Va'era*. In *Bo*, the plagues are removed immediately, without waiting until the next day, as in the past. The plague of locusts is the first place that it says that Pharaoh called for Moses and Aaron *"in haste"*; previously, it had merely said that Pharaoh called them, but from that point on there is great urgency. The climax is reached, of course, in the plague of the smiting of the firstborns when Pharaoh is forced to run to Moses in his house and plead before him.

IV. THE NEGOTIATIONS

The negotiations between Pharaoh and Moses in the aftermath of the plagues of locusts and darkness should be understood in this light as well. Following the threat of the locusts, Pharaoh proposes to Moses that he would be willing to allow the men alone to go out into the wilderness to serve God, but Moses refuses the offer and demands that the entire people be allowed to go. Later, during the plague of darkness, Pharaoh agrees to send the children as well, but Moses insists that even the sheep and the cattle must go with them. We are not dealing here with the sort of haggling that takes place between two merchants, with Moses raising the price at every turn, and Pharaoh being forced into ever greater concessions, but rather with Pharaoh's misunderstanding of the change that has taken place in the objective of the plagues. Since Moses had originally spoken of a three-day journey into the wilderness followed by Israel's return to Egypt, Pharaoh proposed that they go in partial formation in order to observe their religious feast. At first he thought that his proposal that only the men should go would suffice, for they are the ones who would be offering the sacrifices. Even afterwards, his readiness to agree that the children would go but not the animals assumed that in question was a religious feast at the end of which Israel would return to Egypt. He insisted that the animals stay behind not because of their economic value, but because that served as a sign that Israel was planning to return to Egypt. This, however, is precisely the reason that Moses refuses to agree. Pharaoh's proposal to leave for three days was valid in *Parashat Va'era*, when the matter in dispute was recognition of God. From the moment that this objective was achieved, Moses' demand became that Israel be sent out from Egypt. Hence he insists on the departure of all of Israel, including their sheep, cattle and other property.

V. BETWEEN THE *HAFTAROT*

The *haftarot* of *Parashot Va'era* and *Bo* also reflect this distinction. The focus of the *haftara* of *Va'era* (Ezek. 28:25–29:21) is "And all the inhabitants of Egypt shall know that I am the Lord" (Ezek. 29:6). The *haftara* for *Parashat Bo* (Jer. 46:13–28) deals with the price that Egypt will pay, and the human angle of the smiting of Egypt.

The background for *Parashat Bo's haftara* is found in the previous prophecy, where the prophet Jeremiah prophesies the ascent of Babylon and the geo-political failure of Egypt to halt Babylon's takeover of the entire region. That prophecy relates to a battle fought on the shores of the Euphrates River, where Egypt tries to take the initiative and stop Babylon in the north. The *haftara* of *Bo* relates to the next stage in the process; the war is not at the Euphrates, but in Egypt where Nebuchadnezzar comes to strike at Egypt itself.

What this means is that behind every political and military deci-sion there is a human price that will be extracted from Egypt. Pharaoh's struggle over his geo-political standing will not end with Egypt's decline but with the conquest of Egypt itself. The prophet's concern, however, is not with the significance of the conquest on the standing of Egypt, but with the sword that will devour the Egyptian people. The situa-tion is described by the words "for the sword shall devour round about you" (Jer. 46:14), and Egypt's feeling is "Arise, let us go again to our own people, and to the land of our nativity, from the oppressing sword" (v. 16). In addition to the sword, they are also threatened by exile and the destruction of their country: "O you daughter dwelling in Egypt, furnish yourself with the baggage of exile: for Nof shall be waste and desolate without inhabitant" (v. 19). The contrast with Ezekiel who also prophesies about the desolation and destruction of Egypt ("Behold, I will bring a sword upon you, and cut off man and beast out of you. And the land of Egypt shall be desolate and waste"; Ezek. 29:8–9) is striking. Ezekiel's argument is "and they shall know that I am the Lord," whereas Jeremiah ignores all that and focuses exclusively on the destruction itself.

VI. THE COST OF POPULAR SUPPORT

On this point there is a similarity between the *haftara* and the *parasha*. In the *parasha* as well, the Egyptian man on the street pays the price for Pharaoh's war against the people of Israel: his grain and sustenance are destroyed, his life comes to a halt, and his firstborn son dies. In this context, it is fitting to cite what I once heard from Rav Soloveitchik. The Rav asked why is it that God killed all the firstborns in Egypt and did not suffice with that which was said in *Parashat Shemot*, that God would kill Pharaoh's firstborn son. He answered as follows: "As a child in Russia, who suffered from constant anti-Semitism – from whom did I suffer? When I ran home from those who wished to hit and humili-ate me – from whom was I running? Not from the czar, but from the neighborhood bully." Without the support and cooperation of the Egyptian people, Israel would not have suffered as they did in Egypt. The popular support is what allowed for the oppression of the people of Israel, and the people of Egypt were full partners in the subjugation. In the *haftara* as well, "the daughter dwelling in Egypt" is perceived as identifying with Pharaoh and assisting him, and therefore she too is punished along with him.

VII. THE DIFFERENCE BETWEEN THE CROCODILE AND THE FAIR HEIFER

Regarding this point, let us contrast the two main metaphors found in the two *haftarot*. In Ezekiel's prophecy, the main metaphor is the crocodile, whereas Jeremiah prophesies about a very fair heifer, and describes Egypt as "fatted bullocks." The crocodile symbolizes power and primality, and as such it is a fitting symbol of the creation, but it has no importance for human consumption. The heifer, on the other hand, is identified with human survival, and supplies man with his basic needs. As a domesticated animal, it does not radiate power and energy, but rather the human economy. The heifer is not a force in nature that rules over animals, but rather it is ruled by others. All this turns the heifer into a poor metaphor for Ezekiel's purposes, but a very good one for the issue that Jeremiah is dealing with. So too, the heifer symbolizes the sated middle class, and its slaughter at the hand of Babylon ("But destruction comes; it comes out of the north"; Jer. 46:20) symbolizes the destruction of the easy life of the Egyptians.

VIII. A MODEST PROMISE

The *haftara's* conclusion with the promise to Israel is also focused on the perspective of the suffering individual, rather than on the theological or national ramifications of redemption:

> But fear not you, O My servant Jacob, and be not dismayed, O Israel; for, behold, I will save you from afar, and your seed from the land of their captivity; and Jacob shall return, and be quiet and at ease, and none shall make him afraid. Fear you not, O Jacob My servant, says the Lord: for I am with you, for I will make a full end of all the nations where I have driven you: but I will not make a full end of you, but correct you in due measure; yet will I not utterly destroy you. (46:27–28)

The emphasis here is on the fact that the people will enjoy peace and ease and that their fears will disappear. No mention is made here of the raising of Israel's horn or a declaration that the nations will recognize God, but merely that the people will enjoy peace. If we examine the second verse, we see that its promise is minimal, its essence being that God will not utterly destroy Israel. So too, both verses emphasize "Fear you not, O Jacob My servant" – the fear and concern about the very existence of the sword. The consolation in this prophecy is directed not only at Israel's survival as a nation, but also towards its individual members.

We might add that it is possible that the redundancy in these two verses corresponds to the two prophecies that Jeremiah prophesied about Egypt. The first verse is directed toward the prophecy that precedes it, and it focuses on the peace promised to the individual members of Israel. The second verse relates back to the previous prophecy which dealt with the political fall of Egypt as a nation, and it prophesies by way of consolation about the destiny of Israel as a nation that it will not be utterly destroyed, but rather that it will survive as God's people.

Parashat Bo

Representing God or Representing Israel

Rav Ezra Bick

The ten plagues are divided into two *parashot* – the first seven in *Parashat Va'era* and the last three in *Parashat Bo*. Is this merely a division of convenience, or is there an important distinction between these two groups of plagues?

Parashat Bo begins with God explaining to Moses the purpose of the plagues:

> Come to Pharaoh, for I have hardened his heart and the heart of his servants, in order that I set my signs in his midst; and in order that you recount to the ears of your son and your son's son that which I have wrought in Egypt and the signs which I have placed in it, and you shall know that I am HaShem. (10:1–2)

This is clearly a break in the continuous narrative of the plagues, though nothing has occurred which seems to warrant this interruption. Several commentators surmise a reluctance on Moses' part to keep coming to Pharaoh, seeing that Moses' warnings have not had any apparent effect on him. God tells Moses that he is commanded to go to Pharaoh anyway, not to convince him to let the Jews go, but in order to demonstrate the opposite, and justify continued plagues and signs of God's might. However, there is no evidence in the verses for this hesitation on Moses' part, nor any explanation why it takes place precisely after the seventh plague.

What's more, this explanation is qualitatively different from similar explanations given in the past. Before the first plague, *in Parashat Va'era*, God told Moses:

> And I shall harden the heart of Pharaoh, and will multiply my signs and wonders in the land of Egypt. But Pharaoh will not listen to you, and I shall set my hand against Egypt.... And Egypt shall know that I am HaShem, when I stretch out my arm over Egypt and take out the Jews from their midst. (7:3–5)

Similarly, when Moses removes the frogs, he tells Pharaoh to choose the hour, "so that you know that there is none like HaShem our God." Finally, before the plague of wild animals, Moses tells Pharaoh that there will be a dividing line between the land of Egypt and Goshen, "in order that you know that I am HaShem in the midst of the land."

In all these instances, the purpose of the plague, or at least some aspect of the plague, is that Egypt, or Pharaoh, recognize God's power and presence. Before the eighth plague, however, we find a new emphasis:

> In order that you recount to the ears of your son and your son's son that which I have wrought in Egypt and the signs which I have placed in it, and you shall know that I am HaShem.

The target of the signs and wonders is Israel, that they should know that He is HaShem. Something has changed!

The most striking change is also the key to understanding what has happened. God commands Moses to "come to Pharaoh." This is the first time such a command appears before a plague without the message that is to be delivered. Before all previous plagues, we find one of two forms: Either Moses is told to accost Pharaoh somewhere (usually on the Nile) and warn him of the impending plague, or Moses is told to simply perform an action which brings on the plague.

In some cases, God does not tell Moses to first speak to Pharaoh – but in those cases, there also is no command to "come to Pharaoh." In our case, we have the anomalous situation of God telling Moses to visit Pharaoh, without telling him what to say, followed immediately by Moses going to Pharaoh and delivering a speech, warning of the next plague, the locusts. Ramban (commentary to 10:2) explains that it must be assumed that if Moses speaks to Pharaoh, God had first told him what to say, just as previously in the case of the hail we must assume that Moses does tell Pharaoh what God had commanded him to say, even though it is not explicitly stated. The Torah, claims Ramban, does not have to repeat both the command and the fulfillment. This strengthens my question. Had the original command been totally absent, we would have a conservation of unnecessary repetition. But the Torah here does have both the command and the fulfillment – but they are not parallel. God does command Moses to go to Pharaoh, followed by Moses' explicit fulfillment of that command – it is just that in the command, there was no mention of the content of the speech; and instead, we find the totally unexpected explanation of God's purpose in artificially lengthening the Egyptian ordeal by hardening the heart of Pharaoh.

Starting with this plague of locusts, the Torah noticeably stresses the comings and goings of Moses, beyond the detail necessary to explain where he is. It seems as though the coming before Pharaoh, and the leaving his presence, is an independent focus of the story, without reference to what happens or what is spoken during the encounter.

First, the opening command – "Come to Pharaoh," with no particular content to the visit explicated by God. I think Ramban is undoubtedly correct – God must have told Moses what to say, and this is the opportune time to do so. But filling in that lacuna does not in itself explain the structure of the verse, which gives the appearance that God did not tell Moses what to say. So, having accepted Ramban's comment, we still have to explain why the explicit structure of the verse has God commanding Moses to make an appearance, to go, without telling him what to do. The unavoidable impression is that there is now special importance in the visit itself, regardless of the content of Moses' speech.

This is mirrored and emphasized in the actual events of the following three plagues.

A. Moses delivers the warning about the locust, and "he turned and left the presence of Pharaoh."

B. After hearing his servants' fears, Pharaoh has Moses returned, only to "drive them away from the presence of Pharaoh."

C. Moses is called to Pharaoh after the plague of locust and then "goes out from the presence of Pharaoh" in order to pray to God.

D. After calling Moses in response to the plague of darkness, Pharaoh tells him, "Get away from me; be careful not to see my face again, for on the day you see my face you shall die." Moses answers, "So be it, as you have spoken; I shall not again see your face." It seems, then, that the Torah is drawing attention to the significance of the face-to-face meetings between Moses and Pharaoh. The tension here is palpable, and it centers, not around the content of the communication between Pharaoh and Moses, but on the direct personal confrontation between them. It is not hard to imagine the scene – these two men staring at each other, the grim hardness of their words, the challenge in the supercharged air.

E. Apparently, before leaving, Moses continues and gives Pharaoh the final message of God, the impending plague of the first-born. The final line of this warning is: "And all these, your servants, will come down to me and bow down before me, saying, 'leave, you and all the people at your feet, and then shall I leave'; and he left the presence of Pharaoh with consuming anger." The circle begun with "*bo el Pharaoh*" – come to Pharaoh – has been finally closed with Moses walking out on him.

Of course, we all are familiar with the final scene:

F. "And Pharaoh rose in the night, he and all his servants…and he called to Aaron and Moses in the night and said: 'Get up and leave from my people, you and the children of Israel.'" The Midrash (Rashi 11:8; see also 12:31), based on the closing line of Moses in his last meeting with Pharaoh, claims that Pharaoh came to the house of Moses to plead with him to leave. Again, another closing of the circle of "*bo*" – Pharaoh comes to Moses rather than Moses coming to him.

The different nature of *Bo* is clear – starting with this plague of locust, God is telling Moses that the confrontation with Pharaoh is to be a personal one – he is to go to face Pharaoh directly and engage in a test of wills with him. The verbal content of Moses' speeches is now secondary in importance to the actual personal appearance that he must make. Moses is to overcome Pharaoh on the personal level – as Moses says, "all your servants shall come and bow down to me" (Rashi explains that "servants" was a respectful way of hinting at Pharaoh himself). Moses "squares off" with Pharaoh, in a battle of wills, and eventually wins – of course, the reason is that God's miracles are behind him.

To explain the reason for this personal confrontation, let us place it in a wider perspective. At the beginning of *Va'era*, Moses is introduced through the filter of the lineage of the Jews as a member of the Jewish nation rather than as an extraordinary individual possessing unique talents. Because he is to represent God, rather than himself, he is placed in the context of the genealogical tree of *Benei Yisrael*. If I can widen that idea slightly, the genealogy which eventually reaches Moses (and Aaron) basically has the effect of assimilating Moses – he is just another Jew, so to speak. The reason is that it is the Jews as a whole who are demanding of Pharaoh that he let them go – Moses is just a representative Jew. Moses' own personality is submerged – what is important is the message he carries in the name of HaShem, God of Israel.

By the time we get to *Bo*, the message is really unimportant, for at least one very simple reason. Pharaoh will not in any event listen to the message, for his heart is hardened by God. Indeed, I think the conversations between Pharaoh and Moses in *Parashat Bo* are characterized by a lack of anything approaching genuine communication, unlike *Parashat Va'era*, where at least at times, Pharaoh seems to be wavering or genuinely considering the power or truth in Moses' demands. In *Bo*, although Pharaoh asks Moses for his position, he then rejects it out of hand without any hesitation. Moses' position, even backed by the plagues, makes no impression on Pharaoh. I am arguing that the purpose of the conversation was not to persuade Pharaoh, was not in fact to communicate with him at all, but should be found in the confrontation itself. Moses is not presenting the Jewish position – he is locking himself in battle with Pharaoh, facing up to him, waiting, as it were, for him to blink. These are not negotiations any more, this is confrontation for the sake of confrontation.

Why? The answer is given by God:

> Come to Pharaoh, for I have hardened his heart and the heart of his servants, in order that I set my signs in his midst; and in order that you recount to the ears of your son and your son's son that which I have wrought in Egypt and the signs which I have placed in it, and you shall know that I am HaShem.

The purpose of God's elaborate plan is that "you [plural] shall know that I am HaShem." Now we all know who is the ultimate protagonist of the battle with Pharaoh; it is not Moses but God Himself. As this verse says, "that which I have wrought in Egypt." *Ḥazal* expressed this most clearly in the passage from the Pesaḥ Haggada:

> "And I shall pass through the land of Egypt" – I and not an angel – "and I shall strike every firstborn" – I and not a seraph – "and I shall pass judgment on all the gods of Egypt" – "I and not an agent – I am HaShem" – I am He and no other.

The final confrontation, the plague of the firstborn, takes place with the Jews locked in their homes, and God Himself, alone, passing through Egypt. (The same theme is explicitly repeated in *Parashat Beshallaḥ* – "God shall fight for you and you shall be still"). It is striking, however, that during the prelude to the last plague, Moses openly identifies himself with God.

> Moses said: "So says HaShem: At midnight I shall go forth in Egypt. And every firstborn in the land of Egypt shall die.... And all these, your servants, will come down to me and bow down before me, saying, 'leave, you and all the people at your feet', and then shall I leave."

Who is the reference of the pronoun 'I' in this sentence? Since Moses' speech begins with the very formal opening "*ko amar HaShem,*" which is also immediately followed by the statement "I shall go forth in the land of Egypt," it would seem to clearly be God. Yet the last line – "and then shall I leave," seems to be clearly referring to Moses, and was undoubtedly understood that way by Pharaoh. The previous line – "will bow down before me" – would also seem to refer to Moses. I would like to suggest that these lines are deliberately equivocal. It is indeed God who is speaking, and ultimately, Pharaoh's subservience is before God. But this will be fulfilled when Pharaoh comes down to look for Moses on that last night and humbles himself before Moses. Pharaoh began his conversations with Moses by dismissing God – "Who is HaShem that I should listen to His word?" Now Pharaoh will "go down to Him" and bow down before Him."

Why is this necessary? Not, God tells Moses in the beginning of the *parasha*, so that Pharaoh should know that HaShem is God – for that will have been accomplished earlier, during the original plagues. Now the purpose is that "you should know that I am HaShem." God sends Moses to battle Pharaoh, and strengthens Pharaoh in the doing, so that Moses should experience first-hand the clash of titans, the battle of God's word against the vainglory of human power, of emperors and tyrants. This is qualitatively different than merely observing the battle from the side-lines, as the Egyptians and the Jews were doing. God wants Moses' personal involvement, and he switches Moses' role from the representative of the Jewish people, speaking in God's name, to the representative of God Himself. For this it is necessary to divinely empower Pharaoh as well, giving him the added strength to represent the powers of resistance to God, beyond what Pharaoh the mortal could have mustered on his own, though perhaps not beyond what he would have wanted to muster. The *parasha* is intensely personal, so that Moses should feel personally the involvement of God in this struggle. Ultimately, God will take on the last blow completely alone, leaving even Moses at home to await the coming of Pharaoh to surrender.

The moment that this identification of Moses with the personal struggle of God becomes complete is, I think, when he "turns and leaves in consuming rage." The anger Moses feels at Pharaoh is rooted in his complete identification with God who has been belittled by Pharaoh. Until now, Moses did not have such a spontaneous reaction despite all the words of Pharaoh. And Pharaoh, I think, recognized this change in Moses as well. Right before that moment, Pharaoh threatens Moses with death. It is striking that never before had Pharaoh sought to silence Moses. At first, he treats Moses with disdain – "Why, Moses and Aaron, do you disturb the people from their work" (5:4). Later he treats him with respect, but never before did he feel personally threatened by Moses. Pharaoh reacts at this moment with anger and fear, which leads him to threaten Moses personally – "If I see you again, you shall die." Now that the confrontation is personal, now that Pharaoh has felt the power that is in Moses, God tells him of *makkat bekhorot*, of the ultimate encounter, and Moses in turn walks out in anger.

But why does God want this to take place. The answer is, once again, "that you should know that I am HaShem." This has two levels. One is for all Jews. The pronoun "you" is in plural form (*"vida'atem ki ani HaShem"*). But I think that there is also a hinted goal for Moses alone. The verse combines singular and plural pronouns: "In order that you [singular] should tell your son and your son's son … and you [plural] should know that I am HaShem." Moses will, it is hinted, have a personal story to tell. This is the personal identification that he experienced when God struck Pharaoh. I would like to suggest that this is the moment when Moses becomes more than a leader. This is when he begins to become "*Ish HaElokim*," who will bring the Torah down from the mountain.

"This Month Shall Be to You the Beginning of Months"

Rav Yair Kahn

I. FROM NARRATIVE TO HALAKHA

The closing segment of *Parashat Bo* begins with the section: "*HaḤodesh hazeh lakhem Rosh Ḥodashim*" (This month is the first month for you) (12:1). In his commentary on the first verse in the Torah, Rashi quotes the famous question of Rabbi Yitzḥak – why didn't the Torah begin with this section? The assumption underlying this question is that the Torah is essentially a book of law, and it should therefore begin with the first law that was given to Israel. Whether or not that assumption is valid is not the topic at hand. It is, however, important to note the shift from narrative to halakha that occurs at this point in the Torah.

The Torah relates the historical events that took place up until the heated exchange between Moses and Pharaoh. Pharaoh warns Moses to never come see him again, and Moses storms out of the palace in anger. The stage is set for the final plague, which will bring about freedom from bondage. However, before continuing, the children of Israel must be told the laws of the Pesaḥ sacrifice. In other words, the presentation of the laws of Pesaḥ at this point is actually a continuation of the narrative.

However, when considering this halakhic section, one is struck by a redundancy. Chapter 12 contains three separate subsections, each of which deals with the various laws of Pesaḥ. The first subsection goes from verse 1 until verse 20. The second follows immediately and continues until verse 28. The third picks up after a brief narrative section and goes from verse 43 until verse 50. Why couldn't all the laws be given in one section? What is the purpose and meaning of this division?

II. FROM HASHEM TO THE PEOPLE

In truth, the first two sections are not actually redundant. The first begins, "And HaShem spoke to Moses and Aaron in the land of Egypt saying," and documents the prophecy revealed to Moses and Aaron. The second section begins, "And Moses called all the elders of Israel and told them." This section describes the transmission of the Pesaḥ laws to the people. There are many examples where the Torah only documents the divine command to Moses, and we assume that Moses passed it on (see 10:2). Conversely, there are cases where only the command to the people is explicit, and we conclude that this was preceded by a divine command (see 16:32; Ramban on 16:4). However, in our *parasha*, which introduces us to the halakhic narrative, the Torah documented both the divine command as well as its transmission to the people.

It therefore comes as no surprise that the first section is more detailed than the second, as was already noted by Ramban:

> "And Moses called to all the elders of Israel and said to them" –
> this section is abbreviated, as it was commanded by HaShem in
> the previous section, since it is obvious that Moses told Israel
> everything in detail and taught them the entire topic.

Indeed, the basic format and content of both sections are the same. The beginning of each deals with *"Pesaḥ Mitzrayim,"* the laws of Pesaḥ that were practiced that particular year in Egypt. Both sections then shift to *"Pesaḥ dorot,"* the laws that are to be practiced in future generations.

It is noteworthy that the second section is not merely a brief summary of the first; it contains information not previously mentioned. Clearly, this "additional" information was part of the original divine message, but it was only revealed to us when the Torah documented the transmission of the Pesaḥ laws to the people.

An exhaustive study of this section would demand noting all the differences between the two sections. For our purposes, it is sufficient to note that the details added in the second section regarding *Pesaḥ Mitzrayim* appear to be technical; they are relevant to the instruction given to the people themselves, as they are about to perform the *Korban Pesaḥ* (paschal offering). For instance, in the first section, we read the general command:

> And they shall take the blood, and put it on the two side posts and on the upper door post. (12:7)

In the second section, we are supplied with the pragmatic details of the performance:

> And take a bunch of hyssop, and dip it in the blood that is in the basin, and touch with it the lintel and the two side post. (v. 22)

This explains most of the additional information found in the second section. The only interesting exception is the prohibition that no one should leave their house until morning (v. 22), which does not appear in the first section at all. Was this prohibition said explicitly to Moses but only written when the laws were given to the people? Or perhaps it was said to Moses only implicitly, when HaShem said:

> And the blood shall be to you for a token upon the house where you are: and when I see the blood, I will pass over you, and the plague shall not be upon you to destroy you when I smite the land of Egypt. (v. 13)

It therefore had to be spelled out explicitly to the people.

Regarding *Pesaḥ dorot*, however, the respective descriptions of the two sections are totally distinct. The first section shifts from the one night of *Korban Pesaḥ* practiced in Egypt to the seven day festival during which Ḥametz is prohibited. In contrast, the second section continues to discuss the *Korban Pesaḥ*:

> And it shall come to pass, when you shall come to the land which the Lord will give you, as He has promised, that you shall keep this service. And it shall come to pass, when your children shall say to you, "What do you mean by this service?" That you shall say, "It is the sacrifice of the Lord's Passover, who passed over the houses of the children of Israel in Egypt when He smote Egypt and delivered our houses. And the people bowed their heads and worshipped." (v. 25–27)

The people are commanded to instill within their children the relevance of the *Korban Pesaḥ* for future generations. They are commanded to pass on a living, dynamic tradition by internalizing and eternalizing the meta-historical experience of *Yetziat Mitzrayim* – the exodus. This unique message, which must become integral to the essence of the children of Israel, is emphasized specifically when the Torah repeats what the people themselves were told.

III. THE DEVELOPMENT AND EMERGENCE OF NATIONAL IDENTITY

The most puzzling part of the halakhic narrative is the third section. As we mentioned, the first two halakhic sections actually constitute a continuation of the narrative. Following those sections, the Torah continues the story of the exodus: "And it came to pass, in the middle of the night, and HaShem smote every firstborn in Egypt" (12:29). The Torah recounts the events of that night and those of the following morning when the children of Israel marched to freedom. The section concludes:

> And it came to pass on that very day, that all the hosts of the Lord went out from the land of Egypt. It is a night of watchfulness to the Lord for bringing them out from the land of Egypt; this is the Lord's watch-night, for the children of Israel in their generations. (12:41–42)

Then, for some unexplained reason, the narrative ends and another halakhic section dealing with the *Korban Pesaḥ*, which according to the narrative had already been sacrificed, is inserted. Immediately following this, the Torah repeats itself:

> And it came to pass on that very day that the Lord did bring the children of Israel out of the land of Egypt by their hosts. (12:51)

What is the explanation for the "artificial" insertion of the third halakhic section? Moreover, what is the significance of the concluding verse, which is both redundant and out of context?

Rashi simply notes that this section was given on the fourteenth of Nisan, before the actual exodus. His solution is based on the rule *"ein mukdam ume'uḥar baTorah,"* the Torah does not maintain chronology. However, he offers no suggestion for why it was written where it was – after the exodus took place, on the fifteenth of Nissan.

Ramban, unlike Rashi, offers a reason to justify the sequential break. Ibn Ezra, on the other hand, suggests that the *parasha* deals with *Pesaḥ dorot*, which would explain its post-exodus location.

Before attempting to explain the odd location of this *parasha*, it is important to make an additional note. The term *"be'etzem hayom hazeh"* ("on that very day") appears only eleven times in the entire Torah, and three of those instances are in our chapter in reference to the exodus. The first time is in verse 17, in the first halakhic section, when HaShem tells Moses about *Pesaḥ ledorot*:

> for on this very day have I brought your hosts out of the land of Egypt.

The second time is in verse 41, during the narrative that describes *Yetziat Mitzrayim*:

> and it came to pass on that very day, that all the hosts of the Lord went out from the land of Egypt.

The third time is in verse 51, after the third halakhic section:

And it came to pass on that very day that the Lord did bring the children of Israel out of the land of Egypt by their hosts.

Why does the Torah repeat itself three times?

There are subtle differences in the wording of these three verses, which may point to a solution. In the first verse, HaShem refers to the children of Israel as *"tzivoteikhem"* (your multitudes). In the second verse, the children of Israel are referred to as *"tzivot HaShem"* (God's multitudes). In the third verse, they are referred to as *"Benei Yisrael"* (the children of Israel). Perhaps by repeating the same idea almost verbatim, the Torah is emphasizing the development of the Israelite nation.

The first reference, which took place on the first day of Nisan, relates to the people as an undefined human mass ("your multitudes"). In the second reference, this human mass is characterized as God's multitudes. What generated this change? What dramatic event took place since the first of Nisan that led to such a radical reformulation of collective identity of the people? The third reference introduces us to the "children of Israel." This human mass now has a national identity. What brought about this change?

According to our sages, Pesaḥ begins the national process of *gerut*, conversion, of *Benei Yisrael*. *Gerut*, in its ideal form, is comprised of three components: circumcision, immersion in a *mikveh*, and offering a sacrifice. This is derived from the collective *gerut* of Israel, which began with the circumcision that preceded the *korban Pesaḥ* and continued with the *mikveh* and sacrifice that also took place at Sinai.

Rav Soloveitchik noted that *gerut* has a national element as well as a religious one. On the one hand, a convert accepts the yoke of heaven and the rules of Torah. On the other hand, he joins the national entity of Israel. Therefore, it is reasonable that *Yetziat Mitzrayim*, which signals the beginning of the *gerut* process, contains both elements. Moreover, it may be that both of these elements are connected to the *Korban Pesaḥ*.

Rabbi Meir Simḥa of Dvinsk suggested that the *Korban Pesaḥ* can function as a *korban gerut*. The religious component of the *korban* is clear: a sacrifice is an act of worship. The transformation from *"tzivoteikhem"* to *"tzivot HaShem"* was accomplished through the collective act of worship of the *Korban Pesaḥ*.

However, the *Korban Pesah* is also associated with the national element of *gerut*. In fact, there are only two positive commandments that are punished by *karet* ("cutting off") if unfulfilled – *Korban Pesah* and circumcision. Both are expressions of being part of the national covenant; failure to fulfill either is punished by being cut off from the nation. This aspect of the *Korban Pesah* is expressed in the third halakhic section, which was intentionally separated from the first two. There, the Torah stresses that the *korban* is unique to the children of Israel and prohibited to non-Jews. Emphasis is placed on the national covenantal act of circumcision as a prerequisite for partaking of the Pesah. Finally, the Torah concludes, "And all the children of Israel did as HaShem commanded Moses and Aaron, so they did" (v. 50). This verse should be contrasted to the parallel verse concluding the first two halakhic sections (v. 28), where the word "all" is left out.

I propose that the Torah intentionally separated the laws of Pesah into two distinct sections. The first section, which flows as part of the narrative, is intended to document the religious development of the people. It traces the dramatic transformation of a group of slaves serving an idolatrous nation into a committed people, involved in worship and sacrifice. The narrative continues to relate how the people became free from Egyptian bondage and became servants of HaShem. The narrative concludes with verse 41, "And it came to pass on that very day, that all the hosts of the Lord went out from the land of Egypt," which, shifting from the original "*tzivoteikhem*," refers to the people as "*tzivot HaShem*."

At this point, there is a break in the narrative. The Torah returns to the laws of Pesah in order to document the national development of a disparate group of slaves into a national unit. The laws of Pesah relevant to the collective identity of Israel as a covenantal nation are documented separately, and the Torah symbolically returns to the narrative by repeating the verse, "And it came to pass on that very day that the Lord did bring the children of Israel out of the land of Egypt by their hosts." At this point, it is the nation of *Benei Yisrael* who leave.

Based on the above, we can return to the divine command that preceded the ten plagues. In *Parashat Va'era*, when God commands Moses to go to Pharaoh and free the children of Israel from bondage, He says:

> That I may lay My hand upon Egypt and bring out *My hosts, My people, the children of Israel,* out of the land of Egypt by great judgments. (7:4)

This verse contains a redundancy. "I will take out (1) *My hosts* (2) *My people, the children of Israel* – from the land of Egypt." It is possible to interpret this repetition as an explanation. Who are My hosts? The answer is "My nation, the children of Israel." However, based on our analysis of the halakhic narrative in *Parashat Bo*, the repetition should be interpreted as relating to two distinct ideas. The term *"tzivotai"* ("My hosts") is a reference to the religious development of the people in attaining the status of *"tzivot HaShem."* "My people the children of Israel," on the other hand, emphasizes the unique covenantal nationalistic status. Only by combining the two do we fully understand the fullness of the exodus from Egypt.

Ḥag HaPesaḥ and Ḥag HaMatzot

Rav Mordechai Breuer

What is Passover? "Passover" is the literal translation of Pesaḥ, but a careful analysis of the Torah's discussion of this holiday yields a more complex picture of its meaning. The *Korban Pesaḥ* (paschal offering) is indeed slaughtered on the afternoon of the fourteenth of Nisan and eaten on the night of the fifteenth; but this night is merely the beginning of a weeklong festival (*Ḥag*) known in the Torah as *Ḥag HaMatzot*.

We may see this clearly in Exodus 12:1–20, which divides into two sections. The first section talks about Pesaḥ in Egypt (*Pesaḥ Mitzrayim*), describing the first *Korban Pesaḥ* and the events surrounding it; the second part describes *Ḥag HaMatzot* as it is observed for all generations. Between these two parts, we find a verse of ambiguous orientation – difficult to determine whether it concludes the passage dealing with *Pesaḥ Mitzrayim* or if it opens the passage which deals with *Ḥag HaMatzot*.

> And *this day* shall be a memorial for you, and you shall celebrate it as a festival for God for your generations; you shall celebrate it as an eternal law. (12:14)

According to Rashi, "this day" which is to be "a memorial for you" is the single day of the exodus from Egypt; because this is what the verse states later on: "Remember this day on which you have left Egypt, the house of slaves" (13:3). However, the exodus from Egypt takes place "on the fifteenth day of the first month, on the morrow following the Pesaḥ" (Num. 33:3); this indicates that the holiday mentioned in this verse is *Ḥag HaMatzot*, which starts on the fifteenth day of Nisan.

However, according to this view, it is very difficult to understand the phrase "this day" ("*hayom hazeh*"), as the preceding passage does not discuss at all the day of the exodus from Egypt, but rather the day of the offering of the *Pesaḥ*. *Pesaḥ Mitzrayim* requires taking an animal "on the tenth of this month" (v. 3), keeping it "until the fourteenth day of this month" (v. 6), slaughtering it "in the afternoon" (ibid.) and eating it "on this night" (v. 8); and close to the time of eating the *Pesaḥ*, the firstborn are slain "on this night" (v. 12). As the Torah says immediately afterwards that "this day" will be a memorial, the intent can be only to refer to the day of the offering of the *Pesaḥ*, which includes the night of its consumption as well; and this is only the fourteenth of Nisan, including the night after it. (Although the day follows the night for most applications of Jewish law, the reverse is true when it comes to sacrifices.) If we assume that "this day" is tied to redemption, the intent cannot be to refer to the day of the exodus in practice – which is the morning of the day of the fifteenth of Nisan – but rather only to the time of the slaying of the firstborn, which is the previous night, the one following the day of the fourteenth of Nisan.

On this question, Rav David Zvi Hoffman suggests a novel view in his commentary to Leviticus 23:6. According to him, "this day" refers to "this night" which is mentioned in the previous verses (8, 12). This night may be linked to one of two days. In the previous passage, it concludes the day of the *fourteenth of Nisan*, because we are talking there about the offering of the *Pesaḥ*, and when it comes to sacrifices, the night follows the day. In our verse, on the other hand, this very same night is considered to be the beginning of the day of the *fifteenth of Nisan*; since we are talking about a festival which is celebrated everywhere, and not only in the holy precincts, the day follows the night. This would then be the explanation of this verse: the (following) day which includes "this night" is meant to be "a memorial for you."

However, though this approach is feasible, it is undeniably a stretch. The simple meaning of the term "this day" is not the day which includes "this night," but rather the day which has been discussed until now, the fourteenth of Nisan, which draws the night of the fifteenth after it. Furthermore, in the view of Rashi, the Israelites are commanded to remember the fifteenth of Nisan because on the morning of this day they left Egypt. However, the exodus from Egypt in the morning has not yet been mentioned in this paragraph; rather, it has discussed only the offering of the *Pesaḥ* and the slaying of the firstborn at night. It is nearly inconceivable that the Torah would demand that one remember "this day" without relating the crucial event which has occurred on it!

Apparently, this is what motivates Ibn Ezra to explain that "this day" should be interpreted simply as the day discussed in the passage above. With this approach, he explains another feature – the absence of the phrase "wherever you may dwell" in the first passage, despite the fact that it is mentioned at the conclusion of the *Ḥag HaMatzot* section (v. 20). This phrase is inappropriate for *Ḥag HaPesaḥ*, as the *Korban Pesaḥ* cannot be offered outside the holy precincts once the Jews arrive in Israel. According to this explanation, the verse before us does not open the laws of *Ḥag HaMatzot*; rather, it concludes the passage of *Pesaḥ Mitzrayim*.

Different considerations may have dissuaded Rashi from accepting this approach. One reason becomes clear in his words: we have not found another verse in which one is commanded to remember the paschal offering in Egypt. However, this is hardly compelling, as there are many commandments which are mentioned only once, and it is conceivable that this is one of them.

Furthermore, it is possible to say that the exodus truly begins at the time of the slaying of the firstborn, as this final plague is the direct cause of the exodus from Egypt. It is possible that the mitzva of remembering the exodus includes the mitzva to remember the slaying of the firstborn. It turns out that this mitzva is identical with the mitzva stated here, because "this day" – the day of offering the *Korban Pesaḥ* – is also the day of the slaying of the firstborn.

Even the terminology of *Ḥag* written in our verse seems to contradict Ibn Ezra's view. It states here that the day must be celebrated (*"vehagotem"*) as a "festival (*Ḥag*) for God." However, there are only three days classified as *Ḥag* in the Torah: *Ḥag HaMatzot*, Shavuot and Sukkot. The day of offering the *Pesaḥ* is not counted among them.

In truth, however, this argues *for* Ibn Ezra. The verse states: "And *this day* shall be a memorial for you, and you shall celebrate it as a festival for God for your generations; you shall celebrate it as an eternal law." We are talking here of a festival which lasts only one day. Since *Ḥag HaMatzot* lasts for seven days, it is clear that the verse here is not referring to it. We are compelled to say that we are talking about the paschal "*Ḥag*" here, as all of the procedures of the *Korban Pesaḥ* last only one day.

Furthermore, our verse is not the only place in which the day of the *Pesaḥ* is called a *Ḥag*. There are two additional parallel verses which appear later, in *Parashat Mishpatim* (23:18) and *Parashat Ki Tissa* (34:25), after the three pilgrimage festivals are enumerated, each bearing the title of *Ḥag*. In *Parashat Mishpatim* the Torah says: "Do not sacrifice the blood of my sacrifice upon leaven, and do not let the fat of my festival (*Ḥag*) lie until morning"; while *Parashat Ki Tissa* states: "Do not slaughter on leaven the blood of my sacrifice, and do not let lie until morning the sacrifice of the Passover festival (*Ḥag HaPesaḥ*)." There is no doubt that the *Ḥag* referred to in each case is the festival of bringing the *Pesaḥ*.

Ibn Ezra also struggles with the rest of the paragraph. According to him, we are talking about *Ḥag HaPesaḥ*, but the paragraph in its latter part is indubitably talking about *Ḥag HaMatzot* (v. 15): "For seven days shall you eat matzot," etc. However, this is not a clear proof either, as the juxtaposition is difficult according to everyone. If this verse is talking about *Ḥag HaPesaḥ*, it does not fit in with the verses after it (which discuss *Ḥag HaMatzot*); if this verse is about *Ḥag HaMatzot*, it does not fit with the previous verses, which address the topic of the *Pesaḥ*. Moreover, the laws of *Ḥag HaMatzot* should not have been stated here at all; the appropriate place for them is after the exodus actually occurs. Clearly, the Torah appends *Ḥag HaMatzot* to the passage of the *Pesaḥ* here, without adequately separating them. The Torah writes it here for some reason which must be explicated according to all views.

The Torah does not clearly explain the content of *Ḥag HaPesaḥ*; however, there is no doubt that that its main mitzva is to offer the *Korban Pesaḥ*. The date of this *Ḥag* is also known; it falls out on the fourteenth of Nisan. Unlike all of the other Jewish festivals, the day does not follow the previous night, but rather the night follows the day. Since the essence of the Ḥag is bringing a sacrifice, the rule that applies is, as we have already mentioned, that when it comes to offerings, night follows day.

There is another distinction between all other festivals and Ḥag HaPesaḥ. All other festivals have at least one day defined as *"mikra kodesh"* (a holy convocation), on which certain forms of labor are forbidden. Ḥag HaPesaḥ, on the other hand, does not have the title of *mikra kodesh*, and in no place does the Torah state that any labor is forbidden on this day.

As such, Ḥag HaPesaḥ is an independent festival and is not counted with the three pilgrimage festivals – unlike Ḥag HaMatzot. The essential mitzvot of Ḥag HaMatzot are tied to the laws of ḥametz (leaven) and matza. Ḥag HaMatzot lasts seven days – from the fifteenth through the twenty-first of Nisan. Since the essential ceremony of the festival occurs outside the Temple, the day follows the night. Similar to the other two pilgrimage festivals, Ḥag HaMatzot has both *mikra kodesh* status and a prohibition of labor. In this matter, there are some contradictions between the passages which discuss this festival. Exodus 12, Leviticus 23 and Numbers 28 state that both the first and the seventh days have the status of *mikra kodesh*, and "laborious work" is prohibited on them. However, Exodus 13 says, "For seven days shall you eat matzot, and on the seventh day, a festival for God" (v. 6). It appears from here that there is a greater holiness to the seventh day alone. Similarly – though with different phrasing – we find in Deuteronomy 16: "For six days shall you eat matzot, and on the seventh day, a holiday for Lord your God, you shall not do labor" (v. 8).

Sometimes Ḥag HaPesaḥ and Ḥag HaMatzot are mentioned independently, but sometimes consecutively. In *Parashat Mishpatim* and *Parashat Ki Tissa*, the verse discusses Ḥag HaMatzot without mentioning that it is preceded by Ḥag HaPesaḥ; later, it talks about the laws of Ḥag HaPesaḥ and does not mention that Ḥag HaMatzot comes right afterwards. The same is true of Exodus 13. The Torah there explains the specifics of the laws of Ḥag HaMatzot, but there is no mention of Ḥag HaPesaḥ or *Korban Pesaḥ*. In other places, these two festivals are mentioned consecutively. Leviticus 23 states that the fourteenth of Nisan is "a Passover for God," and the fifteenth of Nisan is "Ḥag HaMatzot for God." Numbers 28 contains similar phrasing. Therefore, we should explain our section in the same way – after the Torah mentions that "this day" (the fourteenth of Nisan) is "a festival for God," it adds the laws of *Ḥag HaMatzot*: "For seven days shall you eat matzot," etc.

It appears that *Ḥag HaPesaḥ* and *Ḥag HaMatzot* are two festivals which may exist independently, but practically fall one after the other. They have, however, some common aspects. The laws of *ḥametz* and matza relate not only to *Ḥag HaMatzot* but to *Ḥag HaPesaḥ* as well. This is what is stated in our section, that one should eat matzot with the *Korban Pesaḥ* (v. 8). Furthermore, the Torah states that it is forbidden to "sacrifice" or "slaughter" the paschal sacrifice "upon leaven" (23:18 and 34:25 respectively); and it says in Deuteronomy that it is forbidden to eat any *ḥametz* "upon" the *Korban Pesaḥ*.

The fact that matzot must be eaten together with the *Korban Pesaḥ* is not an absolute proof that there is a similarity between *Ḥag HaPesaḥ* and *Ḥag HaMatzot*. It is indeed possible that these matzot are akin to those eaten with other offerings, such as the thanksgiving offering, and they do not point to anything special about *Ḥag HaPesaḥ* and its link to *Ḥag HaMatzot*. On the other hand, the prohibitions to slaughter the *Korban Pesaḥ* upon *ḥametz* or to eat *ḥametz* upon the *Korban Pesaḥ* are proscriptions unique to *Korban Pesaḥ*; there is no analogous ban for any other offering. These prohibitions must consequently point to the unique character of the *Korban Pesaḥ* and the *Ḥag* to which it lends its name. Based on this, there is a clear link between *Ḥag HaPesaḥ* and *Ḥag HaMatzot*.

Despite their commonalities, however, *Ḥag HaPesaḥ* and *Ḥag HaMatzot* are fundamentally different. The essence of *Ḥag HaPesaḥ* is the offering brought during it. The laws of *ḥametz* and matza which are observed on this festival are not independent laws, but rather they are dependent on *Korban Pesaḥ* – it is a mitzva to eat matzot with the *Korban Pesaḥ*, it is forbidden to slaughter the *Korban Pesaḥ* over *ḥametz*, and it is forbidden to eat *ḥametz* over the *Korban Pesaḥ*. On the other hand, *Ḥag HaMatzot* has no special offering of this type; therefore, the laws of *ḥametz* and matza observed on it are independent laws, irrespective of any offering.

In light of these points, one may understand the festival mentioned in the book of Ezekiel:

In the first, on *the fourteenth day of the month*, it shall be for you the Passover, a festival; *for seven days, matzot shall be eaten.* (45:21)

The festival described appears to be an amalgam of Ḥag HaPesaḥ and Ḥag HaMatzot. It is similar to Ḥag HaPesaḥ in that it starts on the fourteenth of Nisan, which is the time of offering the paschal sacrifice. It is similar to Ḥag HaMatzot, because it lasts seven days, and we eat matzot all the days of the festival.

However, these seven days do not constitute here an independent festival; rather, it appears as if Ḥag HaMatzot has been moved up by one day, and its first day is the day of offering the Korban Pesaḥ. As a result, Ḥag HaMatzot loses its independent identity, and turns into a part of Ḥag HaPesaḥ; the boundary of Ḥag HaPesaḥ expands and the power of the Korban Pesaḥ wins out. We no longer eat matzot only at the time of eating the offering, and we do not eliminate ḥametz only at the time of slaughtering the Passover. Rather, the impression of the offering is noticeable for a full week – it is a mitzva to eat matzot throughout this week, which begins on the day of bringing the offering. Since eating matzot is now contingent on the Korban Pesaḥ, the entire Ḥag is no longer called Ḥag HaMatzot, but rather Ḥag HaPesaḥ; indeed, its laws of ḥametz and matza are part of the laws of the Korban Pesaḥ.

A seven-day Pesaḥ is also mentioned in *Parashat Re'eh*: "And you shall sacrifice a Passover for Lord your God…do not eat leaven upon it; for seven days shall you eat upon it matzot, bread of affliction" (Deut. 16:2–3). The mitzva to eat matzot for seven days is not an independent mitzva here, connected to Ḥag HaMatzot, but is a mitzva dependent on Korban Pesaḥ, a mitzva of eating matzot "upon [the Passover]" – not only on the night of Pesaḥ, but throughout all seven days of Pesaḥ. We see the matzot eaten on these seven days as if they are eaten "upon [the Passover]" because they are eaten throughout the days of Pesaḥ.

Thus, it turns out that there are *three* festivals which fall in the month of Nisan:

1. Ḥag HaPesaḥ begins on the fourteenth of Nisan and lasts one day. Its main mitzva is offering the Korban Pesaḥ; its laws of ḥametz and matza are part of the laws of the Korban Pesaḥ.
2. Ḥag HaMatzot starts on the fifteenth of Nisan and lasts seven

days. Its main laws are the laws of *ḥametz* and matza; these laws do not relate to any *korban*.

3. *Ḥag HaPesaḥ* has *Ḥag HaMatzot* joined to it. For the sake of this juxtaposition, *Ḥag HaMatzot* is moved up by one day. As a result of this, *Ḥag HaMatzot* becomes part of *Ḥag HaPesaḥ*; the laws of *ḥametz* and matza on it are part of the laws of the *Korban Pesaḥ*.

Ḥag HaPesaḥ – in all of its forms – has no *mikra kodesh* status and no prohibition of labor. Conversely, both the first and the last days of *Ḥag HaMatzot* have *mikra kodesh* status, and on these days laborious work is forbidden. In other places, the Torah states only that there is special holiness to the seventh day.

We will now try to understand the significance of these three festivals.

The redemption from Egyptian slavery takes place in discrete stages. On the fourteenth of Nisan, in the afternoon, the Israelites slaughter the *Korban Pesaḥ* and eat its flesh "on this night." At that time, nothing has yet happened to indicate their imminent redemption. Pharaoh still holds them as slaves, and there is no reason to assume that in the future they will go free. Even so, the Israelites have already become free men in their own eyes, for when they eat the *Korban Pesaḥ*, they thereby enter the category of God's servants, and no servant of God can be enslaved to a human being. As it were, they are sitting by "the royal table" and eating from the divine larder – like emancipated slaves. This emancipation is not merely a promise destined to be fulfilled; rather, everything which is about to happen has already occurred in principle. Accordingly, the Israelites act practically as if the exodus is a *fait accompli* – despite the reality that their bill of emancipation has not yet been issued. The firstborn of Egypt have not yet been slain – but the Israelites are already prepared and decked out for the road, with their loins girded, their feet shod and their staffs in their hands. In the geographical reality, they are still slaves to Pharaoh in Egypt; the taskmasters are insistent, demanding that they finish each day's tasks on time. However, in the Godly reality that they have embraced, their former oppressors are insistent, demanding that they leave the land hurriedly. Because of this, they do not eat the meal casually – as would be appropriate for one invited to the king's table – rather they eat in haste, *hipazon*; their ears are already ringing with the clamor of the Egyptian mob, pressing them to leave the land.

More than anything else, eating the *Pesah* hastily testifies to the actual reality of freedom. Their loins girded, their feet shod and their staffs in their hands – all of these elements declare that the Israelites are destined to go out to war; and the haste of eating the *Pesah* testifies that they are already being pushed to leave, and there is almost no opportunity for them to finish their meal. Because of this, we find that the element of *hipazon* is not only one of the laws of the *korban* – it is the very essence of the *korban*. The *Pesah* not only alludes to the fact that God "passed over the Israelites' houses"; the *korban* is called *Pesah* because of the *hipazon*: "Eat it with haste; it is a Passover for God" (v. 11).

Everything which happens first on the ideal level happens afterwards in the terrestrial-tangible reality. The Egyptians see their dead lying before them, and they can no longer continue to enslave Israel. This is how the Israelites go free – not only in the vision of their intellect – but before the eyes of all Egypt. At the time of eating the *Korban Pesah*, they had been only prepared and ready for the road – now they are actually departing. The *hipazon* with which they have eaten the *Pesah* is the *hipazon* with which they are leaving Egypt. The hand of Egypt is heavy upon them "to hurry to send them out of the land." They do not depart casually and comfortably, but rather "they were driven out of Egypt, and they could not hesitate, and they did not make provisions for themselves." At that time, the Godly reality of the *Korban Pesah* becomes the terrestrial reality of the exodus from Egypt.

At the border between these two events – of eating the *Pesah* on the one hand and departing Egypt on the other – stands the event of the slaying of the firstborn. Its roots are hidden in the Godly reality, and only its branches extrude into the terrestrial reality. For God is passing through to smite Egypt, and when He sees the blood on the door, He passes over the Israelites' houses. This fact, which is tied directly to the *Korban Pesah*, is known only to the *Pesah*-eaters. Nevertheless, the plague and the salvation are visible to the physical eye, for the firstborn of Egypt perish while the firstborn of Israel are saved – and this is a tangible fact which is discernable by all. In the framework of the natural world, only this plague, which is visible to the eye, brings in its wake the exodus from Egypt.

Consequently, we must say that the slaying of the firstborn is the last of the acts of the *Pesaḥ* – and simultaneously, it is the beginning of the exodus. In the framework of the relationships between Israel and its God, the people have completed all of the acts tied to the *Korban Pesaḥ*. This emerges from our section, wherein the Torah describes in exacting detail all of the acts and events of *Pesaḥ Mitzrayim*: from the slaughtering of the *Pesaḥ* on the afternoon of the fourteenth of Nisan through its eating "on this night" – all the way until the slaying of the firstborn and the salvation of Israel, which also take place "on this night." To this, the verse adds that the Jewish people must remember "this day," on which all of these things happened, and celebrate it as "a festival for God." It makes sense that this is also the idea of *Ḥag HaPesaḥ* as mentioned in *Parashat Mishpatim* and *Parashat Ki Tissa*. Since the essence of *Ḥag HaPesaḥ* is the redemption acquired via the *Korban Pesaḥ*, the matzot of the *Ḥag* are only for the *Korban Pesaḥ*. This why is the time of the festival overlaps the time of the *korban*. It starts on the fourteenth of Nisan in the afternoon, and it ends at midnight or dawn; this is the time which passes from the slaughtering of the *Pesaḥ* until the end of the time of its consumption. Since the spiritual-ideal redemption of the *Korban Pesaḥ* occurs with *ḥipazon*, the acts of the *Pesaḥ* testify to this haste. Because of this, there is a mitzva to eat the *Pesaḥ* with matzot (v. 8), it is forbidden to eat *ḥametz* over the *Pesaḥ* (Deut. 16:3) and it is forbidden to slaughter the *Pesaḥ* over *ḥametz* (Ex. 23:18, 34:25). One who wants to make *ḥametz* must tarry, kneading the dough until it rises; the matza, on the other hand, is baked hurriedly, evoking *ḥipazon*.

Ḥag HaMatzot, which lasts seven days, recalls the essence of the exodus from Egypt. This *Ḥag* is described in Exodus 13 (v. 3–10), stated immediately after the departure from Egypt. The exodus, as described there, is a wholly terrestrial-political affair: the Egyptians see "that there is no house with no dead"; because of this, the Israelites are urged to abandon the land quickly. Since the Israelites "were driven out of Egypt, and they could not hesitate," they are forced to carry their dough "before it could become leaven"; in the end, "They baked unleavened cakes of the dough, because it had not become leaven." In order to commemorate this event – which is wholly within the tangible reality – *Ḥag HaMatzot* is instituted. Therefore, all of the laws mentioned in relation to this *Ḥag* are the laws of *ḥametz* and matza. On the day of the exodus, "leaven shall not be eaten" (v. 3); when they arrive in the land of Israel, matzot are to be eaten for seven days (v. 6–7), and all forms of leaven must not be seen anywhere on their property (ibid. v. 7). Conversely, there is no mention of the *Korban Pesaḥ*; the "service" mentioned here (v. 5) is only the "service" of eating matzot. This festival does not commemorate the spiritual redemption of the *Pesaḥ*; rather, it is a memorial to the tangible, practical redemption of leaving Egypt. Because of this, the matzot borne on the shoulders of those who depart are the matzot eaten by the celebrants.

According to this approach, one may understand the meaning of the third *Ḥag*, *Ḥag HaPesaḥ* which lasts for seven days. This *Ḥag*, described in *Parashat Re'eh* and the book of Ezekiel, expresses the point of encounter between *Ḥag HaPesaḥ* and *Ḥag HaMatzot*. Like *Ḥag HaPesaḥ*, it expresses the spiritual-ideal redemption which comes to expression in the *Korban Pesaḥ*. However, the climactic point of that redemption is at midnight, when God passes through to smite Egypt and passes over the Israelites' houses. At that time, the tangible redemption of the exodus begins. The firstborn of Egypt have already died, and as a result of this, Pharaoh's release of Israel is inevitable. It appears that the *ḥipazon* of the exodus, its realization as banishment, is not an expression of the heartfelt vision anchored only in the Godly, spiritual reality – it is instead built on the tangible, terrestrial reality, in which the dead of Egypt already lie before them. Since there is no further need for God's direct intervention, all who are about to go free are already considered free. It turns out that even the tangible exodus is already complete at the close of the day of the *Pesaḥ*. Therefore, this aspect of the redemption as well may be realized in the *Ḥag HaPesaḥ*.

This is this festival's meaning. It expresses the spiritual redemption of the *Pesaḥ*; therefore, it starts on the fourteenth of Nisan, on the day the *Korban Pesaḥ* is brought. At the same time, the *Ḥag* expresses also the tangible exodus from Egypt; therefore, matzot are eaten for seven days. However, these seven days also begin on the fourteenth of

Nisan; eating matzot on them is considered eating matzot "upon [the Passover]"; indeed, during this *Ḥag*, the tangible departure from Egypt is also part of the redemption of the *Pesaḥ*, as it is embodied and hidden in its potential.

"The House of Bondage": Exoduses from Egypt and from Sodom

Rav Chanoch Waxman

I. TWO KEY-WORDS: "LEAVING" AND "HOUSE"

Towards the end of *Parashat Bo*, as part of a series of legal imperatives (12:43–13:16) that close out the story of the actual exodus from Egypt (11:1–13:16), Moses commands the people to remember this day.

> And Moses said to the people: "Remember this day that you went out (*yatzatem*) from Egypt, from the house of bondage (*beit avadim*), for with a mighty hand God brought you out (*hotzi HaShem etkhem*)." (13:3)

A few verses later, the Torah presents a similar formulation. When faced with an inquiring son who wants to know what all the laws and rituals are about, who asks the brute question of "What is this?" (13:14), we are supposed to respond:

> With a mighty hand, God brought us out (*hotzi otanu*) from Egypt, from the house of bondage (*beit avadim*). (13:14)

These repeated references to God's "mighty hand" and *"yetzia,"* the leaving or being brought out of Egypt (13:3, 14; see 13:9, 16), comprise not only the rationale for the surrounding legal material (12:43–13:16), but also an appropriate literary and thematic note on which to conclude the story of the exodus.

All the way back at the burning bush, God had informed Moses that Pharaoh will let the children of Israel go only after being forced to do so by a "mighty hand" (3:19). Likewise, throughout the story of the exodus, the text utilizes the image of the "hand of God" to denote the cause of the plagues (3:20, 6:1, 7:5, 9:3, 15). Reemphasizing the image near the end of the story is not surprising.

Similarly, the root *y-tz-a* (.א.צ.י – leaving, going, removal, etc.) assumes the role of a dominant motif in the text beginning with Moses' receiving the warning prefacing the death of the firstborn (11:1–10), which is the start of the action of the actual exodus. Utilizing the verb in various permutations, the Torah informs us both of God's "going out" into Egypt to perform the plague of the firstborn (11:4) and of Moses' storming out from the presence of Pharaoh (11:8). Sometimes we are told of "the taking out" of dough by the Israelites from Egypt (12:39), and other times of the prohibition of "leaving" the house during the night of the plague (12:22). However, most commonly, the verb refers to the "leaving" or "taking out" of the Israelites (11:8; 12:17, 31, 41, 42, 51; 13:3, 4, 8, 9, 14, 16). Altogether, in a stylistic flourish that dovetails nicely with the content of the story of "leaving Egypt," the term appears a remarkable eighteen times. Once again, finding the term at the tail of the story fails to surprise. The image fits both stylistically and thematically.

In contrast, the phrase *"beit avadim,"* here translated as "house of bondage," presents somewhat of a problem. Unlike its partners in the triad of images presented in these summary verses (13:3, 14), the phrase *"beit avadim"* has never appeared before in the story of the exodus. In its place we might naturally have expected a simple reference to Egypt or "slavery." Alternatively, if for some reason the Torah prefers a more elaborate phrase, we may reasonably have expected a descriptive phrase used at some earlier point in the narrative. Something like "from under the burdens of Egypt" (6:6–7), "the hand of Egypt" (3:8), or some sort of reference to "affliction" (3:7) and "oppression" (3:9) would seem to have constituted a natural choice.

In fact, the coining of the unique phrase *"beit avadim,"* the house of bondage, here at the end of the narrative, seems part of a larger trend present in the latter part of the story of *"Yetziat Mitzrayim,"* the exodus from Egypt. As mentioned previously, the final stage of the exodus begins with Moses' receiving and conveying Pharaoh's final warning (11:1–10). At this point, the topic shifts from instructions for Pharaoh to instructions for the children of Israel. God delivers to Moses the instructions for that fateful night, the instructions for the selecting, slaughtering and consuming of the paschal lamb (12:1–13).

Concurrent with this shift, the term *"bayit,"* meaning house or household, enters the narrative. God commands the children of Israel to "take each man a lamb according to the house of their fathers, a lamb for a house" (12:3). If there are insufficient souls in the household to consume a lamb, one joins with his neighbor, literally, "the neighbor near his house" (12:4). The blood of the lamb must be placed on "the doorposts and lintel of the house" in which the lamb will be consumed (12:7). The blood serves as a sign on the "houses," and causes God to pass over the homes of the children of Israel, thereby sparing their firstborn (12:13, 23, 27). Finally, no one can "go out of the door of his house until morning" (13:22).

The centrality of the term *"bayit"* continues into the legal portions of the narrative delineating the rituals that commemorate the exodus (12:14–20, 43–50). The prohibition of unleavened bread is phrased as a requirement to expunge it from your "houses" (12:15), and a few verses later as a prohibition of finding it in your "houses" (12:19). Likewise, the laws of the paschal sacrifice for future generations include the requirement to eat it in "one house" and the prohibition of "taking it out of the house" (12:46). Altogether, in its various guises, the term appears fifteen times in the narrative of the actual exodus and its accompanying legal instructions (12:3, 3, 4, 4, 7, 13, 15, 19, 22, 27, 27, 46; 13:3, 14).

But this constitutes the problem. While we may no longer need to wonder about the strange phrase *"beit avadim,"* house of bondage, we do need to wonder about the centrality of the term and symbol *"bayit"* to the actual exodus. Why does the story of *"Yetziat Mitzrayim,"* the leaving of Egypt by virtue of God's mighty hand, revolve around the object, theme and literary image of *"bayit"*? In other words, how does "house," as both object and symbol, connect to the fundamentals of the story?

II. THE EXODUS FROM SODOM AND
THE EXODUS FROM EGYPT

Back in Genesis, the Torah presented the story of the destruction of Sodom and the rescue of Lot (Gen. 19:1–29). Like the story of the exodus, the narrative revolves around the root *y-tz-a* (.א.צ.י), both textually and thematically. The angels sent to rescue Lot advise him to "take out" (*hotzei*) his family from Sodom before the moment of destruction arrives (19:13). Likewise, when Lot procrastinates, the angels grab hold of him and "take him out" (*vayotziuhu*), setting him outside the city (19:16). Similarly, the men of Sodom previously demand the "bringing out" (*hotzi'em*) of Lot's guests, Lot "goes out" (*vayetzeh*) to negotiate, and offers to "bring out" (*otziah*) his two virgin daughters (19:5–8). Altogether, in the course of describing the various negotiations and movements of Lot throughout the story, the text utilizes the term *"yetzia"* eight times (19:5, 6, 8, 12, 14, 14, 16, 17).

Interestingly enough, in this other *"yetzia"* story, what might be thought of as *"Yetziat Sedom,"* the leaving of Sodom, the text and story also contain the term "house" (*bayit*). Lot invites the angels into his "house" (19:2) and eventually persuades them to come into his "house" (19:3). Likewise, the men of Sodom immediately surround the "house" to demand the "bringing out" of the guests (19:4–5).

Much of the ensuing action involves the setting of the house and its component parts. Lot insists that the men should not be harmed, as they have entered the "shadow of his roof" (19:8). When the Sodomites try to break down the "door," the angels draw Lot into the "house," close the "door," and then smite the men clustered around the "entrance to the house" (*petaḥ habayit*) with blinding light, making it impossible to find the "entrance" (19:9–11). On the thematic plane, when Lot is *"taken out"* from the city by the angels (19:16), he is in fact taken out of his "house," his previous place of refuge from the danger of the mob just outside the entrance to his home.

This last point should make us realize that we have stumbled upon far more than an overlap of imagery between the story of the exodus and the story of the rescue of Lot. In fact, we have here two stories of *"yetzia,"* of being brought out by God. In both stories, the dual imagery of "leaving" and "house" plays a prominent role. On the thematic plane, in both stories, a family unit, the households of the Israelites in Egypt and the family of Lot in Sodom, face danger right outside their front doors. Just as Lot and his family face danger right outside the "entrance to their house" and are trapped inside (19:10–12), so too the children of Israel are ordered not "to go out of the entrance of your houses" (12:22) and are trapped inside. Just as Lot and his family are saved from both the mob and destructive plague that has been visited upon the mob outside their door (19:9–11), so too the children of Israel are saved from the destructive agent, the plague of the firstborn that reigns outside their door (12:23).

Following both stories chronologically brings us to a third and crucial element of the parallel. Before daybreak, the angels pressure Lot to leave, telling him to "get up" (19:15). But Lot delays (*vayitmahma,* 19:16). At this point we are told the following:

> And the men seized (*vayahaziku*) his hand and the hands of his wife and two daughters, in God's mercy upon him, and they brought him out and placed him outside the city. (19:16)

Lot's nighttime order to leave and his exit are forced upon him. Likewise, the order for the children of Israel to leave Egypt occurs sometime before dawn. After God strikes the Egyptian firstborn in the "middle of the night" (12:29), Pharaoh summons Moses and Aaron and tells them to "get up" (12:31) and leave. Just as in the story of Sodom, Lot is forced to leave without a second for delay, so too here "the Egyptians urged (*vatehezak*) the people on, hurrying them to leave the land" (12:33). In only the second usage in the Bible of the word *"mitmame'a,"* meaning delay, we are told that the Israelites had no time for delay, and were "expelled" from Egypt (12:39).

Furthermore, the key terms used to structure this "forced exit" parallel, *"vayahaziku"* (19:16) and *"vatehezak"* (12:33), are both based upon the root *h-z-k* (.ק.ז.ח), connoting strength, power or force. This of course is the same root that serves as the basis of the phrase "*yad ḥazaka*," the mighty hand that God uses to smite the Egyptians and redeem the Israelites. In fact, when reassuring Moses after Pharaoh's initial stubborn behavior and crackdown, God explicitly links the mighty hand of redemption with the concept of forced exit. God promises that as a consequence of the divine "mighty hand," Pharaoh will "expel" the people with a "mighty hand" (6:1). In other words, the force and strength (*vateḥezak*) by which Egypt hurriedly expels the Israelites is but a manifestation of the divine "mighty hand" (*yad ḥazaka*).

So too, and even more blatantly, in the case of "*Yetziat Sedom.*" The divine emissaries have previously "sent their hand" (19:10), "smitten" (*hiku*) the Sodomites (19:11) and declared their status as divine emissaries sent to "destroy" Sodom (19:13). They are the mighty hand of God, parallel to the "destroyer" that roams across Egypt smiting the firstborn (12:23). When the angels forcefully seize the hands of Lot and his family (*vayaḥaziku*), they no doubt use their "hands." In other words, it is angelic "hands," a physical manifestation and symbol of the "mighty hand" of the divine, that performs the plague, the destruction and the forced exit of Lot – just as later on in Egypt.

But this is not all. In commenting on the fact that Lot served his guests unleavened bread (matza), Rashi (19:3) pithily states, "It was Pesaḥ." This comment highlights yet another parallel to the story of the exodus. The story of "*Yetziat Sedom*" opens with the angels evening-time arrival in Sodom (19:1). They promptly enter Lot's house, termed by Lot in his invitation "*beit avdekhem*," the house of your servant (19:2), and engage in a repast of matza. As evening blends into "night" (19:4–5), the people of Sodom gather around and the action ensues. This of course eerily resembles the story of "*Yetziat Mitzrayim.*" The children of Israel, "*avadim*" (slaves) in Egypt, gather in their houses as evening blends into night and consume matza (see 12:3, 6, 8, 18). As evening turns into night, the redemption ensues.

In other words, our two "*yetzia*" stories have similar settings and props. Just as the setting of "*Yetziat Sedom*" involves evening-time, the house of an "*eved*" (servant) and unleavened bread, so too the setting of "*Yetziat Mitzrayim.*" In a kind of pun on our starting point, the children of Israel are in fact literally taken out from "*beit avadim*," not the house of bondage, but the house of slaves.

To put all of these points and texts together, we can summarize the complex overlap between the story of the exodus, *"Yetziat Mitzrayim,"* and the story of the rescue of Lot, *"Yetziat Sedom,"* by grouping the various parallels around the three images we began with.

1. The imagery of leaving – the inability to go outside the house due to the danger and divinely wrought destruction outside; being taken out/rescued from a plagued place; the prominence of the root *y-tz-a* throughout the story
2. The mighty hand – forced exit sometime during the night, near daybreak; no time for delay; God's rescue from a plagued and destroyed place
3. The house of bondage (*beit avadim*) – the setting of evening, unleavened bread and a house of a servant/slave (*eved*); the protective role of refuge in that house; the rescue of family units; the prominence of the word "house" throughout the story

By now we no longer need wonder about the prominence of the term and symbol *"bayit"* in the story of the exodus. Quite obviously, "house" comprises part of a paradigm, shared by both *Yetziat Mitzrayim* and *Yetziat Sedom*. To phrase this a little differently, and perhaps more radically, apparently God and the Torah have modeled the leaving of Egypt upon the leaving of Sodom.

But this explains nothing. If anything, we seem to have moved from the frying pan to the fire. Beforehand we faced merely the problem of the connection between "house" and a story of "leaving" by virtue of God's "mighty hand." Now we face the problem of the reason for the modeling, the inner meaning of the parallel between leaving Sodom and leaving Egypt.

III. RELUCTANT RESCUE?

As pointed out above, as part of the "forced exit" component of the parallel, both stories contain the rare term *"mitmame'a,"* meaning delaying or lingering. When the angels order Lot to leave, he lingers (19:16). Only their firm grasp upon his arm forces Lot out of Sodom. In contrast, the usage of the phrase in the story of the exodus carries no such implication of willful lingering. We are simply told that since there was no time for lingering, and hence no time for the dough to rise, the children of Israel baked their dough into unleavened bread (12:39). The absence of any particular reason for Lot's delay implies that the lingering stems from an inner impulse, not a practical need to prepare supplies.

This theme, Lot's difficulty in parting with Sodom, picks up speed as the story moves along. After the angels physically remove him from Sodom, his rescuers give him a threefold instruction. Warning him of being swept up in the incipient destruction, they tell him to flee for his life, not to look back and, finally, to get to the mountains, somewhere off the plain (19:17). But Lot refuses to follow the third order. He tells the angels that he can't flee to the mountains lest some "evil" befall him and he die. Following this strange explanation, Lot requests to flee to a small city nearby and the angels grant his request (19:21). Apparently, whatever drew Lot to the area of Sodom and whatever attracted him to Sodom itself still beats deep within him. He cannot bear to part and wishes to stay nearby.

What for Lot seems difficult, turns out to be downright impossible for his wife. She violates the angels' second instruction and looks back. In accord with their warning, she is swept up in the destruction of Sodom and turned into a pillar of salt (19:26).

The point seems to be that being rescued from Sodom, leaving Sodom, carries the implicit challenge of breaking with Sodom. The angels command Lot to part with Sodom not just physically but also mentally. Lot's lingering, his desire to remain nearby in one of the cities of the plain, his wife's looking back and Lot's eventual retreat into a mountain cave (19:30) all signify the fundamental failure of Lot and his family to part with Sodom.

If so, the paralleling of *"Yetziat Mitzrayim"* to *"Yetziat Sedom"* highlights the presentation of the same challenge to the children of Israel, the newly freed slaves. Can they break with Egypt? Can their fleeing from Egypt and slavery become a full-fledged parting with their lives as slaves in Egypt and their exposure to Egyptian culture? When they leave, can they truly become, as God has put it in His instructions to Moses, a people that "knows that I am the Lord" (6:7)? Will they give themselves over wholeheartedly to the "service of the Lord" (12:31) that constitutes the rationale for Pharaoh's freeing them? Or will they continue to be Egyptian slaves, forever entrenched in an identity determined by their experience in Egypt, and eternally pining for the familiar surroundings of their former home?

In other words, the paralleling of the two stories serves to raise the crucial questions that confront the Israelites during their desert journey.

IV. THE PASCHAL SACRIFICE: BREAKING WITH EGYPT

In elaborating on the parallel between the exodus from Egypt and the rescue of Lot, I chose to utilize the labels "*Yetziat Mitzrayim*" and "*Yetziat Sodom*." Theoretically, given the centrality of the paschal lamb to the events of the night of the exodus, and the parallel of that night to the night in Sodom, we could have chosen different terminology. For example, some interpreters have recently begun to refer to "*Pesaḥ Mitzrayim*" and "*Pesaḥ Sodom*." However, for obvious reasons I eschewed this choice. The story of Sodom contains none of the symbols of the paschal sacrifice itself, neither the lamb nor the blood. In fact, we may think of it as a story of "*yetzia*" (leaving), of God's "mighty hand," and the imagery of "*bayit*" minus whatever it is that the paschal lamb contributes to the story the second time around. This constitutes the crucial difference between the two stories. But what do the lamb and blood on the house accomplish? What do they add to the story?

After the fourth plague, the plague of the swarming gnats or beasts, Pharaoh offers a compromise. He suggests to Moses that the people need not bother with journeying into the desert, and can instead sacrifice to their God right at home in Egypt (8:21). Moses replies that this is impossible. The Israelites will sacrifice the "*to'eva*" of Egypt to their God. The Egyptians will never stand for this and will surely stone the people (8:22). The mysterious term "*to'eva*," best translated as "untouchable," has already appeared in the context of Egyptian-Israelite relations. Joseph instructed his brothers to inform Pharaoh that they are shepherds. Joseph hopes that since shepherding, the keeping of sheep and goats, is "*to'evat Mitzrayim*," untouchable or abomination to the Egyptians, Pharaoh will settle his brothers in the outlying land of Goshen.

This brings us back to the paschal sacrifice. As pointed out by many commentaries, the ritual of the paschal offering clearly plays off the concept of "the untouchable of Egypt." The procuring of a lamb from either the goats or sheep, guarding it until the fourteenth of the month and the mass slaughter and roasting by every household (12:1–6) will surely strike the Egyptians as an "untouchable" act. Placing the blood of the "untouchable" on your house as a sign to your God surely violates Egyptian sensibilities. But what is "untouchable" and "abominable" about the keeping of sheep and goats or their sacrifice to God? What does Moses intend when he tells Pharaoh that this kind of sacrifice is an "untouchable-abomination"?

Did the Egyptians worship sheep and goats? Does untouchable here mean "holy" in the sense of godly (Rashi 8:22, Abarbanel 12:1–13)? Perhaps. Ibn Ezra (8:22) suggests the variant possibility that the Egyptians were proto-Hindus, vegetarians who were disgusted by the shepherding, slaughtering and consuming of meat. Or maybe cattle that literally consume precious agricultural space and produce along the holy Nile were considered destructive, vile, un-holy and disgusting objects (see Rashbam 8:22). Either way, a religious ritual that involves the sacrifice of "*to'evat* Egypt," either a holy or disgusting object, constitutes a fundamentally un-Egyptian act. The smearing of the blood of the lamb on the house constitutes a declaration of religious independence, a shattering of Egyptian cultural norms and taboos. It defines a new identity, a non-Egyptian culture loyal to the instructions of the Lord, the God of the forefathers.

As such, the inclusion of the paschal sacrifice and its symbolism of religious and cultural disjunction with Egypt in the story of "*Yetziat Mitzrayim*" defines the difference between the exodus and "*Yetziat Sedom.*" Lot never broke with Sodom. The story of leaving Egypt is precisely about differentiating not just from Egypt but also from Lot.

V. CENTRALITY OF THE HOUSE

This brings us full circle back to the image of Section I, and the problem of the centrality of the symbol and object of the house in the two stories.

Lot's house was a hospitable place. It was a place where he maintained the traditions of Abraham, acted with kindness, and hosted guests (19:1–3). It served as a physical and cultural barrier against the evil of Sodom that surrounded his home (19:4–10). Part of the tragedy of

Lot lies in the fact that his house turns out to be no more than a semi-permeable barrier, a mere membrane, which the pernicious influences of Sodom had long breached. His sons-in-law consider the possibility of God destroying the evil city no more than a joke (19:14). His two virgin daughters (19:8) turn out to be sophisticated enough to seduce him (19:31–35). His wife is so unable to separate from Sodom that it literally kills her. Finally, even Lot himself, the student of Abraham, cares so much for his guests that he offers his virgin daughters to the mob (19:8). He, too, has been absorbed into Sodom.

In other words, the symbol of "house" represents the failure of Lot, his integration into Sodom and his attachment to Sodom. It foreshadows his lingering and his eventual retreat to the cave. The Sodomite without Sodom is a broken man.

If so, it is understandable why the symbol of "house" enters the story of leaving Egypt, and at the same time as the paschal sacrifice. Putting the blood on the house, the place of the household, implicitly symbolizes the need to construct a barrier, to cut the cultural tendrils that have snaked across the threshold. The Israelites must break with Egypt. They must construct a physical and cultural space that truly contains the tradition of Abraham. They must succeed where Lot had failed. They must move from the "house of bondage" to the "house of Abraham."

Lot's Pesaḥ and Its Significance

Rav Yoel Bin-Nun

Anyone who has studied Genesis with Rashi has come across the verse describing Lot's hospitality towards the angels in Sodom: "And he prepared a banquet for them, and baked matzot, and they ate" (Gen. 19:2), and Rashi's laconic comment: "It was Pesaḥ."

Rashi's explanation is most surprising, for several reasons:

1. Does the mere fact that matza was baked and eaten indicate that it was Pesaḥ? Why does Rashi not deduce that Lot baked matza because it took less time to prepare than bread? (Indeed, this is the explanation offered by Radak, who regards the verse as an important lesson in hospitality: guests should not have to wait long to be offered food.)

2. What significance could there be to a Pesaḥ before there was a nation called *Am Yisrael* and before they left Egypt? Does Rashi's explanation not undermine the special character of the festival of Pesaḥ as a commemoration of the miracle of *Am Yisrael*'s departure from Egypt?

In my youth, I spent much time pondering the reason that Rashi reached this conclusion, whose textual basis seemed so weak. Admittedly, the idea that "it was Pesaḥ" has its source in a midrash of Ḥazal (*Rosh HaShana* 11a; *Bereshit Rabba* 50:22), but Rashi does not always interpret a verse in accordance with such midrashim. Why, then, does he choose in this instance to rely on a midrash whose encounter with the literal text gives rise to such serious questions?

At some stage, the realization hit me. I read the chapter as it is written, and was suddenly struck by the depths of the insight possessed by Ḥazal and by Rashi. It is specifically when one reads the text itself directly – rather than through the eyes of the commentaries – that Ḥazal's view emanates from the words of the verses.

The narrative in Genesis 19 describes a house that is closed up, in which the family and the guests have just completed a meal with matzot. At the doorway to the house, the angels save the family members, strike the people of the city (Sodom), and then bring Lot's family out of the city, by virtue of the hospitality shown to them.

The following table presents a comparison between the expressions in this chapter and the description of Pesaḥ in Egypt:

GENESIS 19 – LOT AND THE ANGELS	EXODUS 12 – THE EXODUS
(6) And Lot went out to them at *the entrance*, and shut the door after him.	(22) And none of you shall go out from *the entrance* of his house until morning.
(11) And they struck the men that were at *the entrance* to the house with blindness … and they wearied themselves to find the entrance.	(23) God will pass over *the entrance* and will not allow the destroyer to come into your houses, to smite you.
(3) And he made them a feast, and baked *matzot*, and they ate.	(8) And they shall eat the meat on that night, roasted with fire, with *matzot*; they shall eat it with bitter herbs.
(14) …*get up; get out* of this place, for God is going to destroy the city…	(31) And he called for Moses and Aaron by night, and said: *get up; get out* from among my nation – you and *Benei Yisrael.*
(16) And he *lingered* … so they brought him out.	(39) And they could not *linger.*
(24) *And God rained down* upon Sodom and Amora brimstone *and fire* from God out of the heavens.	And God sent thunder and hail, *and the fire* ran down to the ground, *And God rained down* hail upon the land of Egypt. (9:23)

Duration: All night until the morning	Duration: All night until the morning
Lot's family is saved, producing two nations: Moav and Ammon.	The Exodus from Egypt gives rise to the nation of Israel.

The many parallels between the overturning of Sodom and the plagues on Egypt practically shout out, "Pesaḥ!" There is the closed house, the angels of destruction/deliverance, and the events that continue "all night until the morning," when the day dawns and the sun rises (which is the same timetable followed in the exodus). Most specifically, there is the command, "Get up, get out," and the word "linger"; these are expressions that are intrinsically bound up with the exodus. *Benei Yisrael* "could not linger – because they were driven out of Egypt." Similarly, in leaving Sodom, Lot could not linger because the angels held firmly (perhaps forcibly) onto his hand, and his wife's hand, and the hands of his two daughters, "and they brought him out and left him outside of the city" (19:16).

Ḥazal had all these parallels in mind when they drew their conclusion in the Midrash. The "literal school" of commentators, on the other hand, did not see all of this. Their approach is generally to read a verse within its local context, not to offer a synchronic reading of "biblical parallels." In this respect, as in certain others, the Midrash offers more than the literal interpretation does. In this manner we are able to draw a distinction of depth between the literal text and the Midrash.

Unfortunately, there are people in our times who are so protective of the honor of Rashi and Ḥazal that they are unwilling to read a chapter of the Torah in a simple, fluent, straightforward manner lest they find themselves encountering questions and difficulties. Furthermore, they seem to fear that a person who starts off ignoring Rashi and Ḥazal and their interpretations or midrashim may (Heaven forefend) come to scorn their moral teachings and halakhic instruction, as well… and this, in turn, may lead to skepticism and perhaps, God forbid, even heresy. For this reason, they issue a sweeping, all-inclusive directive (by which no intelligent, thinking person can abide): that none of us should imagine himself capable of a fluent, straightforward reading of the text, and therefore none of us is worthy of raising serious questions.

In this manner, we lose out on the treasures of the biblical text, which fill a person with supreme joy and with the love of God. We lose out on the joy of the simple, plain reading (no less inspiring than the "secret" readings based on codes and the counting of intervals between letters), as well as on an understanding of the midrash, since we receive it through "faith in the sages," an acceptance brimming with anxiety and denial of the intellect.

The proof of this is that I have presented above the treasures that I discovered through a simple reading and through which I exposed the source of the Midrash and its greatness. The Midrash recognizes expressions characteristic of the exodus from Egypt, within the story of Lot's exodus from Sodom.

Indeed, "it was Pesaḥ."

Does this mean that the scene took place in the "month of spring," the season of Pesaḥ? A study of the chapter from all angles offers no reason to assume this, and therefore we must conclude that the Midrash also comprises two levels. The "literal level of the Midrash" is the idea, or concept, of "Pesaḥ": the salvation of one lone family from the chaos, by virtue of their hospitality, which is the characteristic of the household of Abraham. This idea or concept preceded the exodus from Egypt, and it produced two nations, descendants of Lot: Ammon and Moav. These two nations are prohibited from joining *Benei Yisrael* for all time because they did not observe and maintain the custom set down by Lot, their father, by virtue of which he had been saved from Sodom. They did not welcome *Benei Yisrael* "with bread and with water, on your way as you came out of Egypt, and they hired Bil'am … to curse you" (Deut. 23:4–7).

The deeper level, the "Midrash of the Midrash," introduces into the story the date of "Pesaḥ," not only the idea of it. This is the source of the Midrash recorded in the Gemara: "Isaac was born on Pesaḥ" (*Rosh HaShana* 11a).

This obligates us to re-examine the "Pesaḥ of Egypt" experienced by *Benei Yisrael*, which had been preceded by the "Pesaḥ" experienced by Lot (together with his wife, daughters, and sons-in-law). It becomes immediately clear that the unique character of the "Pesaḥ of Egypt" lies not in the fact that it was the first such occasion, but rather in that it was a "Pesaḥ" of salvation and redemption for an entire nation. The entire nation was "at home" – each family in its own home with its own Pesaḥ sacrifice, and all of Israel was saved, family by family, and continues to celebrate, family by family, to this day.

Even though "Pesaḥ for all generations" is the commemoration of the deliverance and redemption of all of Israel for all generations, it retains its fundamentally family-orientated foundation and character from the family of Lot, from the household of Abraham. Even when the "Pesaḥ for all generations" was established as a "communal sacrifice," such that it is offered even on Shabbat (Yerushalmi *Pesaḥim* 6:1), it never for a moment ceased being a "family offering" – albeit of all the families together. The Yerushalmi (ad. loc.) regards the Pesaḥ as a communal sacrifice (as does the Tosefta, *Pesaḥim* chapter 4), while the Bavli (*Pesaḥim* 66a) omits the deduction by Hillel the Elder concerning the communal sacrifice.

Pesaḥ is a unique sacrifice in that it is offered by all of *Am Yisrael* – by its families.

Finally, the "hospitality" of the Seder night, which is formulated in the Haggada in Aramaic (with its source in the Bavli) in "*Ha laḥma anya*" has its true source in the very first Pesaḥ in the Torah – the Pesaḥ of Lot, whose essence was the hospitality of Abraham's household. It was by virtue of this quality of hospitality that Sara received the news that her son Isaac would be born, and by virtue of this same quality Lot was saved from Sodom.

Therefore, we learn that hospitality (both monetary and physical) is one of the central elements of Pesaḥ, and the secret of the deliverance and salvation.

Parashat Beshallaḥ

The Prohibition on Returning to Egypt

Rav Yoel Bin-Nun

It happened that when Pharaoh sent the nation forth, God (*Elokim*) did not guide them along the way of the land of the Philistines, which is close; because God said, "Lest the nation have a change of heart when they see war and return to Egypt. So God led the nation roundabout, along the way of the desert by the Red Sea; the Israelites left Egypt armed." (13:17–18)

Despite the many interpretations that have been offered, the meaning of these verses is very problematic and they seem as baffling as ever. There are three basic questions:

1. What is the meaning of "which is close" (*ki karov hu*)?
2. Which war is being referred to in the phrase "if they see war"?
3. Why is the phrase, "the Israelites left Egypt armed," included in this context?

We must raise three further difficulties:

1. Why do these verses refer to God as *Elokim* (אלקים), the only such instance in the exodus narrative, rather than God's

"personal" and "historical" name *Y-H-v-H* (HaShem), the only
name which appears from the burning bush story onward?

2. The goal of the exodus has been repeatedly defined in relation
to Mount Sinai, which lies on the "way of the desert" and not
the "way of the Philistines." God stated, "When you bring the
nation out of Egypt you will worship the Lord on this mountain"
(3:18). Indeed, Pharaoh's permission to worship at Sinai is the
expressed goal of all Moses' negotiations, threats, and wonders,
and it is with this understanding that Pharaoh finally gives his
permission: "Get up and leave my nation – you and the Israelites;
go and worship the Lord as you say" (12:31).

But this is diametrically opposed to our verses, which
imply that the logical path of the exodus would have avoided
Sinai. Hence, the revelation at Sinai was virtually accidental,
merely an outcome of God's concern that "the nation would
have a change of heart" if they encountered war on the shorter,
more direct coastal road.

3. The traditional interpretations assume that God wanted to avoid
confronting Israel with war, at least at the outset, since He was
concerned that this would inspire them to abandon their cause
and physically turn around and return to Egypt. The difficulty
is that in actuality, the alternate, supposedly more peaceful,
route through the desert led them into war with Egypt almost
immediately, causing an instant public outcry to return to Egypt.
God's action seems to have achieved the opposite of its intention.
The reaction of the Jews when the Egyptian army caught up with
them – "for it is better for us to serve Egypt than to die in the
desert" – was exactly the reaction that God feared "should they
see war," and God nevertheless dealt with it – "God will fight
for you and you shall be still." This repeated itself several times
during the journey to the land of Israel, so that it is clear that
changing the route did not solve the problem. The longer route
did not, in fact, lead them away from war.

The classical commentators proposed solutions which
seem somewhat contrived. Rashi suggest that "if the *circuitous*
route resulted in their saying: 'Let us return to Egypt,' how much

worse would the *direct* route have been!" Accordingly, the phrase "which was close" means "close to Egypt," making it easier to return there. Taking the nation to Canaan along the more distant desert road would deter the people from returning.

Rashbam reads "close" – to *Eretz Yisrael* (the Land of Israel); the shorter route would have brought the war for the Land earlier. By delaying the Canaanite wars, the people were less psychologically connected to Egypt when the crisis struck. Rambam similarly suggests:

[I]t is contrary to human nature that a person be raised in slavery, doing the most menial of tasks, and promptly wash the filth off his hands and go wage war with the gigantic Sons of Anak.... God's wisdom led them roundabout, through the desert, until they learnt to be brave. It is well-known that traveling in the desert without luxuries such as washing and the like gives rise to bravery, while the opposite gives rise to cowardice. (*Guide to the Perplexed*, 3:32; see also chapter 24)

On the other hand, Ramban interprets "which was close" as referring to the path traversing the land of the Philistines. Even though this route was shorter, God wished to avoid war with the Philistines. However, on the longer route they meet Amalek instead.

All of these interpretations contain important points but do not address the cardinal problem: the confrontation at the Red Sea with Egypt, the superpower to whom they had been enslaved for centuries and with whom they had struggled for independence. This confrontation was potentially far more deadly than any war with the Amalekites, Canaanites or Philistines could have been. This war came immediately, and at a time when Israel was weak and confused.

Modern scholars offer a different solution to our problem, which resembles Ramban's interpretation. Bas reliefs on the walls of the temple at Karnak, dating to the rule of Pharaoh Seti I (toward the end of the thirteenth century B.C.E., show that the entire northern Sinai coastal region was under direct Egyptian sovereignty, with Egyptian military outposts all along the way. Israel, fearing a trap, avoided the coastal road from the outset. Plausible though this theory may sound, the reason it proposes for the change of route is not that mentioned in the Torah. God did not fear an Egyptian trap but rather the desire of the Jews to return to Egypt.

Therefore, I would like to propose a different interpretation for these verses:

> "which is close" – and therefore should have been the route of travel (following Ramban),

> "God said, 'Lest the nation have a change of heart if they see war'" – any war, whether for the Land or at any point in history,

> "and return to Egypt" – to request aid and patronage from Pharaoh,

> "so God led the nation roundabout, along the way of the desert by the Red Sea" – so that Pharaoh would pursue them, guaranteeing that war would take place,

> "and the Israelites left Egypt armed."

Contrary to the accepted opinion, God's intention was not to avoid war and save Israel undue fear, but precisely the opposite – to drag them straight into a confrontation, and achieve final, total liberation at the Red Sea. The Jews need to be liberated not only politically and economically, but also mentally, as is evident from their demand: "leave us be and we will serve Egypt, because we prefer serving Egypt to dying in the Wilderness" (14:12). Complete liberation will result from the experience of war ("the Lord will fight for you") and through the rejoicing and singing of victory.

The expression "to return to Egypt" refers to seeking support from Egypt in several places in the prophets.[1] Returning, or "going down," to Egypt does not necessarily refer to the physical emigration of all or part

---

1. Isaiah states: "Woe to those who descend to Egypt for aid, who rely on their multitude of chariots, and on the immense power of their horsemen, but did not desire

of the nation to Egypt. Suffice it that an Israelite king send messengers to Pharaoh saying, "I am your servant and son" (1 Kings 16:7), and the prohibition against "returning" has been violated.

The Torah commands the king that he "not return the nation to Egypt in order to acquire many horses" (Deut. 7:16). Clearly, this refers to seeking military support from Egypt. King Solomon, for example, disobeyed the commandment not by sending his entire royal house to Pharaoh, but rather by dispatching a handful of merchants (1 Kings 10:28, 29). "Returning to Egypt" not to dwell there but rather to gain support and patronage is the spiritual opposite of the independence gained via the exodus.

The *tokheḥa* (rebuke) in Deuteronomy ends similarly: "The Lord will return you to Egypt in ships, on a route I told you that you would never see again; there you will be offered to your enemies for sale as slaves, but no one will buy you" (Deut. 26:68).

Did Israel leave Egypt in ships, that God is threatening them with return along the same route? The Torah is not describing the geographical route of return to Egypt, but rather the implication of return to Egypt – renewed bondage. The common denominator of a request for Egyptian protection, physical return to Egypt of one's own free will, and sale into Egyptian captivity is forfeiture of independence. The route God said Israel should never see again is the route of slavery.

The Rabbis understood this point as being the crux of the commandment to pierce the ear of the voluntary slave: "An ear which heard [at Sinai], 'I am the Lord your God' and went and bought itself a master – should be pierced" (Rashi to Exodus 21:6, based on Yerushalmi *Kiddushin* 1:2; *Sifra Vayikra* ad loc.).

At this point, we can take a new look at the prohibition against returning to Egypt and serving her:

and *the Lord said* you would never return this way again. (Deut. 17:16)

Israel's Holy (God) and did not consult the Lord" (31:1; see also 30:2, 31:3, Jeremiah 2:36, 37 and Hosea 7:11, 8:13).

on the road *I told you* that you would never see again. (28:68)

Where and when did God previously tell Moses that they would not return this way? The recurring theme of "never seeing Egypt again" leads us to Moses' words to Israel before the parting of the Sea as they cried out, in their panic, that they preferred slavery.

As such, we can understand the verse "The Lord will fight for you... for as you have seen Egypt today you will never see them again" (14:13) as follows: "as you have seen Egypt today" – in the *manner* that slaves look up to their masters – "you will never see them again."

That the halakha understood patronage to be the true meaning of "returning to Egypt" is clear from the following midrash:

> The Torah warned Israel three times against returning to Egypt [here the Talmud quotes the three verses we saw above]... but Israel returned to Egypt three times, and as is written, "Woe to those who descend to Egypt for aid"; three times they failed. The first was in the time of Sanḥerev; the second was in the time of Yoḥanan ben Kare'aḥ; and the third was in the time of Torginos. (*Mekhilta Beshallaḥ*, mas. 2, par. 2; Yerushalmi *Sukka* 5:1; Bavli *Sukka* 51b)

Three prohibitions and three "returns" mean three different kinds of submission. The first is asking for Egyptian patronage, as Ḥezkiyahu did when he was threatened by Sanḥerev. The second is actual physical emigration to Egypt, as the Judeans, led by Yoḥanan ben Kare'aḥ, did (Jer. 40–43). The third kind of "return" is that of the Jewish community of Alexandria, which lived under Egyptian patronage from the time of Alexander the Great (c. 333 BCE) until the period of the Roman emperors Trajan (evidently the Torginos of our text) and Hadrian. The defeat spoken of is the decimation of the Alexandrian community after hatred and persecution drove the Diaspora Jewry to all-out revolt, forty-five years after the destruction of the Temple.

It is submission that the Rabbis see as the true meaning of "return," as is evidenced by the conclusion of the Yerushalmi:

One may not return to Egypt to live there, but one may return there for trade, for business, and for conquest. (Yerushalmi *Sanhedrin*, end of chapter 10)

Financial dealings do not imply submission, and are therefore permitted.

Returning to our *parasha*, we note that the exodus came about based on Pharaoh's consent. Therefore, our verses call God "*Elokim*," the universal name known to all, which is used, as a rule, when the Torah presents dialogue with gentiles (see Gen. 20, 31:40–41; Ex. 5:1–4; see also Ibn Ezra to Exodus 3:15; *Kuzari*, chapter 4). The reason for its use here is precisely because the Jews left Egypt with Pharaoh's permission. This account of the exodus describes a political-historical event which takes place along natural, political lines; its goal is not revelation at Sinai.

Only when the Torah returns to describe the "other" exodus, the inner psychological exodus, the journey towards complete freedom, with no foreign protection whatsoever, and where the goal is the Torah, does it speak of revelation and lawgiving, and does God reveal Himself through His transcendental, historical attribute *Y-H-v-H*.

Had *Benei Yisrael* left Egypt on the "Way of the Land of the Philistines,"[2] Pharaoh would never have pursued them at all. He could have granted them the mountain region and even made them his representatives there. In times of war, the people would have returned to Egypt to seek protection. Needless to say, this exodus would not have been conducive to revelation. A slave-nation which progressed from

---

2. This road was an official route under Egyptian jurisdiction, as were considerable portions of Canaan. Had Israel taken Pharaoh's road, they would have displayed good faith to him, and de facto recognition of his protection. At every checkpoint along the road, they would have shown Pharaoh's letter of safe passage; and whenever they found themselves in danger, especially in situations of war, they would have sent Pharaoh letters similar to the petition for aid sent to Pharaoh by Biridia, king of Shekhem:

> To my king, my lord and my sun: So speaks Biridia, the king's faithful servant. Beneath the feet of my king, my lord and my sun, I grovel on my belly and on my back. (from the Tel El Amarna letters)

slave status in Egypt to vassal status in Canaan would not have achieved true freedom, even if it would have been freed from hard labor. A nation which is not free could not have received the Torah. God's sovereignty is possible only after all other sovereignties have been renounced:

> I am the Lord your God ... you will not have other gods beside Me.

Moses' prophecy and leadership – including God's revelation at Sinai and giving the Torah – stem from a state of total liberation from yoke of Pharaoh. For this reason, God led them on the desert route, into confrontation, into war, into victory and singing, and into complete freedom –

> You will never see them [through the eyes of slaves] again.

Pillar of Fire, Pillar of Cloud

Rav Tamir Granot

I. INTRODUCTION

In this *shiur* we shall address how Tanach describes a certain aspect of God's revelation in the world. The commonly-held conception is that of God's presence in the heavens; the heavens are His dwelling place, and from there He reveals Himself from time to time within the world. On the other hand, it is clear that God's transcendence in Tanach is not absolute – for God is, indeed, revealed in the world; He appears, directs, influences.

It appears that the characteristics of divine manifestation in the world may be presented schematically as follows:

1. Speech – prophecy
2. Phenomena contravening the laws of nature – miracles
3. Management of history – divine providence, reward and punishment
4. Appearance – revelations of God's glory

The entire Tanach is based on the assumption that the timing and frequency of these manifestations rests with God alone. There is no way of understanding biblical history, or the Torah with its concept of religious obligation, without a recognition of God's ability to speak with people – and especially His prophets, to manage history according to His will, and to change the laws of nature so as to fulfill His objectives.

We will try to understand the fourth manner of divine manifestation – appearance and revelations. God's appearance may occasionally remind the prophet of a human form in his mind, but he does not see it manifested in reality. I wish to address those verses that refer to actually seeing God, in reality, in the world. The Tanach offers various terms for describing the manifestation of God: "vision," "form (of God)," "face (of God)," and sometimes directly – as in the verses in chapter 6 of Isaiah. But the most frequently used term to describe God's appearance is the term "*kevod*" – glory. We shall examine the exact meaning of this term, but we may already say that the expression "God's glory" means His embodiment, or concretization, within some real, worldly entity.

We shall address the fundamental significance of revelation through some tangible entity. What this means is that God is revealed as an object or phenomenon within nature. When He is revealed, whoever views the revelation knows that he is experiencing a divine manifestation. The occurrence of revelation is an extraordinary phenomenon; on the other hand, it is not necessarily miraculous, in the strict sense of the word – meaning, it does not necessarily involve a deviation from the laws of nature.

Using the divine appearances in pillars of cloud and fire in our *parasha*, we can begin to understand the significance of an aspect of God's revelations through nature.

II. IN FIRE AND CLOUD

In most of the Tanach's descriptions of divine revelation, God appears in the form of fire and cloud. In some cases, the description includes both phenomena at the same time, while in others the revelation involves only one of them. In describing revelation, biblical texts adopt a range of different styles in accordance with the occasion and the character of the book in question. The fire in which God is revealed is mentioned as plain fire, and also as a "flaming torch," a "pillar of fire," a "consuming fire," a "flaming fire," "smoke," and a "brilliant flame of fire." Similarly, the cloud in which He is revealed is described simply as a cloud, and also as a "smoking oven," the "smoking furnace," a "pillar of cloud," a "thick cloud," a "black cloud of darkness," and "darkness like walls, a mass of water, the thick clouds of the sky."[1]

Revelation in cloud often has consequences and ramifications that are related to its meteorological essence – darkness, opacity and concealment on one hand, and on the other hand, phenomena related to water – a river of peace, a flowing brook, "upon many waters." Similarly, revelation in fire has consequences related to its physical essence, on one hand, destruction – "a fire is kindled in My anger," "He is a consuming fire"; on the other hand, light – "The glory of God has risen over you," "the land is illuminated by His glory," "from the brightness in front of Him," "at night – in a pillar of fire, to illuminate for them" etc.

The key to understanding these manners of revelation is to be found, to my view, in an examination of the relationship between visions of fire and visions of cloud. As stated, in many instances we find these visions independently of one another. Thus, in the exodus, the text describes God going before the Israelite camp to lead it – by day He is revealed as a pillar of cloud and by night as a pillar of fire. Some opinions maintain that these are two functionally distinct revelations that are fundamentally different from one another. The pillars are emissaries of God, sent to guide His nation; God creates a pillar of cloud in the day and fire by night so that both will be visible.

But it is clear that the manifestation in fire and in cloud here is more than merely functional. God does not reveal Himself in fire and in cloud on a merely *ad hoc* basis; rather, He is always manifest specifically in a cloud and/or in fire, and hence *Benei Yisrael* have not only a guide, but also the very Presence of God going before the camp.

Are there really two revelations here – one in a pillar of clouds and the other in a pillar of fire? In order to answer this question we must grapple with a most problematic literary unit: the description of the journey of *Benei Yisrael* to the Red Sea.

1. See Gen. 15:17; Ex. 3:2, 14:21, 16:10, 19:9, 24:15–17, 33:10; II Sam. 22:9–13; Isaiah 4:5, 66:15; Ezek. 1:4.

III. TO THE RED SEA

Let us focus on chapters 13 and 14, describing the journey of *Benei Yisrael* from Egypt. The description of the journey consists of four clear sections:

1. The description of the expulsion of *Benei Yisrael* and Pharaoh's subsequent change of heart (*Exodus* 13:17–14:8)
2. The description of *Benei Yisrael*'s fear as they encamp by the sea and notice the Egyptians in pursuit (14:9–15)
3. The description of *Benei Yisrael*'s entry into the sea (14:16–22)
4. The description of the Egyptians' entry into the sea and their drowning (14:23–29)

Right now we are interested in the third section, because it is here that God begins to act through the essences that represent Him. Let us review the verses:

> God said to Moses, "Why do you cry to Me? Speak to *Benei Yisrael*, and let them journey. And you – raise your staff and stretch your arm over the sea and divide it, such that *Benei Yisrael* will come into the midst of the sea on dry land. As for Me – behold, I shall harden the hearts of the Egyptians and they shall come after them, and I shall be glorified through Pharaoh and through all of his army, through his chariots and his horsemen. Then all of Egypt will know that I am God." (14:15–18)
>
> Then the angel of God who was proceeding before the camp of Israel travelled and went to their rear, and the pillar of cloud went from before them and stood at the back of them. And it came between the camp of Egypt and the camp of Israel and there was the cloud with darkness, and it illuminated the night. (14:19–20)
>
> Then Moses stretched out his hand over the sea, and God drove the sea with a strong east wind all night, and made the sea dry land, and the water was divided. So *Benei Yisrael* came into the midst of the sea on dry land. (14:21–22)

In the above excerpt we find the command for *Benei Yisrael* to enter the sea and God's promise that He will harden the hearts of the

Egyptians so that they too will enter the sea. The basic storyline consists of verses 15–18, and then verse 21 onwards. It is not clear what purpose verses 19–20 serve, describing the relocation of the pillar of cloud and the pillar of fire. The problem is a dual one. It is difficult to understand how this relocation of the pillar of cloud from its regular place in front of the camp to the rear is necessary. It is also difficult to picture what the verses here are describing, and the purpose of the relocation of the manifestation of God.

We may list the internal difficulties arising from these two verses as follows: Who, or what, is this "angel of God" described as journeying behind the camp of Israel? Why does the angel and/or pillar of fire change its location? From verses 20 and 21 it would appear that all of this happened at night – but during the night the pillar was of fire, not of clouds! Finally, the following phrase is a peculiar one: "There was the cloud with darkness, and it illuminated the night." How does the cloud with darkness illuminate the night?

Rashi is sensitive to these difficulties, and posits that at first, the pillar was a pillar of cloud because the beginning of the journey was during the day. However, on this particular one-time occasion, the pillar of cloud remained even when it was dark. Its purpose in moving to the back of the camp was to bring darkness upon the Egyptians and to protect Israel from their arrows. The pillar of fire remained in its usual place, and it was this that illuminated the night for Israel, so that they could see their way to the sea. Thus, according to Rashi, each of the pillars fulfills a distinct function, with the overall objective being the same – to protect Israel and to lead them safely towards the sea. The major problem with Rashi's explanation is that the crux of what he is saying is missing from the text. Nowhere does the Torah say anything about the purpose of the pillar being to protect Israel. The verse appears to tell us only that the pillar of fire "illuminated the night" – i.e., it was there for illumination and not for any other purpose.

Furthermore, Rashi assumes that the pillar of fire gave light, as it usually would. But the text seems to be telling us that it was specifically the cloud with the darkness that illuminated the night. If we assume that the formulation here is in abbreviated form, and the Torah meant that the pillar of fire illuminated, then the problem is that the pillar is now located at the rear of the camp rather than in front. How, then, did it give light from behind?

The difficulties inherent in Rashi's explanation demand another look at the verses, with special attention to two points: the significance of God's promise to harden the hearts of Pharaoh and the Egyptians so that they would enter the sea, and the meaning of the revelation of the cloud and the fire.

To my mind, most of the exegetical difficulties with Rashi's interpretation are due to his assumption that there are two distinct pillars: one of cloud and the other of fire. Let us propose instead that the text is speaking not of two separate pillars, but rather of one single pillar of fire and cloud together – fire on the inside and a cloud on the outside. According to this understanding, the distinction between day and night is not a change in the essence of the revelation, but rather in the manner in which it is perceived by the viewer. The cloud is what is seen by day, and the fire is what they see at night. This is the only difference between them. Indeed, when we find the description of the defeat of the Egyptians in the sea, we read, "And it was, *at the morning watch*, that God looked upon the camp of Egypt *through the pillar of fire and cloud*, and He confounded the camp of the Egyptians" (Ex. 14:24). At the morning watch – when there is already light, but the moon and stars are still visible – the fire and clouds could be perceived together. And indeed, according to the description here, *there is only one pillar, of both fire and cloud*, rather than of one of them alone.

This being the case, the pillar of fire and cloud, the only pillar that exists, moved to the rear of the camp of Israel and gave light – not for Israel, but for Egypt. God's angel traveling before the camp is itself the pillar of cloud – as we read previously, "And God went before them in a pillar." The text emphasizes that God placed Himself, as it were, between the two camps. Accordingly, our interpretation of the verse should be:

"The pillar of cloud moved from before them" – close to evening,

"and came between the camp of Egypt … and there was a cloud" – the cloud placed itself, return to what was said before,

"and darkness" – the night became dark, immediately afterwards, "and it illuminated the night" – the pillar of cloud which has been the subject all along – i.e., the angel of God, i.e., the fire of God within the cloud. All of this happens just after it grows dark.

Immediately thereafter Moses stretches his hand, and then "God drove the sea with a strong east wind all night." This development sits well with the chronology that we have proposed, according to which the pillar of fire illuminates at the beginning of the evening, and then Moses stretches out his hand and the wind starts up; it then blows all night and dries the middle of the sea. It is in the middle of the night that *Benei Yisrael* enter the sea and also emerge from it, and the Egyptians enter the sea on their heels, by the light of the pillar of fire. At the morning watch God casts confusion among them with His pillar of fire and cloud, Moses stretches out his hand, and the sea returns to its strength.

But the picture that emerges from the above interpretation is a very strange one! It seems paradoxical that at the most critical moment, the divine pillar of fire works to the benefit of the Egyptians, rather than to the benefit of *Benei Yisrael*!

In order to understand this point, let us return to our first question, concerning the hardening of Pharaoh's heart.

IV. HARDENING PHARAOH'S HEART

God promises Moses that He will harden the hearts of the Egyptians, and the Egyptians will follow them into the midst of the sea. How did God harden Pharaoh's heart and the hearts of the Egyptians?

We ask this question with respect to the point in time when they entered the sea, but clearly the question is of central importance in understanding the story of the exodus as a whole. In all the plagues save for the last, the text notes that Pharaoh hardened his heart, or that God helped him to do so. Even after *Benei Yisrael* leave Egypt, there is a need for God to harden Pharaoh's heart in order that he will decide to go off to the desert in pursuit of them:

> Then Pharaoh will say of *Benei Yisrael*: "They are lost in the land, the wilderness has closed in on them"; and I shall harden Pharaoh's heart, so he will pursue after them, and I shall be glorified

through Pharaoh and through all of his army, and the Egyptians shall know that I am God.

The purpose of hardening Pharaoh's heart is, as we learn from the verses quoted above, to teach the Egyptians to recognize God, by having God multiply His wonders among them. Indirectly, *Benei Yisrael* also come to learn this – along with the other nations ("The nations heard and were afraid"). But understanding the purpose of the hardening of his heart in no way alleviates the difficulty inherent in the concept of using this tactic. The commentators discuss at length the problems arising here in relation to the principle of reward and punishment. Ḥazal's major line of response – adopted also by Rambam, in his *Laws of Repentance* (chapter 6) – is that the hardening of Pharaoh's heart was a means of punishment after his fate had been sealed. If the time had come for punishment, then hardening the heart could indeed be fair and just. There is no difference between God causing someone to suffer or to die, and hardening his heart in order to cause him pain. As such, the commentators make almost no attempt to understand how the mechanism of "hardening the heart" operates. We must assume that most of them accepted that the hardening of his heart is achieved by manipulative intervention in the person's consciousness or will, and that it is miraculous and not given to human understanding The reactions of a person whose heart has been hardened are automatic; they are, in fact, non-human. Hence, they can only be justified as a punishment that comes to a person as a stage on the path to death.

It would seem that close inspection of the narratives in which expressions of "hardening of the heart" appear could lead to a different understanding of the issue. Let us examine the opening section of chapter 14, the story of the Egyptian pursuit:

> God spoke to Moses, saying: "Speak to *Benei Yisrael*, and let them go back and encamp before Pi HaḤirot, between Migdol and the sea, before *Ba'al Tzefon*; you shall encamp facing it, at the sea. And Pharaoh will say of *Benei Yisrael*, 'They are lost in the land; the wilderness has closed about them.' And I shall harden Pharaoh's heart, so that he will pursue after them, *and I shall be*

*glorified through Pharaoh and through his army, and the Egyptians
shall know that I am the Lord."* And they did so. When it was told
to the King of Egypt that the nation had fled, the heart of Pharaoh and his servants turned, and they said: "Why have we done
this, that we have let Israel go from serving us?" So he readied
his chariot and took his people with him. And he took six hundred choice chariots, and all the chariots of Egypt, with captains
over all of them. *And God hardened the heart of Pharaoh,* King of
Egypt, and he pursued after *Benei Yisrael,* and *Benei Yisrael* went
out with a high hand. (14:1–8)

Here, too, there is a divine promise concerning the hardening of
Pharaoh's heart, but in this case its purpose is to reverse Pharaoh's despair
and submission and to "turn his heart" such that he will stop being
afraid, and go out to pursue Israel. We may suffice with the assumption
that God manipulated Pharaoh's heart, but there is no need to resort to
this, as the text itself supplies the answer. The narrative here is built in a
chiastic structure with its climax – the point of the entire story – being,
"the Egyptians shall know that I am God." It is around this central point
that the story is set out, with symmetrical "arms" preceding and suc-
ceeding it. Thus, the hardening of Pharaoh's heart occurs by means of a
simple manipulation of historical events. *Benei Yisrael* escape, and this
becomes known and is reported to Pharaoh. Pharaoh need only make
his simple calculation: My nation of slaves is lost in the desert; there is
apparently no one to lead them. This may confirm the prophecy of his
astrologers: "They are heading towards evil." Possibly, the internal pressures that had always weighed in favor of refusing Israel's request were
effective this time, too. The need for slaves, the honor of the kingdom,
and the ego of the humiliated king, all desperate to be shored up – these
are the elements that count once the external circumstances calm down.
God has no need to miraculously intervene; it is enough that the surrounding factors be organized such that their general constellation will
bring about a certain *pharaonic* reaction.

This may also be the intention behind the textual conclusion of
each of the plagues with the record of God hardening Pharaoh's heart.
The limited nature of the plagues in terms of time and quality (they were

neither too long nor too severe) allowed the Egyptians, and Pharaoh, to act in a way that was subject to their fixed interests, rather than out of pressure caused by the plagues. The "hardening of Pharaoh's heart," according to this hypothesis, is not the forcing of his will, but rather the creation of circumstances that allowed for choice and guided the reaction in a certain direction, without actually dictating it.

I propose that the withdrawal of the pillar of cloud and fire to the rear of the camp of Israel represents a fulfillment of the promise to harden the heart of Pharaoh and the Egyptians so that they would pursue *Benei Yisrael* into the sea. It is an absurd move – but that is precisely its purpose. Precisely at this dramatic moment, when God is ready to split the sea in order to save Israel and to exact revenge on the Egyptians, an obvious question arises. There is no reason why Pharaoh and his army, upon seeing the sea split in half, should take their lives in their hands and enter. It is for this reason that the pillar of cloud (at the end of the day, immediately becoming a pillar of fire as night falls) moves from its regular position. The Egyptians see the pillar of fire approaching to lead them, and they see that *Benei Yisrael* are left without any guiding figure. They have an excellent view of the Israelite camp, thanks to the illumination of the pillar of fire-cloud, while *Benei Yisrael* themselves are shrouded in darkness. These conditions inspire the Egyptians with confidence to enter the sea despite what must have been great astonishment at the fact of its splitting.

A study of the structure of this narrative lends support to our hypothesis:

A. And you – raise your staff and stretch out your hand over the sea and divide it; and *Benei Yisrael* will come into the midst of the sea on dry land.

  B. As for Me – behold, I shall harden the heart of the Egyptians, and they shall come after them.

   C. And I shall be glorified through Pharaoh and through all of his army, his chariots and his horsemen.

    D. That Egypt may know that I am the Lord.

   C1. When I am glorified through Pharaoh, through his chariots and through his horsemen.

B1. And the angel of God that went before the camp of Israel journeyed and went to the back of them, and the pillar of cloud journeyed from before them and stood at the back of them. And it came between the camp of Egypt and the camp of Israel, and there was the cloud with darkness, and it lit up the night, and one did not come close to the other all night.

A1. And Moses stretched out his hand over the sea and God drove the sea with a strong east wind all night, and He made the sea into dry land, and the water was divided. And *Benei Yisrael* came into the midst of the sea on dry land.

The story clearly bears a chiastic structure, with the central axis expressing the point of the whole development: "That Egypt may know that I am the Lord." On either side of this central axis pairs of clearly parallel statements are arranged, lending the unit its perfect structure. But the parallel causes us to understand that B, the announcement concerning the hardening of Pharaoh's heart, is parallel to B1, the description of the relocation of the pillar of fire and cloud. It is by means of this relocation that God hardens Pharaoh's heart.

According to the above interpretation, the phrase, "One did not come close to the other all night" actually implies a "nevertheless." Despite the fact that God lit up the night for the Egyptians and made it dark for *Benei Yisrael*, such that the Egyptians could seemingly have managed quite easily to capture them, they did not do so. Perhaps there was something miraculous about this, or perhaps the Egyptians feared some sort of trap. They continued to pursue – but at a distance.

To summarize: the pillar of fire and cloud is one and the same. The relocation of this pillar at the end of the day created a night in which the pillar of fire gave illumination to the Egyptians. Later, God was revealed at the morning watch and He cast confusion amongst them. As noted above, because this was a time of transition between day and night, the pillar was perceived as being both fire and cloud simultaneously.

V. BETWEEN SINAI AND THE *MISHKAN*

Earlier, we proposed that the revelation in fire and cloud is one and the same thing, and the differences between the various descriptions lie in the eye of the beholder, rather than in any objective quality of the revelation itself. God is always manifest in fire from within a cloud. The cloud conceals and veils the fire in its midst. It is possible that the cloud is the result of the waves of heat and moisture around the fire. This is not necessarily a cloud of water. It should be remembered that Tanach offers various expressions in its description of the cloud: "*arafel*," "*ashan*," etc.

A striking and relatively clear description is provided in Exodus, where the Torah speaks of the Divine Glory resting upon Mount Sinai, and later on the descent of God's glory to dwell in the *Mishkan*. There is a clear literary parallel between the two descriptions, and they point to one another.

Exodus 24 – Mount Sinai	Exodus 30 – *Ohel Moed*:
The cloud covered the mountain.	The cloud covered the Ohel Moed.
God's glory dwelled upon Mount Sinai.	God's glory filled the *Mishkan*.
The cloud covered it for six days.	For God's cloud was upon the *Mishkan* by day.
He called to Moses on the seventh day from the midst of the cloud.	He called to Moses.
The appearance of God's glory was like a consuming fire at the top of the mountain.	And fire was in it by night.

The parallel is clear. God dwells upon Mount Sinai, the glory of God rests within the cloud. The expression "the glory of God" means the revelation of the Divine Presence. In this context, the main function would seem to be speech. But how is it recognizable to those witnessing it? The text explains, "Like a *consuming* fire at the top of the mountain." In other words, God's glory appears like a fire and the fire is covered with a cloud. God's glory calls to Moses – who previously was not able to approach. In the case of the *Ohel Moed*, we are told this explicitly. Why could Moses not come to the *Ohel Moed*? "For the cloud dwelled upon it." What kind of explanation is this? How and why does the cloud prevent him from approaching? The answer is to be found in the second part of the verse: "And the glory of God filled the Mishkan." Moses is prevented from coming before the glory of God which is fire! The same message arises from chapter 40: "Fire was in it by night." Specifically "in it" – for previously we were told that the cloud was covering, therefore now the text is explicit: "For the cloud of God was *upon* the *Mishkan* by day." But His glory "fills the *Mishkan*" – and is therefore "in it." Clearly, Moses is not able to enter, for the very same reason he is prevented from approaching God at Mount Sinai – for the appearance of God's glory is like a consuming fire. This is an expression implying threat: "For the Lord your God is a *consuming* fire, a jealous God." This is the full description of the revelation, both at Mount Sinai and in the introduction to the Divine Presence coming to dwell in the *Ohel Moed*. God's glory, appearing as a fire, is revealed with a veil of a cloud. The cloud is on the outside; the fire is on the inside. The cloud is above the *Mishkan*; the fire is within it. Hence, the last verse of Exodus, describing the apparently dual revelation of the cloud by day and the fire by night, is recounted from the perspective of the nation that is watching. From an objective point of view, the fire (God's glory) and the cloud both remain there all the time.

Attention should also be paid to the following parallel:

Exodus 14 (our *parasha*)	Exodus 40 – the *Mishkan*
God went before them …	And the cloud covered the *Ohel Moed*, and God's glory filled the *Mishkan*.
by day – in a pillar of *cloud*, to show them the way…	For God's *cloud* was upon the Mishkan – by day…
and at *night* – in a pillar of *fire*, to make light for them.	and *fire* was in it *by night*.

Thus we learn that in the same way that God was revealed when *Benei Yisrael* left Egypt, so He was revealed to them on Mount Sinai and in the *Ohel Moed*. And just as in the two latter cases His glory was manifest as fire within a cloud, so it was in the first case. Thus, there are not two separate pillars, but rather only one. By day it is perceived as a cloud; by night it looks like fire. And thus the final verse of Exodus ends: "In the sight of all of *Benei Yisrael*, throughout their journeys."

What!? – Manna and Quail

Rav Ezra Bick

Let us ask the question the Jews asked in the desert, when they first encountered the manna:

> The Israelites saw, and they said to each other, "*what* ('mann') is it," for they did not know what it was. (16:15)

Changing the question slightly – what is the point of having manna fall from the sky, with its special quality of being unhoardable? Why connect the manna to Shabbat observance? Finally, what is the meaning of the manna, within the context of the narrative of *Parashat Beshallah*?

Looking at the verses, we note the following apparent anomalies and difficulties.

> They traveled from Eilim, and the entire congregation of the children of Israel came to the desert of Sin, which is between Eilim and Sinai, on the fifteenth day of the second month of their exodus from Egypt. (16:1)

Why are the location and the time here detailed so extensively? With the previous two movements, we do not find a comparable specificity – "They came to Mara" (15:23), "They came to Eilim" (15:27). In neither case is there a date, or an attempt to exactly locate the station within the larger, and presumably better known, geographic locus.

> The entire congregation of the children of Israel complained against Moses and Aaron in the desert. (16:2)

This verse should have been preceded by a statement that there was no food in Midbar Sin, or that their original store of food ran out. When they complained in Mara, the Torah first explained that "they could not drink the water in Mara, for it was bitter" (15:23). Similarly, in Refidim, we first find "there was no water for the people to drink" (17:1), and only then, "And the people argued with Moses and said, give us water" (17:2). Why, in our case, is the reason for the complaint not explicated?

Similarly, why specify that "Israel complained... *in the desert*"? We already know the location. Why append the geographic location to the complaint?

The complaint of the Jews is followed by a confusing list of speeches of God, Moses and Aaron. This is the order as described in the verses:

1. God tells Moses that He will send down "*bread* from the heaven" to be collected each day, except for Friday, when there will be a double portion (16:4–5).
2. Moses *and Aaron* tell the Jews that in *the evening and the morning* they will witness that God will hear their complaint, "but what are we that you should complain about us?" (6–7).
3. Moses then seems to say exactly the same thing again (8).
4. Moses tells Aaron to gather the Jews before God (9).
5. God tells Moses that He will give the Jews *meat in the evening and bread in the morning* (11–12).
6. After the manna falls, Moses explains to the Jews what the rules for collecting manna are, without mentioning Shabbat (15–16).

God promises meat by evening, and indeed the camp is covered with quail (13). But there is no further reference to the quail, nor are we told of the reaction of the people to this event, even though previously Moses had predicted that "in the evening, and you shall know that God has taken you out of Egypt." What is the status and the meaning of the quail, especially in relation to the manna, which is clearly the central focus of the story?

NO FOOD?

Let us start from the second and third question. Ramban already suggests that the answer to the second is found in the third. The reason the Jews complained was *because* they were in the desert. They "complained…in the desert" means that their complaint was formed and caused by their being in the desert. Now, you might understand this to be no more than a shorthand way of saying that they had no food, since the desert is associated in our minds with a shortage of food. However, had that been the case, the Torah would state that "there was nothing to eat," just as when there is no water, that is explicitly stated. I suggest that there was, at least for the moment, plenty of food. It was the fact that they were entering the desert, a place where there is no *assured supply of food in the future* that led to the complaints. It was not hunger, but uncertainty, that caused the unrest.

In fact, the desert is not necessarily a place where there is no food. More importantly, the Jews were only a few weeks from Egypt, and they had originally planned a trip that would have to take at least that long. Even the short route ("the way of the land of the Philistines") would have necessitated a trek of several weeks. If we assume that their immediate goal is Mount Sinai (as God had promised Moses), they have yet some distance to go, and presumably they should have prepared food. We know that they had their flocks with them, and there is, as yet, apparently no shortage of water. So why are they complaining about imminent death from starvation?

The answer is not that they are feeling hunger but that they are scared. In the desert, it is difficult to know where your food will come from. They are no longer sure of the path (since they are not on the "way of the land of the Philistines"), and they are now "in the middle of nowhere" (between Eilim and Sinai). They lack not food but assurance. In other words, they lack faith.

This is indicated by the picturesque language used to describe Egypt – the pot of meat. The contrast between the desert and Egypt is between a land of unknown resources and a full pot. They remember not the fullness of their bellies but the fullness of the pot; in other words, the guarantee of food tomorrow. This is what they find so disturbing in the present – not the lack of food per se, but the lack of a pot brimming with an abundance of food. What was so special about Egypt was that there was more food than they could eat, and that is what they miss now.

In fact, we cannot be sure that they always ate well in Egypt, for, as slaves, they might well have been deprived by their masters. But they undoubtedly had enough to survive and continue working, and, since this was Egypt, they had no fear for the future in that respect.

This situation, the assurance of tomorrow's meal without necessarily being richly fed now, is in fact the essence of being a slave. The slave has no riches of his own, but he relies on his master, who is rich. The complaint of the Jews when they reach the desert is a direct expression of their slave mentality, and their memories of Egypt are a form of nostalgia for the security of enslavement. To a slave, whose meal comes every day at the same time from the hands of his master, the desert is truly a terrifying place, even if at the moment he still has food in his hands.

We now understand the answer to the first question. The geographic location is "the desert of Sin, which is between Eilim and Sinai"; in other words, halfway between a place of abundant food (seventy palms and twelve springs) and their direct goal, Sinai. The time frame is "on the fifteenth day of the second month of their exodus from Egypt"; in other words, halfway between the crossing of the sea and the revelation of Sinai. (Actually, there were twenty-four days from the sea and twenty-one days from the giving of the Torah, but that is close enough.) The Torah is stressing to us the feeling of "being in the middle" – away from Egypt, but not yet at their goal. The open-ended future, cut off from their origin but not yet in sight of their destination – between worlds, as it were – is the background to their situation. The actual distance from Egypt is not great, nor is the time that has transpired sufficient to actually exhaust their food-supply, but mentally, psychologically, they are halfway from everywhere.

The manna is God's answer to this complaint. We all know the special conditions of the manna – it fell every morning, but could not be stored for the next day. Everyone received the same amount. The attempt to hoard resulted in its becoming wormy and spoiled. God explicitly tells Moses that this is not merely a blessing but a "test" (*nisayon*) – "will they follow My Torah or not" (16:4). Rashi explains this test as referring to the laws associated with the manna. Following Ibn Ezra, I suggest that it refers not to any specific law, but to the entire relationship of the Jews to God in the desert. "'In order to test them' – because they will need Me every day" (Ibn Ezra on 16:4). The Manna is, in one sense, a recreation of the assured dependence of the slave on his master, only that God has replaced the Egyptian master. On the other hand, because God is not a natural cause, and His bounty cannot be seen with the same sense of natural assurance that the overflowing Nile gives to the population of Egypt, this is a test of faith. The manna will fall daily without failure, God promises, and you will be totally dependent on that promise, because it is impossible to accumulate manna and save it for a rainy day. The experience of the manna is a kind of education, training the Jews to have faith in the providence of God, weaning them from a dependence on hoarding, which would have been, perhaps, a natural reaction to their separation from the fleshpots of Egypt. It is learning to live with natural uncertainty, based on faith in, and dependence on, God.

This helps us to understand the deep connection between the manna and Shabbat. One of the messages of Shabbat is that everything has to be prepared beforehand. On Shabbat one does not accumulate anything at all, but relies only on what has been prepared. This message is explicated in our *parasha* – "On the sixth day, they shall prepare that which they shall bring" (16:5). Shabbat is, for all generations, a small trial of dependence, where one enjoys what one has without gathering for the morrow. Imagine the feeling of the recently released slave, when finally, on the sixth day, he has managed to put aside a small nest-egg, a small security for the rainy day he knows in his Jewish heart will surely come – and then, on the next day, Shabbat, he has to eat his savings and go back to living on the edge of penury! Naturally, he can barely resist and goes out and tries to gather on the Shabbat, in order to protect his savings. "And it came about on the seventh day, some of the people went out to gather, but they did not find" (16:27).

This lies at the heart of the mysterious unknown nature of the manna as well. Were the manna to be any form of a familiar food, no matter how unexpected it were initially, the Jews would have come to view it eventually as the natural food found in this particular desert. It would have become a natural resource, a form of security for the inhabitants of the desert. But God wishes the Jews to remain on the edge of insecurity, with the desert remaining a land that does not provide assured food. Hence, manna is not the food of the desert but "bread from the heavens" (16:4), and the only thing the Jews can say when they encounter it is "what!?" What is it – its name is a question. "*Mann hu?*" – what is it? Therefore "The house of Israel called it *mann*" (16:31).

In the initial speech of Moses to the Jews, he tells them that there will be meat in the evening and bread in the morning. Indeed, that is what takes place – quail covering the camp in the evening and the manna in the morning. We do not find the quail mentioned again except in exceptional circumstances (the episode of *Kivrot Hata'ava*, Numbers 11). This *parasha* itself concludes with the statement, "The Israelites ate manna for forty years, until they arrived at an inhabited land; they ate manna until they arrived at the edge of the land of Canaan" (16:35). While this does not necessarily mean that they ate nothing else, it definitely seems to imply that their only regular food was manna. (See Ramban on 16:12, who states that the quail fell for forty years). What happened to the quail, and what was the purpose of its falling in the evening?

To answer this, we have to follow very closely the multiple speeches of God and Moses. When God first responds to the people's complaint, He does not mention the quail. "Now I am going to rain down bread from heaven, and the people shall go out to gather every day's amount" (16:4). At this point, God already mentions that on the sixth day there will be a double portion. Immediately afterwards Moses and Aaron speak to the people, and for the first time, and without apparent command from God, tell them,

in the evening, you will know that God has taken you out of
Egypt; and in the morning, you will see the glory of God, when
He hears your complaint against God, but who are we, that you
should complain against us. (v. 7–8)

Moses then makes explicit the meaning of "evening and morning," telling them,

when God gives you *meat in the evening* and bread in the morning in satiation, when God shall hear your complaints which you
complain against Him, but who are we; your complaints are not
against us but against God. (v. 8)

Only subsequently, after Aaron gathers the people, do we find
God saying to Moses:

Say to them, you shall eat meat towards evening and in the morning be satiated with bread, and you shall know that I am HaShem
your God. (12)

What is happening here? Apparently, there are two different
issues. One is the faith issue I described above. God's answer to that is
the manna, with Shabbat emphasized. But Moses and Aaron have seized
on another issue. The Jews, in their complaint, have complained to Moses
and Aaron and placed the responsibility for their plight squarely on their
shoulders. "Would that we had died by the hand of God in the land of
Egypt…for *you* have taken us out to this desert, to kill all this congregation by hunger" (v. 3). Moses perceives a basic error of religious knowledge here. The Jews fail to see the guiding hand of God in the exodus
and in the path in the desert. Moses therefore speaks to the people and
admonishes them, telling them that their complaint is not against him
and Aaron, but against God. Moses emphasizes that when they see the
miracles of the quail and the manna, they will "know that God has taken
you out of Egypt" (v. 6). It appears to me that the manna is the basic
answer to the slave mentality of the Jews, which is not so much a sin as

a condition. God does not give the manna as a punishment or a rebuke, but as a gift. The quail, on the other hand, although food, carries within it a rebuke, similar to what happens in *Parashat Beha'alotekha*, when the Jews rebel against the regimen of the manna and God bombards them with quail (Num. 11). The purpose of the quail is to correct directly the theological transgression and to show them that God is in charge of their destiny. Precisely because the quail is a natural solution (though miraculous in its appearance in this place and time), it demonstrates God's mastery over nature, and therefore His responsibility for their fate. Moses does not mention the Shabbat here, not wishing to emphasize the divorce from nature, even divinely controlled nature. The manna, on the other hand, shows that those who are God's servants are completely out of the bounds of nature and are fed directly from "His table."

How could Moses and Aaron have promised the quail if God did not first tell them? The answer presumably is that God did tell them, since it is inconceivable that they made it up on their own. Nonetheless, the Torah gives the impression that God is initially only concerned with the manna and its message of dependence on God, whereas Moses and Aaron are interested in the problem which concerns them directly, the misplaced "blame" and responsibility which the Jews have placed on their shoulders.

This difference between the message of the quail and the message of the manna is hinted at even in the language with which Moses introduces the double miracle:

> Moses and Aaron said to all the Israelites:
> "Evening, and you shall know that God has taken you out of Egypt.
> And morning, and you shall see the glory of God, when He hears your complaints against God." (v. 6–7)

As Rashi points out, the first verse contains a note of displeasure, especially when compared to the second. The evening is directed only to correcting their theological error. The morning, by contrast, contains an element of religious excitement and uplifting – you shall witness the glory of God! The sages state that the evening is "not with a shining face" and the morning is with "a shining face." Their complaint in terms of food is met graciously by God in the morning. The evening is not an answer to their complaint, but only a lesson in who is in charge.

Since there is a difference between God's main concern and Moses', the conversations between them, and between them and the people, become rather convoluted. First God speaks to Moses about the manna (and Shabbat), then Moses and Aaron speak to the people, stressing the proper address for their complaints, then, after they bring the people to the proper address, gathering them to hear the word of God, God appears and adopts their double plan. Once, however, the morning dawns and the Jews experience the manna, the primacy of God's plan is manifest, as the rest of the *parasha* deals exclusively with the manna and its ramifications.

I think there are two reasons for the primacy of the manna issue over the quail issue. The first is that it is genuinely more central to the main purpose of the exodus – to turn the nation of slaves into the servants of God. In the immediate future it is a precondition for receiving the Torah. The recognition of God's leadership of Jewish destiny can wait – perhaps until they are about to enter the Land of Israel and begin political life.

The second reason, which admittedly at least partially contradicts the first, is that the message of the quail was not absorbed in the short run. The Jews continued to turn to Moses as the source of their problems and to accuse him of responsibility for what happens on the way through the desert. In the case of the golden calf, this is especially evident:

> The people saw that Moses was tardy in descending from the mountain, and they gathered on Aaron and said to him: "Arise and make us a god, for this man Moses, *who took us out of Egypt,* we do not know what has happened to him." (32:1)

This perception of Moses as the actual leader and decision-maker in the desert continues to be expressed throughout the events in the desert, throughout the complaints of the book of Numbers, until the original generation has disappeared. God's plan turns out to be correct. First one must take Egypt out of the soul of the Jews; only then can they reach full recognition of God's mastery of nature and their destiny.

The Wanderings of Benei Yisrael in the Desert

Rav Yaakov Medan

I. INTRODUCTION

Several biblical sources indicate that the wanderings of *Benei Yisrael* in the wilderness had additional significance, aside from the need to circumvent the land of the Philistines (13:13–14) and apart from the punishment decreed on the nation as result of the sin of the spies (*Num.* 14:28–35). These sources point to another message: the wilderness is a place with no means of subsistence. There, *Benei Yisrael* learn that it is God who feeds and sustains them – whether with manna, with quails, or with water. The precise significance of this message differs from one source to the next. Some emphasize that our food comes from God, and we must therefore not become arrogant and forget Him when we have plenty of everything, in *Eretz Yisrael* (Deut. 8:14–18). Elsewhere the emphasis is that our hearts should not be tempted to believe that the foreign gods of the land are the source of our sustenance (Hosea 2). Yet another source notes the loyalty of the nation that believed in God in an unsown land with no food (Jer. 2:2).

Of all of these, we choose here to understand the wandering in the desert as depicted in the prophecy of Amos (2:9–12; 5:25), who describes the trek entirely from a social perspective, in terms of justice and righteousness:

Let justice roll down like water, and righteousness like a mighty stream. Did you offer sacrifices and offerings to Me in the desert for forty years, O House of Israel? (Amos 5:24–25)

Wandering in the desert, with the threat of starvation, served to transform the rag-tag group of slaves that left Egypt into a nation that bears the standard of righteousness, justice, and social equality, concerning which the nations of the world are destined to comment:

Which nation is so great, that has righteous statutes and judgments, as all of this Torah which I place before you today. (Deut. 4:8)

II. LAW AND JUDGMENT

A review of the *"Mei Meriva"* (15:22–26) narrative demonstrates that the water that Moses sweetened was meant to do more than merely quench the thirst that had built up over three days:

He called out to God, and God showed him a tree; he cast it into the water and the water was sweetened. There He made for them a statute and a judgment (*ḥok umishpat*), and there He tested them. (Exodus 15:25)

The Torah gives no indication of what the "test" was, but from the context we may conclude that it was related to the "statute and the judgment" mentioned together with it. We must clarify, then, which "statute and judgments" were given at Mara.

Among *Ḥazal* we find different opinions. The Gemara mentions civil laws (*dinim*), *Shabbat*, and honoring parents, and explains:

Dinim, as it says, "There He made for them *ḥok umishpat*"; *Shabbat* and honoring parents, because [in the Ten Commandments in Deuteronomy, both of these commandments mention] the words, "as the Lord your God *has commanded* you" [Deut. 5:11, 15]. (*Sanhedrin* 56b)

Hence we deduce that *Benei Yisrael* were given these command-ments earlier, prior to the revelation at Sinai.

But what is the "statute" that is referred to as having been given at Mara? I would like to suggest that the word "statute" (*ḥok*) is meant here as a specified measure – particularly, a specified ration of food. When the waters of the well were sweetened, God established a "*ḥok*" – a ration, or measure – as to how much water each person was entitled to draw for himself, for his family, and for his cattle. If no ration was deter-mined per person from the waters of the well, it is difficult to describe the chaos that would have ensued when six-hundred-thousand thirsty people, after three days of wandering in the desert, were to grab water for themselves, their families, and their cattle. The "*ḥok*" (ration) required "*mishpat*" – an actual rule as to the ration of each family. At Mara, the group of slaves who had just been freed, and who did not recognize each other and their rights, faced their first test of mutual respect, con-sideration for others, and – especially – discipline. All of these are fun-damental, elementary concepts on the road to building a properly-run society and nation; they are elementary concepts on the road to freedom. The test of freedom is not whether a person is able to do whatever he wishes, but rather whether he is able to act in accordance with his will, out of free choice, but at the same time – to remain a human being, in the moral and cultural sense of the word. Therefore, this is also the test of a free society and of a free nation.

The "statute and judgment" concerning the water are also the test of "there He tested them," as the continuation of the story proves. When *Benei Yisrael* reach the wilderness of Sin, their bread runs out. In their hunger, they complain against Moses and Aaron. And just as God sweetened the water for them at Mara, so too He rains down food for them from heaven – the manna. Again, the manna is given at the price of a test:

> Behold, I rain down for you bread from the heavens, so that the people can go out and gather each day's rations, in order that I may test them as to whether they will follow My Torah or not. (16:4)

In the *parasha* dealing with the manna, an explicit commandment is given, and this becomes the test:

> This is the thing that God commanded: Gather of it each person according to his eating, *an omer per person* according to your numbers; each person shall take for those who are in his tent. (16:16)

We do not know how much manna descended each day, but even if there was a great abundance – no one could know in advance what quantity would be needed to feed millions of hungry mouths with manna. Clearly, the manna had to suffice for everyone. People who took more than they needed would cause their neighbors to suffer a shortage. Again, this was a test of respect presented to free people who were not receiving their set rations from their masters, but rather were able to gather it themselves, and could – were it not for the commandment, and had they so wished – take more for themselves.

Furthermore, it should be noted that the test of gathering a set measure of manna was not an easy one. In two separate places the Torah praises the taste of the manna: "Its taste was like a wafer with honey" (16:31); "its taste was like an oil cake" (Num. 11:8). At the same time, the Torah states: "He afflicted you and made you hungry, and fed you with the manna, which you had not known" (Deut. 8:3). A comparison of the sources leads us to conclude that although manna was good and tasty, it was provided in small measure, which was enough for survival but not enough to fill one's stomach; it did not give a feeling of satiety. If we add the sense of hunger – experienced also by the elderly, the children, and the sick – to the fact that it was forbidden to put any aside even for emergencies, we may begin to understand the extent of the test involved in "gathering by measure." The purpose of this measure was "statute and judgment" – to enable everyone to gather and to eat in equal measure, to prevent a situation in which "may the best (strongest) man win."

III. SHABBAT AND SOCIAL JUSTICE

As mentioned above, two additional commandments were given at Mara: Shabbat and honoring parents. Therefore, concerning these commandments – as they appear in the Ten Commandments in Deuteronomy –

we are told, "as the Lord your God commanded you." Let us devote some discussion to the commandment of Shabbat in this context.

Two main reasons are given for the commandment of Shabbat. Firstly, Shabbat is a testimony to the fact that God created the heavens and the earth within a given time (Ex. 20:10); secondly, "in order that your manservant and maidservant shall rest like you, and you shall remember that you were a servant in the land of Egypt" (Deut. 5:13; Ex. 23:12). These two reasons may be viewed as addressing the two focuses of our faith – the creation of the world and the exodus from Egypt.

The Gemara mentioned above (*Sanhedrin* 56b), as well as Rashi on Deuteronomy (5:11) assume that Shabbat, as commanded at Sinai, is a sign of the Creation, while Shabbat as commanded at Mara (and as mentioned in the Ten Commandments in Deuteronomy) is a remembrance of the exodus from Egypt, and "in order that your manservant and maidservant shall rest like you." This assumption fits what we said above – that the crux of the commandment at Mara concerned the "*hok umishpat*" – the emphasis is on equality, on the "like you." "Like you" in resting on Shabbat, "like you" in the ration of water from the well, and – later on – "like you" in the *omer* measure of manna.

Let us explain further. The Gemara provides no details as to which of the laws of Shabbat were commanded to *Benei Yisrael* at Mara. It is difficult to imagine that all of the thirty-nine categories of *melakha* (creative activity) were taught there, since these are derived from the *melakhot* performed in the *Mishkan*, while the stop at Mara preceded the commandment to build the *Mishkan*. Similarly, the juxtaposition of the *parashot* discussing the *Mishkan* and Shabbat respectively, which is the source for the derivation, only appears later, in chapters 31 and 35. It seems, therefore, that *only* at Sinai were *Benei Yisrael* commanded concerning the thirty-nine categories of *melakha*. The categories of creative *melakha* associated with the *Mishkan* are a remembrance of the creative *melakha* of Creation, and the cessation from such *melakha* on Shabbat is a remembrance of the Shabbat of Creation, as stated in the Ten Commandments as they appear in Exodus, and in the Shabbat command in the context of the *Mishkan*: "For in six days God made the heavens and the earth, and on the seventh day He ceased and rested" (Ex. 31:17).

The mitzva of Shabbat that was given at Mara consisted, in

my opinion, of one single prohibition of *melakha* – a category of *melakha* whose connection with the work of the *Mishkan* is weak: the act of carrying from one sort of domain (*"reshut"*) to another. This *melakha* is explicitly mentioned in the *parasha* of Shabbat in the wilderness of Sin, as part of the regulations of the manna, and from the rebuke over the breach in Shabbat observance it appears that this prohibition was not given there for the first time, but rather was already known to them. Apparently *Benei Yisrael* were commanded in this regard at Mara.

According to Rashi's understanding, the Shabbat commandment given at Mara is the Shabbat mentioned in the Ten Commandments in Deuteronomy, whose essence is a remembrance of the exodus from Egypt, social justice, equality between the master and slave in rest and in the rations of water and manna whose essential command concerns the *melakha* of carrying from one "domain" to another. The Shabbat commanded at Sinai, on the other hand, and mentioned in the Ten Commandments in the book of Exodus, reminds us of the creation of the world within a set time. This is the Shabbat mentioned in connection with the work of the *Mishkan*, and whose essence is the commandment concerning the thirty-nine categories of *melakha*.

At Mara and in the wilderness of Sin, until God revealed His glory to them at Har Sinai and they were commanded with regard to the essence of faith, the challenges the people faced were different ones. In the desert, *Benei Yisrael* were not engaged in action and creativity, and their food was available to them without their having to exert much effort. Either they found a desert oasis with streams and date palms, or they obtained food miraculously – in the form of the manna or the quails.

Possibly, the main occupation of those who left Egypt during this period was commerce. Basic nourishment was provided to all from on High, other requirements – such as vessels and clothing – were traded amongst each other, or with foreign caravans that they encountered along the way. Many owned assets that they took from the Egyptians when they borrowed their vessels and from the booty seized at the Red Sea. Under these conditions, the water and manna might have served as additional property for trade and an additional factor in the accumulation of capital, had it not been for the explicit prohibition against gathering more than the requirement for each individual.

At Mara – and specifically there – the Torah comes to place limits on commercial activity and the efforts to accumulate capital. This is done in two ways:

1. By placing a *"ḥok umishpat"*; essentially a setting down of the ration of water for each family and each individual, as in the case of the manna later on. At the same time, the other rules of *"ḥok umishpat"* were set down – the concepts of uprightness, loyalty, and justice in national life in general. "There He gave them *ḥok umishpat*, and there He tested them."

2. Through the mitzva of Shabbat; The creative *melakha* that was prohibited in this command concerned carrying from one domain to another – the only category of *melakha* whose connection with the creative work of the *Mishkan* is weak.

The unique character of the category of *melakha* that involves carrying between domains, and its associated prohibitions, is emphasized not only in the *parasha* of Shabbat in the wilderness of Sin, and in the source for Shabbat at Mara (as explained above). Nehemiah introduced Shabbat enactments specifically concerning carrying:

> In those days I saw in Judah some people treading the winepress on Shabbat, and bringing in sheaves of corn, and loading donkeys even with wine, grapes, figs, and all kinds of burdens, and bringing them to Jerusalem on Shabbat. I warned them on the day when they sold produce. And there were people of Tzor who lived there, who brought fish and all sorts of wares, and sold them on Shabbat to the inhabitants of Judah and in Jerusalem…. It happened, when the gates of Jerusalem grew dark before Shabbat, I commanded that the gates should be shut, and I commanded that they should not be opened again until after Shabbat, and I posted some of my servants at the gates so that no burden should be brought in on the Shabbat day. So the merchants and sellers

of all kinds of wares lodged outside Jerusalem once or twice. I warned them and said to them: "Why do you lodge around the wall? If you do this again I will lay hands on you." From that time onwards they did not come on Shabbat. (Neh. 13:15–21)

The reason for the widespread violation of Shabbat specifically in the area of carrying is clear from Nehemiah's testimony; it relates to commercial life in Jerusalem. Those who brought merchandise into Jerusalem were mostly non-Jews. Merchants dictated the city's commerce; they chose business days that were convenient for them. The inhabitants of Jerusalem had very little possibility of engaging in agriculture and industry, and the pressures exerted by their non-Jewish environment made things no easier for them. The Jews were a minority living in cities, while most of the fields were in the hands of non-Jews who had settled there before the return of the exiles from Babylon. The Jews, then, were forced into adopting an urban lifestyle; they bought their agricultural produce from the non-Jews. Commerce occupied an important place in their lives, and when the business day was set by the non-Jewish merchants as Shabbat – the violation of Shabbat concerned mainly the *melakha* of carrying. Nehemiah took steps to halt the phenomenon: he chased the merchants away from the gates of the city and enacted the prohibitions of carrying from one sort of domain to another in order to reinforce this specific aspect of Shabbat observance. Since then, carrying from one domain to another is the Shabbat activity with the greatest number of protective enactments.

The situation towards the end of the First Temple Period, as summed up in the story of the Rekhavites, was no better:

It happened, when Nebuchadretzar, King of Babylon, came up to the land, we said: "Come, let us go to Jerusalem for fear of the army of the Kasdim and for fear of the army of Aram" – and so [now] we dwell in Jerusalem. (Jer. 35:11)

This being the situation, it is no surprise that most of the produce was in non-Jewish hands, while the inhabitants of Jerusalem engaged mainly in buying the produce from non-Jews who dictated the business calendar. The main warning against this violation of Shabbat was applied specifically to carrying burdens of wares and produce through the city gates, as Jeremiah declares:

> Thus said God to me: "Go and stand at the gate of children of the nation, by which the kings of Judah enter and by which they leave, and at all the gates of Jerusalem. Say to them: 'Hear the word of God, O kings of Judah, and all of Judah and all the inhabitants of Jerusalem who enter these gates: So says God: Guard yourselves lest you bear a burden on the Shabbat day and bring it into the gates of Jerusalem. Nor shall you carry a burden out of your houses on the Shabbat day, nor shall you do any *melakha*. You shall sanctify the Shabbat day as I commanded your ancestors.'" (Jer. 17:19–21)

Shabbat, as it relates to the place of business, does not come to testify to God's creation of the world in six days. The cessation of the *melakha* of carrying does not involve cessation from creative *melakha*, since it involves no creativity. The Shabbat of the workplace is not meant to stop productivity and development; it is meant to halt the unending pursuit of money which is related to commerce. The greatest danger in this pursuit of money is the overt and covert deceit, the villainy which may technically be permissible or may not. All of these involve the same result: injustice towards the weak and the innocent.

For one day in the week God commands that a person halt his battle for survival, his desire for riches. For one day in the week a person must remember the waters of the well at Mara and the manna, by which Shabbat was sanctified and blessed (see Rashi on Gen. 2:3). In this way he will recognize that his sustenance comes from God, and it is God who determines how much he will receive. He will recognize that we borrow from Him and He gives – that all eyes are turned to Him, and He gives them food at the proper time. Throughout the forty years, beginning with the Shabbat at Mara and the Shabbat in the wilderness of Sin, all those who left Egypt, and their children, ate the same food and in equal quantities. Together they quenched their thirst and together they suffered hunger. A merchant who thinks to himself, "When will the

New Month be over, that we may sell corn, and Shabbat – that we may set forth wheat," making the *'efa'* small and the shekel great, falsifying their deceitful balances" (*Amos* 8:5), will remember, when commerce is postponed on the seventh day, that all of God's children are equal in His eyes, and He opens His hand to feed all of them. No amount of effort on man's part will achieve anything unless his Father in heaven sets aside sustenance for him. He who redeemed him from the slavery of Egypt, and also from the fleshpot there, is the same One who promises to provide food for him and for his family; He asks only one thing: "That your manservant and your maidservant shall rest like you" (Deut. 5:14).

Before we conclude our discussion of Shabbat, we must mention the parallel between the two Shabbats – the Shabbat of Mara and the wilderness of Sin (mentioned in Deuteronomy) and Sinai (mentioned in the Ten Commandments in Exodus), and the Shabbat (*Shemitta*) of the seventh year, when the land is left to lie fallow. The subject of *Shemitta* is clearly divisible into two separate commandments: First,

> For six years you shall sow your field, and for six years you shall prune your vineyard and gather all of your produce. But in the seventh year there shall be a Shabbat of Shabbats for the land, a Shabbat to God. You shall not sow your field, nor shall you prune your vineyard. You shall not reap what grows by itself of your harvest, nor shall you gather the grapes of your undressed vine; a Shabbat of Shabbats shall there be for the land. (Lev. 25:3–5)

The reason for this command is reflected in the explanation for the commandment concerning the *'yovel'* (jubilee) year which follows immediately afterwards: "For the land is Mine; you are strangers and sojourners with Me" (v. 23). The nation that reaches its land and inherits it may be mistaken into thinking that they own it, believing that they till it by virtue of their ownership of it. In the seventh year, every supposed landowner is required to abandon work on his land and to commemorate a Shabbat for God, thereby declaring, as the prophet Jeremiah did, "I [God] formed the land ... by My great strength and by My outstretched arm I give it to whomever is upright in My eyes" (Jer. 27:5).

It is not the nation that hosts the *Shekhina* in their land, but rather the opposite – "You are strangers and sojourners with Me." That which is said of the *Mishkan* on the seventh day is said also of the entire land in the seventh year.

A second commandment of the seventh year, with no direct connection to the prohibition of *melakha* in the seventh year, is:

> The produce of the land in the seventh year shall be food for you, for you and for your manservant and for your maidservant, for your hired servant and for the stranger that dwells with you, and for your cattle and for the beasts that are in your land shall all its produce be, for food. (Lev. 25:6)

The sages explain: "'for food' – but not for trade" (*Avoda Zara* 62a). The Torah here is not prohibiting work, but rather commerce. The purpose of this prohibition is to achieve equality between the landowner and the stranger who has no land. For one out of every seven years, man halts his pursuit of money. Together with his neighboring stranger, he eats a sort of "manna," from the Table on High:

> If you will say: "What shall we eat during the seventh year, for we shall not sow nor shall we gather our produce?" – I command My blessing to you in the sixth year, and its produce will suffice for three years. (Lev. 25:20–21)

Again – the landowner's obligation concerning food for the stranger and for his servants is the Master of the Universe's own obligation concerning food for His children and His servants, food for His nation dwelling in His inheritance as "strangers and sojourners." The acceptance of His mastership and ownership of the land is the Shabbat described in the Ten Commandments in Exodus; it is the Shabbat of the land and its prohibition of agricultural *melakha*. The faith that the Master of the Universe and the God of the land will sustain us from His open hand, and that He alone determines our sustenance, rather than our own unceasing efforts – that is the Shabbat of Mara, of the wilderness of Sin and of Deuteronomy, and this is the *Shemitta* of the land for the stranger and for the sojourner: "for food – and not for commerce."

IV. HONORING ONE'S FATHER AND MOTHER

At Mara, in addition to the mitzva of Shabbat, *Benei Yisrael* were also commanded to honor parents. We must now explain the mitzva of honoring parents and its connection to the "*hok umishpat*" of Mara.

One of the *parashot* that is most obviously connected to the mitzva of honoring parents is the matter of the rebellious and wayward son:

> If a man shall have a wayward and rebellious son – he does not listen to his father and to his mother, and they punish him but he does not listen to them – then his father and his mother shall take hold of him and bring him out to the elders of his city, and to the gates of his place. They shall say to the elders of the city: "This son of ours is wayward and rebellious, he does not listen to us; he is a glutton and a drunkard." (Deut. 21:18–20)

The only sin that is explicitly mentioned in connection with the rebellious son is that he is a "glutton and a drunkard." The Gemara, however, expresses surprise that solely the volume of a child's culinary habits would define the law of the wayward and rebellious son:

> Rabbi Yossi HaGelili says: "Is it then because this boy ate a '*tartemar*' of meat and drank a half-'*log*' of Italian wine that the Torah commands that he be taken out to the *Beit Din* to be stoned? [Surely not]; rather, the Torah understands the full depth of the rebellious son's mind: ultimately he will squander all of his father's assets, he will seek his habit [meat and wine] and not find it, and so he will go out to the crossroads and rob the passersby. So the Torah says: Let him rather die innocent, rather than waiting for him to die guilty." (*Sanhedrin* 72a)

Rabbi Yossi HaGelili's explanation removes the *parasha* of the rebellious son altogether from the issue of honoring parents, and moves it to the sphere of robbery and violence. The Torah understands the full extent of the rebellious son's thinking: he does not get what he wants from his father, so he stands and robs passersby.

When we return to the "*ḥok umishpat*" – the fair distribution of resources – during the desert wanderings, we note that so far the Torah has not insisted that every individual must take exactly the same amount as his fellow does. Thus far, the Torah has enforced equality only on the family level:

> Gather of it each person according to his eating; an omer per person, according to the number of you; each person shall take for those who are in his tent. (16:16)

Every person took for the number of people in his household, and the Torah relies on the natural system of distribution within the family. Within the family there is certainly no reason for concern as to an unjust distribution, for it is impossible that when it comes to doling out food, the parents will favor one child over the others.

But when the family includes a son who is rebellious, a glutton and a drunkard – a son who appropriates all of the family's food for himself and has no consideration for his siblings, a son whose rations consist of a '*tartemar*' of meat and a half-'*log*' of wine – then how can the rationing of an *omer* per person remain justified? And if the son has no concept of fair rationing even between himself and his siblings, how is he going to act towards his neighbors, towards everyone else? Will he really keep himself to taking an *omer* and no more? And how will he treat his parents, who provide him with only an *omer* instead of a '*tartemar*'; the same *omer* concerning which it is written, "He afflicted them and made them hungry" (Deut. 8:3)?

When those who left Egypt stood in line next to the well at Mara, when God gave them a "*ḥok umishpat*," the Torah also commanded the honoring of parents. This is honor which means – first and foremost – a son's respect for the parents' right to distribute food among their children according to their best judgment and in keeping with their sense of fairness.

V. REFIDIM

Refidim brought the first major crisis. There *Benei Yisrael's* sin was memorialized in the name of the place – *Masa uMeriva* – and there they were punished for the first time, in the battle against Amalek.

In the simplest terms, their sin was a dual one: *'masa'* and *'meriva'*:

"For the quarrel (*riv*) of *Benei Yisrael*" (17:7) – the quarrel against Moses, as the verses emphasize, "The nation quarreled with Moses"; "why do you quarrel with me?"

"and for their challenging (*nasotam*) God, saying: 'Is God in our midst or not?'" (ibid.) – a challenge to God, as Moses says: "Why are you testing God?"

We tend to view them as a single sin, encapsulated in their words to Moses, "Why then have you brought us up from Egypt" (17:3). This was a quarrel with Moses who, they claimed, had brought them on his own initiative out of the land of the Nile to a wilderness with no water; it was a challenge to God in that they ignored the fact that He had brought them out of Egypt, and in their declaration which implied that God was not amongst them.

But if this was their whole sin – how could God accede to their complaint and provide water in a miraculous way and with a revelation at Ḥorev, even making the elders witness to the miracle and to the revelation? And why does God then immediately punish them, with no additional sin? The only comparable example that we have of such a chain of events – the story of the quails, at *Kivrot Hata'ava* – actually serves to contradict our hypothesis: There, although God provided them with quails, and while the meat was still between their teeth, He struck the nation with a plague (Num. 11:33); prior to that He had provided the meat in anger and with rebuke. He tells them explicitly, "Because you despised God who is in your midst" (Num. 11:20).

Moreover, in the *parasha* that parallels the story of Refidim – the *parasha* of *Mei Meriva* at Kadesh (Num. 20:1–13), the complaint of the nation was the same as that at Refidim, but we find no punishment meted out to them.

The principal difference hinted to in the verses between *Benei Yisrael*'s behavior at Refidim and their behavior at *Mei Meriva* concerns the words they spoke at Refidim: "Why then have you brought us out of Egypt to kill us and our children and our cattle [all written in the singular: me and my children and my cattle] with thirst" (17:3). This style is somewhat unusual, hinting at the fact that the nation was concerned not for the collective, but rather each man for himself, his own family and his own cattle.

I propose that when Moses was commanded to pass before the nation and to go with the seventy elders to the rock at Ḥorev, which was located at some distance – the movement from Refidim to Mount Sinai is described as a "journey" in the list of journeys in *Parashat Masei* – a fight broke out over the water, which was not being distributed according to the order of "*ḥok umishpat*" which Moses had established at Mara. Let us explain this picture more clearly: God's revelation was, as we have said, at the rock at Ḥorev (another name for Sinai), the place where the Ten Commandments would eventually be given. Later, Moses will cast the ashes of the golden calf into the "stream that came down from the mountain" (Deut. 9:21), sprinkling it over the water in the middle of summer – on the seventeenth of Tammuz (see Ex. 32:20). It is impossible for there to have been a running stream on that date in the middle of the wilderness of Sinai. We must therefore conclude that the stream was created miraculously – meaning that the rock at Ḥorev, where the water emerged, was at Mount Sinai rather than at Refidim.

No elaboration is needed for the reason why the place of the revelation concerning the water was at the place of the *Shekhina* – the place where the Torah was to be given. The same pattern had played itself out at Mara – with the "*ḥok umishpat*" being given over water, and likewise also the rock of Ḥorev. Still, we must ask why the miraculous emergence of the water from the rock was not performed before the entire nation, but rather only in the presence of the elders:

> God said to Moses: "Pass over before the nation, and take with you some of the elders of Israel." (17:5)

This was a contrast to what had happened at Mara, at *Mei Meriva*. Instead, the miraculous flow of water at Ḥorev was similar, in this respect, to the plague bringing death to the firstborn in Egypt, where *Benei Yisrael* were commanded, "You shall not come out, any one of you, from the entrance to your houses until the morning. And God passed over to strike Egypt with the plague" (12:22–23). The fact that the miracle of the water was performed in this way, such that *Benei Yisrael* did not witness the actual splitting of the rock at Ḥorev, but only the water which flowed to them at a great distance from the rock – must certainly have been a result of their sin; they were not worthy of the miracle. The result – water flowing through the camp while the *Shekhina* was not in the camp and Moses and the elders of Israel were also absent – can only be imagined. Two facts are known to us: 1. No song of praise was sung there, in contrast to the song of the well during the fortieth year; and 2. No *"ḥok umishpat"* were given from the moment that the water emerged until *Benei Yisrael* arrived, in complete *teshuva* (see *Mekhilta*, "in the third month," *parasha* 1; *Rashi* on 19:2), at Mount Sinai.

VI. AMALEK

According to the literal account, it would appear that Amalek arrived at Refidim when they heard about the water flowing there (although the generally accepted understanding follows the opinion of Ramban, that Amalek "came pursuing a quarrel that was not theirs"). This battle took place towards the end of Iyar (they moved to Mount Sinai on the first of Sivan, see 19:1), at the beginning of the summer. As desert dwellers, Amalek claimed ownership of the water, and it was over this that the war broke out. Perhaps their daring in storming the camp arose from the disorderly allocation of water that was happening there, with the fighting on all sides in the absence of the leadership and with the people's short temper. The mighty blow that Amalek delivered to the nation – despite the fact that *Benei Yisrael* were undoubtedly more numerous – is explained, in our view, by the fact that on the day when Amalek struck, the nation's entire leadership – Moses, the seventy elders, and presumably Moses' disciple Joshua – was at the rock in Ḥorev. Amalek had no difficulty attacking a leaderless nation divided against itself.

As soon as Moses found out what was going on, he sent Joshua to the camp, to Refidim, to select soldiers. Moses remained at Ḥorev, where he raised his arms and his staff of God. Therefore *Benei Yisrael*'s counter-attack was delayed by a day, as we read: "Tomorrow I shall stand" (17:9), and this is what allowed the catastrophe to happen.

Who were the soldiers selected for this battle? Let us compare this battle against Amalek and their neighbors, Midian (see Judges 6:33), with the battle waged by Gideon against Midian and Amalek many generations later. There, too, Gideon was commanded to select men:

> God said to Gideon: "Those who lap with their tongue from the water, as a dog laps, shall you set apart, and likewise those who bend down on their knees to drink." (Judges 7:5)

The uncontrolled scramble for water, in which Gideon's candidate soldiers throw their weapons upon the ground, is the same drive that leads *Benei Yisrael* in Refidim to drink with no thought of quantity, with no consideration for others, with no fair allocation – and this is what brings Amalek to the camp. The minority who did not behave in this manner are the soldiers who defeated them. When *Ḥazal* discuss the sin that brought in its wake the war against Amalek, they note the juxtaposition of *parashot* in Deuteronomy:

> You shall not have in your bag diverse weights, great and small. You shall not have in your house diverse measures – great and small. [Rather,] you shall have one perfect and just weight, one perfect and just measure, in order that your days may be lengthened upon the land which the Lord your God gives you. For all those who do this, all those who perform injustice, are an abomination to the Lord your God. Remember what Amalek did to you on the way, when you came out of Egypt. (Deut. 25:13–17)

Ḥazal comment:

> If you are dishonest with measures and weights, then beware of enemy attacks. For it is written, "Deceitful weights are an abomination to God," and it is also written "Where there is malice, there will also be disgrace." (Rashi on Deut. 25:17; *Tanḥuma Ki Tetze* 8, and *Pesikta deRav Kahana, Zakhor*)

The fair allocation of resources and the entire *parasha* of measures and weights are founded on the "*ḥok umishpat*" of Mara. *Benei Yisrael* passed the test of the water at Mara and the manna in the wilderness of Sin, but failed at the water of Refidim – and it was then that Amalek attacked.

VII. YITRO AND HIS ADVICE

At the conclusion of the war against Amalek, Yitro comes to the Israelite camp. There are two ways of understanding his visit:

1. The reason that he himself provides: the news of the exodus (18:1). Yitro has a strong personal connection with the exodus, since he is the father-in-law of Moses, the savior of Israel. Therefore, he comes to the camp with Tzipora, Moses' wife, and their two sons.

2. A second reason is left unstated, but seems very likely, on the basis of the juxtaposition of the two episodes in the text: Yitro the Midianite, as a neighbor and ally of Amalek, comes to make peace with Israel after Amalek's defeat at Refidim.

While the beginning of the *parasha* presents the exodus as the exclusive reason for Yitro's appearance, both reasons find expression in the Torah:

> Moses told his father-in-law all that God had done to Pharaoh and to Egypt for the sake of Israel; all the tribulations that had come upon them on the way, and how God had saved them. *Vayiḥad Yitro.* (18:8–9)

Both possible explanations that Rashi provides for the expression, "*vayiḥad Yitro*" (18:9), which appears no-where else in Tanach, are correct. It expresses pleasure ("*ḥedva*") over the exodus and Yitro's sense of partnership in the wonders of God's miracles, or alternatively (or at the same time) sorrow ("his flesh became covered with goose-bumps – '*ḥidudin*'; *Sanhedrin* 94a) over the defeat of his ally, Amalek. In his declaration of praise to God, Yitro gives thanks for the exodus while ignoring Israel's victory over Amalek:

Yitro said: "Blessed is God who has saved you from the hand of Egypt and from the hand of Pharaoh, who has saved the nation from the hand of Egypt." (18:10)

When Yitro comes to offer a sacrifice to God, Moses builds an altar for this purpose. To our understanding, this is the altar of "God is my banner (*HaShem nissi*)," over which Moses proclaims God's war against Amalek for all generations (17:15).

The episode of Amalek does not conclude with Yitro's appearance; it continues in the following verse: "And it was, on the next day, that Moses sat to judge the nation; the nation stood before Moses from the morning until the evening" (18:13).

What were these lengthy legal procedures about? I think it likely that Moses was occupied with the distribution of the booty from the war against Amalek (admittedly, I have found no midrashic source to support this possibility). Many years later, David was to set down most forcefully his rule as to a just allocation of the booty of the war against Amalek:

Then all the evil and worthless men of the people who had gone with David said: "Since they did not go with us, we shall not give them of the spoils that we have recovered; only to each man his wife and children, that they may lead them away and go." Then David said: "You shall not do so, my brethren, with that which God has given us – who has preserved us and given the troops that came upon us into our hands. Who will obey you in this matter? Rather, the portion of he who goes down to battle shall be the same as he who remains by the equipment; they shall share alike." And it was so from that day onward, and it became a statute and law for Israel until this day." (1 Sam. 30:22–25)

The reason that David gives for the fair distribution of the booty from the war against Amalek is the same reason that the Torah provides for a fair allocation of water and manna – "That which God has given us."

Two separate laws, then, pertain to the war against Amalek. Both share the same foundation: "God is at war with Amalek" – the war against Amalek is God's war. Sometimes the booty is for God alone, sometimes it is shared equally among all of Israel. Saul sins in this regard – he sets aside the best of the sheep and cattle – and the prophet rebukes him:

> Why have you not listened to God's voice, diving upon the spoils and doing that which is evil in God's eyes? (1 Sam. 15:19)

If the war against Amalek is God's war, then the spoils are His.

The second law is realized in David's war against Amalek. If the booty belongs to God (and there is no special command to destroy it all), then it must be allocated in the same way as the manna that descended from the heavens: "Gather of it each man according to his eating" – a fair and equitable distribution, since we are all God's children and we are all equal in His eyes.

Similar to David's war was the war against Amalek in Refidim. On the day after the altar was established, Moses sat in judgment to allocate the booty through "*hok umishpat*" – "statute and ordinance." Just like David, Moses faces a difficult task. His camp, too, includes "evil and worthless men." Moses' father-in-law, witnessing his difficulty and the stress of the nation (and perhaps remembering Moses' equitable allocation of the well-water among Yitro's daughters and the other shepherds, in Midian), offers his suggestion: to appoint officers of thousands and officers of hundreds, officers of fifties and officers of tens.

"Do the Hands of Moses Wage War?"

Rav Mordechai Sabato

I. INTRODUCTION

In this article, I wish to re-examine the account of Israel's war with
Amalek, discuss its meaning, and consider the ramifications upon the
story's location within Exodus, and the book's structure as a whole. I
wish to begin by presenting the entire story, dividing it into sections
and emphasizing the keywords that run through it.

> Amalek came, and fought with Israel in Refidim. And *Moses* said
> to Joshua, "Choose us out men, and go out, fight with *Amalek*;
> tomorrow I will stand on the top of the hill with the rod of God
> in my *hand.*" Joshua did as *Moses* had said to him, and fought with
> *Amalek*; and *Moses*, Aaron and Ḥur went up to the top of the hill.
> And it came to pass, when *Moses* held up his *hand*, that
> Israel prevailed; and when he let down his *hand*, *Amalek* prevailed.
> But *Moses'* *hands* were heavy; and they took a stone, and put it
> under him, and he sat on it; and Aaron and Ḥur supported his
> *hands*, the one on the one side, and the other on the other side;
> and his *hands* were steady until the going down of the sun. And
> Joshua vanquished *Amalek* and his people by sword.
> And the Lord said to *Moses*, "Write this for a memorial in

a book, and place it in the ears of Joshua: that I will utterly blot
out the remembrance of *Amalek* from under the heaven." And
Moses built an altar, and called the name of it, "The Lord is My
Banner." And he said, "The *hand* upon the throne of the Lord;
the Lord will have war with *Amalek* from generation to generation." (Ex. 17:8–16)

What stands out is that the battle against Amalek is being fought
on two different planes. There is a war being waged in the camp below,
under Joshua's command: "So Joshua did as Moses had said to him, and
fought with Amalek." The real battle, however, is being decided above,
on the hilltop, through Moses' hands: "And it came to pass, when Moses
held up his hand, that Israel prevailed; and when he let down his hand,
Amalek prevailed." Joshua vanquishes Amalek with the the sword, below,
but the power of that sword depends upon the state of Moses' hands on
the top of the hill, above. Joshua's war against Amalek below is, then, a
reflection of Moses' battle with Amalek above.

This struggle between Amalek and the hands of Moses is also
highlighted by the *leitvorten* (keywords) used in this passage. Three
leitvorten run through this story, each one repeating itself seven times:
Amalek, Moses, and hand. The first six instances of the word "hand" refer
to the hand of Moses. Thus, it may be argued that in this story Amalek
struggles with the hand of Moses.[1]

What is the significance of this conclusion and how are we to
understand the supernatural power of Moses' hands which finds expression in this story? This question is the key to understanding the story,
as well as to uncovering its objective.

At first glance it seems that the Torah praises Moses. Through
the merit of Moses' hands, Joshua succeeds in vanquishing "Amalek and
his people with the edge of the sword" – so that it is Moses' hands that
wage the war. Already the sages questioned this: "Do the hands of Moses
wage war or break war?"[2] The sages' question sharpens the strangeness

---

1. Regarding the significance of the fact that the last instance of the word "hand" apparently refers to the hand of God, see below.
2. *Rosh HaShana* 3:8. In *Mekhilta DeRabbi Yishmael, masekhta deAmalek, Beshallaḥ,*

of the story. As a rule, the Torah is careful to emphasize God's absolute rule and man's dependence upon Him. Our story, in contrast, seems to emphasize the supernatural powers of Moses' hands, and this demands explanation. This anomaly is even more puzzling in light of the fact that the Torah had always emphasized the divine source of the miracles performed by Moses and Aaron. Nowhere does Scripture describe a miracle as an act performed solely by them. Every miracle performed by Moses and Aaron until now is preceded by an explicit statement attributing the miracle to God, and we do not find a single instance where Moses performs a miracle by way of his own power. Moses and Aaron are merely agents who were chosen to carry out God's will. Even in the story of Korah, where Moses decrees that the earth should open its mouth and swallow up Datan and Aviram, Moses explicitly attributes the miracle to God: "But if the Lord creates a new thing, and the earth opens her mouth" (Num. 16:30). In contrast, the miracle in our story is attributed to Moses alone, with no mention of God's part in the matter. As stated above, this requires explanation.

The sages answer this question as follows: "Rather, as long as Israel looked upwards and subjected their hearts to their Father in Heaven, they prevailed, but otherwise they fell." This answer, however, does not accord with the plain sense of the text. According to the simple understanding, it is not Israel who stands at the heart of the story, but rather the hands of Moses. Nowhere does the story discuss whether or not the people of Israel are looking upwards.[3]

The sages' question demands a different solution, one that fits in with the text's plain meaning.[4] To answer this question we must first analyze the story's structure.

---

parasha 1, the reading is: "Now did the hands of Moses make Israel prevail or did the hands of Moses break Amalek?" and similarly in *Mekhilta DeRashbi, parasha* 1.

3. The sages' answer is more appropriate for the Mishna's second question: "Now did the serpent kill or did it keep alive?" for in the biblical story it says: "Every one that is bitten, when he looks upon it, he shall live" (Num. 21:8), although there too there is no mention of subjection of the heart. It stands to reason that the answer to the first question was formulated based on the answer to the second.

4. Some of the commentators try to explain the verse in a realistic manner. Thus, for example, Rashbam writes (and in his wake also Ḥizkuni): "When he held up his

II. BETWEEN PREPARATIONS AND EXECUTION

The story itself may be divided into three sections. The first three verses, 8–10, describe the preparations for the war; the next three verses, 11–13, describe the war itself; and the three verses that follow, 14–16, describe God's and then Moses' reaction – the conclusions from the battle.[5] Let us first address the relationship between the first two sections that comprise an account of the war.

A closer examination of the verses reveals tensions between the account of the preparations for battle and the story of the war itself, evident in two ways:

1. The account of the preparations emphasizes the part played by "the rod of God in my hand." In contrast, in the story of the war itself, no mention is made of the rod, and only the hands of Moses are emphasized.

2. In the account of the preparations, Moses says: "Tomorrow I will *stand* on the top of the hill," whereas in the story of the war, it says: "And they took a stone, and put it under him, and he *sat* on it." What is the significance of these discrepancies?

We could ignore this question and argue that one should not be excessively precise with the words of Scripture, for often the words of the Torah in one place fill in what is missing in another. Accordingly, when Scripture says: "And it came to pass, when Moses held up his hand, that Israel prevailed; and when he let down his hand, Amalek prevailed," the reference is not exclusively to the hand of Moses, but first and foremost

---

hand and the rod, Israel prevailed, for it is the way of soldiers of war, as long as they see their banner uplifted, they prevail, but when it is cast down, they usually flee and are defeated." The text, however, does not mention that Israel saw the rod; rather it is the supernatural significance of Moses' hands that is emphasized.

5. As stated, the first two sections are more strongly connected to each other than is the third section to the first two. The division of this passage into three sections was already noted by E. Samet (*Iyyunim beParashat haShavua*, second series, *Bereshit-Shemot*, Jerusalem 5764, pp. 286–306), but his presentation of the overall structure of the story is different from ours.

to the rod of God in his hand.[6] Similarly, when Moses says: "I will stand on the top of the hill," he merely wishes to describe where he will be found, but he does not mean to rule out the possibility of sitting, should that become necessary.

However, given our story's concise and concentrated nature, we cannot disregard these gaps, and it is not by chance that Scripture emphasizes the differences between them regarding these two points. Furthermore, while the verse, "And it came to pass, when Moses held up his hand, that Israel prevailed; and when he let down his hand, Amalek prevailed," can be understood as referring to the rod in his hand, only with great difficulty can we explain the verse that immediately follows, "But Moses' hands were heavy... and Aaron and Hur supported his hands, the one on the one side, and the other on the other side," as referring to the rod, for the rod is found in only one hand. Why would it be necessary to support both of Moses' hands?

This tension between the role of the rod and the lifting up of Moses' hands was already noted by Ramban, who writes as follows:

> The reason that Moses commanded Joshua to fight against Amalek was so that he should be able to pray with the lifting of his hands on the top of the hill. And he went up there so that he should be able to see Israel fighting and set his eye upon them for good, and so that they too should be able to see him lifting his hands to heaven and prolonging in prayer, and they will rely on him, and add greater courage and valor....
>
> If so, the words "with the rod of God in my hand" mean that when he went up to the top of the hill and saw Amalek, he stretched out his hand with the rod to bring upon them the plague, the sword and destruction, as it is stated regarding Joshua: "Stretch out the spear that is in your hand toward Ay,

---

6. This follows from the words of Rashbam, cited above, note 5. Similarly, in Exodus 10:12: "And the Lord said to Moses, Stretch out your hand over the land of Egypt for the locusts," as opposed to verse 13: "So Moses stretched out his rod over the land of Egypt." It should also be noted that we find the lifting of a hand with respect to a rod in Numbers 20:11: "And Moses lifted up his hand, and with his rod he smote the rock twice"; see also Exodus 7:20, 14:16.

for I will give it into your hand" (Joshua 8:18), *for when he was praying and his hands were spread out to heaven, he could not hold anything in his hand.*

According to Ramban, the role of the rod was to bring upon Amalek the plague, when Moses stretched out his hand. In contrast, Moses' lifting of his hands involved spreading his hands out towards heaven in prayer. Ramban emphasizes that these two objectives cannot be realized at the same time – "for when he was praying and his hands were spread out to heaven, he could not hold anything in his hand." Ramban implies that we have two stages: First, Moses went up to the top of the hill, saw Amalek, and he stretched out his hand with the rod to bring plagues upon them. Afterwards, he put the rod down and spread out his hands in prayer.

Ramban's assumption that the rod's role was to bring plagues upon Amalek seems to accord with the text's plain sense, as this was the rod's function up until this point. His assumption that the lifting of his hands implies spreading out his hands in prayer also fits in with the text's plain sense, as we find with the removal of the plague of hail: "And Moses went out of the city from Pharaoh, and spread out his hands to the Lord" (Ex. 9:33). However, his assumption that these two things occurred in stages is exceedingly difficult. As stated above, the rod is mentioned only in the account of the preparations, whereas the lifting of hands is mentioned in the description of the war itself, with no hint of two stages in Moses' actions.

We are forced to conclude that the difference is not between two stages in the execution of the plan, but between the plan and the execution. Moses intended to stand on the hilltop with the rod in his hand, and bring upon Amalek the plague, just as had happened in Egypt. This, however, is not what happened. During the battle, the rod is entirely absent, and in its place, we find the lifting of Moses' hand or hands. There are fundamental differences between Moses' stretching out his rod and his holding up his hands in prayer. Stretching out the rod is a clearly miraculous act, expressing the absolute power of the person holding the rod; while lifting up hands to heaven involves turning to God, expressing the dependence of the person holding up his hands upon the One to whom the hands are lifted. Second, stretching out the rod is meant to be an action that has immediate consequences. It doesn't require special physical powers, and thus it is not exposed to the weakness of the hand holding it. In contrast, lifting up hands to heaven is a continuous action that demands continued physical strength, and as such it is subject to the weakness of the human hand. As a result, Israel encountered the surprising situation in which, "And when he let down his hand, Amalek prevailed."[7] It became clear suddenly that changing the plan from stretching out the rod to lifting up Moses' hands was liable to lead to the opposite results – the weakening of Israel and the victory of Amalek. Moses' decision to accept upon himself the responsibility for victory in battle could, God forbid, have led to defeat. This is emphasized in the words, "But Moses' hands were heavy," which clearly express the limits of Moses' powers. Even Moses, the man of God, who brought ten plagues upon Egypt and then split the sea for Israel – is in the end a man of flesh and blood. He too feels the heaviness of his hands.

In addition to the tension between the preparations and the battle itself described above, attention should also be paid to the differences regarding Moses' exclusivity regarding the battle's outcome. From Moses' words in verse 9, "Choose us out men, and go out, fight with Amalek; tomorrow I will stand on the top of the hill with the rod of God in my hand," the exclusivity that Moses attributes to himself regarding the outcome of the battle and the active nature of his behavior is clearly evident. Moses decides that Joshua will conduct the battle in the camp, while he himself will stand on top of the hill with the rod of God in his hand, and thus decide the battle. In contrast, from verse 11 onwards, we

---

7. An allusion to this unexpected situation is found already at the beginning of the verse: "And it came to pass, when Moses held up (*yarim*) his hand, that Israel prevailed." The form of the word "*yarim*" indicates an action that is repeated over and over, which implies that this was not always the case. Ramban refers to the parallel in Joshua 8:18: "And the Lord said to Joshua, 'Stretch out the spear that is in your hand toward Ay; for I will give it into your hand.' And Joshua stretched out the spear that he had in his hand toward the city." There, however, Scripture emphasizes (v. 26): "For Joshua did not withdraw his hand, wherewith he stretched out the spear, until he had utterly destroyed all the inhabitants of Ay." This account retroactively highlights the heaviness of Moses' hands in our story.

detect a certain passivity in Moses' actions. First, Moses finds himself forced to let down his hands, thus causing Amalek to prevail. Then Scripture explicitly notes his weakness: "But Moses' hands were heavy." Next, Moses no longer stands erect on the hilltop, but rather sits on a stone, another expression of his weakness. Moses did not even decide to do this on his own, but rather it was done to him by others: "And Aaron and Hur supported his hands, the one on the one side, and the other on the other side." Moses, who had announced that he would stand on the hilltop, is now forced to sit down and be supported by Aaron and Hur. Only then does Moses succeed: "And his hands were steady until the going down of the sun."

What is the significance of these sharp transitions and significant deviations from Moses' plan to his actions during the war itself? Until now, the rod worked without any difficulties – why now, all of a sudden, does Moses finds it difficult to hold his hands up? Before I propose my answer to these questions, I wish to briefly discuss a midrash relating to our passage.

III. MOSES' HEAVY HANDS

The sages expounded as follows:

> "But Moses' hands were heavy." From here [we learn] that a person should not delay [performing] the commandments. Had not Moses said to Joshua, "Choose us out men," he would not have suffered so. They said: "Moses' hands at that time grew heavy like a person from whom two jugs of water hang." (*Mekhilta* of Rabbi Shimon bar Yohai, 17:12)

The sages understood the words "But Moses' hands were heavy" not merely as a statement of objective fact, but also as a punishment meted out to Moses. What shortcoming did the sages find in Moses' conduct?

Similarly, Rashi writes:

> "But Moses' hands were heavy" – because he had shown himself remiss in the duty, and had appointed someone else in his place, his hands grew heavy.

According to Rashi, the fact that Moses appointed Joshua and did not lead the battle himself is what caused the heaviness of his hands. On the other hand, the Targum Yonatan renders the verse as follows: "But Moses' hands were heavy because he put off the battle to the next day, and did not quicken himself on that day for the deliverance of Israel." That is to say, Moses' delaying the battle to the next day is what caused his hands to grow heavy.

The wording of the midrash, "From here [we learn] that a person should not delay [performing] the commandments," implies that the criticism here relates to Moses' putting off the battle to the next day, as suggested by the Targum Yonatan. However, the continuation of that same midrash, "Had not Moses said to Joshua, 'Choose us out men,' he would not have suffered so," supports Rashi's understanding, that the main criticism is that he had appointed another person in his stead.

It appears that we see two alternative critiques of Moses. What is not clear is what shortcoming the sages see in Moses' casting the mission upon Joshua. Surely Moses only sent Joshua because he assigned a different role to himself: "Tomorrow I will stand on the top of the hill with the rod of God in my hand." Why should this be judged to his discredit?

It seems to me that the sages are criticizing Moses for the role that he assigned to himself. Moses wanted to decide the outcome of the battle being waged through the rod in his hand as he stood on the hilltop. He wished to continue to exploit the power of the rod of God as it expressed itself until now in the ten plagues and in the splitting of the sea. Just as there, where every time that Moses stretched out his hand with his rod a miracle took place – plague and destruction came upon Egypt, the sea split so that Israel could pass through and then returned to its original state to drown the Egyptians – so too here, with the stretching of his hand with his rod, Amalek would be routed and the battle would be quickly decided. But a subtle but critical difference distinguishes between the previous cases and the case before us. In all the previous cases, the use of the rod followed an explicit command from God. In contrast, against Amalek, Moses decides on his own to make use of the rod. It should be noted that in the entire story (until the conclusion) there is no mention whatsoever of God's name. Thus, the dividing line between the agent and the One who sent him was liable to become blurred. Anyone could erroneously have concluded that it was Moses himself who possessed the power latent in the rod.[8] This erroneous conclusion would have found support in the division of roles between Joshua and Moses. Joshua wages the battle in a natural manner in the camp below, while Moses decides the outcome of the battle in a supernatural way, from the top of the hill above.

Moses' conduct stands out against the background of the story that preceded the war against Amalek – the incident in Masa and Meriva (17:1–7). Several elements link the two adjacent stories. In both cases, Scripture emphasizes that the incident took place in Refidim; in both cases use is made of the rod; in both cases, the story ends with the calling of a name: "And he called the name of the place Masa and Meriva" (v. 7), and "And he called the name of it, The Lord is My Banner (*Nisi*)" (v. 15) (note the similarity in sound between the two names). In the story of Masa and Meriva, the rod's miraculous role is evident. By hitting the rock with his rod, Moses brought forth water from it. However, Moses used the rod only after God explicitly commanded him to do so. What is more, Moses' reaction to the people's complaints there was: "And Moses cried to the Lord, saying, What shall I do to this people? They are almost ready to stone me" (v. 4). This reaction, both the cry to God, and the words, "What shall I do," teach us that Moses was aware of the limits of his power and his absolute dependence upon God. Moses' conduct in the story of the war against Amalek stands in total opposition to his behavior in the story of Masa and Meriva. In the story of Masa and Meriva, Moses clearly expresses his powerlessness and dependence upon God; here in the story of Amalek, Moses creates an impression through his words that he is capable of accepting upon himself the role reserved for God, and deciding the battle by way of the rod in his hand.

God's words to Moses in the story of Masa and Meriva should also be compared with Moses' words to Joshua in the account of the war against Amalek. In the story of Masa and Meriva, God says to Moses:

---

8. Compare to Israel's error at the time of the sin of the golden calf: "Arise, make us gods, which shall go before us; for as for this man Moses, who brought us up out of the land of Egypt, we know not what is become of him" (Ex. 32:1).

pass before the people, and take with you of the elders of Israel; and your rod, with which you smote the river, take in your hand, and go. *Behold, I will stand before you there upon the rock in Ḥorev*; and you shall smite the rock, and there shall come water out of it, that the people may drink. (Ex. 17:5–6)

In the account of the war against Amalek, Moses says to Joshua:

choose us out men, and go out, fight with Amalek; tomorrow *I will stand on the top of the hill* with the rod of God in my hand. (v. 9)

In both cases there is a division of roles. In the story of Masa and Meriva, God commands Moses to pass before the people and act in such a way that will relieve the distress, but He adds that He will stand before him upon the rock. In the account of the war against Amalek, Moses commands Joshua to fight against Amalek, and he emphasizes that he will stand on the top of the hill. Thus Joshua will draw his strength from Moses' presence on the top of the hill. This parallelism reinforces the impression that Moses took upon himself a role ordinarily reserved for God.

This erroneous impression can impair the most important lesson that the Torah wishes to impress upon us – God's absolute rule, and the essential difference between man – all human beings – and God. Moses' plan cannot be carried out in its literal sense.

According to this, Moses' ascent to the top of the hill with the rod of God in his hand should not have succeeded at all. But God governs the world in His own way. "For as the heavens are higher than the earth, so are My ways higher than your ways, and My thoughts than your thoughts" (Isaiah 55:9). He directs man to mend his ways little by little until he recognizes and explicitly declares the absolute rule of God.[9] In

---

9. Compare with what I wrote in my article, "*Sipur HaShunamit*," *Megadim* 15, 5752, pp. 45–52. I argued there that in the story of the Shunamite (11 Kings 4:8–37) Scripture levels the critique at Elisha that his conduct gives the impression that there is no limit to his miraculous powers, and that he can even bring life into the

my opinion, this is the key to understanding the relationship between the description of the preparations for battle and the battle itself, and to resolving the tension between the two sections.

IV. WHAT HAPPENED?

> And it came to pass, when Moses held up his hand, that Israel prevailed; and when he let down his hand, Amalek prevailed. (v. 11)

With these measured words Scripture describes what occurred. We already noted that no mention is made here of the rod, nor does it mention that Moses put the rod down, as one might have expected according to Ramban. Additionally, the verse speaks of Moses' holding up his hand in the singular, and this may include the lifting of the rod. In any case, it is not explicitly stated here that Moses lifted his hands to God in prayer, as Ramban wished to understand.

It seems to me that this verse describes the change from the original plan to what happened in practice. Moses lifted up his hand, and it stands to reason that his rod was in his hand, as Moses had stated earlier. The verse, however, says nothing about the rod or its being stretched out. By ignoring the rod, the Torah teaches that the rod itself accomplished nothing – practically speaking, it did not exist at all. It becomes clear that it was not the rod, but the lifting of Moses' hand which caused Israel to prevail. It may be argued that the miraculous power passed from the rod to the hand of Moses, but this transfer led to two changes. First, Moses' hand had an effect only as long as it was lifted upwards. This change exposed the wondrous power of his hand to its natural weakness – "and when he let down his hand, Amalek prevailed." Second, lifting the hand and leaving it in its raised position changed the miraculous character of the action. It was no longer a miracle stemming from the power of the rod as it was stretched out towards the enemy, but a strengthening stemming from lifting the hand upwards toward heaven. These changes are

---

world without first turning to God or at least explicitly attributing the wonder to Him. There too Elisha's decree is realized at first, but later he himself is forced to concede that his powers are limited and that he is dependent upon God.

two sides of the same coin. On the one hand they reveal the limitation of Moses' power owing to the fact that he is flesh and blood, while on the other hand, they symbolize the source of Moses' strength, God in heaven.

> But Moses' hands were heavy; and they took a stone, and put it under him, and he sat on it; and Aaron and Ḥur supported his hands, the one on the one side, and the other on the other side. (v. 12)

Once it has become clear that the power is in the hand raised toward heaven and not in the rod, "hand" in the singular is changed to "hands." It is precisely when the power passes into the hands of Moses himself, that the weakness of his hands becomes evident, for "Moses' hands were heavy." Exposing the weakness of Moses' hands is a necessary link in the narrative and in the process of correcting the erroneous impression created by the earlier words of Moses. Since on the one hand, "Moses' hands were heavy," and on the other hand, "and when he let down his hand, Amalek prevailed," there was no possible way to prevent the fall of Israel, and bring about a victory over Amalek, without supporting Moses' hands. Sitting Moses down on the stone with Aaron and Ḥur's support clearly symbolizes Moses' limitations. Moses is no longer the party who determines the outcome of the battle. Like any other human being, he needs others' support. This expresses man's limitations, as opposed to God's absolute power. Only then can it be said: "And his hands were steady until the going down of the sun."

The only difficulty with this explanation is that Aaron and Ḥur went up with Moses even before Moses' limitations became evident, which implies that it had been Moses' intention to make use of them from the outset. However, when Moses spoke to Joshua he made no mention of Aaron and Ḥur, emphasizing only his own presence: "Tomorrow I will stand on the top of the hill with the rod of God in my hand."

The answer is that there is a difference between the original purpose for which Aaron and Ḥur went up with Moses and the actual role that they later filled. They went up with Moses because it would have been beneath his dignity for such an important person to go by himself. As the sages said: "This is the way of the world that an important person who sets off on the road needs two people to minister to him" (*Tanhuma Balak* 8). Only later, after the original plan had gone wrong, did their role change. Aaron and Hur initially went up with Moses to show him honor and minister to his needs, but in the end they turned into a source of support which Moses was forced to accept. From now on everyone understood that the source of Moses' power is not his rod, and that the source of the rod's power is not Moses. The power of both of them lies in Him, towards whom his hands were raised.

In light of this we should go back to the beginning of the story and explain the meaning of the name of the place where this incident occurred: "Then came Amalek, and fought with Israel in Refidim." Already the sages sensed that the name of the place mentioned here demands explanation, and they suggested that the people of Israel let their hands drop (*rafu* = weak) from holding the Torah.[10] In this exposition, the sages wished to draw a connection between this passage and the concluding verse of the previous passage: "And he called the name of the place Masa and Meriva because of the strife of the children of Israel, and because they tempted the Lord, saying, 'Is the Lord among us, or not?'" We noted that in the previous passage, Scripture emphasizes that the incident took place in Refidim. If we wish to explain the name based exclusively on what is stated in our passage, it may be suggested that the place was called Refidim because it was there that the hands of Moses dropped, for Moses' hands were heavy. This weakness of the hands, in contrasting manner, highlights the strong hand of God.

V. "THE LORD IS MY BANNER"

Let us now discuss the concluding section of the story, verses 14–16: "And the Lord said to Moses, Write this for a memorial in a book, and rehearse it in the ears of Joshua: that I will utterly blot out the remembrance of Amalek from under the heaven." God's reaction emphasizes the severity with which He judges Amalek's action. The wording, "I will utterly blot

---

10. *Mekhilta DeRabbi Yishmael, masekhta deAmalek, parasha* 1 (ed. Horowitz-Rabin, p. 177; ed. Kahana, p. 156); *Sanhedrin* 106a; and elsewhere. "*Rifyon yadayim*" is a common term in Scripture. See: II Samuel 4:1, 17:2; Isaiah 13:7, 35:3; Jer. 6:24, 47:3, 50:43; Ezek. 21:12; Zeph. 3:16; Ezra 4:4; Nehemiah 6:9; II Chron. 15:7.

out," however, might come to emphasize the lesson emerging from the story. The blotting out of Amalek and the war waged against that nation will be done by God Himself and not by mortal man.[11] This might also explain the words, "And place it in the ears of Joshua." Joshua who had heard Moses say, "Tomorrow I will stand on the top of the hill with the rod of God in my hand," and might have understood that the battle would be decided by way of the rod in Moses' hand, must now hear from Moses himself that the blotting out of Amalek will be done by God. Attention should also be paid to the difference between "And Joshua vanquished Amalek" and "That I will utterly blot out the remembrance of Amalek." The battle that was decided through Moses' hands ended only with the vanquishing of Amalek and his people, but God's war will end with the blotting out of Amalek's remembrance from under the heaven.

"And Moses built an altar, and called the name of it, The Lord is My Banner [*nisi*: my *nes*]." In Scripture the word "*nes*" denotes a pole or a banner, as we find, for example, in Numbers 21:8: "Make you a venomous serpent, and set it upon a pole (*nes*)," and similarly in Isaiah 30:17: "Till you be left like a flagpole upon the top of a mountain, and as a banner (*nes*) on a hill." This brings to mind Moses' hands which were lifted up during the entire duration of the battle on the hilltop. Moses wishes to proclaim: "The banner is not the rod that was in my hand as I stood on the top of the hill, nor my hands that were lifted up during the course of the battle, but rather God to whom my hands were raised – He is my banner." Possibly, the altar in this verse refers to the stone upon which Moses sat. Corresponding to the stone that demonstrated the limits of Moses' power, there is now an altar that is called "The Lord is My Banner."

"For he said, 'The hand upon the throne of the Lord.'" As stated

---

11. While it is true that in the book of Deuteronomy it says: "You shall blot out the remembrance of Amalek" (Deut. 25:19), nothing may be learned from the account in Deuteronomy to the account in Exodus, for the account in Deuteronomy differs on important points from Exodus. This is not the place to discuss at length the relationship between the two accounts. For our purposes, it may be argued that after the emphasis of God's part in the war against Amalek in the book of Exodus, the mission can once again be cast upon the nation itself. Compare to the wording of Samuel's command to Saul: "Thus says the Lord of hosts, I remember that which Amalek did to Israel.... Now go and smite Amalek" (1 Sam. 15:2–3).

above, the first six instances of the word "hand" in our passage refer to the hand of Moses. In this last instance, the word "hand" refers not to Moses' hand, but to the hand of God. This minor detail expresses the essence of the entire story. It now becomes clear that the hands of Moses depend upon the hand of God.

"The Lord will have war with Amalek from generation to generation." Neither the rod in Moses' hand nor the hands of Moses will fight against Amalek, but rather God Himself. It should be noted that the name of God which was absent from the story of the war itself in verses 8–13 is mentioned in the concluding section in each of its three verses.

This is the idea that will later be expressed by David: "Give us help against the foe; for vain is the help of man. Through God we shall do valiantly; for it is He who will tread down our enemies" (Psalms 60:13–14, 108:13–14).

VI. BETWEEN AMALEK AND YITRO

We have already noted the connection between this story and the previous story, the incident at Masa and Meriva. In this section I wish to discuss the connection between this story and the story that follows, the arrival of Yitro.

The Midrash already noted the contrasting parallelism between the stories of Amalek and Yitro, saying: "It is written: 'Smite a scorner, and the simple will beware' (*Mishlei* 19:25). 'Smite a scorner' – this refers to Amalek; 'and the simple will beware' – this refers to Yitro."[12] This contrasting parallelism between the story of Amalek and that of Yitro was developed by Ibn Ezra:

> Now I shall explain why the story of Yitro was inserted in this place: Since [the Torah] mentioned above the evil perpetrated by Amalek against Israel, it mentions in contrast the good that Yitro did for Israel. And it is written: "And Yitro rejoiced for all the good" [Ex. 18:9], and he gave good and correct advice to Moses and to Israel, as Moses said to him: "And you may be to us

---

12. *Pesikta deRav Kahana, parasha* 3, ed. Mandelbaum, p. 35; *Midrash Tanḥuma Yitro* 3; and elsewhere.

instead of eyes" [Num. 10:31], this meaning that he illuminated their eyes. And Saul said: "And you have shown kindness to all of the children of Israel" [1 Sam. 15:6]. Since mention was made above of God's war with Amalek, which Israel is obligated to wage, mention is also made of Yitro, because [his descendants] lived together with the people of Amalek, that Israel should remember the kindness shown by their father, and not harm his descendants. And indeed we find the Rekhavim, descendants of Yitro, who were with the people of Israel in Jerusalem and in the days of Jeremiah, Yonadav the son of Rekhav [Jer. 35:19]. (Ibn Ezra, long commentary on Exodus 18:1)

Ibn Ezra adopts the view that Yitro arrived after the Torah was given at Sinai, and is therefore forced to account for the location of the story of Yitro's arrival. According to Ibn Ezra, the story of Yitro was intentionally placed here next to the story of Amalek in order to highlight the contrast between them. Amalek came to fight against Israel, whereas Yitro came to give them good and correct advice. As a result Israel was commanded to wage war against Amalek, whereas Yitro was given a reward. Ibn Ezra also alludes to Saul's war against Amalek, noting that it was in this frame-work that Saul, prior to his campaign against Amalek, suggested to the Kenites, who were descendants of Yitro, that they remove themselves from Amalek because they had shown kindness to Israel. This story illustrates the contrast for all generations between the attitude toward Amalek and the attitude toward Yitro. Indeed, it can be demonstrated that the book of Samuel wished to contrast the attitude toward Amalek to the attitude toward the Kenites. Even the wordings are similar: "I remember that which Amalek did to Israel, how he laid wait for him in the way, *when he came up from Egypt*" (1 Sam. 15:2), and "Go, depart, go down from among the Amalekites, lest I destroy you with them; for you have shown kindness to all the children of Israel, *when they came up out of Egypt*" (ibid. v. 6).

The contrast between Amalek and Yitro also finds expression in the words of Bil'am:

And when he looked on Amalek, he took up his discourse, and said, "Amalek was the first of the nations; but his latter end shall be everlasting perdition." And he looked on the Kenites, and took up his discourse, and said, "Strong is your dwelling place, and you put your nest in a rock." (Num. 24:20–21)

Here too the Kenites are mentioned immediately following Amalek, as was already noted by *Ḥazal* and the commentators.

Cassuto, in his commentary to Exodus, reinforced this idea by demonstrating the many linguistic parallels between these two stories. He says as follows:

> Even the formulation of the two sections in the form before us is intended to underline the antithesis between the two episodes. Above (xvii, 8) it is stated: "And Amalek *came* and *fought* with Israel," and here (vv. 5, 7): "And Yitro, Moses' father-in-law, *came* ... and they asked each other of their welfare [literally, 'peace']"; in the previous narrative (xvii, 9) it is written: "*Choose* for us men" – a selection for war, whereas in our passage (v. 25) it is recorded: "And Moses chose able men" – a selection for judgement and peace; there (xvii, 12) we are told of Moses: "and he *sat* upon it" – upon the stone to pray for the victory of his people in battle, and in our section it is said (v. 13): "Moses *sat* to judge the people." There are also other parallels: "and Moses' hands *grew heavy*" (xvii, 12) – "for the thing is too *heavy* for you" (xvii, 18); "*stand*" (xvii, 9) – "*stand*" (xviii, 14); "*until the going down of the sun*" (xvii, 12) – "*till* (*the*) *evening*" (xviii, 13, 14); "*tomorrow*" (xvii, 9) – "*on the morrow*" (xviii, 13); "*war ... from generation to generation*," at the end of the section on Amalek (xviii, 6) – "and all this people also will go to their place in *peace*," at the conclusion of Yitro's speech (xviii, 23).[13]

Cassuto explains the correspondence in line with the words of Ibn Ezra: "In order to emphasize the fundamental difference in the relations between the two tribes and the people of Israel."

While there is no doubt about the correctness of his explanation

---

13. U. Cassuto, *Commentary on the Book of Exodus*, Jerusalem, 1967, p. 212.

of the correspondence, I think that additional meaning can be assigned to it.[14] The main point in Yitro's advice to Moses is the understanding that "this thing is too heavy for you; you are not able to perform it yourself alone." That is to say, certain things are too heavy even for Moses to do by himself, and thus it is necessary to join others in the mission. According to what we said above, this is also the central lesson of the story of Amalek. Moses is not able to decide the battle all by himself on the top of the hill, and there too this difficulty expresses itself in the fact that his hands, which were supposed to decide the battle, became heavy. For this reason Moses needed the support and assistance of Aaron and Ḥur. The story of Amalek deals with Moses' limitations in a struggle with an external enemy, whereas the story of Yitro emphasizes Moses' limitations in his handling of the internal affairs of his people.

It is interesting that *Ḥazal* criticized Moses' conduct with respect to his appointment of the judges, in a way that is very reminiscent of the criticism that we saw earlier, in the *Mekhilta*, of Moses' conduct in the war against Amalek (according to our proposed understanding). The sages expounded the verse, "And the cause that is too hard for you, bring it to me, and I will hear it" (Deut. 1:17), as follows:

> "And the cause that is too hard for you." The Holy One, blessed be He, said to Moses: "You [say that you] will judge the hard matters. By your life, I tell you that you will not judge hard matters. I will bring you a matter that a disciple of your disciple is able to hear, but you are not able to hear it. What is that? This is the law governing the daughters of Tzelofḥad." And thus it says [Num. 27:5]: "And Moses brought their cause before the Lord." (*Sifrei* par. 17, ad. loc.)

Here too we can ask: What fault did the sages find in the words of Moses? Surely the most difficult matters should be brought to Moses! The sages appear to criticize what might be misunderstood from Moses' words, that he is at the highest level and there is nothing that he is unable

---

14. My son David enlightened me about this point (I found a similar comment in the commentary of Amos Ḥakham).

to decide. Moses should have added: "And the cause that is too hard for me, I will bring it before the Lord." Here too, just as in the war with Amalek, one who hears this might err and attribute Moses' knowledge to his own wisdom. According to this midrash, Moses had to be rebuked in order to correct this erroneous impression. Only if a case would come before Moses, and Moses would not know how to deal with it, forcing him to bring it before God – only then would it become clear to all that indeed there is a level above Moses, and everyone would understand the source of Moses' knowledge and from where he draws his power. Attention should be paid to the linguistic similarity between "Bring it to me" and "And Moses brought their cause before the Lord." The level that Moses omitted in the story of the appointment of the judges was filled in by Moses himself in the story of the daughters of Tzelofḥad.

VII. THE MEANING OF THE STORY WITHIN EXODUS

Finally, I wish to discuss the location of the stories of Amalek and Yitro in the framework of the entire book of Exodus. Various proposals have been put forward to explain the internal division of Exodus, each expressing a certain dimension of the book's components and the relationship between them. I will mention here the proposal put forward by Cassuto in his commentary. Cassuto divides the book into three parts: (1) chapters 1–17: Israel's servitude and liberation; (2) chapters 18–24: the Torah and the commandments; (3) chapters 25–40: the *Mishkan* and the service. It may be added that this division expresses the relationship between Israel (the first part), the Torah (the second part) and the *Shekhina* (the third part).

I wish to suggest two emendations of this proposal. First, in my opinion, the first part ends in chapter 18. As stated above, and as Cassuto himself discerned, there are strong connections between the story of Amalek and the story of Yitro. Chapter 18 should therefore be seen as completing the story of Israel's liberation from Egypt. The story of Amalek and the story of Yitro present two opposite reactions to Israel's exodus. Second, it should be noted that the last two sections of the book are strongly linked, both in the narrative and in substance. At the end of the second part, Moses is commanded to go up the mountain in order to receive the Torah and the commandments, but when he goes up the mountain he receives also all of the material regarding the *Mishkan*, the essence of the third part. There is also a substantive connection between the two parts: they both describe God's kingdom over Israel, whether through the revelation at Sinai and the giving of the Torah, or through the command to build the *Mishkan*. It is therefore possible to divide the book more precisely into two parts: the first part describes Israel's exodus from Egypt and becoming God's people; and the second part – consisting of parts two and three in Cassuto's formulation – describes the actualization of God's kingdom over Israel.

In light of this, I wish to compare the end of the first part of the book with the end of the second part (which effectively closes the entire book). As was stated above, the first part ends with two stories: the war against Amalek and the story of Yitro. The common denominator between them is that they both describe the limitations of Moses' powers and his inability to act all by himself, whether on the battlefield or when judging the people.

The second part of the book, and the book as a whole, ends with a description of the resting of the *Shekhina* on Israel:

> Then a cloud covered the Tent of Meeting, and the glory of the Lord filled the tabernacle. And Moses was not able to enter the Tent of Meeting, because the cloud rested on it, and the glory of the Lord filled the tabernacle. And when the cloud was taken up from over the tabernacle, the children of Israel went onward in all their journeys. But if the cloud were not taken up, then they journeyed not till the day that it was taken up. For the cloud of the Lord was upon the tabernacle by day, and fire was on it by night, in the sight of all the house of Israel, throughout all their journeys. (41:34–38)

The *leitvort* in this section is "cloud," repeated in each of the five verses. This section divides into two parts, consisting of verses 34–35 and verses 36–38. Each part describes a different aspect of the cloud, i.e., the resting of the *Shekhina*. At the heart of verses 36–38 stands the journey of Israel as determined by the state of the cloud of the *Shekhina*. In practice, all of Israel's journeys in the wilderness after the revelation at

Sinai and the resting of the *Shekhina* in the *Mishkan* are concentrated in the book of Numbers. It may be argued then that the book of Numbers expands on the issues raised in verses 36–38.

What is the central theme of the first part, verses 34–35? Its structure teaches that its main point is found in the verse: "And Moses was not able to enter the Tent of Meeting." In this verse, Scripture wishes to express the intensity of the *Shekhina*'s resting in the Tent of Meeting which did not allow Moses to enter inside. The commentators already noted that the beginning of Leviticus, "And the Lord called to Moses, and spoke to him from the Tent of Meeting, saying," is a continuation of this verse. Since Moses was unable to enter the Tent, God had to call to him so that he would be able to enter.[15] Moses' entry into the Tent of Meeting was to receive the commandments, as is stated at the beginning of the command to erect the *Mishkan*: "And there I will meet with you, and I will speak with you from above the covering … of all things which I will give you in commandment to the children of Israel" (Ex. 25:22). Indeed, the entire book of Leviticus is a series of God's communications to Moses. It may be argued that just as the book of Numbers continues the second part of the concluding section at the end of Exodus, so too the book of Leviticus continues the first part of that section.

The verse, "And Moses was not able to enter the Tent of Meeting," is very puzzling. If Moses was not able to enter the Tent of Meeting, how then could God meet with him there, as had been planned? The answer is found in the verse: "And the Lord called to Moses, and spoke to him from the Tent of Meeting." Why did the Torah see fit to conclude one book with such a puzzling verse, and delay the resolution to the beginning of the next book?

It seems to me that here too Scripture meant to end the book on a note that emphasizes the limitations of Moses' power. Precisely because of Moses' special standing, precisely because elsewhere Scripture emphasizes Moses' elevated level – "And the Lord spoke to Moses face to face, as a man speaks to his friend" (Ex. 33:11), and "With him I speak mouth to mouth" (Num. 12:8) – precisely because Moses was

---

15. See, for example, the commentaries of Rashbam and Ibn Ezra to the beginning of Leviticus.

the man of God "whom the Lord knew face to face" (Deut. 34:10), it was important for Scripture to end the book of Exodus and the account of the resting of the *Shekhina* by emphasizing the essential chasm that lies between the *Shekhina* and man, even if he is Moses. Only after we internalize the fact that no man can stand by himself in the place of the *Shekhina*, only then can we also understand the solution proposed by the verse, "And the Lord called to Moses, and spoke to him from the Tent of Meeting."

It turns out then that both parts of Exodus end, each in its own way, with emphasis placed on the limitations of Moses' powers. Note should also be taken of the linguistic similarity between "You *are not able* to perform it yourself alone" and "And Moses *was not able* to enter the Tent of Meeting."

Only after Scripture labored to engrave this point in our consciousness, could it emphasize in other places Moses' elevated status as a man of God, and even end the Torah with words that stress the mighty hand of Moses:

> And there arose not a prophet since in Israel like Moses, whom the Lord knew face to face, in all the signs and the wonders, which the Lord sent him to do in the land of Egypt to Pharaoh, and to all his servants and to all his land, and in all that mighty hand, and in all the great terror which Moses performed in the sight of Israel. (Deut. 34:10–12)

Parashat Yitro

Moses' Family

Rav Amnon Bazak

I. GERSHOM AND ELIEZER

One of the Torah's most mysterious subjects concerns Moses' family. That the text talks about this great leader more than it does about any other person is not strange; but in light of the extensive documentation of his leadership career, the lack of details about his family, and the mystery surrounding the very little that we are told, stand out even more starkly. We shall attempt here to extract what we can from what the text tells us about his wife, Tzipora, and his sons Gershom and Eliezer, and perhaps also attain an understanding of why the discussion of these characters is so sparse and brief.

Let us begin with the new fact with which our *parasha* opens: the existence of Moses' second son. Until now we knew only of his first son, Gershom, from chapter 2:

> And she bore a son, and he called him Gershom, for he said: I was a stranger (*ger*) in a foreign land. (Ex. 2:22)

Gershom is mentioned again at the beginning of our *parasha*, but here the Torah adds that Moses now has a second son:

> And Yitro, Moses' father-in-law, took Tzipora, Moses' wife (after he had sent her back), and her two sons, one of whom was named Gershom – for he had said, "I was a stranger in a foreign land," and the other who was named Eliezer – for "the God of my father was my help and delivered me from Pharaoh's sword." (18:2–4)

We learn much about Moses from the names that he gives to his children. The name "Gershom" immediately arouses our curiosity, since the words "in a foreign land" refer to Midian, which is a foreign land to the Egyptian-born Moses. It must be remembered that this name was given prior to God's revelation to Moses, while Moses – who had been raised by Pharaoh's daughter – has been described as an "Egyptian man" (2:19). This name, then, expresses Moses' attachment to Egypt, and his sorrow at having been forced to flee.

Eliezer, in contrast, appears to have been born after God's revelation, in which God presents Himself as "the God of your father, the God of Abraham, the God of Isaac, the God of Jacob" (3:6), and commands Moses repeatedly (see 3:13–16) to present Him to *Am Yisrael* as "the God of your fathers." Apparently, the name Eliezer – commemorating that "the God of my father was my help and delivered me from Pharaoh's sword" – was given against the backdrop of the revelation at the burning bush. This name expresses Moses' religious personality and his connection to God, which was solidified through that experience.

In any event, the most puzzling aspect of this mention of Moses' two sons is that this is the last we hear of them; from this point onwards the Torah records nothing about either Gershom or Eliezer, nor about Tzipora.[1] What is the meaning of this silence? Why does the Torah ignore Moses' family?

The absence of Moses' family is felt most acutely in those narratives where we would expect to find them. In *Parashat Va'era*, for example, the story of God sending Moses and Aaron to Pharaoh is interrupted with the genealogy of the family of Levi. The Torah lists Aaron's descen-

---

1. Assuming that the "Kushite woman" mentioned in Numbers (12:1) is not Tzipora, as Rashbam maintains.

dants as far as Pinḥas, as well as Koraḥ's lineage, but nary a word about Moses' own children. Another such passage is found at the beginning of the book of Numbers. Following the census of *Benei Yisrael*, the Torah records the special census of the tribe of Levi. The passage opens with the words, "These are the generations of Aaron and Moses on the day God spoke to Moses at Mount Sinai" (Num. 3:1), but the continuation fails to supply the information we expect to read, listing only the descendants of Aaron and ignoring Moses' descendants. How are we to understand this?

II. "AFTER HAVING SENT HER BACK"

An important clue to understanding the phenomenon lies in the enigmatic "sending back" of Tzipora, from the beginning of our *parasha*:

> And Yitro, Moses' father-in-law, took Tzipora, Moses' wife, after he had sent her back (*le'aḥar shiluḥeiha*). (18:2)

What does this mean? Nowhere until now did we hear anything of this, but apparently, after setting out for Egypt together with Moses, Tzipora had parted from Moses and returned with her sons to Midian. Moreover, the term "*shiluḥeiha*" seems to indicate a form of divorce, as we find in Deuteronomy:

> When a man takes a woman and marries her, and it happens that she does not find favor in his eyes, for he has found some unseemliness in her, and he writes her a bill of divorce and gives it into her hand, and sends her away (*veshilḥa*) from his home…. And if the latter husband comes to hate her, and writes her a bill of divorce and gives it into her hand, and sends her away (*veshilḥa*) from his home. (Deut. 24:1–4)

With this possibility in mind, Ibn Ezra writes in his short commentary:

> Some say that "after she was sent back" means [he sent her] to her father's home, from the road to Egypt, while others interpret this to mean that [he] gave her a divorce.

Either way, what is certain is that at some point in time Moses had "sent" Tzipora away, and her sons had gone with her. What were the circumstances of this "sending"?

Seemingly, the explanation must have something to do with the sole incident known to us from the period of their marriage – the mysterious drama that takes place on the way to Egypt, at the lodge:

> And it was, on the way, at the lodge, that God met him and sought to kill him. And Tzipora took a sharp stone and cut off her son's foreskin, and cast it at his feet, and said, "For you are a bloody bridegroom to me." And He let him go, then she said, "A bloody bridegroom in the matter of circumcision." (4:24–26)[2]

We shall not attempt here to address all aspects of this cryptic narrative. For our purposes, what is important is that after God sought to harm Moses, and Tzipora saved him by circumcising her son, she twice calls Moses a "bridegroom of blood" (*ḥatan damim*).[3] This expression is enigmatic in itself, and many different interpretations have been offered, but its general mood seems to be negative, as in the somewhat similar words that Shimi ben Gera directs to David: "Behold, you are in an evil situation, because you are a man of blood (*ish damim*)" (II Sam. 16:8). Tzipora seems to be telling Moses that living with him involves mortal danger, and that she is not willing to live such a life. In response, Moses sends her back to her father's home, in Midian.

The connection between this incident at the lodge and the beginning of our *parasha* is clear. Our *parasha* describes Yitro's arrival and his welcome by Moses:

> And Yitro, Moses' father-in-law, and his sons and his wife, came to Moses, to the wilderness where he was encamped, at the moun-

---

2. See Rabbi Yoel Bin-Nun, "Moses' Identity Crisis: Who Is the Uncircumcised Child?" in this volume.
3. Rashi understands Tzipora as addressing the angel of God: "You are a (thwarted) killer of my husband to me." However, it is difficult to justify a literal understanding of the words 'a bloody bridegroom' as 'a killer of my husband.'

tain of God .... And Moses came to meet his father-in-law, and he prostrated himself and he kissed him, and they asked each other as to their welfare, and he came into the tent. (18:5–7)

This description is strongly reminiscent of what we read immediately after the incident at the lodge:

And God said to Aaron: "Go to meet Moses, to the wilderness"; and he went and he met him at the mountain of God, and he kissed him. (4:27)

In both instances, a close relative of Moses goes to the mountain of God (Mount Sinai) in the wilderness in order to meet him, and the warm encounter includes a kiss. These two meetings seem to form a circle which begins with Moses' first experiences after the confrontation with Tzipora, following which she had returned to Midian, and concludes with their reunion.

We must now ask what led to Tzipora's return, with her sons, to Moses? Here the answer is explicitly provided:

Yitro, the priest of Midian, father-in-law of Moses, heard all that God had done for Moses and for Israel, His people; that God had brought Israel out of Egypt. (18:1)

Yitro's amazement at the events of the exodus prompt him to return to Moses, who recounts to him "all that God had done to Pharaoh and to Egypt" (v. 8), until Yitro declares, "Now I know that God is greater than all gods, for in the matter in which they plotted against them" (v. 11). Yitro completes his spiritual journey with recognition of God's kingship, and bequeaths to *Am Yisrael* an orderly system of justice, as we read later on.

I suggest that from the time Moses left Midian for Egypt, Yitro was left in a state of suspense, waiting to hear what would come of the campaign, and which side would emerge victorious. For this reason he refrained from any attempt to return Tzipora and her sons to Moses.[4]

---

4. From this perspective, Yitro's conduct resembles that attributed by the Midrash to

Once he heard the great events of the exodus, he decided to renew his connection with Moses.

III. THE RESULTS

Did Tzipora and her sons experience the same spiritual transformation that had been experienced by Yitro, or did life in Midian mold them in a different direction? It would seem that this very issue is addressed by the Torah's silence. The complete absence of Tzipora, Gershom and Eliezer from this point onwards seems to indicate that the three of them were not fully integrated amongst *Am Yisrael*, and they played no active part in Moses' conduct.[5] Moreover, Moses took another wife, in addition to Tzipora – the "Kushite woman."

We conclude that Moses paid a heavy price for the severance

Abraham's brother Ḥaran: "Ḥaran's heart was divided, and he retained his father's words. All the people came to him and said, 'Whose side are you on?' He said to himself, 'Abraham is greater than I; if I see that he has managed to escape, I shall say – I am with Abraham. If not, I shall say – I am with you'" (*Midrash Tehillim* 118:11).

5. Indeed, the possibility that Moses' sons would take their father's place after his death never arises. This is especially apparent against the backdrop of the numerous parallels between Moses and Samuel, as discussed in the first chapter of my book, *Makbilot Nifgashot – Makbilot Sifrutiyot beSefer Shemuel*, Alon Shvut 5766. While Samuel hints at the possibility that his sons might succeed him (see II Sam. 12:2), Moses appears convinced that in his own case there is nothing to discuss.

Nevertheless, surprisingly enough, the midrash criticizes Moses, viewing his request that God appoint a leader to succeed him as a veiled hint at the possibility of his sons taking his place: "After the daughters of Tzelofḥad inherited their father's estate, Moses said: 'Now is the time for me to ask for what I want. If daughters can inherit, then surely it is lawful that my sons inherit my honor.' God said to Moses: 'He who watches over the fig tree shall eat its fruits [Prov. 27:18]. Your sons sat (idle) and did not engage in Torah; Joshua, who ministered to you, is worthy of ministering to Israel'" (*Tanḥuma Pinḥas, parasha* 11). Why do Ḥazal attribute such a thought to Moses when there is no hint of it in the text? Nechama Leibowitz (*Iyyunim beSefer Bemidbar*, Jerusalem 5756, p. 328) writes: "This was not the manner in which our verse was explained by Ḥazal, the sages of the Midrash, who often viewed the narratives of the Torah not as one-time, transient events, but rather as archetypes of human phenomena which are always recurring; not as that which transpired then, but rather as that which is always repeating itself and happening before our very eyes. Within even the greatest of the great they perceived man in all his weakness and nakedness; the desires of the heart and the human inclinations."

from his wife and sons for a lengthy period – and especially during that period in which the national identity of *Am Yisrael* was being formed. His wife and sons were not present at the time of the exodus, nor did they experience the splitting of the sea, concerning which we are told, "Israel saw the great power with which God had acted in Egypt, and the people feared God, and they believed in God and in Moses, His servant" (14:31). They no doubt heard of these events, as Yitro did, but the impact of hearing about it was not the same as experiencing it personally. For this reason, even when they stood at the revelation at Sinai, they were not full partners in the collective experience of internalizing the words, "I am the Lord your God Who brought you out of the land of Egypt, out of the house of slavery" (20:2) – they had never themselves been in the "house of slavery," nor had they been taken from there with great strength and an outstretched arm.

Tanach offers us one further clue to what happened to Moses' family, the story of the "idol of Micah" (Judges 17–18). Towards the end of the story we discover the name of the Levite youth who had served as priest to the idol which Micah had fashioned:

> And the children of Dan set up the idol; and Yehonatan, son of Gershom, son of Menashe – he and his sons were priests to the tribe of Dan until the day of the captivity of the land. (Judges 18:30)

The letter '*nun*' in the name "*Menashe*" is traditionally written in "super-script" (*Menashe*). Rashi comments: "Out of respect for Moses, the '*nun*' is added so as to change his name. And [the letter '*nun*'] is written 'hanging' to teach that [his father] was not *Menashe* but rather *Moshe*" (*Bava Batra* 109a and elsewhere). According to Rashi, then, the '*nun*' is added to Moses' name out of respect for him, but in truth the 'Yehonatan' and his progeny who ministered to this idol for several generations, were in fact Moses' own descendants. This certainly makes sense in light of our discussion above.

If the text takes care to protect Moses' honor, why did Ḥazal reveal the secret and thereby bring him dishonor? Is our discussion above not a further desecration of Moses' memory? It would seem that what

Ḥazal are teaching is that on the one hand we must indeed take care to maintain Moses' honor; at the same time, the awareness of the fate of his descendants is a message which we dare not ignore. It is only thus that we may understand and internalize the colossal tragedy of the greatest of the prophets, the teacher of all of Israel, Moshe Rabbenu. By taking on God's mission to lead Israel out of Egypt, this great leader paid a huge personal price. Was this the inevitable price that the greatest leaders of *Am Yisrael* must necessarily pay, or could things have been done differently? Can we really arrive at an answer to this question?

The Dual Revelation at Sinai

Rav Tamir Granot

At the heart of *Parashat Yitro* lie the Ten Commandments that God proclaimed at Sinai. The discussion concerning the stature of the commandments is both ancient and critical. During the time of the sages, this issue carried significant weight due to what the Talmud refers to as *kefirat haminim* (the heretics' rejection) – the rejection of the mitzvot among Christian sects and the viewing of the Ten Commandments as the basis of the New Testament. *Hazal* therefore instructed that the ritual role of the Commandments be minimized.

In this *shiur* we will explore the status of the Ten Commandments within the general framework of God's revelation at Sinai.

A study of the narrative progression from *Am Yisrael*'s arrival at Sinai, as described in chapters 19, 20, 21 and 24, reveals a number of fundamental difficulties in understanding the function of the Commandments.

The Ten Commandments are introduced with the header, "God spoke all these words, saying" (20:1), indicating that the Commandments are spoken by the Almighty. The verse does not tell us, however, to whom they are spoken. Who hears this divine proclamation?

It is commonly assumed that God here speaks to the entire nation, but this is not explicit at all. Moreover, several verses point us in a different direction:

> 1. Earlier, when God explains to Moses the purpose of the revelation at Sinai, He says to him,
>
> behold, I am coming to you in the thickness of the cloud, in order that the nation hear when I speak with you, and also they will believe in you forever. (19:9)

Accordingly, the purpose of the revelation is to establish the belief in Moses' prophecy, as the nation hears God speak to Moses. God does not proclaim His intent to speak to the people, nor is there any need for this. If the objective is the belief in Moses' prophecy, it suffices for the nation to know that God spoke to Moses; no direct revelation to them is necessary.

> 2. After the Commandments, it says,
>
> The entire nation beheld the sounds, the torches, the sound of the shofar, and the smoking mountain…. They said to Moses, "You speak with us, and we will listen; let not God speak to us, lest we die." (20:14–15)

If God indeed spoke to the people and completed what He had to say, the nation's request seems difficult to understand. They mention the sounds and lightning, but make no mention of God speaking to them, which is perhaps the most frightening experience of all. Furthermore, if God already spoke to them, then either they should already be dead, or they should have nothing more to fear. It appears that the people are afraid that now God will speak to them, something that has not occurred until this point.

Ḥazal seem to have addressed this difficulty, and explained that the people submitted this request after the proclamation of the first two Commandments: "They heard *Anokhi* and *Lo yihyeh lekha* [the first two Commandments] from the mouth of the Almighty." This explanation is based on a difference in style between the first two and subsequent eight Commandments. The first two are written in first-person form – "*I* am the Lord your God who has taken you" ("*Anokhi HaShem Elokekha asher hotzeitikha*"); "beside *Me*" ("*al panai*") – indicating that they were spoken directly from God. However, the final eight Commandments are said in third-person form: "You shall not take the name *of the Lord your God* in vain…. For in six days did *the Lord*…on the land that *the Lord your God is giving* you." These Commandments, it appears, were not heard directly from God, and were rather conveyed through Moses. Ḥazal understood that this transition sheds light on the rest of the Torah: just as *Benei Yisrael* heard these eight Commandments from Moses, even though they were transmitted on Mount Sinai, so did they learn the rest of the Torah from Moses. As mentioned, in this manner Ḥazal resolve the difficulties we raised above: the nation was struck with fear after the first two Commandments, and Moses granted their request that he convey to them the rest of God's instruction.

Nevertheless, although this explanation neatly resolves the discrepancy in style between the first two and subsequent eight commandments, it leaves us unsatisfied for a number of reasons:

A. The Ten Commandments are presented as a single unit, and we find no indication whatsoever in the text that their proclamation was disrupted at any stage.
B. Moses' response to the people's request that they not hear God does not appear to reflect his granting of their request: "Moses said to the people, 'Have no fear, for it is in order to test you that God has come.'" If, as Ḥazal explain, God has already spoken to the people, then He should have continued doing so once Moses calmed their fears. Thus, there is no indication that He stopped speaking, with the exception, of course, of the shift in style as we have already discussed.
C. Earlier, the Torah describes the revelation as follows: "Moses would speak, and God would answer him in a voice." The speaker is Moses; God is not described as speaking to the nation. The expression "*ya'anenu bekol*" ("would answer him in a voice") is a difficult one, but in any event it seems not to refer to plain speech.

Let us now return to our main contention, namely, that it does not appear that God speaks to the nation directly. This claim is reinforced by a verse that appears later, after the presentation of the laws (*mishpatim*) to the people: "Moses came and spoke to the people all the words of the Lord and all the laws. The entire nation responded in a single voice, saying: 'All the things that the Lord has spoken – we will do and we will hear'" (24:3). Moses there speaks to *Benei Yisrael* about two areas: "the words of the Lord," and "the laws" (*mishpatim*). "*Mishpatim*" clearly refers to the laws presented before this narrative, in the section that begins, "*Ve'eileh hamishpatim*" (21:1). To what, however, does "*divrei HaShem*" ("*words of the Lord*") refer? Seemingly, the Torah refers here to the verse that introduces the Ten Commandments: "God spoke all these *words*, saying." If so, we can draw evidence from the *mishpatim* to the Commandments. The *mishpatim* were most certainly spoken only to Moses, as the Torah tells, "and Moses entered the mist…. The Lord said to Moses: 'So shall you say to *Benei Yisrael*…. And these are the *mishpatim* that you shall present to them.'" Moses was instructed from the outset to convey to the people the laws that he now receives from God, and this is what he does. Presumably, this is true also of the *divrei HaShem*: "Moses came and spoke to the people all the words of the Lord and all the laws." Seemingly, until now only Moses heard God's words, and now he conveys to the people what he heard.

Moreover, the ambiguity of the introductory verse to the Commandments requires some explanation. In all instances where the Torah relates that God spoke, it informs us to whom He spoke. Here, however, the Torah writes simply that He spoke: "God spoke all these things, saying…."

In order to understand the progression of events in this narrative, I would suggest the following theory, and that we read the verses in this light. There is an inherent contradiction in the verses' description of the nation's conduct. Three times in chapter 19, God sends Moses to admonish the people not to approach the mountain, lest they be harmed as a result:

You shall restrict the people around [the mountain], saying: "Beware of ascending the mountain." (v. 12)

The Lord said to Moses: "Descend and warn the people, lest they burst forth towards the Lord to see." (v. 21)

The Lord said to him: "Go, descend … and the kohanim and the people shall not burst forth to ascend." (v. 24)

The Almighty's primary concern is the possibility of "*pen yehersu*" – "lest they burst forth," and approach the sacred mountain. God's revelation arouses both feelings of closeness and spiritual yearning, and a degree of curiosity and tension. It causes the people to want to come forward. Even when Moses refuses to descend to warn the people, claiming that the people are already barred from ascending the mountain, having already been admonished to keep back (v. 23), God insists that he go and issue the warning.

But this does not correspond to what is described in the verses following the Commandments: "The entire nation beheld the sounds.... The people saw and they trembled, and they stood from afar" (20:15–16). The people's reaction proves that the main problem was specifically awe, which is manifest as an actual, existential fear and a desire to flee, rather than overabundant "love" which arouses a desire to burst forth towards the sacred ground. How, then, can we understand God's concern?

We will attempt to find a key to the solution in the corresponding verses in Deuteronomy, where Moses describes *Ma'amad Har Sinai*:

The Lord spoke with you at the mountain face-to-face from amidst the fire. (Deut. 5:4)

I was standing in between the Lord and you at that time to tell you the Lord's word, *because you were afraid* of the fire and did not ascend the mountain. (5:5)

In verse 4, he asserts that God spoke "face-to-face," whereas in verse 5 he tells that he himself served as the intermediary bringing God's word to the nation. Each verse could be stated independently, but presenting the two together is inherently contradictory.

We can read the verses as follows: God wanted to speak with

the nation directly, but the people's fear resulted in Moses' mediation between them and God. Moses' role as intermediary apparently had physical implications, as well. "Face-to-face" communication means closeness, and if Moses served as intermediary, then God spoke to only him from up close, "face-to-face," whereas the people stood from afar. It stands to reason that although the nation *de facto* stood from afar and was not privileged to behold a direct revelation, the revelation is nevertheless considered to have occurred "face-to-face." Our memory can portray the revelation at Sinai as a revelation to the entire nation, even if, factually speaking, this never materialized.

Verse 5 concludes with the word "*lemor*" (saying), which introduces the Ten Commandments, presented immediately thereafter. It possibly serves as the conclusion of verse 4, which would then be read as, "The Lord spoke with you...face-to-face...saying: 'I am the Lord your God.'" If so, then the explanation in verse 5 should be read as a parenthetical remark.

Either way, according to these verses, the Ten Commandments were said after the nation expressed its fear, and Moses served as intermediary bringing God's word to the people. It is thus clear from Deuteronomy that God did not speak at all directly to the nation; the Commandments were all conveyed through Moses' mediation.

In light of this information from Deuteronomy, let us now suggest the sequence of events as portrayed in Exodus, working off the assumption that the verses do not necessarily reflect the chronological sequence.

In my opinion, verses 15–18 of chapter 20 in Exodus belong (chronologically) after verse 19 of chapter 19. The chronological presentation would thus appear as follows:

> The sound of the shofar continued with great force; Moses would speak and the Almighty would answer him in a voice.

Immediately thereafter,

> The entire nation beheld the sounds, the torches, the sound of the shofar, and the smoking mountain; the people saw and they trembled.

The nation's fear and request that Moses convey to them God's word preceded the Commandments and resulted from the sounds, torches and shofar blast described in the earlier verses ("And Mount Sinai was entirely in smoke"). The people, who know that God will soon speak, are frightened and ask that He speak only with Moses. Moses assuages their fears, and it is unclear whether he grants their request. If we insert the Ten Commandments immediately at this point, a reasonable progression emerges:

> Moses said to the people: "Have no fear...."
> The people stood from afar, and Moses entered the mist, where God was.
> God spoke all these words, saying: "I am the Lord."

In other words, read 20:15–18 as having preceded the pronouncement of the Commandments, as they parallel Moses' description in Deuteronomy of what transpired before the pronouncement.

God ultimately did not speak to the nation, and spoke only to Moses, due to the people's fear, as explicitly described in Deuteronomy. The verses leave two points unclear:

1. The introductory verse does not clarify to whom God speaks;
2. Did Moses grant the people's request that he serve as intermediary, or did he simply assuage their fears?

We can explain this ambiguity according to the two levels that exist in the description in Deuteronomy. The Torah wishes to convey the message that, fundamentally, the Ten Commandments were indeed said at *Ma'amad Har Sinai* to the entire nation. Factually speaking, this did not happen, and the nation instead stood from afar. The ambiguity in the description enables us to accept both premises: on the one hand, the Commandments were proclaimed to the people (again, this is the impression given by the flow of the narrative, without being mentioned explicitly), while at the same time, the people were frightened and therefore God did not speak to them.

Ḥazal's distinction between the first two and final eight

Commandments, while not accommodating the simple reading of the verses, beautifully expresses the theory we have proposed. God indeed spoke to the people, but He spoke very little, perhaps just enough to confirm the occurrence of revelation. That small amount that He spoke contained the expression of *"Anokhi"* and its derivative prohibition – "You shall have no other gods" – but no more. Anything considered a mitzva that does not necessarily flow from the actual knowledge of revelation was said – according to Ḥazal – by Moses, and not by God.

In this same fashion we can perhaps explain the awkward sequence of the verses. If the nation's request indeed preceded the Commandments, why does the Torah present it later? We may suggest two answers:

1. In light of what we said earlier, we might similarly explain that the Torah seeks to create the impression that the Commandments were indeed proclaimed directly to the people from God, an impression that would not have emerged had the nation's request been recorded before the Commandments. In Deuteronomy, Moses achieves this goal by employing contradictory descriptions (v. 4–5, as explained above).
2. Presenting the nation's concerns before the Commandments would have made the narrative incomprehensible. It would be impossible for the Torah to tell of God's requests that Moses warn the people not to ascend the mountain if at that moment the nation flees. Placing the commandments in between these events gives the impression of a distance in time that is necessary for the cohesiveness of the narrative.

Of course, in truth this difficulty is indeed very troubling. God's instruction to Moses to warn the people appears to contradict the description of the nation's fears, and also appears to undermine our approach.

To resolve this difficulty, let us address another angle that we have yet to consider. Throughout the entirety of chapter 19, the Torah refers to God with the divine name of *Havaya* (*Y-H-v-H*). When recording God's words and actions, it employs only this name, the name in which God appeared to Moses during the story of the exodus. For example (we will employ the term *HaShem* to represent the name *Havaya*): "*HaShem* calls to him from the mountain"; "All that *HaShem* spoke, we will do"; "the nation's words to *HaShem*"; "*HaShem* said"; "because *HaShem* had descended upon it with fire." In all these instances, the Torah employs specifically the divine name of *Havaya*.

In the first section of chapter 20 (until verse 18), in contrast, God is referred to as either *Elokim* or *HaShem Elokim*: "*Elokim* spoke"; "Let not *Elokim* speak with us"; "it was in order to test you that *Elokim* has come"; "entered the mist, where *Elokim* was." In the Ten Commandments themselves, the reference to *HaShem Elokim* appears quite frequently: "*Anokhi HaShem Elokekha*"; "*ki HaShem Elokekha*" "*Shabbat laShem Elokekha*," etc.

Very often, a shift in the terms used in reference to the Almighty indicates that the Torah addresses the given subject from different perspectives, and even tells the same story from two different viewpoints. In these instances, we have two parallel descriptions of a single event, told from two differing perspectives.

It would seem that here, too, the story of *Matan Torah* contains two different, concurrent processes. The beginning of the narrative, in chapter 19, includes both perspectives. God here declares two things: the establishment of a covenant between Him and the people, with the condition of "if you keep My covenant"; and His plan to reveal Himself to Moses, in order for the people to listen to and believe in Moses' prophecy, through which the Torah will be given and regarding which God said earlier, "If you indeed heed My voice."

This description includes both the instruction to create a boundary around the mountain, and the fact that "All the people in the camp trembled." Verse 18 describes God's revelation: "Mount Sinai was entirely in smoke, because the Lord had descended upon it with fire.... Moses would speak, and God would answer him in a voice." In effect, the revelation reaches its peak at this point. Nowhere until this point has the Torah led us to anticipate that God will turn to the nation and speak to them; and if we read only the verses written with the divine name of *Havaya*, this in fact never occurs.

The sequence of the events, according to the perspective of the

Name *Havaya*, is as follows: God descends upon the mountain, Moses speaks, and the voice of God responds from behind him like an echo. People hear actual speech only from Moses, but an echo-sound of the *Shekhina* creates the impression that indeed God's word is in his mouth, as if God speaks with them. Some time thereafter, God tells Moses to descend from the mountain and issue a warning, the reason being, presumably, that this communication would last for quite some time, such that even if the people were initially frightened, they are now right beneath the mountain ("Moses brought the nation to greet God from the camp, and they took their place beneath the mountain"), and the moment they grow accustomed and the initial shock subsides, they may burst forth and ascend towards God.

Moses ultimately comes down the mountain and issues this warning to the nation, as it says, "Moses descended to the people and said to them." The Torah does not clarify what he said to the people, because it is self-explanatory. Thus, the nation hears from Moses what God had commanded him, and Moses returns to the top of the mountain to hear God's words to him, which are apparently no longer said with sounds and lightening, but rather from a mist. (This once again reinforces the concern that the people might seek to ascend the mountain.) God then immediately begins speaking to Moses:

> The Lord said to Moses, "So shall you say to *Benei Yisrael*: 'You have seen that I spoke with you from the heavens. Do not make with me gods of silver or gods of gold.'"

This verse refers not to the Ten Commandments, but rather to what is written before the Commandments: "Moses would speak and God would answer in a voice." It was therefore necessary to command the people not to fashion gold or silver images. According to the simple sequence of the Torah's presentation, this command unnecessarily repeats the second of the Commandments: "You shall not make for yourself an idol, any image." But now we understand the correct sequence. *The mitzvot are said only to Moses.* But once the people witness that God speaks to Moses, anything that Moses tells them subsequently will be regarded as God's direct word to the nation. It must again be emphasized that according to the narrative using only the name of *Havaya*, the primary concern involved the prospect of the nation's ascent to the mountain upon the conclusion of the main event, where Moses speaks and God answers him in a voice; this event does not include the Ten Commandments at all.

If we read the continuation of chapter 19 according to the verses employing the divine name of *Elokim* (20:1–18), a different picture emerges. After the nation sees the sounds and torches, they are frightened and do not want God to speak to them directly. Why were they afraid of God's direct communication? It appears that their fear stemmed from what God said: "If you indeed heed My voice." They anticipate hearing God's command, but are concerned that He might issue it to them directly. Moses understood their concerns and calmed their fears, and they then retreated and stood at a distance (20:18), while Moses approached the mist and heard God proclaim the Ten Commandments. According to this presentation, the Ten Commandments were indeed proclaimed at this point, but only to Moses, and not to the people.

The two parallel accounts, told with two different names of God, express two different, otherwise self-contained perspectives on what transpired.

According to the narrative employing the name *Havaya*, the revelation's primary objective, as stated, is *establishing the belief in Moses' prophecy*. To this end, the Ten Commandments are unnecessary. The moment the nation is convinced and believes, God speaks to Moses alone and conveys to him the mitzvot mentioned at the end of the *parasha* (regarding the altar) and in *Parashat Mishpatim*. The divine name of *Havaya* always expresses the notion of *prophecy and closeness to God*. The primary concern is that the sense of closeness to God felt during this event will result in the nation's desire to approach God – thus the need for boundaries and warnings.

According to the narrative using the name of *Elokim*, the Ten Commandments indeed stand at the center of this event, but they are said only to Moses and not to the people. In the story as told in the name of *Elokim*, the purpose of the revelation is in fact the establishment of a covenant regarding the words of God: "Now, if you indeed heed My voice and observe My covenant." The Ten Commandments form the basis of this covenant; the covenant depends on their observance. According to what is told from the perspective of the name of *Elokim*, God had, in fact, intended to speak directly to the people, but their fear and request to stand back resulted in Moses' serving as intermediary to convey to them God's word. Indeed, the name *Elokim* always signifies the notion of justice and covenant.

The development of fear among the people likewise accommodates the name *Elokim*. The revelation of *Elokim* is a source of *fear* – a concept closely related to the name *Elokim*. The nation is distanced, and this distance remains even at the end of *Ma'amad Har Sinai*.

Moshe Rabbenu serves a moderating role with respect to both perspectives. He is charged with preventing a destructive outburst of love, from the perspective of *Havaya*, and he likewise faces the task of assuaging the nation's fear and assuring them that God does not wish upon them evil, and has rather revealed Himself "in order that His fear be upon you, so that you do not sin."

The story, as presented before us, bridges these two ideal possibilities. Theoretically, each story could be told separately, but practically, it all occurs simultaneously. The Almighty and His names are all one, and thus His revelation includes all the objectives, and generates both love and fear. It stands to reason that the nation's reactions to the revelation were mixed, and included both the desire to escape from and run towards it. The Torah is not interested in presenting a detailed account of what transpired among each group in the nation or in the heart of each and every individual. Rather, it seeks to give the essential message, and hence the arrangement in which the story is told, which synthesizes the two separate progressions.

The two objectives of the revelation are described in chronological sequence at the beginning of chapter 19, one following the other: First – the establishment of the covenant, and second, "they will believe in you forever." Thereafter begins the revelation, and the Torah describes specifically the concern of overabundant closeness, which is entirely true – from one perspective. The concern for excessive closeness obviously does not negate God's revelation and speech, and God is therefore described as the one proclaiming the Commandments, such that one could conclude that they are proclaimed to the entire nation. Only after the proclamation of the Commandments does the Torah mention the problem that arose from the *Elokim* perspective of revelation – the fear that gripped the people. The description of this problem before the proclamation of the Commandments could have potentially diminished the force of the covenant, the essence of which entails the fulfillment of God's commands. The Torah presented this in such a way as to lend the Ten Commandments their status as the very basis of our covenant with God; hence the importance of their having been proclaimed specifically by God Himself.

In summary, I once saw a remark cited in the name of Rabbi Menaḥem Mendel of Rimanov concerning the enlarged letter *Aleph* in the word *Anokhi* with which the Ten Commandments begin. He commented that only the *Aleph* was heard by the people. The *Aleph* represents the voice that marks the very beginning of the utterance. According to this remark, only the endless, undefined voice is what was heard directly from the Almighty. The constriction of that sound into actual words, in the sense of a "utensil" lending the sound shape and form, belongs strictly to the realm of prophecy.

Ma'amad Har Sinai:
The Love and Fear Dialectic

Rav Menachem Leibtag

I. INTRODUCTION

Thus far, the Torah has presented the story of the exodus and how God has fulfilled His covenant with the *Avot*. However, that covenant included not only a promise of redemption, but also the promise that the Israelites would become God's special nation in Canaan. As they now travel to establish that nation in that Promised Land, God brings them to Mount Sinai in order to teach them the mitzvot that will help make them His special nation.

Therefore, the primary purpose of their arrival at *Har Sinai* was to receive God's laws. Nevertheless, the Torah describes in no less detail the experience of how those laws were given. We will undertake a careful reading of chapter 19 (i.e. the events that precede the Ten Commandments), highlighting its complexities, in an attempt to better appreciate *Hazal's* understanding of *Ma'amad Har Sinai*.

II. THE PROPOSAL

Chapter 19 opens as *Benei Yisrael* arrive at Mount Sinai – presumably to receive the Torah. However, before the Torah is given, God first summons Moses to the mountain, instructing him to relay a certain message to the people. Reviewing these verses, we note how they form a "proposal":

> [T]hus shall you say to *Beit Yaakov* and tell *Benei Yisrael*:
>
> "You have seen what I have done to Egypt ... so *now*:
>
> IF – you will *obey* Me faithfully and keep My *covenant* ... and be my treasured nation, for all the Land is Mine.
>
> THEN – You shall be for Me a *mamlekhet kohanim vegoy kadosh* (a kingdom of priests and a holy nation)." (19:3–6)

The "if / then" clause proves that these instructions constitute a proposal (and not just a decree) – to which *Benei Yisrael* must answer either 'yes' or 'no'. And that's exactly what we find:

> And the people answered together and said, "Everything that God has spoken we shall keep," and Moses brought the people's answer back to God. (v. 8)

Clearly, Moshe Rabbenu acts as the middle-man – who must relay the people's answer to this proposal back to God.

Let's take a minute to discuss the meaning of the two sides of this proposition.

The first part of the IF clause – "if you will obey Me" – makes sense, as God must first clarify if *Benei Yisrael* are indeed now ready to follow His laws; in contrast to their previous refusals (see Ezek. 20:5–9; Ex. 6:9, 15:26). However, the precise meaning of the second clause – "and if you will keep My covenant" – is uncertain, for it is not clear if this covenant refers to something old – i.e. "*Berit Avot*"; or something new – i.e. "*Berit Sinai*."

It would be difficult to explain that the word 'covenant' in this verse refers to "*Berit Avot*," for *Berit Avot* doesn't seem to include any specific action that *Benei Yisrael* must keep. More likely, it refers to "*Berit*

Sinai" – whose details will soon be revealed, should *Benei Yisrael* accept this proposal.

However, this ambiguity may be intentional, for this forthcoming *Berit Sinai* could be understood as an upgrade of *Berit Avot*. In other words, *Berit Avot* discusses the very basic framework of a relationship (see Gen. 17:7–8), while *Berit Sinai* will contain the detailed laws which will make that original covenant more meaningful.

If so, then the proposition could be understood as follows: *IF Benei Yisrael* agree to obey whatever God may command, and to remain faithful to this covenant, and act as His treasured nation (see Ex. 19:5) – *THEN*, the result will be that *Benei Yisrael* will serve as God's model nation, representing Him before all other nations [a *"mamlekhet kohanim vegoy kadosh,"* see 19:6].

As a prerequisite for *Matan Torah* (the giving of the Torah), *Benei Yisrael* must both confirm their readiness to obey God's commandments while recognizing that these mitzvot will facilitate their achievement of the very purpose of God's covenant with them.

Whereas a covenant requires the willful consent of both sides, this section concludes with *Benei Yisrael's* collective acceptance of these terms (see again 19:7–8).

Now that *Benei Yisrael* had accepted God's proposal, the next step should be for them to receive the specific mitzvot (i.e. the laws that they just agreed to observe). However, before those laws can be given, there are some technical details that must be ironed out, concerning *how Benei Yisrael* will receive these laws. Note how the next verse describes God's plans for how He intends to convey these mitzvot:

> And God said to Moses, "I will come to you in the thickness of a cloud, in order that the people hear *when I speak with you,* and in order that they believe in you [i.e. that you are My spokesman] forever." (19:9)

God plans to use Moshe Rabbenu as an intermediary to convey His laws to *Benei Yisrael,* consistent with Moses' role as His liaison heretofore. Nonetheless, God insists that the people will overhear His communication with Moses, so that they believe that these laws truly originate from God, and not from Moses.

In the middle of verse 9 we encounter our first major difficulty in the flow of events. Note that God has just informed Moses of how He plans to convey His laws. Hence, we would expect Moses to convey this message to *Benei Yisrael* (just as he did in 19:7). However, something very strange takes place:

> then Moses reported the *people's* words to God.

The second half of the verse seems to omit an entire clause – it never tells us the people's response. Instead, it just says that Moses relayed the people's response back to God, without telling us what the people said!

III. BE PREPARED!

This question is so glaring (and obvious) that Rashi, taking for granted that the reader realized this problem, provides an answer based on the Midrash that fills in the missing details:

> "*Et divrei ha'am* (the words of the people)" – The people responded: "We want to hear from *You* [God] directly, for one cannot compare hearing from a *shali'aḥ* (messenger) to hearing from the King himself. We want to see our King!"

Note how Rashi adds an entire line to this narrative. According to his interpretation, *Benei Yisrael* do not accept God's original plan that they would hear the mitzvot via Moses. Instead, they demand to hear them directly – from God Himself!

What allows Rashi to offer such a bold interpretation?

There is an apparent contradiction between God's original plan in 19:9 and what appears to be His new plan, as described in the next two verses:

> And God told Moses, "Go to the people and get them ready…for on the third day God will reveal Himself *in view of all the people on Mount Sinai*." (19:10–11)

God commands *Benei Yisrael* to ready themselves, for in three days they will actually see God. This declaration that He plans to reveal himself before the entire nation suggests that God now plans to convey His mitzvot directly to the people. These instructions appear to describe a new plan for *Matan Torah*.

From now on, we will refer to the original plan (Commandments via Moses) as *Plan A* (based on 19:9), and to the new plan (Commandments Direct) as *Plan B* (based on 19:11).

Rashi claims that God's suggestion of *Plan B* stems from the people's unwillingness to accept *Plan A* – for *Benei Yisrael* want to hear the Commandments directly.

This change of plan explains why the people now require three days of preparation. In order to prepare for this direct encounter, *Benei Yisrael* must first attain a higher level of spiritual readiness, as reflected in the three-day preparation period. Note how the details of this preparation continue until 19:15.

In 19:12–13, Moses is commanded to cordon off the entire area surrounding the mountain. In 19:14–15, Moses relays these commands to the people. Hence, from now on, we refer to this section (19:9–15) as "Preparation."

Are *Benei Yisrael* capable of reaching this level? Are they truly ready to receive the *Dibrot* directly from God? If so, why did God not suggest this direct encounter in the first place? If not, why does God now agree to their request?

To answer these questions, we must analyze the verses that follow to determine which of these two divine plans actually unfolds.

IV. RUNAWAY BRIDE

According to the new plan, on day three God should reveal Himself on Mount Sinai and speak the *Dibrot* directly to the entire nation. Let's continue now in chapter 19 and see what happens:

> And it came to pass on the third day in the morning, and there were loud sounds and lightening, and a *thick cloud* on the mountain, and the *shofar* sounded very strong, and all the people in the camp became frightened. (v. 16)

Apparently, *Benei Yisrael* never came to Mount Sinai that morning! Instead, they were so frightened of God's awesome revelation that they remained in the camp. This explains the next verse, where Moses goes back to the camp, and brings everyone to the foot of the mountain (see 19:17). Now it's time to try again:

> And Mount Sinai was full of smoke, for God had descended upon it in fire, and its smoke was like a furnace, and the entire mountain shook violently. (19:18)

This verse certainly describes God's revelation, and it appears to follow according to *Plan B*. Note how God *descends* onto the mountain (note the word *"vayered"* in both 19:11 and 19:18). Nevertheless, one could also understand the intense smoke as reflective of the protective cloud described in 19:9 (*Plan A*).

The stage has now been set for *Matan Torah*. The people are standing at the foot of Mount Sinai, and God has revealed Himself upon Mount Sinai. Therefore, the next verse should describe God's proclamation of the Ten Commandments.

> The sound of the shofar grew louder and louder; as Moses would speak, God would answer him with a *kol*. (19:19)

This verse is quite ambiguous, for it does not give us even a clue as to *what* Moses was saying or what God was answering. It is not even clear as to *whom* Moses is speaking, to God or to the people!

If Moses is speaking to the people, then this verse would be describing how he conveyed the Commandments. If so, then Moses speaking and God responding with a *"kol"* implies that the Commandments were given according to *Plan A*, as Moses serves as the intermediary.

However, if *"Moshe yedaber"* (19:19) refers to Moses speaking to God, then it not at all clear what their conversation is about; nor can we make any deduction in regard to how the Commandments were given.

V. PLAN B – MYSTERIOUSLY MISSING

Rashi's commentary on this verse is simply amazing. He claims that Moses is speaking to the people, telling them the Commandments. However, what's amazing is Rashi's explanation that the clause "*Moshe yedaber*" describes the transmission of the *last eight* Commandments, but not the first two. This is because Rashi understands that the first two *Dibrot* were given *directly* from God – in accordance with *Plan B* – while the last eight were given via Moses – in accordance with *Plan A*. As this verse (19:19) describes *Plan A*, it could only be referring to the transmission of the last eight *Dibrot*.[1]

Note that according to Rashi, chapter 19 intentionally omits two key events relating to *Plan B*:

1. *Benei Yisrael's* original request for *Plan B* (in 19:9)
2. The story of the two Commandments given at the level of *Plan B*

For some thematic reason that remains unclear, chapter 19 prefers to omit these two important details, leaving us with the impression that *Plan B* may have never taken place!

Ramban rejects Rashi's interpretation of 19:19 (as do many other commentators), arguing that 19:19 does not describe how the *Dibrot* were

---

1. As we saw, Rashi, following the *Mekhilta*, understands this verse as referring to the procedure of the transmission of the *Aseret HaDibrot* (Ten Commandments). Ramban disagrees, claiming that it describes the manner in which the laws in the following verses – concerning the "limitation" – were presented. This is the general approach of Abarbanel and Rabbenu Yosef Bekhor Shor, as well. Ibn Ezra claims that the verse does not reveal what it is that Moses says here, but it definitely does not refer to the *Aseret HaDibrot*. The point of the verse is to stress that despite the overpowering sound of the shofar, it did not interfere with Moses' conversation with God. The *Or HaHayyim* writes that Moses here spoke words of praise to God, and He would then respond. According to all these views, this verse does not refer to *Aseret HaDibrot*, as Rashi claims.

   A particularly interesting interpretation is suggested by the Malbim, Netziv and *HaDrash VeHaIyun* (though with some variation). They claim that the sound of the shofar proclaimed, "*Moshe yedaber veHaElokim ya'anenu bekol.*" In other words, they place a colon after the word "*me'od*" in this verse. The shofar blast thus informed the people that Moses will serve as the intermediary between God and *Benei Yisrael* in transmitting the Torah.

given. Instead, Ramban explains that *"Moshe yedaber"* describes the conversation between God and Moses that immediately follows in 19:20–25:

> God descended upon Mount Sinai to the top of the Mountain and summoned Moses to the top of the Mountain, and Moses ascended.... Then God told Moses: "Go down and warn the people lest they break through toward God to see, and many of them will perish. And even the kohanim who are permitted to come closer must prepare themselves." (19:20–22)

According to Ramban, this additional warning is given *before Matan Torah,* and serves as the final preparation before the *Dibrot* are given. However, according to Rashi's interpretation, it remains unclear when, where, and why this conversation (in 19:20–25) takes place.

This final warning clearly reflects the mode of transmission that we have referred to as *Plan A* – God will appear only to Moses (at the top of the mountain), while everyone else must keep their distance down below. Only Moses will be privy to witness the descent of the *Shekhina* onto the *top* of the mountain, while *Benei Yisrael* are prohibited from ascending to see, "lest they die."

As this section describes how God is now limiting His revelation to the top of the mountain, we refer from now on to this section (19:20–25) as "Limitation." Chapter 19 now divides into four distinct sections:

I.   Proposition (19:1–8)
II. Preparation (19:9–15)
III. Revelation (19:16–19)
IV. Limitation (19:20–25)

What happened? Has God reverted to *Plan A* (that Moses is to act as an intermediary)? On the other hand, if *Plan B* remains in operation, why does God restrict His revelation to the *top* of the mountain? Could this be considered some sort of compromise? There appears to have been a change in plans, but why?[2]

---

2. An interesting variation on this theme is suggested by the Malbim. According to

Even though chapter 19 does not seem to provide any explanation for what motivated this change, a story found later in chapter 20 seems to provide us with all the missing details.

VI. POST-SINAI TREPIDATION

Immediately after the Torah records the Ten Commandments, we find yet another story concerning what transpired:

> And the people all saw the *kolot*, the torches, the sound of the shofar and the mountain smoking; the people saw and retreated and stood at a distance. And they told Moses: "You speak to us, and we will listen to you, but God should not should speak to us, lest we die."
>
> Moses responded saying: "Do not be fearful, for God is coming to test you and instill fear within you so that you will not sin."
>
> But the people stood at a distance, and Moses [alone] entered the cloud where God was. (20:15–18)

This short narrative provides us with a perfect explanation why God chooses to revert from *Plan B* back to *Plan A*: the people changed

his explanation, *Plan B*, which the people requested, involved their hearing directly from God the entire Torah, not only the Ten Commandments. (Ramban – 20:14 – writes that *Benei Yisrael* feared that this was God's plan, though in actuality He had never intended to transmit the entire Torah to them directly.) God initially agrees, but their sense of terror upon experiencing the thunder and lightning signaling God's descent onto the mountain (19:16), and their consequent hesitation to go to the mountain ("*vayotzei Moshe*" – 19:17), reflected their unworthiness for this lengthy exposure to divine revelation. God therefore presented directly either the Ten Commandments or the first two. Only Moses received the rest of the mitzvot directly from God.

We should note that in contradistinction to our understanding of Rashi, the Maharal of Prague (*Gur Aryeh* on 19:9) explains Rashi to mean that Moses simply confirms God's plan. God tells him that He plans on revealing Himself to Moses as the nation hears, and Moses replies, "Indeed, this is what the people want." Apparently, the Maharal understands "*hinei Anokhi ba elekha be'av he'anan*" to refer to the same level of revelation that actually occurs, such that there was never any change of plans. (According to the Maharal's approach, it turns out that there is no difference between the approaches of Rashi and Ramban.)

their minds! They were frightened and overwhelmed by this intense experience of divine revelation. But why is this story recorded in chapter 20, and not chapter 19?

Indeed, Ramban does place this story in the middle of chapter 19. Despite his general reluctance towards rearranging biblical chronology, Ramban (on 20:14–15) explains that this entire section (20:15–18) took place earlier, before *Matan Torah*. Based on textual and thematic similarities between 20:15–18 and 19:16–19 (and a problematic parallel in Deuteronomy 5:20–28), Ramban concludes that the events described in 20:15–18 took place before *Matan Torah*, and should be read together with 19:16–18.

Thus, according to Ramban, the people's request to hear from Moses (and not from God) that took place within 19:16–18 explains the need for the 'Limitation' section that follows immediately afterward in 20:19–25.

Rashi and Ḥizkuni offer a different interpretation. They agree with Ramban that 20:15–18 – the Fear Story – is out of place, but they disagree concerning where to put it. While Ramban places this story *before Matan Torah*, Rashi and Ḥizkuni (on 20:15) claim that it took place *during Matan Torah, between* the first two and last eight commandments.[3]

VII. THE TEN COMMANDMENTS: FIRST OR THIRD PERSON

This creative solution solves yet another problem – why the Ten Commandments shift from first to third person after the second commandment. Whereas the first two commandments (20:2–5) are written in the first person, indicating that God conveyed them *directly* to the people (reflective of *Plan B*), the last eight commandments (20:6–14) are written in the third person, suggesting a less direct form of communication (reflective of *Plan A*). This reflects Ḥazal's explanation that: "*Anokhi veLo Yihyeh Lakhem, mipi HaGevura shema'um*" – the first two commandments were heard directly from God (*Makkot* 24a).

---

3. Ibn Ezra (see 20:15) takes an opposite approach, maintaining that the fear story is recorded right where it belongs; it took place only after *Matan Torah*. Therefore, the people heard all Ten Commandments directly from God, as mandated by *Plan B*.

This explanation has a clear advantage over Ramban's, as it justifies the transplantation of the "Fear Story" (20:15–18) from its proper chronological location to after the Commandments. Since this story took place *during* the Ten Commandments, the Torah could not record it beforehand. On the other hand, it could not have been recorded where it belongs, for the Torah does not want to break up the Ten Commandments. Therefore, the Torah records the "Fear Story" as a type of appendix to the Ten Commandments, explaining afterward what happened while they were given.

Although we have suggested several solutions to problems raised by chapters 19 and 20, a much more basic question arises: why can't the Torah be more precise? Why does the Torah appear to intentionally obscure the details of such an important event in our history?

VIII. *AHAVA* AND *YIRA*

One could suggest that this ambiguity is intentional, as it reflects the dialectic nature of man's encounter with God.

Man, in search of God, constantly faces a certain tension. On the one hand, he must constantly strive to come as close to God as possible (*"ahava"* – the love of God). On the other hand, he must constantly retain an awareness of God's greatness and recognize his own shortcomings and unworthiness (*"yira"* – the fear of God). Awed by God's infinity and humbled by his own imperfection, man must keep his distance (see Deut. 5:25–26).

God's original plan for *Matan Torah* was realistic. Recognizing man's inability to directly confront the *Shekhina*, God intends to use Moses as an intermediary (*Plan A*). *Benei Yisrael*, eager to become active covenantal partners, express their desire to come as close as possible to God. They want to encounter the *Shekhina* directly, without any mediating agent (*Plan B*).

Could God say no to this sincere expression of *ahavat HaShem*? Of course not! Yet, on the other hand, answering yes could place the people in tremendous danger, as they must rise to the highest levels of spirituality to deserve such a direct, unmediated manifestation of God.

While *Plan B* may reflect a more ideal encounter, *Plan A* reflects a more realistic one. One could suggest that by presenting the details with such ambiguity, the Torah emphasizes the need to find the proper balance between realism and idealism when serving God.

God is well aware of *Benei Yisrael's* unworthiness to encounter the Divine at the highest level. Nevertheless, He encourages them to aspire to their highest potential. As *Benei Yisrael* struggle to maintain the proper balance between *ahava* and *yira*, God must guide and they must strive.

Our study of *Parashat Yitro* has shown us that what actually happened at *Ma'amad Har Sinai* remains unclear. However, what could have happened remains man's eternal challenge.

The Waters of Sinai

Rav Chanoch Waxman

I. INTRODUCTION

Right before the revelation of the Ten Commandments, God gives Moses some last-minute instructions. After the preliminary negotiations (19:3–9), after the three-day preparatory period (19:10–15), and after Moses has already escorted the people to the mountain and ascended (19:16–20), God tells him to go back down:

> And God said to Moses: "Go down, warn the people, lest they break through to God to see and many of them perish. And also the priests, who come near God, must sanctify themselves, lest God break out against them." (19:22–23)

These last-minute instructions seem to come as somewhat of a surprise to Moses. After all, as part of the command of the three-day preparation period, God has already ordered Moses to set boundaries around the mountain (19:12). The people have already been told "not to go up onto the mountain" or "touch the border." Violation of the prohibition carries the death penalty (19:12–13). If so, why does God need to reiterate the prohibition and the apparent danger of its neglect at the very last minute?

This sense of surprise animates Moses' reaction to God's orders. Moses replies, "The people cannot come up onto Mount Sinai," and "You have already warned us to set boundaries around the mountain and make it holy" (19:23).

In response, God reiterates his orders one last time:

> And God said to him: "Go, get down and then you shall come up, you and Aaron, but do not let the people and the priests break through to come up to God, lest He break out against them." (19:24)

Sufficiently chastised and ever the obedient servant, Moses descends the mountain and informs the people (19:25).

While Moses may have swallowed his sense of surprise at God's last-minute instructions, that would not be the proper response for us, the readers of the story. God's double reiteration of the need for the people not to encroach upon the mountain (19:21–25) seems to break up the flow of the narrative. After Moses' ascent to the mountain (19:20), we expect him to receive the Ten Commandments. Instead, we find the "prohibition of encroachment." Consequently, when the Ten Commandments finally do appear, they seem both anti-climactic and intrusive. Moses is now at the bottom of the mountain reiterating the prohibition of encroachment (19:25). Suddenly, without preface and without bothering to mention Moses' again ascending the mountain, the Torah begins to tell us about God's speaking the Commandments (20:1).

Moreover, the flow of chapter 19 seems to mitigate against the possibility of the people breaking through to "see" God. They have already been warned. More importantly, earlier on in the chapter, the Torah depicts them as "trembling" at the sight and sounds of the thunder, lightning and thick cloud upon the mountain (19:16). Moses must "bring out" the people for their meeting with God (19:17). It seems hard to imagine that these very same trembling people, who have already been warned on pain of death not to approach the mountain, and who must be coaxed into approaching the terrifying presence of God, will suddenly break through and try to "see" God.

Finally, the actions of the people upon hearing God's words further highlight the problem of God's last-minute warning. Immediately after God's stating of the Ten Commandments (20:1–14), the Torah reports the people's reaction:

> And all the people saw the thunder and lightning and the sound of the shofar, and the mountain smoking, and when the people saw it, they fell back and stood at a distance. And the people said to Moses: "You speak to us and we will listen, but let not God speak with us, lest we die." (20:15–16)

Rather than rushing forward to "see" God, the people rush away from the "sight," the overwhelming sensory experience of the signs of God's presence. The people choose distance and ask Moses to serve as their intermediary. If so, what was the need for the last-minute instructions and the double reiteration of the prohibition of encroachment? Accordingly, there seems to have been no real danger of anyone plunging into the Divine Presence. What was God so concerned about?

II. SINAI – DÉJÀ VU

The narrative of the revelation at Sinai commences with the arrival of *Benei Yisrael* in the wilderness of Sinai. The Torah reports that the Israelites departed from Refidim, arrived in the wilderness of Sinai, and encamped facing "the mountain" (19:2). A cursory reading of this relatively standard travel report gives the impression that *Benei Yisrael* have arrived in a new locale, a place they have never been before.

Yet this is not exactly correct. The "mountain" across from which the people camp (19:2), and upon which God "descends" to deliver the Ten Commandments (19:18, 20), has been visited previously by Moses. Back at the burning bush, God had instructed Moses that when he redeems the people from Egypt, "You shall serve God on *this mountain*" (3:12). In other words, when Moses brings the people to Sinai, and to "the mountain" of chapter 19, he in fact brings them to the place he had first encountered God, the mountain of the burning bush. The key term "*sneh*," the unusual term for bush in the burning bush narrative, highlights this point. It constitutes a word-play on "*Sinai*" and hints at the proper name of the place.

This leads us to a crucial point. The narrative of the burning bush opens with Moses' leading his father-in-law's sheep out to the desert, to "the mountain of God, to Ḥorev" (3:1). Similarly, later on, the location of the revelation at Sinai is named Mount Ḥorev (33:6), and in recounting the revelation at Sinai in Deuteronomy, Moses repeatedly refers to Ḥorev and Mount Ḥorev (Deut. 1:6, 4:10, 5:2–5). In other words, Ḥorev, meaning dry or desolate, constitutes an alternative name for the mountain itself, or a name for the immediate desert locale of the mountain. But shockingly enough, Ḥorev is in fact a place already encountered on the journey from the Sea of Reeds to Sinai, a place already known to *Benei Yisrael*.

During their stay at Refidim, *Benei Yisrael* had quarreled with Moses and tested God (17:2, 7). They demanded water and began to question Moses' taking them out of Egypt (17:2–3). The quickly deteriorating situation is resolved by Moses' hitting the rock and bringing forth water for the people. God instructs Moses, "I will stand before you on the rock at Ḥorev and you shall hit the rock, and water will come forth and the people shall drink" (17:6). As pointed out by both Ramban and Abarbanel, when God commands Moses to "pass before the people," and "go," taking the elders and the stick with him (17:5), He in fact commands Moses to continue on just a bit further in the journey. He commands Moses to move on, at least temporarily, to Sinai, a place already known to Moses, where He has previously met Moses and will now be waiting for him. He commands Moses to produce the water out of Ḥorev itself. If so, Sinai has been previously visited not just by Moses, but by the thirsty children of Israel as well. They have all been there before.

III. BETWEEN *MASA UMERIVA* AND SINAI

The story of the revelation at Sinai told in chapter 19, and the story of the quarrel and test (*Masa uMeriva*) told in chapter 17 (17:1–7), may have far more in common than the locale of Ḥorev-Sinai.

In discussing the problem of place in the two stories, the question of where *Benei Yisrael* are located and the geographic relationship of Refidim/*Masa uMeriva* and Sinai, both Ramban and Abarbanel cite Psalm 78, a psalm describing the wilderness years:

He brought forth streams from a rock
And made them flow down like a river....
True he struck the rock and waters flowed
Streams gushed forth. (Psalms 78:16, 20)

Based upon the double reference to a rock from which a flowing stream emerged, Ramban raises the possibility, and Abarbanel concludes, that there really was no need for all of *Benei Yisrael* to visit Ḥorev-Sinai even temporarily. The people remained at a distance, back at Refidim. Only Moses and the elders passed on ahead to Ḥorev-Sinai. Moses performed the miracle and the elders, the select group, witnessed. The people remained behind and drew water from the newly created springs of Sinai, a river flowing down from Ḥorev.

Consequently, Abarbanel claims that God's command to Moses at *Masa uMeriva* to take the elders with him on his journey to Ḥorev (17:5) creates a crucial parallel to the story of Sinai, and to the general structure of Sinaitic revelation.

The Sinaitic revelation was experienced differently by three groups: Moses, an elite faction, and the people. The depiction of the revelation at Sinai included at the end of *Parashat Mishpatim* (24:1–11) constitutes the paradigm. It places Moses alone at the top of the mountain, the elite consisting of Aaron and his sons, i.e. the future priests, and the seventy elders somewhere behind Moses, lower down on the mountain, and the people down at the foot (24:1–2). Unlike the people down at the bottom who glimpse nothing of God's actual presence, the elite group "sees" and "beholds" God (24:10–11). They serve what might be thought of as a "witnessing" function.

Likewise, the first depiction of the revelation at Sinai, the story of the Ten Commandments, refers to three groups: Moses, "the priests who come near to God," and the people (19:21). While according to chapter 19, this elite group must sanctify itself (19:22) and is barred from ascending to God (19:24), the priests do seem to be treated differently than the people. While the people are explicitly barred by God in His last-minute instructions from "breaking forth to see [God]," in contrast, the "priests that *come close to God*" are merely required to "sanctify themselves" (19:21–22). The elite group is not barred from seeing. Once again, there is a three-part structure: Moses, those who are close – perhaps even close enough to see, and finally, the people.

This brings us back to the story of *Masa uMeriva*. Like the Sinai stories, the text refers to three groups: Moses, the elders-elite, and the people (17:6). Like the Sinai stories, Moses meets the Divine Presence at Sinai-Ḥorev. Like the Sinai stories, he is accompanied until the last minute – the actual meeting with the Divine Presence (i.e. the performing of the miracle) – by the elite group. Everything happens "in their sight" (17:6). The elite group witnesses. But the people do not see Moses, the Divine Presence, or the miracle. Abarbanel argues that in this proto-Sinai story, they remain behind, back in Refidim.

Thinking of the story of *Masa uMeriva* as a proto-Sinai story should clue us in to two other crucial linguistic and conceptual overlaps between the two stories. The last verse of the story of *Masa uMeriva* reads as follows:

> And he called the name of the place *Masa* and *Meriva*, because of the quarreling (*riv*) of *Benei Yisrael* and their testing (*nasotam*) of God saying, "Is God present among us or not?" (17:7)

The new name given to the spot in Refidim at which the Israelites had camped and complained literally means "Test (*Masa*) and Quarrel (*Meriva*)." It embodies Moses' interpretation of the incident. While in fact *Benei Yisrael* did not have sufficient water (17:1), their excessive pressuring of Moses, the quarrel (17:2), and the questioning of the exodus from Egypt (17:3) reflect a deeper agenda. *Benei Yisrael* doubt whether God is among them. They view the immediate provision of water at their campsite as a test of God's presence and power. God must prove Himself to the people. Any delay would strengthen the conclusion that it has been Moses, not God, leading them all along.

The term for test, the Hebrew root *n-s-h* (.נ.ס.ה), also appears in the story of the revelation at Sinai. After the people retreat in fright from the thunder, lightning, sounds and smoke which accompany God's revelation of the Ten Commandments (20:15), they request from Moses that he, rather than God, speak to them (20:16). They equate God's speaking to them with death, and request Moses as an intermediary. Moses replies:

> Do not be frightened, for God has come only in order to *test* you, and so that the fear of Him will be upon you so that you will not stray. (20:17)

Like the story of *Masa uMeriva*, the story of Sinai is a test. The purpose of God's revelation is to test the people. Whereas before the people tested God, now God tests the people.

Finally, we may note a fourth connection between the two stories. Both are fundamentally concerned with the presence of God amongst the Israelites. God's presence or lack of presence among the people constitutes the issue at stake in the test of *Masa uMeriva*. Similarly, the story of Sinai (19:1–20:18), while a narrative of lawgiving, is nevertheless primarily a story about God's presence. The story is about God's "coming" (19:9, 20:17) and "descending" (19:11, 18, 20) to Sinai, right in front of the people (19:9, 11, 20:15).

In sum, we face two stories that rather surprisingly bear much in common. They both involve Ḥorev-Sinai, and they both depict a three-part social and physical structure: Moses – elite – people. Moreover, they both involve the concept of "test" and the issue of the presence of God.

IV. GOD AND LIFE

Connecting the two stories confronts us with a crucial question: What possible meaning is conveyed by these surprising connections? How do the stories interact and contribute to one another?

One possibility can be gleaned from the commentary of Abarbanel. On his account, understanding the link between the stories depends upon understanding the symbolism of life and death in the story of *Masa uMeriva*.

Benei Yisrael find themselves in the desert without sufficient water (17:1). While they may not yet be dying of thirst, they do face imminent dehydration and death. In their lack of faith and doubt of God's presence and power, they accuse Moses of bringing them out of

Egypt to cause their deaths, the deaths of their children and the death of their cattle (17:3). The miracle that resolves the situation picks up on the life vs. death issue. It involves taking the stick with which Moses and Aaron hit the river in Egypt (17:6) and striking a rock, in order to bring forth water. In other words, the stick that had turned water into blood, i.e. life into death, will now be used to turn imminent death into life. From the dry and desolate rock of Ḥorev (which means "dry, desiccated"), Moses brings forth a gushing river of life, a stream that sustains and maintains *Benei Yisrael*.

The reversal of the symbolism of the stick causes *Benei Yisrael* to realize that it has not been the magic of Moses and his death-dealing rod that has saved them. Just as God, the ultimate power, can turn water into blood and life into death, so too He can turn rock into water and dry death into a rushing stream of life. God, the source of life, is both present and powerful.

This brings us to the reason the miracle is performed not in the camp or at its edge, but rather at Ḥorev-Sinai, a short distance away. According to Abarbanel, God utilizes the occasion of the Israelites' complaint and their proximity to Sinai to create a psychological connection between water, the source of life, and Ḥorev-Sinai. The waters which save *Benei Yisrael* flow from Sinai. Sinai constitutes the very fount of existence. The answer to the question of *Benei Yisrael* as to whether God is among them, whether His power provides them with life and sustains their existence, can be found only through journeying to Ḥorev-Sinai. The experience is meant to create a mental triangle of life, Sinai and the presence of God.

On this account, the point of the connection between the two stories is to create a yearning for Ḥorev-Sinai in the hearts and minds of *Benei Yisrael*. It is the place of God and the source of life. The story of *Masa uMeriva* constitutes a kind of proto-Sinai, a forerunner and stage in the revelation of the Torah. In a complex psychological process, God intends to transmute the instinctive association of life with water into a complex association of life with the word of God – the Torah learnt at Sinai-Ḥorev.

Alternatively, by factoring in the fourth connection between the stories, the notion of test, we may explain the link in a different fashion. At *Masa uMeriva*, *Benei Yisrael* test God. In demanding water from

Moses, they openly speculate whether "God is among us or not." Mired in their own lack of faith and religious immaturity, they present a front of desiring the presence of God. In a self-righteous and human-centered inversion of the God-man relation, they test God.

Sinai constitutes God's real answer to the problem of *Masa uMeriva*, not so much the technical problem of thirst, but the underlying dynamic of religious immaturity. He now gives *Benei Yisrael* precisely what they had asked for. He descends upon the mountain right before their very eyes and ears (19:9, 11, 20:15). He now is present among them exactly in the simple and tangible way they had claimed to desire. He is immediate and overwhelming. The parallels between our two stories serve not so much to highlight *Masa uMeriva* as a part of a preparatory process for Sinai, but rather to highlight Sinai as a reversal of *Masa uMeriva*. Before, *Benei Yisrael* had tested God and desired His presence; now, God provides them with exactly what they have claimed to want, and tests their reaction.

V. THE YEARNING FOR GOD

Let us return to the problem of God's last-minute instructions to Moses and His strange expectation that *Benei Yisrael* will break bounds and rush forward to "see" the Presence of God.

Whether we interpret the parallel between our two stories as part of a process of psychological preparation for Sinai or as a reversal of the Israelites' testing of God at *Masa uMeriva*, we need no longer wonder about God's last-minute reiteration of the prohibition of encroachment. His "expectation" of the imminent danger, that *Benei Yisrael* will rush forward and break through to "see" the very Presence of God Himself, should no longer seem mysterious.

According to Abarbanel, God has ordered events and structured the miracle of *Masa uMeriva* in order to engender a yearning for God and Sinai-Ḥorev within the hearts and minds of *Benei Yisrael*. They have been taught to associate the place and the presence of God with life itself. While they may well be temporarily jolted by the thunder, lightning and dark cloud (19:16), there exists the real danger that at the crucial moment, forgetting the fireworks and the threat of the death penalty, they will surge forth to life itself. They must be warned, and warned again.

Alternatively, on the view that Sinai constitutes a reversal of *Masa uMeriva*, a case of God's testing of *Benei Yisrael*, the last-minute warning comes not in response to imminent danger but as part of the lesson of the test. As part of the test, God acts as if *Benei Yisrael* are truly able to withstand His presence. He warns them against the religious ideal of plunging forth to greet the Divine, rather than the actual danger of their running away.

On the psychological plane, the warning may very well conjure up the gap between their previous demand for God's presence and their current attitude. Back at *Masa uMeriva*, they presented the front of desiring God's presence. It was they who were present and God who was distant. But now things are clearly different. The people are terrified by even the external special effects of God's actual presence. Upon hearing God's voice they run away. God is present and they are distant. If so, they learn the folly of their previous attitude, and their demand for the constant tangible presence of the Divine. They learn the need for the mediation of Moses, for the "reduction" of God's presence, for the invisible and not-always-immediate presence of God. They learn the need to cling to God's intangible word, the truly special effect of the revelation at Sinai.

After Revelation

Rav Alex Israel

After the climax of the Ten Commandments and the powerful revelation of God at Mount Sinai, we come back to earth with a veritable bump. The verses that immediately follow the *Ma'amad Har Sinai* thrust us from the direct experience of God to His law; from the fire, cloud and shofar sounds, into the technical world of halakhic details, as stated:

> The Lord said to Moses: "Thus shall you say to *Benei Yisrael*: 'You yourselves saw that I spoke to you from the very heavens. You shall not make with Me any gods of silver, nor shall you make for yourselves any gods of gold. Make for Me an altar of earth and sacrifice upon it your burnt offerings (*Olah*) and your peace sacrifices (*Shelamim*), your sheep and your cattle; in every place where I cause My name to be mentioned I will come to you and bless you. And if you make for Me an altar of stones, do not build it of hewn stones; for by wielding your sword (tool) upon them you have profaned them. Do not ascend My altar by steps, that your nakedness may not be exposed upon it.'" (20:19–23)

The very next verses open with a ceremonial formula: "And these are the *mishpatim* that you shall lay down before them," indicating that a new section is beginning. If so, our verses are an independent section of mitzvot which is an adjunct to the revelation of Sinai. From the introduction, "You yourselves saw that I spoke to you from the very heavens," we see that this section is clearly an epilogue to *Ma'amad Har Sinai*. But how? Why these mitzvot in particular? Are they internally connected, and how do they connect with the Ten Commandments or the revelation at Sinai in general?

Let us begin by noticing how this group of mitzvot reflects the three superlative commands commonly known as *Yehareg ve'al ya'avor*[1] – not to be transgressed even in the face of death:

Avoda Zara – The ban on gods of gold and silver;

Shefikhut Damim – The requirement that no metallic cutting tool ("a sword") be utilized in the process of construction of the altar (in rabbinic sources, the altar is a source of life, "life-giving," rather than "life-taking." The altar is the antithesis of violence);

Giluy Arayot – The concern for exposure of the body as one ascends the steps to the altar (of course, the term *"giluy arayot"* relates in its literal translation to the act of bodily exposure).

Now, despite the obvious neatness of this grouping, we should realize that this structure solves little. The foundation of each of these commandments may be found in the Ten Commandments themselves. The second commandment deals with idolatry, the sixth and seventh deal with adultery and murder. Why do we need to review these commands so soon after they have been legislated?

II. CONCLUSION OR INTRODUCTION?

Two approaches might be offered, one that sees these five verses as a sort of conclusion to the Sinai revelation, and another that perceives these mitzvot as a prelude to *Parashat Mishpatim*. Let us expand on each:

One may view this passage as a response to the Ten Command-

---

1. Usually in Judaism all commands can be transgressed in a life-threatening situation. These three are exceptions in that we must suffer death rather than engage in the forbidden act.

ments. We may surely raise the question: What are the Israelites going to do on the day after the revelation at Sinai? Moses will be gone (for forty days and nights). The Israelites will be looking for a way in which to continue. They may wish to commemorate the Sinai experience in some way. They might wish to somehow continue the sense of contact with God, the feelings of connectedness and spiritual elevation that they experienced as they heard God's voice, and felt His presence. They might want to express their fear, their feelings of insignificance and unworthiness in the face of the mighty all-powerful deity.

Am Yisrael will have a need to respond to Sinai. And here lies the danger. They might possibly be led in directions which are not desirable to Judaism. They might build images in order to serve God, to connect with the deity who spoke to them from the top of the mountain, from the fire and cloud. As the Torah warns:

> The Lord spoke to you out of the fire; you heard the sound of words but perceived no shape – nothing but a voice…. Be most careful – since you saw no image when the Lord your God spoke to you at Ḥorev out of the fire – not to act wickedly and make for yourselves a graven image. (Deut. 4:15–20)

It is interesting that with the exodus from Egypt, God was very explicit in instructing us as to the precise mechanism of commemoration. With Sinai, nothing is specified. Maybe these lines, these verses, act as some form of caveat to the Sinai revelation. These lines warn us how *not* to serve God in the aftermath of *Ma'amad Har Sinai*. Be careful of idolatrous responses, we are told. We are also instructed that when we build our sacrificial altar, we are to distance any trace of violence and sexuality. The pagan nations did practice violence and sexuality in the context of their religious ceremonies. Hence, we are being warned.[2]

---

2. It is interesting that, according to Ḥazal, the episode of the golden calf included each of these three primary sins (see Rashi 32:6). According to the *Kuzari*, the golden calf was precisely a response to the revelation upon Sinai. Was it these precisely chosen mitzvot, delivered immediately after *Ma'amad Har Sinai*, that were designed to be the safeguard for the sort of deterioration that occurred in the golden calf disaster?

III. PRELUDE TO *PARASHAT MISHPATIM*

An alternative mode of seeing this section is to view it as attached to *Parashat Mishpatim*. The entire section consisting of Exodus 20–23 is, according to some, a *Sefer Berit* (see Ibn Ezra 24:4) – God creates a covenant with *Am Yisrael* as detailed in these chapters. This section is a summary of the Torah, outlining a comprehensive review of all the areas in which Torah applies to human life.

So, how does Exodus 20:19–23 fit in? The Ten Commandments form the heading of the covenant. The rest is the derivative, the details of that covenant. We might claim that *Parashat Mishpatim* is an expansion of the Ten Commandments. In this context, Ramban views our verses as derivatives of the first of the Ten Commandments:

EXODUS 23:19–23	THE TEN COMMANDMENTS
You yourselves saw that I spoke to you from the very heavens.	First commandment – Belief in God
You shall not make with Me, any gods of silver.	Second commandment – Prohibition of idolatry
[I]n every place where I cause My *name* to be mentioned I will come to you and bless you.	Third commandment – Taking God's *name* in vain

IV. THE *MISHKAN* CONNECTION[3]

Some wider questions present themselves. These laws all seem to relate in one way or another to the *Mishkan* experience. After all, they talk about sacrifices, *korbanot* and an altar, a *mizbeaḥ*. But when one begins to think about the way in which the *Mishkan* deals with these particular questions, we realize that the *Mishkan* dealt with these issues very differently! Let us explain:

1. Here we are told that we may have no "gods" of silver or gold. Does the *Mishkan* not contain images of gold? For example, the *Keruvim* (Cherubs) upon the *Aron*?

---

3. For this section, I am indebted to an article by Rabbi Dr. Chaim Burganski, published in the Bar-Ilan *parasha* pamphlet 5760.

2. The altar is supposed to be of earth or of stone. In the *Mishkan* the altar was constructed from wood and copper (27:1–8).

3. There are to be no steps up to the altar lest the person ascending reveals his nakedness. In the *Mishkan* however, the kohanim wore special undergarments specifically with this in mind! See 28:42 – "linen breeches to cover their nakedness; they shall extend from the hips to the thighs." What is the worry regarding the steps up to the altar?

In other words, from the perspective of the *Mishkan*, these instructions are not only irrelevant, they are contradictory! How should we explain the laws contained in these verses?

Let me try to solve this problem in time-honored Jewish fashion, by posing two further questions, or maybe, more accurately, raising two further observations.

1. Let us note that the notion of the priest, the kohen, is entirely absent within these verses. Why? It is noteworthy that the kohanim *are* mentioned at Mount Sinai (19:22, 24). But here, these "Temple" instructions are addressed to the entire nation.[4] The implication is that anyone may approach the altar, as long as they are appropriately dressed. Is this the case?

2. The notions of *korban* and *mizbeaḥ* in the *Mishkan* are very precisely defined things. Every item in the *Mishkan* is quantified and measured in minute detail. Here, the altar is given a vague, most unspecific definition, based upon restrictions of what not to do. But there are no exact dimensions, clear instructions. One begins to wonder why these laws are written here. If they refer to the Temple altar then they should be mentioned later on in the context of the construction of the *Mishkan*. However, in this context, one is puzzled as to how they do in fact relate to the Temple altar.

---

4. Contrast, for example, with certain Temple laws which are exclusively addressed to Aaron and his priestly sons. See, for example, Leviticus 6:1–2; 9:2; 10:8; 21:1, 16; 22:2, 17.

The classical commentaries are keenly aware of these discrepancies. Regarding the *Keruvim* in the *Mishkan* and the problem of forms of silver and gold, Rashi comments:

> The Torah warns regarding the *Keruvim*, that you not construct them from silver. If you do this – changing the specific plan of the *Mishkan* – then they will be considered by Me as "gods." "*Gods of gold*" – You may make two *Keruvim*, but not four.

Rashi attempts to resolve these lines as an instruction to follow with precision the plans and details of the *Mishkan*. Any deviation will be considered tantamount to idolatry. I would like to suggest a more radical approach, based on ideas previously discussed.[5]

What these verses suggest is that we have here a totally different system of the worship of God. Like certain midrashim and the non-chronological approach of Rashi, we suggest that the *Mishkan* is a response to the golden calf (*Egel haZahav*). This does not mean that there was no concept of a *Mishkan* prior to the *Egel haZahav*: *Shirat Hayam* (the "song of the sea") refers to "*Mikdash HaShem*" (15:17), and *Parashat Mishpatim* introduces the mitzva of *Aliya laRegel* in order to "behold the presence of the Lord, God" (23:17). There was a plan for a place of worship, a *mikdash*, a focal religious center, which was planned *prior* to the *Egel*.

I would like to suggest that its basic rules are set down in these sporadic verses that follow the Ten Commandments. After all, we have discussed how there was a human need for a response to *Ma'amad Har Sinai*, a need to serve God. These verses delineate the plan. In this model, there is no full-scale temple, only a *mizbeaḥ*.[6] Moreover anyone – any

---

5. See the interpretation of Seforno, who first suggests this approach.
6. In the times of the patriarchs, the primary religious expression of worship would appear to be the *mizbeaḥ*. See Genesis 12:7; 13:4, 18; 21:33; 22:13; 26:25; 35:7; 46:1. This would seem to continue with the era of Moses, see Exodus 3:12; 17:15; 18:12; 24:4–5. Is this the standard pre-Sinai mode of worship, or is it the mode of worship up to the golden calf? In this shiur, we shall suggest that even post-Sinai, pre-golden

Jew – may worship God, acting as a kohen upon the altar of God. This is a "democratic" form of sacrificial worship.

What we are suggesting is that in the wake of Mount Sinai, there is to be a method whereby the nation can express their devotion to God. This is via sacrifices, *korbanot*, and they may be brought with certain caveats:

1. A total ban on images. There is a tendency to represent God by physical form. This is banned.
2. The altar must conform to the precise regulations. The tendency is to embellish and to decorate the ritual environment, leading to a slippery slope of indulgence within worship. Here, any embellishment or grandeur is also outlawed. Hence a very simple, earth or stone structure is mandated. No metal, just a simple "natural" altar.
3. When engaging in the act of worship, extreme caution must be taken to distance any immodesty in the ritual context. This affects the architecture of the altar. Since ancient times human beings expressed themselves religiously through the medium of the *korban*. This is a natural human impulse. The Israelites felt it too. God, in these verses, is instructing the Jews how to serve him in *any* location, how to build an altar anywhere. Every Jew was invited to express himself via the *korban* – but with certain restrictions.

In this way, the average Jew may approach God at any time and in any place.

How does this interface with the existence of a single national place of worship as mandated by the Torah? I don't know, because this plan never happened! The sin of the *Egel haZahav* caused a realization that this "freestyle" worship that was loosely regulated was too easily open to corruption. The idolatrous incident of the *Egel* put an end to

---

calf, despite the multiplicity of mitzvot, this mode of worship was supposed to be a central mode of *avodat HaShem*.

the democratic approach to God, to giving each and every individual direct unmediated access to God.

Instead, now we have:

1. A Temple – only one – in a designated location;
2. Priests – kohanim – who are trained in the laws of the Temple, and will prevent any misdemeanor or transgression of the laws of the *Mishkan*. They will allow access but via a trained agent. (Note, incidentally, the Levites were the ones who were zealous to put a stop to the *Egel* fiasco.)

Now, also, the *Mishkan* is more regulated; hence images are allowed if precisely defined. Why? – Because the legalistic nature of the architecture, and the fact that there is only a single *Mishkan*, seriously diminish the likelihood of corruption and deviation. Likewise, the clothing of the kohanim internalizes the lessons of *"tzeniut"* (modesty), and prevents the revealing of nakedness in the first instance.

What we have here then is a proto-*Mikdash*. We have a plan for a very open approach to God, in the same manner in which Sinai was an unmediated experience by the *entire* nation. But this very accessible framework for divine worship is also unstable, and open to all sorts of violations and errors. The first error of this sort took place at the *Egel haZahav*. After the *Egel*, the *Mishkan* continues the "altar" tradition, but in a different manner. Admittedly, it is statelier, grander, and more elaborate. However, a price is paid – it is less democratic, less accessible, and less spontaneous than what God originally intended.

Parashat Mishpatim

The Torah's Attitude to Slavery

Rav Elchanan Samet

I. THE HEBREW SLAVE VS. THE CANAANITE SLAVE

It is easy to illustrate the Torah's essential opposition to slavery by reviewing the laws of the *eved Ivri* (Hebrew slave, or indentured servant) in our *parasha* and in the book of Leviticus (25:39–43). In both sources, the laws represent an almost total nullification of the institution of slavery within Israel. There is no comparison between the slave of the ancient world and the *eved Ivri* described by the Torah. In essence, the *eved Ivri* is simply somebody who is employed for a lengthy period – "He has been worth double a hired servant to you, serving for six years" (Deut. 15:18). The only limitation that he has in common with a regular slave is that within the period of indenture to which he is committed he may not change his mind and leave.

It is no coincidence that our *parasha* introduces these laws with the declaration, "If you should acquire an indentured Hebrew servant – he shall work for six years, and in the seventh year he shall go free, for nothing." This is a declaration nullifying slavery in its traditional sense as pertaining to *Am Yisrael*, and it complements what the nation heard previously at Mount Sinai (20:2), "I am the Lord your God who took you out of the land of Egypt, from the house of slavery." Ramban explains:

> The first law given here is that of the indentured Hebrew servant, because the freeing of this servant in the seventh year serves as a reminder of the exodus from Egypt mentioned in the first of the Ten Commandments, as it is written [Deut. 15:15], "And you shall remember that you were slaves in the land of Egypt, and the Lord your God redeemed you, therefore I command you this thing today." (Ramban on 21:2)

But the laws of the *eved Ivri* do not reflect the Torah's attitude towards the universal institution of slavery, since they reflect the special relationship that must prevail amongst the Jewish nation itself – which in turn is based on God's relationship with them: "*For they are My servants, whom I took out of the land of Egypt*; they shall not be sold as slaves" (Lev. 25:42). The Torah goes on to distinguish between the nullification of slavery amongst the nation of Israel, who are "the servants of God" and whom He took out of Egypt in order that they may be His servants rather than slaves to any mortal, and the continued existence of the institution of slavery as pertaining to the other nations: "And your slave and your maidservant that you may have from among the nations around you – from them you may acquire slaves and maidservants…and they shall be your property" (ibid. 44–45).

The proper way to clarify the Torah's attitude towards the institution of slavery is therefore to examine the laws of the *Gentile slave*, known in rabbinic literature as the "Canaanite slave." The laws that pertain to this slave shed light on the Torah's fundamental attitude towards slavery in general.

Nevertheless, even the laws of the indentured Hebrew servant are of some significance in clarifying the Torah's stand on slavery. The almost complete nullification of slavery within *Am Yisrael* shows that slavery in itself is considered an improper social situation, and therefore it should not exist within the Jewish nation. Although the reason given is historical and religious – the exodus from Egypt made *Benei Yisrael* servants to God alone – the foundation for this reason may be broadened to include all of mankind. Everyone is worthy of being considered a servant of God on some level, by virtue of being His creature and by virtue of the obligation to serve Him. Theoretically, there is no justification for the enslavement of someone who was created in the divine image in order to serve God.

II. THE ORDER OF THE LAWS OF THE CANAANITE SLAVE

Our *parasha* records the laws pertaining to the "Canaanite slave" in three places:

> If a person should strike his slave or his maidservant with a staff, and he/she dies by his hand, he/she shall be avenged. But if the slave survives for a day or two, then he/she shall not be avenged, for he/she is his [the master's] property. (21:20–21)

> If a person strikes the eye of his slave or of his maidservant such that he/she is blinded, then he/she is to be freed on account of his/her eye. And if he causes the tooth of his slave or his maidservant to be knocked out, he shall send him/her free on account of his/her tooth. (21:26–27)

> If the ox should gore a slave or maidservant, thirty shekels of silver shall be given to the master, and the ox shall be stoned. (21:32)

An additional law particular to the Canaanite slave appears in Deuteronomy:

> You shall not give over a slave to his master if he escaped to you from his master. He shall remain in your midst, in the place that he chooses in one of your gates, as it suits him – you shall not oppress him. (Deut. 23:16)

Why are all the laws pertaining to the Canaanite slave not concentrated in one place, but spread out in a seemingly disordered fashion? Deuteronomy's prohibition against handing over an escaped slave clearly does not belong here among the laws of damages. But why are the three laws here – all dealing with injury to a slave – not all grouped together in one place?

The answer relates to the general structure of the section of damages, which is arranged according to a categorization of *the injured party* and his status. The section's first half (21:12–27) deals with one person who injures another. The second half (21:28–22:6) also begins with injury to a *person* (the causing of his death), not as a result of damage inflicted by another person, however, but as a result of being gored by his neighbor's ox. The Torah then deals with damage to a person's *animals* (a pit or an ox that caused damage to animals, or a person who steals the animals of his neighbor); damage to *the produce of his field* (a person who frees his ox to cause damage to his neighbor's field or one who starts a fire that consumes his neighbor's field); and finally to *his possessions* (a person who steals money or vessels from his neighbor). This is a *value-oriented* order, in accordance with the relative importance of the various injured parties, and teaches us that a person's life and his freedom, his physical well-being and the well-being of his possessions – from the most important among them to the least important – are all worthy of protection from the actions or inaction of his neighbor.

Let us now return to the order of the injuries caused to the Canaanite slave. These are arranged in accordance with the *type of damage* discussed in each case, corresponding to a similar damage caused to a free person: a blow that leads to death – the law if the slave dies immediately, the law if he does not die immediately (free person: verses 18–19; slave: verses 20–21); a blow that causes him to lose a limb (free: 22–25; slave: 26–27), and the causing of his death as a result of a goring ox (free: 29–30; slave: 31). The verses deal with these three types of damage in order, and within each type alternates between two cases: damage to a free person and damage to a slave. As a result, the laws specific to a slave are separated from one another.

But the separation between these laws pertaining to the slave is not at all similar to the separation in the laws of the thief discussed above. The thief is the *injuring party*, and it is therefore clear that the *parasha* – whose internal order follows the order of the injured parties – should separate the laws of the thief in accordance with the quality of the thing that he stole. The slave, in contrast, is the *injured party*, and his laws should therefore seemingly be grouped together in their own place within the list of injured parties, in accordance with his relative importance and status within this list – i.e., after damage to a person, before damage to property. The *parasha's* order should be:

1. Damage to the person himself (damage to his life, to his freedom or to his physical well-being);
2. Damage to his property: slave, animal, produce, possessions.

Why are the laws of the slave not grouped in this manner? The answer is clear: the Torah considers the slave as a person, an independent legal personality. The laws pertaining to him are different from those pertaining to a free person, but his damage or injury is not measured from the point of view of his master, concerning whom he represents property, but rather from the point of view of the slave himself. Out of the three laws of damages pertaining to the slave, the first two address damage caused by the master himself to the slave, and these correspond to the damage caused by one person to another ("If a person should strike his neighbor" – "If a person should strike his slave").

Thus, damages caused to a slave are not addressed as damage to property but as damage to a person, and therefore they always appear in proximity to damage caused to a free person. The third law follows the same pattern: although the death of the slave is also addressed as damage to his master ("thirty silver shekalim will be given to *his master*"), the section concludes, "And the ox will be stoned" – for having killed *a person*. In this respect there is no difference between an ox that killed a free person and an ox that killed a slave.

III. A PERSON WHO STRIKES HIS SLAVE WITH A STAFF

I shall address the first two laws of the Canaanite slave in our *parasha*, to clarify the Torah's attitude towards the institution of slavery. In our times, with slavery no longer practiced, it is difficult for us to understand the full significance of these laws. In order to properly understand the importance of these laws *at the time that they were given and for some considerable time thereafter,* some familiarity is required with the general historical background – the laws of slaves that prevailed among nations in ancient times. Only then can we fully grasp the Torah's intention, and only then will the Torah's fundamental attitude towards the institution of slavery become clear.

> If a person should strike his slave or his maidservant with a staff, and he/she dies by his hand, then *he/she shall be avenged*. But if he/she survives for a day or two then he/she shall not be avenged, for he/she is his (the master's) property. (21:20–21)

Let us examine the details of this law. Firstly: what is the meaning of "he/she shall be avenged"? Rambam introduces his *Laws of Murderers* as follows:

> Anyone who kills any fellow Jew is guilty of transgressing a negative command, as it is written, "You shall not murder." And if he murdered knowingly and intentionally, before witnesses, then he is to be put to death by the sword, *as it is written, "he/she shall be avenged"* – it is a tradition passed down from Mount Sinai that this refers to a death penalty by the sword.

The textual foundation for the death penalty for any intentional murderer has its source in the law pertaining to a master who strikes his slave and thereby causes his death!

What is the relationship between the law of the slave who is struck by his master and the law of a free person who is struck by his neighbor, addressed previously in verses 18–19? The principle behind each law is the reverse of the other. If a person strikes his fellow free person, "he is tended until it becomes clear whether he will be healed" (Rashi on v. 19). "And if he dies – even after a long time – the one who struck him shall die" (Rashbam ibid.). Only if the injured party leaves his sick-bed and recovers is the person who struck him acquitted.

The opposite is the case in the event of a person striking his slave, as Rashbam explains:

> But concerning his slave – he is guilty (and deserving of the death penalty) only if "he dies by his hand" (i.e. immediately, as a result

of the injury), but if the slave survives for a day or two, then the master is acquitted (even if the slave dies thereafter).

What is the reason for this difference? Attention should be paid to the difference in weapons: a person who strikes his friend does so using "a stone or his fist," while one who strikes his slave does so using a staff. The staff is not a weapon designed to kill, but an acceptable tool (in biblical times) to discipline a child or a slave, perhaps to force him to work:

> Do not withhold moral teachings from a young child, *for if you strike him with a staff – he will not die!* (Prov. 23:13)

How does the slave die as a result of this blow? Ibn Ezra explains: "God commands that when a master disciplines his slave, he should not enforce cruel discipline; if he sees that his slave will die from his blows, he should leave him. And if he does not leave him, then he is to be put to death on account of him!" (long commentary, v. 21). Since striking a slave with a staff was acceptable at times, the Torah introduces a measure of strict control on this practice. The master is striking his slave with a tool that is not an implement designed for killing, and in circumstances where the use of the staff is theoretically permissible, since the slave is in his hands. However, the master might abuse this situation to practice cruelty and to cause his death – even using a staff. Despite the seemingly mitigating circumstances, the master deserves the death penalty for this!

How can we ascertain that the master indeed meant to kill his slave, and not merely to discipline him? Here the condition of "a day or two" comes to serve as an indication: if the slave "dies by the hand" of the master who strikes him with the staff (or a short time later, the same day), then there can be no doubt that the master did in fact intend to kill him. But if the injured slave dies only "after a day or two," there is room to assume that the master did not mean to kill him, but rather only to discipline him – for he put away the staff when he saw the condition of the slave, and it is only as a result of additional factors that the slave later died. The actual blow that the master delivered to the slave does not represent sufficient grounds for the death penalty.

Proof for this interpretation – that the "day or two" is not a leniency on the part of the Torah concerning the killing of a slave, but, on the contrary, an extra measure of strictness with regard to the one who struck him – may be found in the law pertaining to a master who strikes his slave "with a stone or with a fist" – tools designed to kill. Rambam writes as follows:

> It appears to me that one who strikes his slave with a knife or a sword or stone or fist etc. and he was diagnosed as being likely to die and he in fact dies, then the law of "a day or two" does not apply to the master; even if the slave dies after a full year – he has died as a result of him [the master]. It is for this reason that the text mentions "with a staff" – because the Torah allows him to strike only with a staff, a stick, a strap, etc. – not with something that is designed to kill. (*Laws of Murderers*, 2:14)

What is the law of a person who strikes someone else's Canaanite slave? Rambam writes:

> What is the difference between [striking] his own slave and a slave belonging to someone else? He is entitled to beat his own slave...but one who strikes the slave of someone else – even if the slave dies as a result of the blow only after several days, he shall be executed *on account of the slave as for a free man*, because he struck him with the intention to kill. (ibid. 2:11–12)

We see that the law pertaining to a slave is not fundamentally different from the law pertaining to a free person, and his life is not considered as having less value. The Torah law concerning one who strikes his slave arises from special circumstances that engender the need to ascertain whether there was intention to kill on the part of the master. Such circumstances exist only in the case of one who strikes his own slave, with a staff. It does not apply to one who strikes the slave of someone else, nor to one who strikes his own slave with a stone or a fist.

In contrast, what did the laws of the ancient nations say about a master who killed his slave? They are silent, for it presented no problem for them. A person could treat his property as he saw fit. Just as he could slaughter his horse or his donkey, so too could he kill his slave.

What if someone's slave was killed by someone else? Here a problem arises – for another's property has been damaged. The Hittite laws, for instance, stipulated an exact monetary penalty to be paid to the master if the slave was killed with prior intent (double the slave's worth) or if he was killed unintentionally (the slave's worth). Likewise, a penalty was stipulated for various wounds inflicted on the slave of one's neighbor.

The master-slave relationship, however, remained outside the bounds of legal concepts: the master could not be punished for causing the death of his slave, nor for causing him any wound or blemish, since the slave was his property.

Only against this background can we appreciate the magnitude of the legal and philosophical revolution introduced by the laws of the Torah pertaining to the striking of a slave. Although the slave is his master's "property," this is true only in a contractual sense and in the sphere of work relations that prevail in a world where slavery is acceptable. But his independent human essence is retained. His life is not the property of the master, but rather of the One who gives all life – and it is He who demands his blood from the hands of those who spill it – whether the master or someone else.

IV. THE SLAVE GOES FREE ON ACCOUNT OF A TOOTH

> And if a person strikes the eye of his slave or the eye of his maidservant and blinds him/her, he shall send him/her free on account of the eye. And if he causes the tooth of his slave or of his maidservant to be knocked out, he shall send him/her free on account of the tooth. (21:26–27)

It is not only the life of the slave that is not considered the master's property. Even the slave's body and his limbs are not the master's to treat as he sees fit. What, then, has the master acquired in the slave from a legal point of view? He has acquired only the slave's work power, but the slave's body – in the simple, literal sense – remains outside the sphere of human acquisition.

The sages deduce from the law of the tooth and the eye that twenty-four additional limbs that do not grow back are likewise reason to free the slave (*Kiddushin* 24a–25a). In this case, the law pertaining to the slave is even stricter than the law pertaining to a free person. If someone strikes the limb of his fellow, he pays him only for the eye or for the tooth that was destroyed. However, the slave goes free on account of the eye or the tooth – and clearly, the value of the whole slave is greater than the value of the damage to a single limb. What is the reason for this penalty that the Torah pronounces for the master?

The full significance of this law can only be understood if we familiarize ourselves, again, with the situation of slaves in the ancient world. Shemuel Rubinstein offers the following description:

> The Talmud (*Kiddushin* 25a) teaches: "There are twenty-four protruding limbs of a person, for all of which a slave is set free, and these are they: the tips of the fingers, toes, ears, nose, penis and breasts.... Rabbi says: 'Also testicles.' Ben Azai says: 'Also the tongue.'"
>
> The situation of a slave in ancient times was truly awful. He was like an object owned by his master – the master could beat his slave mercilessly for any major or minor wrongdoing; he could permanently maim his limbs without fear of any punishment. For any purpose desired by the master, the slave could be blinded – likewise, prisoners taken in war were blinded as a sign of slavery, and this was done particularly to kings and officers of the defeated army, as a sign of revenge and enslavement. For the same reason Samson was blinded by the Philistines (Judges 16:21), and this is apparently also the meaning of the words of Naḥash the Ammonite to the men of Yavesh Gil'ad: "By this condition I will make a covenant with you: if you all put out your right eye" (I Sam. 11:2), as if to say, "in order that you will be slaves and prisoners of war to me." This arrogance on the part of the enslavers seems to have lasted until much later times, explaining even Herod's blinding of Bava ben Buta (*Bava Batra* 4a).
>
> For some wrongdoing in his work, or for breaking some vessel, the slave's fingers or hands could be cut off, and this was

apparently also done to prisoners of war as a sign of enslavement. This explains the amputation of thumbs and big toes by Adoni Bezek.... The amputation of a slave's ears was so commonly practiced that it was established as a punishment for slaves.... Slaves were routinely castrated in order that thoughts of women would not interfere with their work, and eunuchs were also used to serve women. This was so common that the term "eunuch" came to be used for all kinds of servants, even those not castrated, like Potiphar, "the eunuch of Pharaoh" (Gen. 39:1), and the royal steward and baker who are referred to as Pharaoh's "eunuchs" (ibid. 40:2).

In summary, nothing prevented a master from doing any of this to his slave. Cicero describes how "it was common among the Romans that if a slave knew some evidence against his master, the master would cut out his tongue in order that he would not be able to testify." And the maiming of slaves, either by purposeless beating or for some purpose desired by the master, was so common that *blemishes were inflicted on the exposed body parts of the slave in order to mark him as a slave.*

It was against all of this that the Torah came to improve the lot of the slaves and their worth, as much as was possible in those days. For beating to death the Torah prescribes, "he shall surely be avenged" – which, in the view of the sages (*Sanhedrin* 52b), refers to the death penalty.

For causing blemishes to the exposed body parts in order to thereby signify that he was a slave – or even without such express intent – the Torah prescribes that "he shall send him free," which is the opposite of the purpose of creating these blemishes. From this we derive the laws stipulating that the master must set the slave free for causing blemishes upon the "exposed" body parts. (*Kadmoniot HaHalakha*, chapter 22)

Thus we learn that both of the laws of damages mentioned by the Torah, where the master is punished for harming his slave, represent overt opposition to the universal institution of slavery. The first law expresses opposition to the concept of ownership of the *life* of the slave, and it raises the slave to the level of a person created in the divine image, with

One who demands his blood. The second law expresses opposition to the concept of ownership of the *body* of the slave, and opposition also to the cruel methods employed in the ancient world to punish slaves or to mark them by means of permanent, visible maiming. Anyone attempting to maim his slave in this way, and thereby to establish his ownership of the slave's body, would achieve the opposite of his aim, "measure for measure" – his slave would go free, against the will of the master.

The ideals expressed here in the concise, legal language of the Torah are expressed more philosophically and poetically by Job, when he declares that he has conducted his life with righteousness:

> If I have despised the just cause of my slave and my maidservant when they strove against me, then what shall I do when God rises up, and when He remembers, what shall I answer Him? Did He who created me in the belly not create him, and was it not the same One who fashioned us in the womb? (Job 31:13–15)

Murdering with Guile

Rav Yaakov Medan

He who strikes a person such that he dies, shall surely be put to death. But if he did not lie in wait for him, only God made it happen, then I will appoint you a place to where he shall flee. And if a person plans against another to kill him with guile – you shall take him from My altar to die. (21:12–14)

Halakha generally recognizes two types of murderers: one who murders knowingly and with premeditation and one who kills unwittingly. But from the above verses a third type arises: one who kills "with guile" (*be'orma*). Halakhically, the special law of "You shall take him from My altar to die" is applied to any intentional murderer, but the literal interpretation of the verse refers specifically and exclusively to the person who murders with guile. This will be the subject of our analysis.

There are two types of murder "with guile." First, a person may deceive his neighbor into trusting him and letting down his guard, thus enabling him to carry out the murder without having to contend with any self-defense on the part of the victim. Concerning this type of deceit, Jeremiah declares:

he speaks peaceably to his neighbor with his mouth, while in his heart he lies in wait for him. "Shall I not punish them for these things," says God? "Shall My soul not be avenged for such a nation?" (Jer. 9:7–8)

A perfect biblical example of this sin is the story of the murder of Gedalya ben Aḥikam by Yishmael ben Netanya – a murder which led to the downfall of the last remnant of Judah:

> It was in the seventh month that Yishmael ben Netanya ben Elishama, of royal lineage, and the chief officers of the king, and ten men with him, came to Gedalya ben Aḥikam at Mitzpa. They ate bread together there at Mitzpa. Then Yishmael ben Netanya and the ten men who were with him arose and struck Gedalya ben Aḥikam ben Shafan by the sword, killing the one whom the King of Babylon had appointed governor over the land.... Then Yishmael ben Netanya came out from Mitzpa towards them, walking and weeping as he went. When he met them he said to them: "Come to Gedalya ben Aḥikam." But when they entered the city, Yishmael ben Netanya slew them [and cast them] into the pit – he and the men who were with him. (Jer. 41:1–7)

This interpretation of "murder with guile," where a person does not have any potential for self-defense, does not sit well with the order of the verses in our *parasha*. One would think that this murder is even more abhorrent than regular premeditated murder. The order of the verses should progress either from the most severe to the least severe or vice versa. How are we to understand the order as it appears in the text: first a premeditated murder, then negligent homicide, and then murder with guile? Moreover, what is the nature of the special punishment reserved for one who murders with guile – that he is taken to die [even] from the holy altar?

A second type of murderer "with guile" is worried about the punishment that a court will mete out to him because of the blood that he has spilled, and therefore uses "guile" to hide the crime. There are two subcategories here: the first does everything in his power to cover up any trace of his involvement with the murder; the other claims that he acted unwittingly or lawfully.

The murderer who seeks to erase all traces of his deed will follow the example of the first murderer – Cain, who killed his brother Abel:

> God said to Cain: "Where is Abel, your brother?" And he said: "I do not know; am I then my brother's keeper?!" (Gen. 4:9)

Perhaps God revealed Himself to Cain while he was offering his sacrifice – as is the case in many other revelations in Tanach. Cain killed his brother in order to "force" God, as it were, to accept his own sacrifice rather than that of Abel. Perhaps, following the murder, Cain went off to achieve his aim and to offer his sacrifice to God. And as he offers it, he protests his innocence, claiming to have no knowledge of where his brother is. While performing the very service at the altar, Cain attempts to deceive the Receiver of his sacrifice.

God does not accept Cain's sacrifice; on the contrary, He banishes him from the altar. Further on in the interchange, God grants Cain a "stay of execution." He suspends the death sentence that the murderer deserves, but does not forgive the attempt to erase the traces of the sin by hiding the spilled blood in the ground:

> He said, "What have you done? The voice of your brother's blood calls to Me from the ground. Now you are cursed from the ground that opened its mouth to accept your brother's blood from your hand: when you work the land, it shall no longer give its strength to you; a fugitive and wanderer shall you be in the land." (Gen. 4:10–12)

In other words, even when God cancels Cain's punishment for willful murder, He does not forego the punishment for murder with guile. Cain is immediately banished from the ground which he used in order to hide his act.

Another *parasha* that emphasizes this point is that of the *egla arufa* (Deut. 21:1–9). Here the Torah describes a situation where the murderer has succeeded in erasing all traces leading to him, as though the earth had "swallowed him up" – just as the earth swallowed up all traces of Abel after Cain murders him. The heifer whose neck is broken in the ravine is the complete opposite of a sacrifice slaughtered upon the altar. Its purpose is to signify that God will accept no sacrifice as atonement for the murder, nor for the guilt of the community as a whole, so long as the murderer goes about freely. On the simplest level, the ravine where the heifer's neck is broken is the site of the murder, and therefore it shall neither be tilled nor sown. This ground is cursed because it opened its mouth and swallowed the footsteps of the murderer – just as the ground cursed Cain after it hid Abel's murder. The elders of the closest city must declare that they were not party to the hiding of the crime, that there has been no situation in which they came upon the murderer but guilefully took no notice of his crime.

The other type of guileful murderer seeking to avoid punishment but unable to cover up his actions, tries to camouflage his intent and to present his act as either a mistake or something that was justified and permissible:

> If a man hates his neighbor, and he lies in wait for him and comes upon him to strike a mortal blow such that he dies, and he flees to one of these cities, then the elders of his city shall send and take him from there, and give him into the hand of the avenger of blood, that he may die. You shall not look upon him with mercy; you shall rid yourself of the innocent blood of Israel, that it may be well with you. (Deut. 19:11–13)

This *parasha* is juxtaposed to the command concerning the cities of refuge, in order to protect those who shed blood by mistake. A willful murderer may not escape to a city of refuge, and therefore this *parasha* speaks about a person who murders with guile, seeking the protection of the elders of the *beit din* (court) in his city against the sword of the avenger of blood. The altar, in this instance, is interpreted – contrary to the previous case, where it implied the place of divine worship – as the place of refuge from the avenger's anger. The avenger, so the murderer believes, will never dare approach "God's altar" with a sword. Therefore the Torah commands us, "You shall take him from My altar to die."

This would appear to explain the order of the murderers listed in our *parasha*. The first is the willful murderer; he is sentenced to death. The second is someone who did not "lie in wait"; the Torah sets aside a place for him to flee to. At this stage the cities of refuge had not yet been established; the command to build them is to be fulfilled only upon reaching *Eretz Yisrael*. Therefore the expression, "I shall make for you *a place* to where he shall flee" would seem to imply that the word *"makom"* (place) is used here in the same way that it is used in many other places in the Torah:

> To *the place* of the altar which he had made there originally; and there Abram called out in God's name. (Gen. 13:4)

> On the third day, Abraham raised his eyes and saw *the place* from afar. (Gen. 22:4)

> He came to *the place* and prepared to sleep there for the sun was setting; he took some of the stones of *the place* and placed them for his head, and he lay down at that place. (Gen. 28:11)

In other words, *"makom"* means an altar, or another site devoted to divine worship. It is to such a place that the murderer flees.

According to our interpretation, the third type of murderer is a composite of the first two types. He murders intentionally, but pretends to have done so unknowingly. It is concerning this murderer that the Torah commands that he be removed from the place of his refuge, from the "altar," and put to death. This includes the murderer who justifies his act as being permissible.

It would seem that the biblical character who best epitomizes the concept of murdering "with guile" is Yoav ben Tzeruya, the commander of David's army. Yoav kills three people, either directly or indirectly: Avner ben Ner, Uriya haHitti, and Amasa ben Yeter. Let us examine each one, beginning with Avner:

> And Yoav went out from David and sent messengers after Avner, and they brought him back from the well of Sira, but David did

not know of it. So Avner returned to Ḥevron, and Yoav took him aside inside the gate to speak to him in private, and he struck him there in the belly, and he died, for the blood of Asa'el his brother. (II Sam. 3:26–27)

Yoav decides to kill Avner: possibly because he suspects that Avner will seduce David and spy against him; possibly to avenge the blood of Asa'el his brother. Perhaps he kills him for a different reason, not mentioned in the verses: the concern that Avner will take over his position as chief of the army as part of the agreement concerning the unification of the kingdom that is to be drawn up with David.

How does Yoav kill Avner? First, he takes him aside at the gate in order to speak with him. Avner does not suspect Yoav of any scheming against him and fails to protect himself; Yoav exploits this and deals him a mortal blow. The Midrash and Rashi describe the scene in more visual terms:

He asked him, guilefully: "A widowed woman who frees her brother-in-law of the obligation to marry her (*yevama*) – if she is an amputee, how does she perform the '*ḥalitza*'?" He began telling him and showing him: "She takes his shoe thus, with her teeth" – and he drew his sword and killed him. (Rashi *Sanhedrin* 49a according to the Midrash HaGadol, Ex. 21:14)

While involved in discussing a halakhic question, Avner lowers his guard and does not protect himself. Yoav exploits this to kill him, in a way that is neither fair nor honorable. This is the way of guile.

But this was not the only guileful aspect of Yoav's act.

"Yoav drew him aside inside the gate, to speak with him in private" – Rabbi Yoḥanan said: "They adjudicated the case. He [Yoav] said to him [Avner]:
– Why did you kill Asa'el?
– Asa'el was a *rodef* [i.e. he endangered Yoav's life].
– You could have saved him with one of his limbs [i.e. you could have wounded him]!

– No, I could not.

– You aimed precisely at his fifth rib…. Could you not have managed one of his [other] limbs?" (*Sanhedrin* 49a)

Yoav judges Avner in accordance with Torah law, as a murderer, and he punishes him in accordance with the law of an avenger. Apparently, everything here is in order. But David, in his eulogy for Avner and in his will, treats Yoav as a murderer:

> David heard afterwards, and he said: "I and my kingdom are guiltless before God forever for the blood of Avner ben Ner. It shall rest upon the head of Yoav and all of his father's household. May Yoav's house never lack a '*zav*,' a '*metzora*,' one who walks with crutches, one who falls by the sword, and one who lacks bread." (II Sam. 3:28–29)

> You, too, know all that Yoav ben Tzeruya did to me – what he did to the two officers of the hosts of Israel, to Avner ben Ner and to Amasa ben Yeter, that he killed them, and shed the blood of war in peace, and put the blood of war upon his belt that was around his loins, and in his shoes that were on his feet. Act according to your wisdom, and do not let him die a peaceful death of old age." (I Kings 2:5–6)

Apparently, a person may judge his fellow in accordance with Torah law and still be considered a murderer, deserving of death. David knew that it was not the avenging of blood that motivated Yoav to kill Avner, but rather his concern that he would lose his own position as chief of the army.

This is guile of the second variety. The murderer is wary not only of the victim's self-defense, but also of his own punishment at the hands of the *beit din*. Therefore, he produces explanations and excuses that are not true, so as to satisfy the judges and assure their protection.

Yoav acts in a similar way when he kills Amasa:

> Yoav said to Amasa: "Are you well, my brother?" And Yoav grasped Amasa's beard with his right hand, to kiss him. And Amasa took

no heed of the sword in Yoav's hand, and he smote him with it in the belly, spilling his bowels to the ground; he did not strike him again, but he died. (II Samuel 20:9–10)

There was guile involved in killing him, but in this case, too, there was seemingly a solid halakhic justification for Yoav's act:

He said to him: "For what reason did you kill Amasa?" He answered: "Amasa rebelled against the king." (*Sanhedrin* 49a)

Despite this justification, Yoav is judged as a murderer for killing Amasa. This shows that the justification was no more than an excuse to get rid of Amasa, who was appointed as commander of the army instead of Yoav after Yoav killed Avshalom, and because David wanted to make peace with the commander of his army. The excuse, then, was nothing more than guile.

Was there truly a justification for killing Uria haHitti, or was the supposed justification again just an excuse? The prophet Nathan rebukes David severely. However, what about Yoav, who fulfilled David's orders? Fulfilling the order of the king of Israel is clearly demanded by halakha, but Yoav did not make any effort to know the limits of the law of obeying the king:

"God will return his blood upon his head for striking two men more righteous and better than he":
"Better" – because they understood the limitations [of their duty to obey: they did not kill the priests of Nov despite Saul's explicit order to do so], while he did not understand.
"More righteous" – because they received their [immoral] orders directly, verbally, and they did not carry them out, while he received his orders [only] in a letter, but he [still] fulfilled them." (*Sanhedrin* 49a)

The fact that Yoav was not blindly obedient towards David at other times gives rise to serious questions as to his true intentions in the matter of Uriya. The manner in which Yoav killed Uriya was also guileful; it exploited military camaraderie and self-sacrifice in order to stab a comrade-in-arms in the back:

> He wrote in the letter, saying: "Bring Uriya to the frontlines of the fiercest fighting, and draw back from behind him so that he will be struck and will die." And it was, when Yoav besieged the city, he assigned Uriya to the place where he knew that the warriors were. When the men of the city came out to do battle with Yoav, some of David's servants fell – and Uriya haḤitti died also. Then Yoav sent and told David all about the battle. He instructed the messenger, saying: "When you finish telling the king all about the battle, then if the king's anger is aroused and he says, 'Why did you come close to the city to fight? Did you not know that they would shoot from atop the wall? Who struck Avimelekh ben Yerubeshet; did a woman not throw a millstone upon him from atop the wall, such that he died in Tevetz? Why did you approach the wall?' Then you shall say: 'Your servant Uriya haḤitti is also dead.'" (II Samuel 11:15–16)

Yoav's punishment is appropriate, as is fitting for one who murders with guile, concerning whom it is written, "You shall take him from My altar to die:"

> Then news came to Yoav – for Yoav had followed after Adoniya, but he had not followed Avshalom – and Yoav fled to God's Tent and he grasped the corners of the altar. It was told to King Solomon that Yoav had fled to God's Tent, and that behold, he was by the altar. Solomon sent Benayahu ben Yehoyada saying; "Go, attack him." Benahayhu came to God's tent and said to him: "So says the king: Come out." But he said, "No, for I shall die here." Benayahu brought word back to the king, saying: "Thus said Yoav, and thus I answered him." The king said to him: "Do as he said; strike him, and bury him, thereby removing the innocent blood spilled by Yoav from upon me and from upon my father's

house. May God return his blood upon his head for killing two
men more righteous and better than he; for he killed them by
the sword, and my father David did not know: Avner ben Ner,
officer of the host of Israel, and Amasa ben Yeter, officer of the
host of Judah. May their blood return to the head of Yoav and
the head of his descendants forever, and may there be peace for
David and for his descendants and for his household and for his
throne from God forever." Then Benayahu ben Yehoyada went up
and attacked him and slew him, and he was buried in his house
in the wilderness. (1 Kings 2:28–34)

Both the Talmud (*Sanhedrin* 49) and Rambam (*Laws of a Murderer,* 5:14) elaborate at length on the two death sentences that Yoav
deserves. The one was for rebelling against the king because he supported Adoniyahu. For this sin the altar protected him, and Benayahu
was unable to kill him. The second death sentence was for spilling the
blood of Avner and Amasa. For this Benayahu took him from the altar
and killed him.

Though he is the paradigm of the "murderer with guile," Yoav's
personality is too rich and complex to discuss fully in such a short space.
Let me nonetheless conclude with one source that balances the negative
picture that emerges from the discussion above:

Rabbi Abba bar Kahana said: "Were it not for David, Yoav would
not have done battle, and were it not for Yoav, David would not
have engaged in Torah. As it is written, 'David performed justice
and righteousness for all his people, and Yoav ben Tzeruya was in
charge of the army.' What does it meant that 'David performed
justice and righteousness for all his people'? [He was able to,]
because Yoav was taking care of the army. And what is the meaning of 'Yoav was in charge of the army'? So that David could perform justice and righteousness for all his people...."

"And he was buried in his house in the wilderness" – Was
his house then in the wilderness? Rabbi Yehuda said in the name
of Rav: "It was like a wilderness. Just as the wilderness is open

to all, so Yoav's home was open to all" [Rashi: to the poor, who were sustained by his household]. Another opinion: "Like a wilderness – just as a wilderness is clean of theft and immorality, so Yoav's house was clean of theft and immorality." (*Sanhedrin* 49a)

Types of Guardianship

Rav Yehuda Rock

T he wording of the verses in the sections dealing with the various types of guardians (*shomerim*) is difficult, nor is the order and structure of these units simple. In this *shiur* we shall attempt to understand the content of these units and the messages that they convey.

There are three *parashot* pertaining to guardianship. We will focus mainly on the first two, but let us begin by reviewing the text of all three:

A. If a person gives to his neighbor some money or vessels to keep, and it is stolen from the man's house, then if the thief is found – he pays double.

If the thief is not found, then the owner of the house is brought to the judges, (to swear) that he did not put forth his hand to his neighbor's goods.

Concerning any matter of transgression, whether it involves an ox, or a donkey, or a sheep, or a garment – for any lost thing concerning which one can say, "This is it" – both parties shall present their case to the judges. Whoever the judges convict will pay double to his neighbor.

B. If a person gives his neighbor a donkey or an ox or a sheep, or any sort of animal, to keep, and it dies, or is injured, or is taken away, unseen, then God's oath shall be between the two of them, that neither put forth his hand to his neighbor's goods. And the owner shall accept [*yikah* – literally, take] this, and [the guardian] shall not pay. But if it is stolen from him, then he shall pay its owner.

c. And if a person borrows [some animal] from his neighbor, and it is injured, or dies – its owner not being with it – then he shall surely make restitution.

> If its owner was with it – he shall not pay. If it is a hired thing, then it is covered by his wages. (Ex. 22:6–14)

In Halakha, these three cases are known as the "guardian for free," the "paid guardian," and the "borrower" respectively.

The obvious difference between the first two units is that the second case requires the guardian from whom the object was stolen to pay the owner, while the first unit exempts him as soon as it is clear that the guardian himself is not responsible for the disappearance of the object. The Halakha bases this discrepancy on the payment conditions of the guardian: a guardian for free, who is performing a favor for the owner of the object, is exempt in the event of the object being stolen. A paid guardian, on the other hand, for whom the task of taking care of the object is part of a bi-lateral deal, is obligated to make restitution in the event of theft.

The terms "guardian for free" and "paid guardian" are not mentioned in the verses, but are later terms employed by Ḥazal in their discussions. What, then, is the basis for the differentiation?

Rashbam explains that on the verses' literal level, the difference concerns not the question of payment to the guardian, but the sort of object that is being kept. The first unit speaks about "money or vessels" – i.e. movable assets, while the second unit deals with a "donkey or ox or sheep or any sort of animal."

Rashbam explains that the discrepancy in the respective levels of responsibility arises from the differing expectations associated with the types of objects that are given to someone for safekeeping. Money or vessels are usually kept inside the house; hence, the owner expects merely that the guardian will place the object in his house, together with his own belongings. Even if the object is stolen from the house, the guardian did what was expected of him. He was not delinquent in his guardianship, and he is exempt from making restitution. In contrast, when taking care of animals, which are kept outside, the owner's expectation is that his animal will be protected from thieves. If the animal is stolen, the guardian has been negligent in his role, and he is required to pay.

If we accept Rashbam's interpretation, it becomes difficult to explain the discrepancy between the Written Law (which discusses money and vessels as opposed to animals) and the Oral Law (which discusses "guardianship for free" as opposed to "paid guardianship"). Admittedly, we might explain the law concerning a paid guardian as being dependent on the *expectations* (the concept introduced by Rashbam) that come with payment (as suggested by Ramban, commenting on *Bava Metzia* 42a, and in opposition to the opinion of Tosafot ad loc.). Thus, both the Written Law and the Oral Law would be making the obligation of restitution in the case of theft dependent on the owner's expectations with regard to the guardianship. However, while the Written Law bases those expectations on the type of object that is being handed over for safekeeping, Halakha (the Oral Law) bases them on the nature of the business agreement between the owner and the guardian.

In contrast to Rashbam, Ramban (in his usual fashion) reads the verses in a way that is not immediately transposed into the Oral Law, but does create a defined link between the literal meaning of the verses and the halakha. Ramban explains that movable property is usually taken for safekeeping for free, while animals are given over to the charge of shepherds, for payment. A person who needs some object to be kept safely will approach his neighbor or relative and ask him to keep it for him. If it is animal that he needs taken care of, he will generally hire the services of a shepherd. We may add that the social reality he describes is actually the phenomenon noted by Rashbam: since movable property is kept inside, it is easy to ask a neighbor or a relative, as a favor, to keep some object in his house. The same cannot be said of taking care of an animal. This requires that a person frequently go out of his house, plus all the activities required to care of the animal. For this reason, it is appropriate that the owner hire a shepherd. To Ramban's view, however, this point may be of sociological interest, but for the purposes of clarifying the verses and understanding the halakha, what interests us is the actual social phenomenon of movable property being kept for free, while animals are usually kept for payment.

Thus, the discrepancy between the Written Law and the Oral Law reflects a process of formalization. The Written Law "speaks in the present" – it sets forth the laws in instances and actions taken from the social reality, in a way that expresses halakhic significance. The Oral Law, on the other hand, presents clear-cut laws and precise definitions, providing their exact conditions. The Oral Law takes a practical, illustrative description and transforms it into a formal legal entity.

In our context, the instance of "money or vessels" is depicted within a social context that is easily identified as an instance of guardianship for free, while the case of "any type of animal" serves as an example of paid guardianship. The Torah provides familiar examples from the existing social reality, without explicitly noting the relevant legal condition that defines each instance. The Oral Law sets the laws upon the relevant formal, legal foundations.

Let us continue comparing between the first two units. Each describes a case in which the guardian is exempt from making restitution: in the first unit, he is exempt in the event of theft; in the second unit, he is exempt in the event that he had no control over what happened ("died or was injured or was taken away"). In both instances we are told that it is necessary to first rule out the possibility of the guardian himself having "put forth his hand to his neighbor's goods." However, there is a significant difference between the two units in the description of the manner of the investigation. The second unit explicitly speaks of an oath: "God's oath shall be between them." In the first unit, we read: "The owner of the house (i.e., the guardian) shall be brought to the judges." *Ḥazal* deduce that "shall be brought" means "in order to make an oath" (*Bava Metzia* 41b), and the commentators interpret the phrase accordingly. However, the second wording gives rise to the question: if the Torah is able to refer to an oath explicitly, then why does it use different language in the first unit?

Apparently, the answer to this question lies in the difference between the two sorts of cases. In the first case, the guardian claims that the item was stolen. The item is not present; it may be sought at his hands. If the stolen item turns up, and witnesses testify that the item is indeed the stolen object, then we know that the guardian himself "put forth his hand" to his neighbor's property and he is the thief.

The second case is different. Here, the animal "died or was injured or was taken away, unseen." At least if the animal "died or was injured," we have the animal in front of us, either dead or injured. (The word "*nishba*," translated here as "taken away," may also be understood as meaning "struck.") This being the case, there is no point in searching the guardian's premises or person; likewise, there are no witnesses to what happened. Therefore, the court and the plaintiff can only rely on the word of the guardian himself: "God's oath shall be between them."

Accordingly, the oath is equally relevant in both cases, but the Torah makes note of it only in the unit where there is no possibility for making any clearer enquiries. Thus it is clear why the halakha stipulates that in the absence of any clear testimony, even a guardian for free is required to make an oath in the event of theft.

This explanation explains the use of the expression, "The owner shall accept (take) this." Rashi and Rashbam understand the phrase as meaning that the owner "accepts" the oath, but there is no linguistic basis for the "taking" of an oath in this sense. The interpretation offered by Ibn Ezra, in his short commentary, is that in such a case of harm to the animal, where the animal is physically present, the owner has the rights to ("takes," or "accepts") the carcass.

In each of the two units there is one verse that we have not yet explained. Let us first address the second unit, which is a simpler matter: "If it is torn to pieces, then he [or 'it'] shall be brought as evidence; he shall not make restitution for that which was torn." The most plausible interpretation is the opinion of Abba Shaul (in the *Mekhilta DeRabbi Shimon Bar Yoḥai*), also from Ibn Ezra: if the animal is torn, then the torn carcass itself is brought as evidence. Then, and only then, the guardian is exempt from payment. In other words, if the guardian claims that the animal was torn, devoured, and nothing remains of it, his claim is not accepted. The assumption is that there is always some evidence that would remain, and so that guardian is required to bring whatever remains of the carcass.

As noted, our discussion here focuses on the first two out of the three textual units concerning guardianship. Out of this selection, the only verse that remains for us to explain is verse 8:

> Concerning any matter of transgression, whether it involves an ox, or a donkey, or a sheep, or a garment – for any lost thing concerning which one can say, "This is it" – both parties shall present their case to the judges. Whoever the judges convict will pay double to his neighbor.

This is the most difficult verse to understand. However, understanding it also opens the door to a new understanding of the order and structure of both units.

The only thing clear from this verse is that there is a plaintiff and a defendant, a clarification undertaken by the *Beit Din* (the "judges"), and in the case of a conviction, the guilty party must pay double – like a thief. But what case is under discussion? What is the meaning of the phrase, "Concerning any matter of transgression," and how are we to understand "Concerning which one can say, 'This is it'"?

The verse presents another problem aside from its linguistic difficulties. We demonstrated that the main difference is the item involved: "money or vessels," as opposed to animals. In verse 8, however, the only "vessel" that is mentioned is the "garment," while the verse explicitly mentions animals! Even if the instance concerning "money or vessels" in the first unit is significant as an example of guardianship for free, and even if the halakhic category is actually one of a guardian for free, as Ramban maintains, nevertheless – since the Torah chooses to illustrate the laws through a depiction of guardianship of movable property, in contrast to guardianship of livestock in the second unit – this is the instance that is being discussed here, and it is not clear how this verse deviates from this framework.

We also ask why this verse does not begin with the word "*im*" (if), in keeping with the detailing of the instances in these units.

Rashi understands the phrase "concerning any matter of transgression" as referring to a situation in which the guardian, who claimed that the item was stolen from him, was himself responsible for the theft. "Concerning which one can say, 'This is it'" refers to the witness, who identifies an item within the guardian's domain as the item that was handed over by the owner for safekeeping. In this case, where the guardian is found to have stolen the item, he is required to pay double.

In practice, this law is implemented only where the guardian actually swears that the item was stolen from him, and thereafter it is found that he lied in his oath (*Bava Kamma* 63). Rashi cites Ḥazal that the owner "being brought to the judges" in the previous verse, refers to the oath. Only after this precondition is fulfilled will a conviction of the guardian for theft entail double restitution. Apparently, the obligation of paying double is actually the fine for the theft, but since this theft was carried out in a passive way, without an actual act of theft, it is only through the oath that it comes to be defined this way.

Rashi's interpretation is problematic from an exegetical point of view. The generalization "concerning any matter of transgression" is unintelligible, in terms of his approach. Second, contrary to what the verse's structure suggests, he does not view the details – "an ox, or a donkey, or a sheep, or a garment" – as elaborating on the general statement "concerning any matter of transgression," since "concerning any matter of transgression" means that the *punishment for* theft perpetrated by the guardian is double restitution, while "for an ox" means that the *transgression* of theft perpetrated by the guardian *concerns* the animal or item. Rashi's explanation also fails to answer our questions: why are animals listed here, if the subject of this unit is movable property, and why does the verse not start with the word "*im*" (if)?

Ibn Ezra (in his long commentary) explains that the word "*pasha*" (translated here as "transgression") can also mean removal of an item from its domain, as in, "Edom revolted (*vayifsha*) (or seceded) from under the hand of Judah" (II Kings 8:22). In light of this, the elaboration "an ox" may indeed be viewed as a detailing or elaboration of the phrase, "Concerning any matter of transgression" – i.e., any item that is lost, whether it be an ox, a donkey, etc.

Ibn Ezra explains the verse in a similar manner to Rashi: the guardian claims that the item was lost, but witnesses then come and testify that the item is being held by him. Ibn Ezra, like Rashi, fails to solve the problems that we raised: what is the list of animals doing here, and why does the verse not start with "*im*"? His explanation also raises a new problem: it suggests that the guardian is obligated to pay double for lying in his claim that the item was lost (and not only for theft), which contradicts the halakha (*Bava Kama* 63).

It appears that "concerning which one may say, 'This is it'" refers to the item being identified. However, the verse does not mean (only) that there are actually witnesses who identify it, but rather that the item is the sort of thing that can in fact be identified. An animal is different from money or vessels in that each is unique and may be identified. Likewise, an animal does not remain hidden inside the house; rather, it stays outside, and may be individually identified. A garment is likewise special, in relation to other "vessels," in that it is worn externally and may therefore be individually identified.

Accordingly, the verse appears not to be speaking about the guardian at all (since in the case of the animal, he is liable in the case of theft or loss). Rather, it is talking about the owner who identifies his lost item (which was stolen from him) within someone else's domain. The verse comes to tell us that an item that was removed (*pasha*) from the hand of its owner – i.e. lost (without any thief being found), if it is an item that may be identified, such as an animal or a garment, then if through identification of the item by another person *Beit Din* comes to convict that person of stealing the item (by bringing testimony that identifies the item and its location within the domain of the thief), then he is obligated to pay double.

Thus, verse 8 actually does not belong to the laws of guardianship at all. It does not begin with the word "if" because it does not provide a further detail in the laws of guardianship of movable property, and it does not maintain the division between movable property and animals because it is fundamentally not connected to the system of laws of guardianship that creates these categories. We must therefore explain why the verse appears here, in between the two units concerning guardians.

The units here have two separate themes. One theme – the more dominant one – describes the various levels of liability pertaining to different types of guardians. A guardian of movable property is exempt in the event of theft; the guardian of an animal is liable in the event of theft; a borrower is liable even in the occurrence of events completely out of his control (the death of the animal, for instance) if the owner is not with it. The second theme is a description of the various ways of tracking down thieves. This theme appears here as a continuation of the preceding unit, which discusses thieves (21:37–22:3). The Torah stipulates that a thief must pay double, with a view to deterring society from theft. Theft which is carried out in secret, hidden from the eyes of society, requires positive action in order to banish the phenomenon.

Fining the thief double, or four or five times the item's value (as specified in the unit on thieves) is an important device within the framework of this social endeavor, but the Torah goes further and points to the different ways in which thieves may be discovered. First, the Torah describes one way of catching a thief: after he has stolen an animal, in secret, he will want to make profit from it, and will therefore slaughter or sell it (21:37). In such a case, it becomes known in the marketplace that that person has an animal, and it may be identified as the stolen animal. The second possibility is to catch the thief in the act: "If the thief is found breaking in…then if the sun has risen on him." (22:1–2).

Verse 3 – "If the theft is found with him, alive, whether it be an ox or a donkey or a sheep, he shall pay double" – is not telling us how to find a thief, but rather is setting forth the law pertaining to him. This is in contrast to the law in the case of the animal having been slaughtered or sold. In the event that the animal is still present and alive, the thief is liable to pay double (and not four or five times).

The third case that describes a way of catching a thief occurs in our unit. The law concerning a guardian, in verses 6 and 7, does not suffice with a stipulation of the level of responsibility of a guardian of movable property, who is exempt if the item is stolen. The verse emphasizes the need to inquire and investigate whether the item is actually located in the domain of the guardian himself. "Then the owner of the house is brought to the judges, [to swear] that he did not put forth his hand to his neighbor's goods." A guardian who claims that the item was stolen from him is the first suspect. Usually it is difficult to locate a thief, because the theft takes place under cover, and there is usually no particular person who can be interrogated or searched. However, there is one case where there is a prime suspect who may be questioned: the case of a guardian, who does not bring the object before the judges, but rather claims that it was stolen from him.

Thereafter the Torah comes to the final method for locating a thief: when the type of item involved is something that may be identified, which usually means something that is outside of the house – such as an animal or a garment – then it is sometimes possible simply to see and identify the object. This is the instance described in verse 8:

> Concerning any matter of transgression, whether it involves an ox, or a donkey, or a sheep, or a garment – for any lost thing concerning which one can say, "This is it" – both parties shall present their case to the judges. Whoever the judges convict will pay double to his neighbor.

The meeting point of the two themes is the instance of the guardian of movable property. The law here specifies the responsibility of the guardian (the guardian of movable property is exempt if the item is stolen), as well as guidance as to locating the thief (if an item disappears while in the safekeeping of a guardian, the guardian himself comes under suspicion, and the item should be sought within his domain). The two themes include additional instances which should come after the case of the guardian of movable property. The Torah chooses to set down first the final instance illustrating the theme of locating thieves, and only afterwards to continue with the rest of the laws of guardianship.

The Akeda and the Covenant of the Basins

Rav Yonatan Grossman

I. INTRODUCTION

Sometimes, a section of the Torah can be explicated by following the literary allusions which connect it in to another. *Parashat Mishpatim* ends with a covenant ceremony on Mount Sinai – the "covenant of the basins" (*berit ha'aganot*). We shall try and understand this section by comparing it to a different incident – *Akedat Yitzḥak* (the binding of Isaac), based on striking parallels between the sections. These parallels extend beyond a common atmosphere, for both stories come to teach similar lessons.

Let us first compare the content of these stories. In both circumstances, a group of people gather at the side of a mountain; a select few ascend, while the rest stay below, commanded to wait the return of those who ascend, gazing from afar. In both of the stories an altar is built.

AKEDAT YITZḤAK – GENESIS 22	BERIT HA'AGANOT – EXODUS 24
Abraham rose *early* in the morning. (v. 3)	[Moses] rose *early* in the morning. (v. 4)
And Abraham said to his servants, "*you wait here* with the donkey. The boy and I will go up there; we will worship and *we will return to you.*" (v. 5)	And to the elders it was said, "*wait here for us until we return to you.*" (v.14)

325

On the third day Abraham looked up and saw the place *from afar.* (v. 4)	Then He said to Moses, "Come up to the Lord, with Aaron, Nadav and Avihu, and the seventy elders of Israel, and bow low *from afar.*" (v. 1)
Abraham built an altar there. (v. 9) And [he] offered it up as a burnt-offering (*ola*) in place of his son. (v. 13)	He set up an altar at the foot of the mountain. (v.4) They offered burnt-offerings and sacrificed bulls as peace-offerings (*shelamim*) to God. (v. 5)
The knife in the *Akeda* is called a *ma'akhelet* (v. 6), based on the same root as "*okhla.*"	Now the Presence of the Lord appeared in the sight of the Israelites as a consuming fire (*eish okhla*) on the top of the mountain. (v. 17)
Do not raise your hands against the boy. (v. 12)	He did not raise his hands against the leaders of the Israelites. (v. 11)

I think it is clear, based on all of the above textual comparisons between the two sections, that the Torah wants the reader to remember *Akedat Yitzḥak* when reading the enactment of the *berit*. It is plausible that we are to use the *Akeda* as a background to the *berit ha'aganot*, as well as a literary model to understand it.

One phrase in the *berit ha'aganot* demands elucidation: "He sent *na'arei Benei Yisrael*, and they offered *olot* and sacrificed bulls as *shelamim* to God" (Ex. 24:5). There is a dispute among the commentators as to the identity of the "*ne'arim.*" Onkelos translates the sentence as "He designated from the first-born of the Israelites." In his footsteps, the commentators explain the word "I" to mean that the *bekhorim*, the first-born men, were chosen to offer the sacrifices.

This understanding is based on the assumption that only at a later date did the tribe of Levi and the sons of Aaron replace the first-born who were initially to have been the priests of God, based on the exchange recounted in *Parashat Beha'alotekha* (Num. 8:14–19).

It makes sense that the first-born would be sent to offer the sacrifices, since at this time they were still the "priests." However, this explanation does not solve the textual problem, for we never find "*na'arei*" to mean the first-born.

The term "*na'ar*" has several definitions in Tanach. Sometimes, it can refer to a baby, for example: "she saw that it was a child (*na'ar*) crying" (Ex. 2:6; see Rashi). It can also refer to someone who has yet to become a grown man, as in Judges (8:14), and 1 Samuel (2:18). Often the term "*na'ar*" means a servant or a slave: "A Hebrew *na'ar* was there with us" (Gen. 41:12; see also Ex. 33:11). Additionally, it also may denote a man of war as seen in I Samuel (30:17), "except four-hundred *ne'arim* who mounted camels and got away" (see also 11 Sam 2:18). However, there is no other place where "*na'ar*" refers to a first-born.

Ramban (on Ex. 24:5) explains:

> Perhaps it is because Scriptures mentioned the elders who are "the nobles of the *Benei Yisrael*" – therefore it called the first-borns "*ne'arim*," for relative to the "elders" they were young. It thus emphasizes that Moses sent them to offer the sacrifices not because of their status in wisdom, for they were not yet advanced in age, but only on account of the *bekhora*, through which they were appointed to offer sacrifices.

According to Ramban, the term "*ne'arim*" suggests that although the first-born are individually unworthy of such an honored position, nonetheless they are granted this position due to their first-born status. Ramban also offers another possible interpretation of the phrase "*na'arei Benei Yisrael*," one which he prefers over his first explanation:

> In line with the plain meaning of Scriptures, *na'arei Benei Yisrael* were the youth of Israel who had not tasted of sin, and had never come near a women, for they were the most select and holy of the people.

We are dealing with one of the most significant events in the founding of *Benei Yisrael* as a nation, the forging of a *berit* with God in preparation of the acceptance of the Torah. Why are the *ne'arim*, whether they are the first-born or young lads, chosen to represent the entire congregation in such a profound moment? Should we not have expected Moses or Aaron to accept the mantle of leadership at such an occasion? What is different about such a moment from the consecration of the tabernacle or the inauguration of the priests, when Moses performs the main role?

In light of the parallel between *berit ha'aganot* and *Akedat Yitzḥak*, perhaps we should see the *berit* as a type of "*Akedat Yitzḥak*," in addition to its other purposes. Just as Abraham as an individual was commanded to sacrifice his son, so too all of Israel, as a congregation, are required to offer their sons, their *ne'arim*, to God. Of course, actual human sacrifice is an abomination. Thus, a ram was offered as a sacrifice instead of Isaac; correspondingly, the *ne'arim* sacrificed burnt offerings as a substitute for themselves. (See Ramban on *Vayikra* 1:9 who explains all animal sacrifices as a substitute for self-sacrifice.)

The *olot* that the *ne'arim* offered were coming as "a soul for soul," a substitute for themselves. The multitude of literary comparisons between *berit ha'aganot* and *Akedat Yitzḥak* enables us to understand why the *ne'arim* were specifically chosen to offer the sacrifices. The burnt offerings were a substitute of the *na'arei Benei Yisrael* themselves, who were supposed to be offered to God just as Isaac, the son of Abraham, was four hundred years earlier.

II. TWO CONFLICTING EMOTIONS

Based on these parallels between the two stories, I would like to suggest another idea, one not necessarily based purely on the textual comparisons.

In some sense, these two accounts are diametrically opposed to one another. Abraham was asked to sacrifice, not only his son, but also his moral conscience. The setting which surrounds the *Akeda* is one of hardship, sorrow and death. After all, the request made of Abraham was to end a life, to alienate himself from reality and his surroundings.

In utter contrast, the *berit ha'aganot* is characterized by the linking of "they beheld God" and "and they ate and drank" (Ex. 24:11). Meeting God at such an occasion is full of happiness and fervor. In addition, there were also feelings of deep identification with God: "and all the people answered with one voice, saying: all the things which the Lord has commanded we will do…. They said: All that the Lord has spoken we will faithfully do" (Ex. 24:3, 7). The central element is a feast, marked by rejoicing and religious exhilaration.

Akedat Yitzhak is characterized by the fear of God, *yirat Elokim* ("for now I know that you fear God," Gen. 22:12), and the offering of an *ola*. In contrast, *berit ha'aganot* is full of jubilation and love, and *shelamim* are brought in addition to the *olot*.

From this distinction we can abstract two diametrically opposing pictures of the encounter with God. One can strive to come close and meet God through personal submission, through feelings of sacrifice, pain, sorrow and trepidation, as demonstrated in *Akedat Yitzhak*. Another method to meet and identify with the Almighty is through feelings of grandeur, elevation of the soul, and joy – actively challenging and building life, and not separating from it, as depicted in *berit ha'aganot*.

This sheds a new light on the two stories. *Akedat Yitzhak* is performed alone and in solitude. Abraham and Isaac ascend the mountain alone, no one knows of their mission. Their awesome experience remains a personal and intimate one, felt in the depths of their hearts. They build an altar high up at the summit of the mountain, where only they could experience the personal and private encounter with God.

In contrast, the altar of the *berit ha'aganot* is built at the "foot of the mountain." The entire people participate in this awesome experience with the Lord. This experience benefits the whole congregation, merging the individual within the larger congregation: "And all the people answered in one voice saying: All that HaShem has commanded we will do" (Ex. 24:3).

The dialectic of these two episodes is related to a difference in the encounter itself. In *Akedat Yitzhak*, Abraham is the one making an offering to HaShem, he is the giver, he is trying to forge a bond with heaven. In *berit ha'aganot*, HaShem is giving the tablets to the people, He is extending an outstretched hand to humankind and descending to a mundane human life. Abraham carries the fire and the knife (*ma'akhelet*) to the mountain, while *Am Yisrael* sees the "glory of God as a consuming fire ("*eish okhla*") at the top of the mountain" (Ex. 24:17). When man initiates the meeting, it takes the form of loneliness and anguish. In contrast, when man merits God's coming to seek him, it is a time of utmost joy and celebration.

Accordingly, we see yet another difference between the two stories. In both of the stories there is repeated mention of the verb "*re'iya*" (seeing). Abraham names the place "*HaShem yireh*, as will be said this day, *behar HaShem yera'eh*" (lit. the Lord will see) (Gen. 22:14). When Abraham recounts the events which took place on the mountain, he chooses the seeing ("*yirat*") of God as the focus of his experience.

In relation to the *berit ha'aganot*, we read, "and they saw the God of Israel: under His feet there was the likeness of a pavement of sapphire.... They beheld God, and they ate and drank" (Ex. 24:10–11). Later on, the glory of God was exposed for the entire nation to behold. "Now the Presence of the Lord appeared in the sight of the Israelites as a consuming fire on the top of the mountain" (Ex. 24:17).

There is major difference between the two events. In *Akedat Yitzhak*, God is the One who is watching the human sacrifice. The main characters in the *Akeda* are the humans who are seen by God, "on the mountain of the Lord there is vision" (Gen. 22:14). God is the One who sees.

In contrast to the story of the *Akeda*, in the *berit ha'aganot*, the people are the ones who do the seeing. In the beginning it is done by the noblemen, and afterwards by the entire nation. This relates back to a previous point, that at the time when man initiates contact with the Almighty, he is the one acting while the Lord passively observes, whereas at times when God reaches towards mankind, He is active and the people are passive.

Possibly, the offering of "sons" is also the instrument of this idea. Perhaps, in order for people to see God and His glory, one must sacrifice one's own life, because "man cannot see Me and live" (Ex. 33:20). When man requests to see the vision of the Lord, it is required of man to sacrifice of himself: "And you must redeem every first-born among your sons. None shall appear before Me empty-handed" (Ex. 34:20).

The Covenant at Sinai

Rav Yair Kahn

I. THE SEQUENCE OF EVENTS

Immediately after the Torah documents *Ma'amad Har Sinai* (Revelation at Sinai) and the *Aseret haDibrot* (Ten Commandments), there is a lengthy legal section containing various *"mishpatim."* This section deals with a wide range of civil laws, including the laws of slavery, damages, guardians, and lending. The end returns to the *Har Sinai* theme and narrates the Sinaitic covenant and the return of Moses to *Har Sinai* to receive the Torah laws.

A simple reading of the Torah indicates that after *Ma'amad Har Sinai* and the giving of the *Aseret haDibrot*, HaShem gave the *mishpatim* section to Moses, who presented these laws to the people. After the people accepted the laws, Moses recorded these *mishpatim*. He then built an altar and erected twelve monuments for the twelve tribes. Various animals were sacrificed on the altar; half of the sacrificial blood was collected in utensils, and half was sprinkled on the altar. Moses than read the *"Sefer haBerit"* (Book of the Covenant) to the people, who subsequently accepted the covenant with the famous statement *"na'aseh venishma"* (we will do and we will listen). The covenantal blood collected in the utensils was then sprinkled on the people. Moses, the seventy elders, and two of Aaron's children, Nadav and Avihu, climbed *Har Sinai* and had a profound religious experience. Moses alone was then summoned to return to *Har Sinai* for forty days to receive the Torah and Tablets.

According to this reading, the *mishpatim* section separates the covenant from the Ten Commandments. However, this separation is a bit strange. Shouldn't the Sinaitic covenant have taken place within the context of *ma'amad Har Sinai* and the *Aseret haDibrot*? Why did HaShem teach Moses *mishpatim* between them? This may have led many commentators to apply the rule of *"ein mukdam ume'uḥar baTorah"* (the Torah is not necessarily in chronological order) to our *parasha*. In *Parashat Yitro*, Rashi comments:

> "And they should be ready for the third day" – which is the sixth of the month. And on the fifth [of the month], Moses built the altar at the foot of the mountain and the twelve monuments, the entire episode as stated in *Parashat Mishpatim. Ve'ein mukdam ume'uḥar baTorah.* (Rashi on Ex. 19:11)

Rashi echoes this position in our *parasha* as well:

> "And to Moses, He said, 'Go up'" – this *parasha* was said prior to the *Aseret haDibrot* – on the fourth of Sivan, Moses was told to go up. (Rashi on Ex. 24:1)

According to Rashi, on the fourth of Sivan, Moses was commanded to make a covenant between Israel and HaShem. The covenant took place on the fifth of Sivan, during the three days of separation and preparation for *ma'amad Har Sinai*, which transpired on the sixth or seventh of the month. The *mishpatim* section was taught only after Moses received the *Aseret haDibrot*.

Rashi's position allows for a seamless transition from the covenant to *Ma'amad Har Sinai*. The application to the biblical narrative, however, is quite a challenge. Why is the covenant documented at the end of *Parashat Mishpatim* and not as part of the *Ma'amad Har Sinai* narrative in *Parashat Yitro*, if that is when it actually occurred?

In general, the rule *"ein mukdam ume'uḥar baTorah"* should not be applied arbitrarily. Ramban notes in the beginning of *Parashat Koraḥ*

(Num. 16:1) that chronological order is the default assumption. The non-chronological rule is applied only when necessary and only if there is a reasonable explanation for why the Torah departed from a chronological presentation. Although there are commentators who apply this principle more liberally, Ramban's position seems quite reasonable and convincing. Apparently, this lack of a compelling reason leads Ramban, in his commentary to Exodus 24:1, to argue with Rashi's explanation, claiming that the order in which these sections are documented corresponds to the sequence in which they occurred.

There is an additional difficulty with Rashi's interpretation. In introducing the covenant, the Torah states, "And Moses came and told the people all the words of HaShem and all the *mishpatim*" (Ex. 24:3). According to Ramban, this is a clear reference to the beginning of the *parasha*, which begins, "And these are the *mishpatim* that you shall place before them" (21:1). However, according to Rashi, these *mishpatim* had not yet been taught to Moses! Rashi is forced to interpret "*mishpatim*" as referring to laws commanded before *Har Sinai*: "'And all the *mishpatim*' – the seven laws of *Benei Noah*, Shabbat, honoring one's father and mother, the laws of the red heifer, and other various laws previously given at Mara." The difficulty here is obvious.

Although Ramban's interpretation fits more smoothly into Scripture, Rashi's position is the prevalent interpretation adopted by our sages. The Talmud states:

> Rabbi Yossi said: On the second day [of Sivan], Moses went up [to *Har Sinai*] and went down. On the third day, he went up and came down…. On the fourth day, he went up and came down. On the fifth day, he built an altar and brought a sacrifice on it. (*Shabbat* 88a)

Another Gemara (*Hagiga* 6a) states that the *hagiga* sacrifice predates the command of HaShem. The only sacrifice that can be considered a *hagiga* that was brought before the word of HaShem was revealed at Sinai is the *shelamim* sacrifice that was brought during the Sinaitic covenant. This again indicates that the covenant took place prior to the commandments.

In his commentary, Ramban claims that the *Tannaim* actually debated this issue in the *Mekhilta* (*Parashat Yitro*). According to Rabbi Yehuda, the altar and twelve monuments were indeed erected on the fifth day, while Rabbi Yossi ben Rabbi Yehuda argued that "on that very day" all the actions were performed. According to Ramban, "on that very day" refers to the day that the *Aseret haDibrot* were given, and he argues that this opinion retains the chronological consistency of these sections. Accordingly, the section of *mishpatim* was taught immediately following the Ten Commandments, and the covenant was made at the end of that day.

Nevertheless, despite the textual difficulties, Rashi's position is clearly more prevalent. We will therefore attempt to present a convincing argument to explain why the Torah chose to depart from the chronological sequence here.

II. ACCEPTING THE *MITZVOT*

According to Ramban, the Torah separated *Ma'amad Har Sinai* and the *Aseret haDibrot* from the Sinaitic covenant. Why were these two events separated, and why was the *mishpatim* section used for the separation?

Ma'amad Har Sinai was a profound moment of divine revelation. Revelation is fundamentally different from covenant. Revelation is unilateral; HaShem decides on His own, as it were, to reveal Himself to finite man. It is an act of divine grace, and man is totally passive in the encounter. Covenant, on the other hand, is bilateral. Two parties are required to make a covenant; even a covenant between man and HaShem requires active human involvement.

The *Aseret haDibrot* were given to man by HaShem – man receives the Torah passively. Our sages describe the *Dibrot* as being imposed on Israel:

> "And they stood at the bottom of the mountain" [literally – under the mountain]. Rav Avdimi the son of Ḥamma the son of Ḥassa said: "This teaches that *HaKadosh Barukh Hu* placed the mountain upon them like a tub and said to them: 'If you accept the Torah – fine, and if not – there will be your grave.'" (*Shabbat* 88a)

This is *"Matan Torah,"* the giving of the Torah. However, there is also an idea of *kabbalat HaTorah*, in which man actively accepts the Torah. The Sinaitic covenant is based on the children of Israel actively and freely accepting the Torah, as they loudly proclaim *"na'aseh venishma."*

According to Ramban, the covenant, in contrast to revelation, can only occur after *"mishpatim."* There must be tangible content to the acceptance of the Torah, and to accomplish that, certain mitzvot must have already been given.

Furthermore, our sages consider the Sinaitic covenant as completion of the collective *gerut* (conversion) of *Benei Yisrael*. The Gemara writes regarding the conversion process:

> Rabbi says: "Like you, like your fathers" – just like your fathers only entered the covenant through circumcision, immersing [in a *mikveh*], and sprinkling sacrificial blood [on the altar], so too, they [*gerim*] enter the covenant only through circumcision, immersing, and sprinkling sacrificial blood. (*Keritot* 9a)

The Gemara explains that we know that our ancestors entered the covenant through *mila*, as circumcision was necessary in order to participate in the *Korban Pesaḥ*. How do we know that one enters the covenant through immersion and sprinkling the blood?

> Sprinkling sacrificial blood – as it says, "And he sent the youth of the children of Israel [who offered burnt-offerings, and sacrificed peace-offerings]." But what is the source for immersing? As it is stated, "And Moses took half the blood and sprinkled it on the people," and there is no sprinkling without [prior] immersion. (ibid.)

The Gemara's source for the requirements of immersing and sprinkling blood is found in the Sinaitic covenant.

Once we define the covenant at Sinai as *gerut*, the necessity of the *mishpatim* is obvious. In describing the process of conversion, the Gemara includes, "You inform him of some easy mitzvot and some hard mitzvot" (*Yevamot* 47a). In other words, entering a covenant of *gerut* requires knowledge of certain mitzvot. Since very few mitzvot were actually taught in the *Aseret haDibrot*, before the covenant was made, a more comprehensive list of laws had to be taught to the nation. This list is that of the *"mishpatim."* When Moses taught Israel the *mishpatim*, the people collectively accepted them; only at that point could the collective covenant of *gerut* be made.

This idea is found explicitly in Ramban's commentary at the beginning of *Parashat Teruma* that, "Upon telling the *Aseret haDibrot* to the nation of Israel face to face, and commanding them through Moses, *certain mitzvot that are paradigms to the mitzvot of the Torah.*"

III. REVELATION AND COVENANT

Perhaps we can enlist the distinction between covenant and revelation to explain the position of Rashi as well. The Torah intentionally separated the covenant from the revelation at Sinai in order to differentiate between these two distinct ideas.

The Torah begins with the revelation, which is of primary importance. At Sinai, HaShem revealed Himself to Israel, and this revelation is the foundation for our trust in Moses and our belief in the Torah. It is a unilateral act of grace on the part of HaShem whose purpose is to eternalize the collective faith in *Torat Moshe*: "I hereby come to you in the thick of the cloud so that the nation should hear as I speak to you and also in you shall they believe for eternity" (Ex. 19:9). Israel at Sinai are passive participants, absorbing the religious experience and the related divine messages.

In contrast, the covenant of Sinai is a bilateral agreement. Both sides make mutual commitments, and the children of Israel are actively involved. They are taught laws, yet must be pro-active and accept them. They issue the famous proclamation, *"na'aseh venishma"* and immerse themselves in ritually pure water, sacrificial blood is sprinkled on them, and they collectively enter a covenant with HaShem.

These two distinct ideas touch upon a much broader issue. When we worship HaShem, are we meant to passively accept divine will? Or are we perhaps charged by HaShem to be similar to Him – so that just as He is the Creator, so too we are meant to be creative? As we have seen above, there is no simple answer to this question. There are areas in which the proper spiritual reaction is to surrender and accept, but regarding other areas, HaShem wills that we be actively involved. For example, *Torah shebikhtav* – the Written Law, which contains the divine word and will of HaShem, cannot be altered at all. Even the distortion of the corner of a *yod* renders a *Sefer Torah pasul* – invalid. The study of *Torah shebikhtav* is accomplished through reading the divine word accurately. With pure faith, we accept the divine word we received at Sinai. *Torah shebe'al peh* – the Oral Law, on the other hand, is given to Israel to understand based on human intelligence; it is left to Israel to study and develop. In fact, even divine signs do not influence its interpretation (*Bava Metzia* 59b). It is noteworthy that the Gemara (*Gittin* 60b) quotes Rabbi Yoḥanan's opinion that the covenant of Torah was made specifically with respect to *Torah shebe'al peh*.

Based on the above, we can explain the Torah's departure from chronological sequence according to Rashi. Had the Torah described these events consistent with historical chronology, it would have been very difficult to isolate either of these distinct ideas. The need to accurately identify the spiritual messages contained in the complexity and dualism of the Sinai experience is sufficient justification for presenting a chronologically inaccurate account.

The default consistency of the Torah with historic reality applies only when the spiritual message of the Torah is not affected. However, since the Torah is not a book of history, it is not bound by the historical chronology. The Torah has a religious agenda, and whenever that agenda is negatively affected by the chronological account, the "*ein mukdam ume'uḥar*" principle can be applied. The importance of clarifying the distinction between divine revelation and covenant is ample justification for a non-historical presentation.

Parashat Teruma

The Mishkan: Ideal First Choice or After-the-Fact?

Rav Menachem Leibtag

EDITORS' INTRODUCTION

One of the major areas of disagreement among the commentators concerns the relationship between the sin of the golden calf and the Mishkan. The instructions for building the Mishkan precede the sin, while the actual construction follows it. Rashi and Ramban disagree whether, text location notwithstanding, the actual command to build the Mishkan preceded or followed the sin.

The specific question concerns the time of the command to build the Mishkan. Rashi delays it until after the sin. The time of the command, however, also suggests the framework for the meaning of the command. Hence, it is natural that Ramban, who holds that the presentation in the Torah follows the chronological order, sees the Mishkan as providing a more permanent "domicile" for the presence of God which first rested temporarily on Sinai. On the contrary, according to Rashi, who distorts the textual order and delays the command to build the Mishkan until after the sin of the golden calf, it is natural to assume that the Mishkan is a means of atonement for the sin, or a response to the new situation created by the sin. Rav Leibtag questions whether according to Rashi there would have been no such thing as a physical sanctuary had the sin not occurred.

Let us first review some of the proofs for both positions.

A. *Rashi* – *Rashi explicitly associates several features of the* Mishkan *with the sin of the* egel *(calf). Rav Leibtag mentions the donation of the half-shekel, the choice of Ḥur's grandson Bezalel, the role of the kohanim and the tribe of Levi, and the bull (= calf) brought by Aaron in the dedication ceremony. To this, various commentators have added the use of gold in the* Mishkan *and the dedication ceremony in Leviticus, which is replete with references to* ḥatat *(sin-offering) and* kapara *(atonement).*

Seforno (24:18) is one commentator who adopts the extreme implications of Rashi's position, claiming that ideally God did not plan to have any earthly building built for Him, and brings an interesting proof for it. Seforno points out that immediately after the revelation on Sinai, God says, "An altar of earth shall you make for Me, and you shall sacrifice on it your burnt offerings (ola) *and your peace offerings* (shelamim), *your sheep and your oxen; in every place where I record My name, I shall come to you and bless you" (20:21). Seforno interprets this to mean that there is no need for any particular place to bring offerings. A simple earthen altar is sufficient. Only after the sin does God command "They shall make me a sanctuary and I shall dwell in their midst." Seforno is clearly claiming that before the sin, there was no plan to establish a central sanctuary with formal rules of operation.*

B. *Ramban* – *Obviously, the main proof of Ramban's position is the order of the Torah text. Ramban is undoubtedly influenced by a more general ideological consideration – he is convinced that* Mishkan *and* Mikdash *are central motifs of the Torah.*

Here too, various commentators searched for parallels between the details of the Mishkan *and the narrative of Mount Sinai. Rav Leibtag has pointed to the walls (meḥitzot) around the* Mishkan *and the boundaries around the mountain, the successive and nested realms where fewer and fewer people are allowed, the altar at the foot of the mountain, etc. In a comment several years ago, Rav Nathaniel Helfgot added the following point: "The first time the root sh-kh-n (ש.כ.נ. – dwell) is used is at the end of chapter 24: "Vayishkon kevod*

HaShem al Har Sinai." *This episode definitely took place at the time of the revelation of Mount Sinai – in fact, according to many commentators, it took place before the revelation. Why does the root of the word* "Mishkan" *appear only here? It appears that the Torah is trying, by the placement and by the use of the root, to connect the revelation on Mount Sinai with the opening of Parashat Teruma immediately afterwards –* "ve'asu li mikdash veshakhanti betokham." *The* Mishkan *is the continuation of Mount Sinai.*[1]

In the *Parashot* of *Vayak'hel* and *Pekudei*, *Benei Yisrael* are commanded to build the *Mishkan* according to the instructions already conveyed to Moses. In between these two sets of instructions we find the story of the golden calf. The commentators debate whether these sections are recorded according to the order in which they occurred, or whether the order is not chronological, and the episode of the golden calf actually preceded the command to build the *Mishkan*. According to Ramban's opinion, it would seem that the concept of the *Mishkan* is a positive ideal, a continuation of the Sinaitic experience, while Rashi's position suggests that the need for a *Mishkan* was "*bediavad*" (*post facto*), i.e., not God's original intention, but rather resulted from the sin of the golden calf.

In this article we shall attempt to prove that even according to Rashi, the idea of the *Mishkan* (and its successor – the *Beit HaMikdash*) is an objective ideal, and that the debate between the two opinions is limited to the reasons for certain details which are part of the command to build it.

Let us begin with a proof that the commandment to build a *Mishkan* represents an ideal. After all, how could it be that were it not for Israel's sinning with the golden calf, they would not have been commanded to build this most significant and central edifice?

---

1. Rav Helfgot's shiur on *Tetzaveh* in this book, listing the differences between the commandment of the *Miluim* in *Tetzaveh* and their fulfillment in Leviticus, is itself a proof of Ramban's position. By finding aspects of the Mishkan in Leviticus which seem to be connected to the golden calf, but which are not found in the original instructions, we may conclude that the basic idea of the Mishkan precedes the sin.

The relationship of the Mishkan to the sin of the golden calf is addressed in a somewhat different manner in the article of Rav Chanoch Waxman which follows this one.

At the end of *Parashat Mishpatim*, in the mitzva concerning the pilgrim festivals, the Torah states:

> You shall celebrate three pilgrim-festivals for Me during the year. You shall observe the festival of matzot ... and you shall not see My face empty-handed. And the festival of the harvest.... Three times during the year all your males shall see the face of the Lord God. You shall not sacrifice the blood of My offerings with *ḥametz*.... The first fruits of your land shall you bring to the house of the Lord your God. You shall not cook a kid in its mother's milk. (Ex. 23:15–19)

There is no doubt that these words were presented to the nation before the incident of the golden calf, and they clearly demonstrates that a "house of the Lord your God" – the *Mikdash* – was meant to exist. The people are commanded to see "the face of the Lord God" (implying – at the place where He is to be found) three times during the year. Hence the general idea of a *Mikdash* certainly exists previous to the commandment to build it, even prior to the sin.

According to Ramban, assuming that the sections are in fact in chronological order, the explanation is quite simple. The *Parashot* of *Teruma* and *Tetzaveh*, with their instructions regarding the *Mishkan*, define more precisely how to go about building the "house of the Lord your God" mentioned at the end of *Parashat Mishpatim*.

However, from Rashi's point of view, there appears to be a difficulty. Why does the commandment to build the *Mishkan* appear before the story of the golden calf, when it should have chronologically appeared only afterward?

Let us understand Rashi's position and the basis of the debate between the commentators by analyzing the order and structure of the *parashot* at the end of Exodus. Looking at the end of the book, we may clearly delineate four units:

A. The giving of the Torah and the *parashot* of Mount Sinai (chapters 19–24)

B. The command to build the *Mishkan* and its vessels, in descending order of importance (chapters 25–31)

C. The sin of the golden calf and the subsequent receiving of the second set of tablets (chapters 32–34)

D. The building of the *Mishkan* (*Vayak'hel-Pekudei* – chapters 35–40)

Ramban's explanation emphasizes the juxtaposition and connection between the command regarding the *Mishkan* (B) and God's revelation on Mount Sinai (A), and hence the logic of the order of the *parashot* as they appear.

> The essence of the *Mishkan* was to allow the Divine Glory which had rested on Mount Sinai to rest upon it [the *Mishkan*] in hidden form... and therefore God first commanded the building of the *Mishkan*, so that He would have a home among them, sanctified for Him.... And in the *Mishkan*, always accompanying Israel, would be the Divine Glory which had appeared to them at Mount Sinai, and when Moses used to approach, God would speak to him as He did on Mount Sinai. (Ramban on Exodus 25:1).

The actual building of the *Mishkan* (D), the execution of the command, was delayed until they had been forgiven for the sin of the golden calf.

Rashi, on the other hand, emphasizes the connection between the commandment regarding the *Mishkan* (B) and the sin of the golden calf (C). Let us examine some other examples of this connection which Rashi observed between these two events:

1. The need for the half-shekel in order to conduct a census of the nation (found at the beginning of *Parashat Ki Tisa*):

   "And you shall give it for the service of the Tent of Meeting" – We learn from here that he (Moses) was commanded to count them at the beginning of the collection for the *Mishkan*, after the episode of the golden calf, because a plague had been upon them (and many had died). (Rashi on Exodus 30:16)

2. Aaron's sacrifice at the end of the dedication ceremonies, in *Parashat Tetzaveh*:

    "One bull" – to atone for the golden calf, which was a bull. (Rashi on Exodus 29:1)

3. The selection of Ḥur's grandson as the chief builder of the *Mishkan*:

    "Bezalel ben Uri ben Ḥur" – Bezalel's grandfather is mentioned ... because Ḥur died as a result of the incident of the golden calf, and the labor of the *Mishkan* came to atone for that sin; that is why Ḥur is mentioned here. (Ḥizkuni ibid, 31:2)

4. The selection of Aaron and his sons (and the tribe of Levi as a whole) to serve in the *Mishkan* (in place of the first-born sons):

    "At that time God set aside the tribe of Levi" – During the first year following your exodus from Egypt, when you sinned with the golden calf and the tribe of Levi did not sin – God set them aside. (Deut. 10:8)

Because of the sin of the golden calf (c), certain details in the commandment to build the *Mishkan* (B) were altered, and therefore Rashi explains that the *parashot* are not in their chronological order:

> There is no chronological order in the Torah. The sin of the golden calf preceded the command regarding the construction of the *Mishkan* by a long period: On the seventeenth of Tammuz the first tablets were shattered, on Yom Kippur God was appeased and forgave Israel, and the next day the collection for the *Mishkan* commenced [Rashi is hinting that there is a connection between the collection of the gold for the building of the *Mishkan* and the collection of gold for the golden calf] and it was erected on 1 Nisan. (Rashi on Exodus 31:18)

Rashi does not state that the sin of the golden calf is the reason for the commandment to build the *Mishkan*. He rather relates specific aspects of the commandment to the influence of that incident, such as who would be involved in the construction, who would serve in the *Mishkan*, which sacrifices were to be brought there, etc.

According to Rashi's opinion, why are the sections not written in their correct chronological order? Why did the Torah see fit to record the commandment regarding the *Mishkan* before recounting the incident of the golden calf?

In his statement, "there is no chronological order in the Torah," Rashi means that the order of the sections in the Torah is determined by thematic connections and not necessarily by the sequence of events. In this light, Ramban's commentary on the thematic connection between the *Mishkan* and the giving of the Torah does not contradict Rashi; it takes on renewed force. The Torah purposefully records the commandment of the *Mishkan* first, despite the fact that it was transmitted to Moses only after the sin of the golden calf, and it is juxtaposed to the section of Mount Sinai in order to emphasize the thematic connection between them. With regard to the entire issue of the importance of the *Mishkan* as an ideal, as a continuation of *Matan Torah*, there is absolutely no need to conclude that Rashi and Ramban disagree.

According to Rashi's position, it seems that the idea of the *Mishkan* appears as early as *Parashat Mishpatim*, long before the sin of the golden calf, but the precise details of "God's house" were not yet enumerated. We do not know what the original plan for the construction of the *Mishkan* would have been had Israel not sinned. (Perhaps the original plans were "shattered" along with the first tablets.) In the wake of the golden calf – and perhaps as part of the atonement process – the original plans regarding the commandment of the *Mishkan* were changed, and some of the details were adapted accordingly. Rashi's explanation is not a negation of the idea that the *Mishkan* was an ideal, but reflects the principle that "there is no chronological order in the Torah." He sees the command to build the *Mishkan* as connected both to Sinai and to the sin of the golden calf.

Ramban believes that we should ignore the chronological order of the stories recounted in the Torah only as a last resort. Since there is no conclusive proof in the section containing the commandments to build the *Mishkan* that would direct us to explain them as an "atonement" for the golden calf, Ramban prefers to leave the chronological order unchanged.

Of Sequence and Sanctuary: Rashi's View

Rav Chanoch Waxman

I. INTRODUCTION

The opening of *Parashat Teruma* marks a major shift in the topic matter of Exodus. Until this point, the book has primarily concerned itself with slavery, redemption and the revelation at Sinai. However, from this point on, the *Mishkan*, the portable sanctuary constructed by the children of Israel, constitutes the focus. Excluding a short break for the sin of the golden calf and its aftermath, the remainder of the book is dedicated to the instructions for building the *Mishkan* and its actual construction. Despite this fundamental thematic turn, the book seems to preserve its linear quality, progressing almost seamlessly from one event to the next. Just as the children of Israel were redeemed from Egypt, traveled through the desert, and received the Torah at Sinai in sequential order, so too the events of the last part of the book appear to unfold in chronological sequence. The story develops as follows:

Upon the culmination of the covenant of Sinai (24:1–14), Moses ascends the mountain and stays there for forty days and nights (24:18).

Section one – During this time, God instructs Moses regarding the gathering of materials for the *Mishkan* and the construction and staffing of the sanctuary (25:1–31:18).

Section two – After Moses has been given the instructions for constructing the *Mishkan*, the incident of the golden calf occurs. Moses eventually achieves atonement for the children of Israel and after another forty days on the mountain returns to the camp carrying a second set of tablets inscribed with the Ten Commandments (31:18–34:35).

Section three – Moses then gathers the people, passes on the instructions for constructing the *Mishkan*, and commences the labor. The book closes with the completion of the labor and the setting up of the *Mishkan* (35:1–40:38).

This sequential reading of the latter part of Exodus constitutes the opinion of the majority of commentaries (Ibn Ezra, Ramban etc.). In marked contrast, commenting on the first verse of the above section two, Rashi makes the following counterintuitive statement:

> There is neither "earlier" nor "later" in the Torah (*ein mukdam ume'uḥar baTorah*). The making of the golden calf occurred many days prior to the command for constructing the *Mishkan*. (Rashi on Ex. 31:18)

Rashi maintains that the literary sequence of events, the textual ordering of the Torah, does not necessarily indicate chronological sequence. While the Torah presents things as if the sin of the golden calf occurred in between the command of the *Mishkan* and building of the *Mishkan*, in reality things happened otherwise.

Factoring in Rashi's comments later on in the same verse (18:1) and his comments on the story of the covenant at Sinai (24:1–18) yields the following time line for the events from chapter 19 until the end of the book:

Section one – The events prior to revelation of the Ten Commandments:
The preparations for the revelation (19:1–25)
The covenant at Sinai (24:1–11)

Section two – The revelation of the Ten Commandments and the aftermath:

The Ten Commandments and the people's reaction (20:1–18)
Moses' ascent to the mountain to receive the stone tablets and
commune with God for forty days (24:12–18)

Section three – The events during Moses' first forty day stay on the mountain and their aftermath:
Moses receives the laws regarding gods of gold and silver, altars
and the rules of *Parashat Mishpatim* (20:19–23:33)
The construction of the golden calf and its aftermath (31:18–34:35)

Section four – The *Mishkan*:
The instructions for making the *Mishkan* (25:1–31:17)
The passing on of the instructions to the people and the actual
construction of the *Mishkan* (35:1–40:38)

Rashi's non-sequential reading of the events in Exodus, his creation of a gap between the real order of events and their textual presentation, raises numerous obvious questions. Most simply, what constitutes the motivation for doing so? While it may be the case that the textual order of the Torah does not necessarily reflect chronological order, this does not mean that the Torah always presents events in this manner. Seemingly, any claim of *"ein mukdam ume'uḥar,"* of the existence of a gap between textual and chronological order, should be accompanied by a compelling reason for making the claim. Furthermore, claiming that a particular group of narratives are not presented in chronological order raises the question of what exactly accounts for the order in which the Torah presents the stories. If chronology doesn't constitute the ordering principle, what does?

Even limiting our analysis to Rashi's position regarding the latter parts of Exodus, we are faced with two questions. What compels Rashi to assume that *Parashat Teruma*, the story of the instructions for building the *Mishkan*, occurred after rather than before the sin of the golden calf? Perhaps more importantly, why does the Torah place things out of "order"? Why present the instructions for the *Mishkan* before the story of the golden calf, rather than afterwards?

II. THE *MISHKAN* AND MOUNT SINAI

The concept of a sanctuary appears relatively late in the story of Exodus. In fact, the first mention of worship and cult after the revelation of the Ten Commandments fails to mention the construction of a full-fledged sanctuary. God tells Moses to inform the children of Israel of the following:

> You yourselves have seen that I spoke with you from heaven. With Me, therefore, do not make any gods of silver, nor shall you make for yourselves any gods of gold. Make for Me an altar of earth and sacrifice on it your burnt offerings and peace offerings…in every place where I cause My name to be mentioned I will come to you and bless you. (20:19–21)

Rather than a full-fledged sanctuary made from precious metals and fine fabrics, God commands the children of Israel to make a simple earthen altar. The commandment comes after the prohibition of making gods of silver or gold "along" with the Lord and seems logically connected to it. But what constitutes the connection?

As pointed out by both Ibn Ezra (on 20:20) and Seforno (on 20:19), the tension between the physical and material on the one hand, and the immaterial and metaphysical on the other hand, constitutes the driving logic of the entire passage. At Sinai, God demonstrated to the children of Israel that His very presence is wholly immaterial. He is but a voice. He is wholly other than the physical and cannot be governed by its rules or symbols. Consequently, representations of God, symbols of God, intermediaries, or attempts to channel His presence to a determined locale, constitute the antithesis of the proper worship of God. Hence the prohibition of "gods" of silver and gold.

Similarly, the cleavage between God and the physical plane determines not just the prohibited form of worship, but also the commanded form of worship. An altar made for the worship of God should be of plain earth, the antithesis of an elaborate physical structure meant to serve as an intermediary, material symbol or abode of God (Seforno). Finally, even this altar constitutes an impermanent rather than fixed holy place. God may "come" to any place where He has set His name in order to be worshipped and in order to bless the children of Israel.

This approach creates quite a problem in reading the story of the *Mishkan*. Unlike our passage above, what might be termed "Introduction to Worship," the instructions for the building of the *Mishkan* are rife with physicality, precious metals, materials and materialism. The *Mishkan* is a permanent, albeit portable, sanctuary described as the resting place of God (Ex. 25:8). The altar is not made from a heap of dirt or stones (20:21–22) but rather out of wood and copper (27:1–8). Finally, the solid gold *keruvim* that top the ark, no matter what their form, or whether their outstretched wings form a throne or not, seem perilously close to the gods of gold made "along" with God, forbidden by the "Introduction to Worship" (20:19–21).

In sum, the very existence of the *Mishkan*, and the dedication of a large part of Exodus to the details of its planning and construction, seem to negate the fundamental principles of divine worship introduced at Sinai.

The answer to this conundrum may lie in exploring the story of the golden calf. Upon growing impatient for Moses' return, the people demand of Aaron to "make us gods" (32:1). This of course is strange. How does one make a deity? To add to the mystery, Aaron seems to know exactly how to go about the matter. He asks the people to donate gold and either by casting it in a mold, or overlaying it on a wooden frame, fashions the golden calf (32:2–4).

At this point, the people paid homage to the image and declared "this is your god(s) O Israel who brought you out of the land of Egypt" (32:4). Do the people believe that the calf is a representation of the Lord? Or perhaps they believe that they have been redeemed from Egypt not by the Lord, the God of their forefathers, but rather by the calf deity. In fact neither of these interpretations is correct. They are engaged in the well-known procedure of making a god of gold "along" with the Lord. In fact when Moses returns to God to pray for the people, he explicitly describes their sin as a "great sin," the act of making "god(s) of gold" (32:31). In other words, the golden calf is meant to somehow embody the power of God, to channel the presence of the Lord and bridge the gap between God and the people.

Aaron's reaction to the people's claim further supports this interpretation. Rather than challenging the people's idolatry, he builds an altar in front of the calf and proclaims a holiday to the Lord the very next day (32:5). The calf constitutes a way to connect with God, a method of seeking His leadership and a means of worship, not a choice of another deity.

When the people get up the next morning to bring their burnt offerings and peace offerings (32:6), they engage in a bizarre parody of the worship instructions given at Sinai (20:19–22). Indeed they bring burnt offerings and peace offerings upon a hastily erected and temporary altar probably made of a heap of dirt or stones. Yet this simple altar stands in front of the "god of gold," the physical and magical device meant to capture the presence and power of God, to embody and confine the infinite in the finite physical realm. Part of God's message at Sinai has somehow been missed.

This brings us back to the *Mishkan*. Just as the golden calf constitutes a contradiction of the Sinaitic rules of worship, so too the *Mishkan* constitutes an apparent violation of the rules of worship. As pointed out above, the very existence of a physical space "containing" God, the precious metals, the wood and metal altar, and the *keruvim* all stand at odds with the theological and legal imperatives of Sinaitic worship. What has happened?

The answer may be the sin of the golden calf. Whether due to the strength of the people's ties to Egyptian conceptions and habits or sheer human nature, the people prove themselves incapable of the rules laid down in the "Introduction to Worship" (20:19–21). They cannot imagine a mode of divine service that strives to be as immaterial and non-physical as the God it serves. They cannot imagine a deity wholly other than the physical, present merely by his word and will. They make themselves a god of gold. In response, God makes what might be thought of as a grand compromise. He provides them with a mode of worship appropriate for the people. Whether as mere symbol, or as an actual metaphysical act of *"tzimzum,"* God confines His infinite Self within the finite space of the sanctuary. It serves as His house. It is His table, His lamp and His chariot-chair represented by the *keruvim* that fill the sanctuary. In stark and marked contrast to ideal theology, He provides the people with physical representation, permanent presence and a glorious golden means to find the divine. In sum, the command of the *Mishkan* comes in response to the crisis of the golden calf.

This brings us back to Rashi and his non-sequential reading of the latter part of Exodus. In line with the textual points and ideas outlined above, Rashi's reading places the sin of the golden calf before the command for the building of the *Mishkan*. While we can never know the precise motivation behind Rashi's interpretation, his reading does indeed dovetail with viewing the *Mishkan* as a response to the crisis of the golden calf and the problem of worshipping an immaterial God.

III. A COVENANTAL CONVERGENCE

While thinking about the *Mishkan* as a response to the golden calf may help explain Rashi's claim of *"ein mukdam ume'uḥar,"* the theory outlined above is in some sense troubling. Can we really view the command of *Mishkan* as a compromise, as something less than an ideal, as a response to either a particular contingent moment in history or human nature? Doesn't this approach subtly undermine the centrality of the sanctuary in Tanach, Jewish Law and Jewish History?

Rather than enter directly into this difficult issue, I would like to approach it by discussing a different problem already hinted at earlier. As pointed out above, a claim of *"ein mukdam ume'uḥar"* must not only possess a compelling reason. It should also include an explanation of the "textual," i.e. non-chronological, ordering of the Torah. Not just the motivation, but also the presentation must be explained. In other words, if the Torah has deliberately arranged the text out of "order," this must serve some purpose or be based upon some set of principles.

At first glance, the explanation advanced above, *Mishkan* as response and compromise, seems to fail this test. What possible literary or pedagogic purpose is served by placing the instructions for the *Mishkan* before the sin of the golden calf, precisely in the wrong place? This placement in fact obscures, rather than elucidates, the true relation between the two. If so, let us take a closer look at the literary placement of the instructions for the *Mishkan* (25:1–31:17).

As noted above, Rashi does more than just transpose the positions of the instructions for the *Mishkan* and the sin of the golden calf in creating his chronology. He also shifts the chronological position of the covenant at Sinai (24:1–11), placing it back in "Group One," the events before the revelation of the Ten Commandments. In addition, he also rereads the timing of Moses' ascent to the mountain to receive the stone tablets (24:12–18), placing this event back in "Group Two," the revelation and aftermath of the Ten Commandments.

In other words, according to Rashi, the Torah engages in a dual displacement of texts. From one direction, it moves the corpus of chapter 25 and onwards, the instructions for the *Mishkan* that occur after the golden calf, to an "earlier" position. From the other direction, the Torah moves the events of chapter 24, both the covenant at Sinai (24:1–11) and the ascent of Moses to receive the tablets (24:12–18) to a "later" position, placing them in direct juxtaposition to chapter 25, the instructions for the *Mishkan*. The purpose seems to be to create a Sinai-*Mishkan* textual flow.

Moreover, numerous literary parallels exist between the Sinai stories of chapter 24 and the *Mishkan*. As pointed out in the past, the story of the covenant of Sinai emphasizes a three-part division of people and space. Moses ascends alone all the way up the mountain to the Lord (24:2, see also 24:12, 18). The elite, the priests and elders occupy an intermediate position somewhere on the mountain and are privileged with some lesser form of the Lord's Presence (24:1, 9–11). The third group, the people, remain down at the bottom of the mountain, along with the altar they have constructed and the sacrifices they have brought (24:4–5). But this in fact constitutes the division of people and space present in the *Mishkan*.

The *Mishkan* is divided into three areas, the Holy of Holies containing the Ark, the remainder of the Tent of Meeting containing the other vessels, and an external area containing the altar. According to chapter 25, God meets with Moses and speaks to him from "above the covering (of the Ark), between the two *keruvim*" (25:22). Moses, and seemingly Moses alone, enters into the holiest space. Similarly, and parallel once again to Sinai, the elite, the priests, enter into the second space, the Tent of Meeting (28:43, Lev. 16:2). Finally, the people remain outside of the two inner spaces, in a "lower," external area where the altar is located (see Lev. 9:23–24).

Moreover, just as the covenant at Sinai emphasizes text and sacrifices, so too the *Mishkan* includes text and sacrifices. The "Book of the Covenant" (Ex. 24:7), containing the "commands of God" (24:4) that the children of Israel react to by declaring "we will do and obey" finds its parallel in the "testimony," i.e. the Torah (see Rashi on 25:16), placed in the ark under the "*keruvim*-throne" of the "King." Likewise, the celebratory, communal and covenantal sacrifices (24:4–5) of Sinai find their parallel in the daily sacrifices performed upon the altar in the *Mishkan*.

To put all this together, the deliberate juxtaposing and paralleling of the covenant at Sinai and *Mishkan* is meant to emphasize that the *Mishkan* constitutes a symbol and physical enshrining of a particular moment in time, the contracting of the covenant at Sinai. The *Mishkan* and its daily function stand as a constant reminder and embodiment of God's visit at Sinai and the children of Israel's commitment to the "book of the covenant," their statement of "we will do and obey."

Alternatively, we may consider not so much the connection of the first half of chapter 24 (24:1–11) to the *Mishkan*, but the link between the second half of chapter 24, the ascent of Moses (24:12–18), and the *Mishkan*. As already pointed out by Ramban (on 25:1), the language and images parallel various *Mishkan* texts. Just as God "rested" upon the mountain in the story of Moses' ascent to receive the tablets (24:16), so too God "rests" in the *Mishkan* (25:8). Just as His cloud "covered the mountain" (24:15–16), so too His cloud covered the *Mishkan* upon its completion (40:34). Finally, and most crucially, just as God summoned Moses to enter and receive the tablets and Torah (24:12, 18), so too God summons Moses into the Tent of Meeting (Lev. 1:1) in order to speak with Moses, and pass His commands on to the children of Israel (Ex. 25:22). Once again, the *Mishkan* constitutes a continuation of Sinai, a means of communication, a method for the ongoing revelation of the Torah.

Needless to say, the two connections between chapters 24 and 25, between Sinai and *Mishkan*, constitute two sides of the same coin. While the *Mishkan* symbolizes revelation and constitutes a means for the ongoing delivery of God's word, it also symbolizes covenant, an ongoing commitment to "do and obey" the word of God.

IV. A SOLUTION BOTH COMPROMISE AND IDEAL

To close the circle, let us return to Rashi, "*ein mukdam ume'uḥar*," the Torah's deliberate choice of textual ordering and the philosophical problem of *Mishkan* as a compromise.

I have tried to argue that Rashi's position regarding the chronology of the latter part of Exodus, a position seemingly rooted in viewing *Mishkan* as a response to the golden calf, winds up emphasizing the link between Sinai and *Mishkan*. The seam between chapters 24 and 25 constitutes not so much an incidental result of the natural unfolding of events, but a deliberate construction meant to emphasize the parallel between Sinai and *Mishkan* and the notion of *Mishkan* as continuation of the communication and covenantal consciousness of Sinai.

If so, something highly complex, but hopefully rather compelling, emerges from Rashi's position. On the one hand, *Mishkan* is a response to the sin of the golden calf and the problem of worshipping an immaterial God. Yet, at the same time, it constitutes far more than a mere forsaking of unrealizable ideals. It constitutes not just a symbol, or perhaps even contraction, of God's presence, but also a representation and continuation of the covenant at Sinai – a means to continue the communication of God's word and will. In other words, it provides the solution of Sinai for bridging the gap between an immaterial God and His people.

To phrase this slightly differently, it was precisely the failure of covenantal consciousness, the ability to connect to God through His word and will, that led to the sin of the golden calf. His presence gone from the mountain, His voice a mere echo and His word a dead text, the children of Israel tried to conjure His presence, to connect to Him through a "god of gold." The *Mishkan* as portable Sinai resolves this fundamental problem. It stands as a reminder of the covenant and serves as a means to hear His ongoing word. While *Mishkan* may indeed emerge from the crisis of the golden calf, it nevertheless teaches the true lesson of Sinai, connecting to God through His covenant and word. It is both compromise and ideal.

The Ark of the Covenant

Rav Elchanan Samet

I. THE ARK – THE HEART OF THE *MISHKAN*

In his introduction to *Parashat Teruma*, Ramban makes several observations crucial for a proper understanding of the role of the *Mishkan* (the Tabernacle, and later the *Beit Mikdash*). He begins by explaining the timing of the commandment to build the *Mishkan*, following the divine revelation to Israel on *Har Sinai* (Mount Sinai) and their acceptance of the Ten Commandments and the commandments of *Parashat Mishpatim*, concluding with the sealing of the covenant between God and Israel (Ex. 24:1–8). Now a new relationship has been established between God and Israel: "From now on, behold, they are a nation unto Him and He will be a God to them." It is appropriate that this relationship between the partners to the covenant be expressed in the construction of "a Temple to rest His *Shekhina* (Presence) amongst them" as a continual expression of this covenant.

However, the *Mishkan* is not a static expression of this covenantal relationship, but rather a tool for its continuation and completion. Israel entered the covenant like converts who had been told "some of the commandments, which were like first principles for all the commandments of the Torah," but the covenant would be complete only

359

when they received the entire Torah. Thus, the Torah specifies several times that the purpose of the *Mishkan* is to serve as a place for continued revelation to Moses in order to complete the giving of the Torah (25:22; 29:42–43; 30:6, 36). The realization of this idea is also mentioned several times after the construction of the *Mishkan* is completed (Lev. 1:1, Num. 7:89, etc.)

Even the name *"Ohel Moed,"* which is repeated many times, means simply "the Tent of Meeting" – the tent in which God meets with Moses and gives him commandments for *Benei Yisrael* (see also Rashbam 25:8). The Torah repeatedly links the concept of *"edut"* (testimony) with the concept of *"hiva'adut"* (meeting); for example, "Before the covering which is upon the *testimony* (*edut*) where I will *meet* (*iva'ed*) with you" (30:6). The *luḥot* (tablets) are testimony to God's covenant with Israel, and therefore it is fitting that the place where the testimony is kept will serve as the place of meeting between God and Moses, with a view to completing this covenant.

Thus we reach Ramban's conclusion that "the secret of the *Mishkan* is that the Divine Glory which rested (publicly) upon *Har Sinai* will rest there privately…and when Moses would come there, the divine word would come to him *as it came to him on Har Sinai.*" On *Har Sinai* Moses was commanded with regard to the construction of the *Mishkan*, at *Har Sinai* he was shown a vision of the *Mishkan* and its vessels, at *Har Sinai* the *Mishkan* was built and dedicated, and when the time came to leave *Har Sinai* and proceed into the desert, *Benei Yisrael* took with them a "portable revelation" in the form of the *Mishkan*.

If this is indeed the significance of the *Mishkan*, then it is clear that the Ark (containing the Tablets of Testimony) and the Ark's covering (with the *keruvim*, from where God spoke to Moses) represents the very heart of the *Mishkan*, as Ramban writes. The two related functions of the Ark – containing the Testimony and serving as a point of meeting – are reflected in the two names of the *Mishkan*: *"Ohel Moed"* (Tent of Meeting) and *"Mishkan haEdut"* (Resting Place of the Testimony). In other words, the entire *Mishkan* is designated by the function of the Ark.

II. THE UNIQUENESS OF THE DESCRIPTION OF THE ARK

The section detailing the construction of the Ark (25:10–22) demonstrates its critical importance in the *Mishkan* in a number of ways:

1. It is the first vessel which they are commanded to make, as Ramban notes: "The ark and its cover are mentioned first, as they are first in order of importance."

2. The *parasha* dealing with the Ark, consisting of thirteen verses, is the longest of all the *parashot* devoted to the vessels of the *Mishkan*.

3. The opening of this *parasha* (25:10) is addressed in the plural – the only time that the plural is used in a command concerning a vessel of the *Mishkan* (even in the continuation of this *parasha*, we find a switch to the singular). Ibn Ezra explains the use of the plural in "And *they* shall make an Ark" as follows: "Because God said in the beginning (v. 8), 'And *they shall make Me* a sanctuary,' therefore He likewise starts here, 'And *they shall make* an Ark.'" Ibn Ezra's connection is compelling in light of the fact that the Ark is the essence of the *Mishkan*.

4. The Ark is not an instrumental vessel – no service is performed with it. At the end of each *parasha* commanding the construction of one of the vessels of the *Mishkan*, its function in the daily workings of the *Mishkan* is mentioned (e.g. 25:30, 37). The corresponding verse in the case of the Ark is different: "And you shall place in the Ark the testimony which I shall give you." This is a one-time action which will turn the Ark into an "Ark of Testimony." Its regular function lies not in the priestly service but rather in meeting with Moses, as we see at the conclusion of the command to build the Ark (25:22): "And I shall meet there with you and I shall speak to you from above the covering."

5. The Ark is one of four vessels of the *Mishkan* which have poles used for carrying it. But only with regard to the poles of the Ark are we told (v.15): "The poles shall be in the rings of the Ark; *they shall not move from there.*"

III. THE PROHIBITION OF REMOVING THE POLES

Ḥazal interpret the verse, "The poles shall be in the rings of the ark, they shall not be removed from there," as a negative command:

> Rabbi Elazar said ... He who removes the poles of the Ark is punished with lashes. (*Yoma* 72a)

This negative command is included as one of the 613 mitzvot (Rambam, *Sefer HaMitzvot*, Neg. 80).

Does a literal interpretation of this verse necessarily entail this conclusion? The Talmud shows that Rabbi Elazar's opinion was not universally accepted (ibid.):

> Rav Aḥa bar Yaakov questioned him: "Perhaps what the Torah means is, attach the poles and place them well within the rings *so that they cannot move.*"

But the Talmud rejects this explanation for linguistic reasons:

> Is it written *"in order* that they do not move"? [Rather, it states "they shall not move," as a direct independent injunction, not a reason for what was written before.]

Ḥizkuni, however, offers an alternative explanation, which does not regard this as a prohibition:

> According to the literal meaning, *there is no need* to remove these poles, for they involve no trouble or taking up of space, since they are in the Holy of Holies where no one but the *Kohen Gadol* enters and leaves ... on one day of the year. But if there were poles [permanently affixed] to the altar of copper which is in the courtyard, where everyone enters and leaves, then people coming in and going out would constantly bump into them. Therefore [the poles] need to be affixed [to the altar] only at those times when they are on the move, as it is written [27:7], "And the poles shall be on the two sides of the altar *to carry it.*"

While this explanation is intriguing, it raises the question: why does the Torah add extra words and tell us something which is obvious – i.e., that "there is no need" to remove the poles? We therefore return to Rabbi Elazar's words, which seem to be the simple meaning of the text.

What is the reason for this prohibition? Rambam (*Laws of the Temple Vessels*, 2:12–13) connects the prohibition to remove the poles from the rings to the positive commandment to carry the Ark upon the shoulders and not on a wagon or an animal (Num. 7:9). The Talmud (*Sota* 35a) explains that King David forgot the law of carrying upon the shoulders, and when he put the Ark on a wagon to bring it to Jerusalem, the priest Uzza (who reached out to steady it) was struck down by God. This is explicit in the account in 1 Chronicles (15:13–15), where David tells the Levites, "Because you did not do this at first, HaShem our God made a breach upon us, because we did not seek Him according to the law." Thereafter we read, "And the children of the Levites carried the Ark of God upon their shoulders, with the poles upon them, *as Moses had commanded according to the word of God.*"

Apparently, the prohibition of removing the poles prevents the possibility of forgetting the obligation that the Ark be carried upon the shoulders. The continuous presence of the poles serves as a reminder that the Ark is to be carried only with the poles. This is not the only instance in which a biblical prohibition serves as a "fence" around another biblical mitzva. For example, the prohibition of making a "sculpture or representation" is a fence around the prohibition of idolatry; the prohibition for the Nazir to eat grapes is a fence around the prohibition of his drinking wine.

This connection between the two mitzvot answers a question raised by many of the commentaries on Rambam. The words "The service of the sanctuary is upon them, upon their shoulders shall they bear it" refer to the service of the children of Kehat to carry *all* the vessels of the *Mishkan*, and for this reason they are not given wagons. Rambam limits this mitzva of carrying upon the shoulders only to the Ark, since the prohibition of removing the poles applies only to the Ark, and not to the other vessels for which the children of Kehat are responsible. It is this prohibition that demonstrates that only the Ark has the positive mitzva of carrying upon the shoulder.

Both the prohibition of removing the poles from the rings of the Ark and the obligation of carrying the Ark upon the shoulders have a common reason. Carrying the Ark upon the shoulders, with a direct relationship between the person and what he is carrying, expresses man's submission to the Ark and to what it symbolizes; it is the maximal gesture of honor. A vessel whose poles are permanently affixed to it and never removed declares that it is carried upon the shoulder, i.e., that man submits to it.

We may take a step further and suggest the following. The poles, which are not completely joined to the Ark, and are yet attached to it without any permissibility of separation, symbolize the proper human attitude towards God, who figuratively "sits upon the keruvim" of the Ark: cleaving with no compromise, assumption of the yoke, expression of admiration towards Him, and submission.

III. STRUCTURE OF THE *PARASHA*

The *parasha* of the Ark is divided into two sections: the first half has the command to make the Ark and its accessories (the rings and the poles), while the second part has the command to make the covering and its accessories (the *keruvim*). The last verse concludes both by indicating the common purpose of the Ark and its covering: "And I shall meet with you there." The two halves correspond to each other in several ways:

1. The vessel itself and its measurements:
   A. *And they shall make an* Ark of *shittim* wood.... And you shall cover it with pure gold. (v. 10–11)
   B. *And you shall make* a covering of pure gold. (v. 17)
2. Its measurements:
   A. Two-and-a-half cubits long and a cubit-and-a-half wide (v. 10)
   B. Two-and-a-half cubits long and a cubit-and-a-half wide (v. 17)
3. Additions to the vessel:
   A. *And you shall make* poles of *shittim* wood and you shall cover them with gold. And you shall put the poles into the rings on the sides of the Ark.... The poles shall be in the rings of the Ark; they shall not move from there. (v. 13–15)
   B. *And you shall make* two *keruvim* of gold.... And make one *keruv* on one side and one *keruv* on the other side; of the

covering shall you make the *keruvim* .... Towards the covering shall the faces of the *keruvim* be. (v. 18–20)

4. Giving testimony:
   A. And you shall put into the ark the testimony that I will give you. (v. 16)
   B. And in the ark shall you put the testimony which I will give you. (v. 21)
5. Purpose of the completed vessel:
   And I will meet with you there and I will speak with you from above the covering, from between the two *keruvim* which are upon the Ark of Testimony, all that I will command you for *Benei Yisrael*. (v. 22)

Analyzing the parallel in reverse, we see the following:

4. Giving of testimony: Why is this repeated? The "tablets of testimony" which are placed in the Ark are connected with *both* parts: the lower part, serving as a holding vessel for them, and the upper part, which serves as a covering for them (the root "*k-p-r*" (כ.פ.ר.) in "*Kaporet*" means covering). Each of the two commands concludes with an indication of its purpose: to serve as a vessel for the testimony.

3. The poles and the *keruvim*: There is a parallel between the poles of the Ark and the *keruvim* which are upon the covering. The poles are two in number, they are made of *shittim* wood and covered in gold (like the Ark); the *keruvim* are also a pair and are made of gold (like the *Kaporet*). The poles are located on either side of the Ark; the *keruvim* are on the two ends of the covering. The poles are attached to the Ark, inside the rings, and do not move from there; the *keruvim* are part of the covering and extend from it as part of one solid unit. To complete this parallel between the poles and the *keruvim*, let us cite Rambam's description of the way in which the Ark is carried: "When they carried it upon their shoulders, they carried it face to face, with their backs facing outwards and their faces facing inwards" (*Laws of the Temple Vessels*, 2:12).

This is clearly reminiscent of the description of the *keruvim*, which faced each other.

1–2. The Ark and the Covering: Since it is obvious that the Ark and its cover must have the same dimensions, why is this repeated? It expresses equality of value and importance. The *Kaporet* is not merely a covering for the Ark; it is part of the entirety with an importance all of its own, and therefore it is deserving of having its own measurements set out explicitly.

IV. SIGNIFICANCE OF THE STRUCTURE

The tablets are testimony to the covenant between God and Israel. God's revelation to His nation is from now on recorded upon the tablets of stone, and the Ark serves as the focus for further revelation. Thus the Ark expresses the mutual connection between God and Israel, with the "testimony" at its center.

The lower portion of the Ark symbolizes the human partner in the covenant – Israel. The covenant begins with the readiness on Israel's part to enter into the covenant and accept God's commandments (19:5–8). Likewise, the Ark must be built starting from the lower portion, the receptacle for the "tablets of testimony" – the revelation of God and His commandments which stand at the center of the covenant.

"For man is a tree of the field" – the human partner to the covenant is symbolized by an "Ark of *shittim* wood," an organic substance that grew in the ground. But the covenant with God elevates this natural aspect, illuminating it with some of the Divine Glory, and therefore "You shall cover it with pure gold."

The poles affixed to the Ark, which "shall not move from it," represent its invariably being carried upon human shoulders – man submitting himself to the yoke of the covenant and, through this method of carrying, expressing his admiration for "He who sits upon the *keruvim*" and who appears to man from between them. If the Ark represents "Israel" the nation, a single unit that is God's partner in the covenant, then the poles represent the individual citizen of Israel who, in every generation, carries the Ark upon his shoulders.

The upper portion of the ark – the *Kaporet* – represents the divine partner to the covenant. The *Kaporet* serves as a symbolic seat for the invisible God (Jer. 3:16–17 and II Sam. 6:2), and it is therefore made of pure gold. "From above the covering" God meets with Moses, and His revelation is accompanied by the two *keruvim*. The *keruvim* spread their wings heavenward, representing the ministering angels who always accompany God in His revelation to man.

Just as the function of the Ark of *shittim* wood is to serve as a receptacle for the "testimony," so the function of the *Kaporet* is to cover and guard that "testimony" from above. The testimony is what joins the two parts of the Ark – the two partners to the covenant, the human and the Divine.

And just as the function of the *keruvim* is to accompany the divine revelation that comes from between them, turning their faces towards the *Kaporet* which covers the testimony (v. 20), so the function of those who carry the Ark upon their shoulders by means of the poles (which are under the open wings of the *keruvim*) is to accompany the divine revelation that goes out towards His nation (see Num. 10:35) and to bear the yoke of the testimony that is within the Ark. We have already noted the parallel between Rambam's description of the carrying of the Ark and the description of the *keruvim* in the Torah.

Just as the *keruvim* are an integral part of the *Kaporet*, so the poles are an integral part of the Ark beneath it. Nevertheless, there is still a difference between them: the *keruvim* are made of a single solid unit with the covering. It is impossible to separate them from it. The poles, on the other hand, are placed in the rings of the Ark, they are independent objects and are not organically joined to the Ark – technically they could be removed. Their closeness to the Ark is based on the prohibition of removing them. This is the essence of the difference between the angels, who have no choice, and man, who is commanded to cleave to God and to His covenant, but who has the choice not to.

Despite the differences between the two parts of the Ark – and the two partners to the covenant – everything in the *parasha* of the Ark is of dual nature: the measurements, the parallel between the poles and the *keruvim*, and the repetition of the placement of the testimony at the end of each half.

At the time of the erection of the *Mishkan*, the Ark began to fulfill its function, and thus the order of the activities was (40:20):

(1) And he took and put *the testimony* into the Ark,

(2) And he placed the *poles* upon the Ark,

(3) And he placed the *Kaporet* (covering) upon the Ark from above.

The Aron HaKodesh

Rav Moshe Taragin

P*arashat Teruma* describes the construction of both the actual structure of the *Mishkan* as well as the utensils which were housed therein. The first item which is detailed is the *Aron* (the Ark) which contained the *luhot* (tablets) and which was placed in the *Kodesh haKodashim* (the inner sanctuary). This section begins in 25:10 and concludes with 25:22. One instruction repeats itself twice – the command to place the (*edut*) (the *luhot*, a *Sefer Torah*, or both) into the *Aron*:

> And you should place in the Aron the *edut* which I will give you. (v. 16)

> And *in the Aron you should place the edut* which I will give you. (v. 21)

This superfluous restatement immediately attracts our attention. Rashi asserts here that the repetition actually reminds Moses to place the *edut* in the *Aron prior* to covering it with the *Kaporet* (the gold "cover" of the *Aron*). This interpretation raises more questions than it solves. Why must

Moses be specifically instructed to insert the *edut* prior to covering the *Aron*? Wouldn't practicality dictate as much? If, on the other hand, the *luḥot* technically can be inserted even after the *Aron* has been covered by its cover, the *Kaporet*, why in fact must Moses insert them prior to covering the *Aron*? Ramban adds an additional question: Shouldn't the *Aron* begin to house the *edut* only after being entirely completed? These difficulties suggest an alternate reason for the repetition of this command.

I. TWO SECTIONS DETAILING THE ARON'S CONSTRUCTION

A closer inspection of the section detailing construction of the *Aron* reveals several features which might suggest that these thirteen verses should be split into two sub-sections. Generally in *Parashat Teruma*, first the actual 'item' is described, and only subsequently does the Torah delineate the ancillary utensils or other material which was placed on or within the actual utensil. With the *Shulḥan* (table), for example, we learn about the various plates and bread-holders which were placed on the *Shulḥan*'s racks only after the dimensions and specifications of the actual *Shulḥan* are given. The breads themselves are only described in the section's last verse. In the case of the *Aron*, however, we learn of the *edut* in the seventh verse, before being informed about seemingly integral aspects of the *Aron*. By describing the *edut* at this early stage the Torah might be signaling that one section of *Aron* instructions has concluded. This first section describes the *edut,* but hasn't yet mentioned the *Kaporet* and the *keruvim* (cherub angels on top of the *Aron*).

An additional issue surrounds the description of the *keruvim*. Though commonly associated with the *Aron*, the Torah itself continuously aligns them with the *Kaporet*. In a span of five verses (25:18–22) the *keruvim* are associated with the *Kaporet* four times and not once directly with the actual *Aron* – despite the fact that it apparently is the base of both the *Kaporet* and the *keruvim*:

> Make two *keruvim* of gold...at the two ends of the *Kaporet*....
> From the *Kaporet* make the *keruvim* on the two ends....
> And the *keruvim* should spread their wings, covering with their wings the *Kaporet*....

And I will speak with you from above the *Kaporet* between the two *keruvim*.

Evidently, the last verses comprise a separate and independent section describing the *Kaporet* and the *keruvim* which arose from it, making little mention of the actual *Aron*.

A "simple" reading of the *parasha* detailing the construction of the *Aron* yields a *parasha* which seems to be subdivided into two distinct sections, each concluded by a separate command to insert the *'edut.'* While the first section (25:10–16) speaks of the *Aron* and makes no mention of the *keruvim*, the second section (25:17–22) firmly associates the *keruvim* with the *Kaporet*. What is the Torah's intent in dividing the *Aron* instructions in two? Apparently, the *Aron* plays two distinct roles, reflected by the double list of instructions.

II. AN *ARON* OF TORAH/AN *ARON* OF TESTIMONY

The most striking feature or function of the *Aron* is that it contained the *luḥot* and/or the *Sefer Torah*. (See Yerushalmi *Shekalim* 6:1 regarding what was actually inserted.) Ibn Ezra likens this *Aron* to a safe or box in which valuables are stored (25:16). It was fashioned from gold to highlight the value of the item which was being stored – similar to a jewelry box, which is adorned or made from precious metal to distinguish it from a breadbox. *Ḥazal* repeatedly emphasized the storing of the *edut* as a characteristic feature of the *Aron*:

[J]ust as Torah preceded all, similarly the construction of the *Aron* was stated first. (*Shemot Rabba* 34:2)

"They should make an *Aron*": why does the Torah employ a plural tense? Everyone should participate in its construction so that they should all merit Torah learning. (*Shemot Rabba* 34:3, cited by Ramban on 25:9)

Why, when describing the crown of the *Aron*, does the Torah write "they should make *above* it (*alav*)" [25:11]? To symbolize that the crown of Torah 'supersedes' the crowns of priesthood and royalty. (*Shemot Rabba* 34:2, see also Rashi on 25:11)

"It should be gold within and without" – from here we learn that any *Talmid Ḥakham* whose inner thoughts do not reflect his outward gestures (*she'ein tokho kebaro*) is not truly a *Talmid Ḥakham* (*Yoma* 72b).

These repeated statements confirm that which is obvious from the text. A primary function of the *Aron* was to store the *edut*, on a practical level protecting them and facilitating transport, and on an aesthetic level glorifying and honoring them. It is this role which lent the *Aron* its title as *Aron haEdut* (25:22; 26:33, 34; 30:6, 26; 39:35; 40:3, 5, 21).

III. THE *ARON* AS THE "SEAT" OF THE *SHEKHINA*

There appears to be a second role played by the *Aron*. The *Mishkan/Mikdash* was intended as the site of the greatest concentration of God's Presence on this world (*Shekhina*). Though this is true of the *Mikdash* in general, the *Aron* served as a miniature throne to the *Shekhina*, as many commentators point out. Throughout Tanach we witness the *Aron* symbolizing no less than the Presence of God Himself during several monumental national experiences:

1. Travel

During travel, the *Aron* paced the nation to select a suitable site for rest (Num. 10:33). This scouting was obviously performed by God as the Torah announces two verses later: "When the *Aron* traveled, Moses declared 'May God arise… and when the *Aron* rested Moses said 'May God return to the tens of thousands of his people'" (Num. 10:35).

2. Parting of the Jordan

The miracle which marked their entry into Israel was centered around the *Aron*'s movement. The book of Joshua describes how the nation's crossing was led by the *Aron*'s crossing: "as soon as the soles of the feet of the kohanim who carried the *Aron* rested in the Jordan… they [the waters] shall stand in a heap" (Joshua 3:13, see also 4:7).

3. The Conquest of Jericho

The first "battle" in the acquisition of the Land is spearheaded by the *Aron* which circled Jericho along with the priests blowing horns. This battle initiated the tradition of carrying the *Aron* out to war, a practice which reflected God's presence in the battle-camp, as indicated in Deuteronomy:

> For God walks in the midst of your camp to deliver you. (Deut. 23:15)
>
> For God goes with you to fight your enemies. (Deut. 19:4)

4. The Oath at *Har Eival*

Upon entering Israel, Joshua fulfills the command given to Moses to recreate Mount Sinai in Israel. The nation assembles as the covenant of *Ki Tavo* is read aloud, with the *Aron* situated at the center to symbolize the presence of God (see Joshua 8:33).

These national events all required the presence of God, supplied by the *Aron*. This role of the *Aron*, as the seat of the *Shekhina*, endows the *Aron* with another title, "*Aron HaShem*," a phrase which doesn't appear in *Parashat Teruma*, but recurs persistently in later sections of the Torah (and more so in Tanach – particularly in the book of Joshua in which this role of the *Aron* is most often manifest).

IV. THE *KERUVIM* AND THE *KAPORET*

Possibly, the *keruvim* and the *Kaporet* are the components of the *Aron* most vital toward establishing it as a throne of glory (*Kisseh HaKavod*). Similar to the actual *Merkava*, God's holy chariot, which is comprised of angelic creatures and serves as the seat of God's presence (see Ezek. 1), the *Aron* contains two angel figures, their *wings* outspread and their *gaze cast down* (a symbolic gesture of the awe in God's presence – see Ḥizkuni and Rabbenu Ḥananel). The wings and the averted eyes are images which are reminiscent of the description of the actual throne in Isaiah (6:1–2): "I saw God sitting upon a throne…. *Seraphim* stood above Him, each had six wings, with two he covered his face." The *keruvim* as components of a miniature *Kisseh HaKavod*, the site of God's Presence, is connoted as well by the recurring phrase "*Yoshev HaKeruvim*" – God who sits upon the *keruvim* (Psalms 80:2, II Sam. 6:2).

The *keruvim* were molded from the *Kaporet* (they were *"miksha"* – hammered from the same piece of gold), rather than fastened to it. The *Aron* as *Kisseh HaKavod* does not require a box capable of storing material items, but only transportation (*keruvim*) and a platform (*Kaporet*). It is understandable that the *keruvim*, the most visible symbol of the miniature *Kisseh HaKavod*, rise specifically from the *Kaporet* and not from the *Aron* proper.

This area of the *Aron* (beneath the *keruvim*, on top of the *Kaporet*) factored heavily in two momentous experiences in the *Mikdash*. It was upon the *Kaporet* under the *keruvim* where the *Shekhina* "appears" on Yom Kippur during the burning of the incense:

> In a "cloud" I will appear upon *the Kaporet*. (Lev. 16:2)
> The "cloud" of the *ketoret* should cover *the Kaporet*. (Lev. 16:13)

It was also through this "window" or "route" that the voice of God was heard by Moses when he entered the *Mishkan*: "And there I will meet you and I will speak with you from above the covering from between the two *keruvim*" (Ex. 25:22). Each of these events demonstrated the ability of the *Kaporet* to serve as the "seat" of the *Shekhina*. During the entire year God's spoken word emanates from this area and reverberates in the *Ohel Moed*. On Yom Kippur a human is actually permitted to approach this *Kisseh HaKavod* for the purposes of achieving atonement (in Hebrew – *kapara*, from the same root as *Kaporet*).

It is now quite obvious why the Torah divided the *Aron* section into two – to underscore the two different functions of the *Aron*. The first verses describe the *Aron haEdut*, an ornate gold chest intended to store the *luḥot* or Torah while the second part of this section describes the *Aron HaShem*, a base upon which stood angel figures, representing a miniature *Kisseh HaKavod* for the presence of the *Shekhina* within the *Mikdash*.

These two roles amply reflect the two functions of the *Mikdash* itself. One the one hand it is the site of the concentrated presence of *Shekhina*. Alternatively it is also an epicenter from which Torah knowledge emits (*Ki miTziyyon Tetze Torah*). As such it was a center of both the written Torah (symbolized by the *Aron haEdut* housing the *luḥot*/Torah) and the Oral Torah. The Sanhedrin, charged with guiding the unfurling of the Oral Torah, resided in the *Lishkat haGazit* adjacent to the *Azara*.

V. COMPLEMENTARY OR INDEPENDENT:

Are these two roles distinct? Are we to view the *Aron haEdut* and the *Aron HaShem* as two different logical structures? Was the *Aron* really one ornate chest storing the *edut*/Torah and a separate platform upon which stood *keruvim* signifying the concentrated presence of the *Shekhina*? Is the *Aron* of Torah distinct from the *Aron* of *Shekhina*? One might have arrived at this conclusion, but the Torah specifically campaigns against this notion. The warrant for a *Mikdash*, for the concept of God revealing himself to human beings, is the fact that we were given His Torah – the closest approximation of His Essence in this world. Were it not for Torah and our ability to understand HaShem by studying and performing His will, there would be no sanction for the concept of *Mikdash*, or for the indwelling of *Shekhina* on this limited physical world. Just as the divine revelation at Mount Sinai was 'channeled' through the experience of Torah, similarly the *Shekhina*'s presence in the *Mikdash* rested – literally and figuratively – upon the presence of Torah within the *Mikdash*. These two roles of the *Aron* reflect the symbiotic relationship between Torah and *Shekhina* which characterizes the *Mikdash* itself.

For this very reason the Torah reiterates the command to insert the *edut*/Torah into the *Aron*. After firmly establishing the concept of an *Aron HaShem* – a miniature *Kisseh HaKavod*, the Torah highlights that this very same *Aron* must contain the *edut*/Torah – else it cannot be a *Kisseh HaKavod* in this world, in this *Mikdash*. Though the *Aron* might have double functions, they are very much integrated and mutually dependent.

Parashat Tetzaveh

מרה יומי 5 say; ואתך ד תאלד?

תאלד? vs. ואתך ד

The Disappearing Moses

Rav Yaakov Beasley

(?)Bring Olives

I. A NOTABLE ABSENCE

And as for you, you shall command the children of Israel to bring
you pure olive oil of beaten olives for lighting, for kindling the
Eternal Lamp. (27:20)

Our *parasha* begins with the divine instruction that Moses should command the Jewish people to bring beaten olives, so that there is oil for
the *Ner Tamid* (the Eternal Lamp). However, God's command – "*ve'ata
Tetzaveh*" – "*And as for you*, you should command," places unusual
emphasis on Moses. The redundant pronoun, "*ve'ata*," replaces what
should have been either the simple future form, "*Tetzaveh*" (you shall
command), or the imperative "*tzav*" (command). This sudden focus
on Moses provoked much discussion among the commentators – has
Moses not been God's agent throughout the entire process of building
the *Mishkan*? Even in the preceding sections, Moses plays a central role:
"And *you* shall make the altar" (27:1), "And *you* shall make the altar's
horns" (27:2), and so forth. What happened that required the Torah to
use suddenly the emphatic form, *ve'ata*?

Ramban suggests a possible answer. In the manufacture of the other sacred items, Moses' role is to instruct and supervise. However, with regard to the sacred olive oil, Moses must personally ascertain its purity. This additional level of involvement that God demands of Moses requires that God emphasize its importance through the usage of the emphatic form, *ve'ata*.

On a homiletical level, the Ba'al HaTurim connects the absence of Moses' proper name here with the self-sacrificing challenge that Moses made to God in defense of the Jewish people after their sin with the golden calf – "Erase me from Your book which You have written!" (32:32).[1] Moses pleaded for the survival of his people by offering his life in exchange. If the people are to be destroyed, then his name must also be deleted from God's book.

Paradoxically, the absence of Moses' name is noted through the repeated emphatic calls to Moses: "And as for you." There is naming and anonymity, both presence and absence. We normally read this *parasha* during the week of the seventh of Adar – which tradition identifies as the date of both Moses' birth and his death – both entry and departure simultaneously.

When we examine the section even closer, we note that the unusual call *ve'ata* – *And as for you* – recurs twice more in the first five verses:

And as for you, bring forth Aaron your brother with his sons, from among the children of Israel, to serve Me as priests. (28:1)
And as for you, you shall speak to all who are wise of heart, whom I have filled with the spirit of wisdom, to make Aaron's clothing, for consecrating him to serve Me as priest. (28:3)

Investigating all three cases, we note a fascinating paradox. In all three cases where Moses is singled out, it is to assume a responsibility that ultimately will not be his own. Aaron (and his children) will attend

---

1. This interpretation clearly assumes that these sections occurred after the sin of the golden calf (the approach of Rashi, echoing the *Midrash Tanḥuma*, and others). Discussions on the chronology of Exodus can be found in the articles by Rabbis Leibtag and Waxman earlier in this volume.

אהרן [handwritten] taking over [handwritten, underlined]

the *Ner Tamid*, Aaron will serve as *Kohen Gadol*, and Aaron will wear the sacred priestly garments. Unlike Moses, whose name has been 'erased' from the text, Aaron's name dominates the beginning of the *parasha*, appearing seven times.

II. PROXIMITY AND STERILITY

The Midrash elucidates the tension created by the text between the vanishing Moses and omni-present Aaron: אשר [handwritten] us Prenu [handwritten] אהרן [handwritten]

vanishing [handwritten]

> "And as for you, bring forth Aaron your brother with his sons, from among the children of Israel, to serve Me as priests." – When God told Moses to bring Aaron forward, He offended Moses.... This is like a wise man who married his relative, and after ten years together, when she had not borne children, he said to her, "Seek me a wife!" He said to her, "I could not marry without your permission, but I seek your cooperation." So God said to Moses, "I could have made your brother High Priest without informing you, but I wish you to be greater than him."

The metaphor is startling. Moses' appointment of Aaron to serve as *Kohen Gadol* in his stead is equivalent to a husband asking his wife to find him a more fertile spouse. Could anyone imagine this metaphor occurring in real life? The nineteenth-century Hasidic leader, Rabbi Yehuda Aryeh Leib Alter (the Gerrer Rebbe – popularly known as the Sefat Emet), suggests several fascinating approaches to deciphering this analogy. In some of his homilies,[2] Rabbi Alter suggests that Moses' elevated spiritual stature was beyond the comprehension of the Jewish people. Therefore, God needed to appoint Aaron in Moses' stead, for his spirituality was more accessible to the nation. In this understanding, it is

---

2. Rabbi Alter, in accordance with Hasidic tradition, would speak to his Hasidim about the weekly *parasha* at the third Shabbat meal. His remarks, which combine sensitivity to text, explorations in Midrashic literature, and discourses on human spirituality and psychology, were then transcribed after Shabbat, and collected posthumously on the work Sefat Emet. It is not uncommon to discover that Rabbi Alter revisited the same theme several times over the years, each year providing a new approach or insight on the previously discussed idea.

the people's unworthiness, not Moses' failing, that removes Moses from the position of *Kohen Gadol*. In other *derashot*, Rabbi Alter proposes that Aaron is simply the external manifestation of Moses [in kabbalistic terms, Moses is the *kol* (the internal voice), and Aaron is the *dibur* (the external sound)]. One year, however, Rabbi Alter suggested a very different rationale for God's decision to reject Moses and choose Aaron in his stead. In his understanding, the very fact that Moses achieved such closeness to God precluded him from serving in roles that were, by nature, hereditary. Fathers can teach royal and priestly functions to their children. Through education and imitation, they can be passed on through generations. Not so with the encounter of an individual with the divine. Moses' spiritual achievements were inimitable. As the very relationship is unique, it defies duplication or imitation. The Rabbis remarked upon this aspect of Moses' service at the beginning of his initiation. God commanded Moses at the burning bush, "Do not come any closer" in response to Moses' exclamation "*Hineni* – here I am" (Ex. 3:4, 5). Here are the underlying echoes that the Rabbis hear in this apparently simple exchange:

> And he said, "Here I am!" – "Here I am," ready for priesthood. "Here I am," ready for kingship…. God replied, "Do not approach closer" – that is, your children will not offer sacrifices [literally – bring close to me], for the priesthood is reserved for your brother Aaron … and the kingship is reserved for King David. Yet, Moses attained both [temporarily], the priesthood when he officiated during the seven days of consecration for the *Mishkan*, and the kingship, as it states, "Then he became a King in Yeshurun" [Deut. 33:5]. (*Shemot Rabba* 2:13)

While Moses did not manage to attain greatness for his descendants, he did reach these lofty levels in his lifetime, even if only for a moment.

III. BROTHERS – GENESIS AND EXODUS

However, there is another theme that runs throughout rabbinic literature regarding Moses' failure to be appointed *Kohen Gadol*. After repeated attempts to convince, cajole, and persuade Moses to serve as His emissary to free the Jewish people, the Torah states, "And God's anger burned" (Ex. 4:14). Rashi comments:

> "And God's anger burned" – Rabbi Yehoshua ben Korḥa stated, "Every 'burning anger' recorded in the Torah leaves a mark. Here, there is no trace recorded, and we have not found any punishment that resulted from that anger." Rabbi Yossi responded, "Here too, we can find a hint. "There is Aaron your brother, a Levite" [continuation of 4:14] – who was destined to serve as a Levite, not priest, while the priesthood I had determined would issue from you. From now on, he will be the priest, and you the Levite, as it is written, "And Moses, the man of God, his sons were named as Levites" [1 Chron. 23:14].

Rashi focuses on the textual links between God's anger and Aaron's appearance. In this understanding, the loss of the priesthood is Moses' punishment for his repeated failure to heed the divine call. We sense though, as the previous Midrash indicated, that God's appointment of Aaron to the role of *Kohen Gadol* is an affront to Moses. Having led the people out of Egypt to Sinai, having entered the fire to receive the divine writ, having been the focus of all of God's instructions about the building of the *Mishkan*, naming Moses as the *Kohen Gadol* would have been the logical culmination. A quick survey of Jewish history also warranted this conclusion. In Genesis, it is the younger brother who achieves greatness at the expense of the older. Suddenly, and ironically, the notion of primogeniture returns. However, as Rashi notes, this reversal was not unjustified:

> "Even now he is setting out to meet you" – when you go to Egypt "and he will see you with joy in his heart." He will not, as you think, resent your rise to greatness. For this, Aaron came to merit the breastplate that is set over the heart.

Unlike Cain, Ishmael, Esau, Reuben, and all the resentful older brothers of Genesis, Aaron felt nothing but joy and gladness at his younger brother's accomplishments and achievements. The Midrash showers praise upon Aaron's altruism:

> Said Rabbi Shimon bar Yoḥai, "The same heart that rejoiced in his brother's greatness, let precious stones be set upon it, as it states, 'And Aaron shall bear the names of the children of Israel on the breastplate on his heart' [28:29]."

The Midrash concludes by commending Moses' wholehearted acceptance of the harsh divine decree:

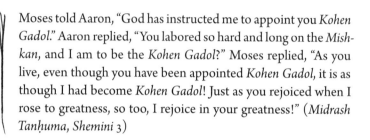

> Moses told Aaron, "God has instructed me to appoint you *Kohen Gadol.*" Aaron replied, "You labored so hard and long on the *Mishkan,* and I am to be the *Kohen Gadol*?" Moses replied, "As you live, even though you have been appointed *Kohen Gadol,* it is as though I had become *Kohen Gadol!* Just as you rejoiced when I rose to greatness, so too, I rejoice in your greatness!" (*Midrash Tanḥuma, Shemini* 3)

Comparing our *parasha*'s emphasis of Aaron over Moses (and the Midrash's sensitivity to this tension earlier in Exodus) with Genesis' almost continuous reiteration of the rivalries, conflicts, and struggles between brothers, the contrast is breathtaking. God's choosing Aaron to serve him as *Kohen Gadol* does not provoke any protest from Moses; just as God's earlier decision to choose Moses as leader does not provoke any protest from Aaron. This togetherness and attachment reflects a concealed transformation that occurs throughout Exodus. Only the emergence of the "*People* of the children of Israel" (Ex. 1:8) from the disparate tribes that comprised "the children of Israel" (1:1) allowed them to stand together at Sinai, as "one person, with one heart." Only if that unity holds will they merit to serve in the *Mishkan.* For this, the selfless example of Moses and Aaron united serves as the Torah's *Ner Tamid,* Eternal Light.

Tamid

Rav Ezra Bick

I. INTRODUCTION

The usual understanding of the division between *Parashat Teruma* and *Parashat Tetzaveh* is that the former deals with the building of the *Mishkan* proper, with all its elements and utensils, while the latter (except for the first two verses) deals with the kohanim; first the preparation of their garments, and then the preparation of themselves as priests. At the end of the *parasha* there is a glaring exception to this rule; the construction of the incense altar.

The section of the kohanim itself is divided into two parts, their garments and their sanctification (chapter 29). The end of this section has a distinct conclusion (before the section on the incense altar mentioned above):

> And I shall sanctify the Tent of Meeting and the altar, and Aaron and his sons shall I sanctify to serve Me. And I shall dwell within the children of Israel, and shall be their God. And they shall know that I am HaShem their God, who has taken them out of Egypt in order to dwell in their midst, I am HaShem their God. (Ex. 29:44–46)

These verses serve as the parallel conclusion to the opening of the "construction sections," which we read at the beginning of *Parashat Teruma*: "And they shall make for Me a Mishkan, and I shall dwell in their midst" (25:8).

However, before this conclusion, there is one section appended to the "*miluim*" (the seven-day ceremony of sanctification of the kohanim) that appears out of place. The previous six verses describe the "*Korban Tamid*," the daily sacrifice. The only connection to the previous section appears to be the mention of the altar. During the seven days of *miluim*, Moses used the blood of the sacrifices to purify the altar. The last verse of the *miluim* reads, "For seven days you shall atone for the altar and sanctify it, and the altar shall be holy of holies; anything that touches it shall be sanctified" (29:37). This is followed by a break (*parasha setuma*), and then the Torah continues, "This is what you shall do on the altar." The Torah then proceeds to present the commandment of the *korban tamid*, the two daily sacrifices, offered every morning and afternoon. That this is a "*mitzva ledorot*," a mitzva for all times, and not part of the special *miluim* sacrifices, is made explicit in the last verse of this section: "A constant offering for your generations" (v. 42). In fact, the entire section is practically identical to the familiar one from *Parashat Pinḥas* (Num. 28:1–8), where it forms the opening to the list of sacrifices offered on every day of the year, beginning with the daily (*tamid*) and followed by the additional offerings for the Shabbat, Rosh Ḥodesh, and holidays.

Our first question is what is this section doing here? Before the *Mishkan* is even constructed, why does God choose to give the command for one particular aspect of the sacrificial ritual immediately after – in fact, as part of – giving the instructions of how to construct the *Mishkan*, and why this particular sacrifice?

There are two other questions that arise, from two other sections to which we should compare our section. The first is the aforementioned section in *Pinḥas*. Although it is nearly identical to ours, there is one dramatic thematic difference, and a host of stylistic ones. The second section is the one describing the fulfillment of the *miluim* instructions, after the *Mishkan* is constructed, in the second half of *Parashat Tzav*. Surprisingly, it is completely absent there. Instead, we have a detailed ritual performed on *the eighth day* (*Parashat Shemini*) which bears no relationship at all with the *korban tamid*. In our *parasha*, no mention is made of an eighth day at all. What is going on?

Comparing the two sections which describe the *korban tamid*, we note one striking difference between the two *parashot*:

Parashat Tetzaveh (Ex. 29:42)	Parashat Pinhas (Num. 28:6)
A continual burnt-offering (*olat tamid*) for your generations, at the entrance to the Tent of Meeting before God, where I shall meet with you [plural] there, to speak to you [singular] there.	A continual burnt-offering (*olat tamid*), which was made on Mount Sinai, for a sweet savour (*re'ah niho'ah*), a fire-offering to God.

Both verses open with the phrase "*olat tamid*," but then refer to two completely different locations. Exodus continues by placing the *tamid* "at the entrance to the Tent of Meeting before God"; whereas the book of Numbers refers to the *tamid* as "which was made on Mount Sinai for a sweet savour, a fire-offering to God." While this presumably means that the *tamid* follows the same rules as a *korban olah* (burnt offering) which was sacrificed at Mount Sinai, it cannot be ignored that this phrase fills the exact spot occupied in Exodus by the reference to the *Ohel Moed*, in what otherwise are two completely parallel *parashot*. Similarly, the phrase "for a sweet savour, a fire-offering to God" is out of place here. Although this phrase appears in Exodus as well, it is at the conclusion of the instructions for the two sacrifices, at the end of the verse beginning "And the second lamb shall you do in the afternoon." In that location, it appears also in the book of Numbers. Its occurrence in the verse we are examining is a *second* appearance, and is parallel to the end of the verse in Exodus. Mount Sinai is parallel to the Tent of Meeting, and "a sweet savour, a fire-offering to God" is parallel to "before God, where I shall meet with you there to speak to you there."

Since we are concentrating on this verse, this is the appropriate time to ask a simple "*peshat*" question. What does "*tamid*" mean? Why does this verse begin with the expression "*olat tamid*"?

II. MISHKAN, THE KOHANIM, AND THE TAMID

It is quite clear from the structure of *Parashot Teruma* and *Tetzaveh* that the entire narrative is about the construction of the *Mishkan*. Hence, the "production" of the kohanim should also, I think, be viewed, not as an independent item which happens to be important to the eventual operation of the *Mishkan*, but as part of its construction. In a halakhic formulation, the kohanim are "*klei Mikdash*"; they are themselves utensils of the *Mikdash* and part of its makeup. This idea is most notably put forward by Rambam, who includes the laws of kohanim in the section of his *Mishneh Torah* called "*Klei HaMikdash Veha'ovdim Bo*" (the utensils of the temple and those who work in it). This explains why the preparation of the altar after its construction is integrated as part of the *miluim* of the kohanim, as explicated in 29:35–7:

> And you shall do to Aaron and his sons thus, all as I have commanded; for seven days they shall fill their hands. And every day you shall prepare a bull of sin-offering, and you shall cleanse the altar by atoning for it, and you shall anoint it to sanctify it. For seven days you shall atone for the altar and sanctify it, and the altar shall be holy of holies, anything that touches the altar shall be sanctified.

The altar, for reasons which we shall not go into here, is not fully sanctified until there are kohanim. In fact, *its* sanctification is part of *their* sanctification and is integrated in their procedure. The very last step, then, in the construction and sanctification of the *Mishkan*, is the sanctification of the altar that takes place in step with the sanctification of the kohanim. The very next thing that the Torah tells us is that this altar will used for the *korban tamid*. How are we to understand this?

I suggest that the Torah is not giving us the mitzva of daily sacrifices here. The place for that is in *Parashat Pinḥas*. This section begins, "This is what you shall do on the altar." The focus is not the mitzva of *tamid*, but an explanation of what the altar which you have just finished is to be used for. The issue is not what sacrifice to bring on a particular day, but what is the altar *for*. The answer to this question is part and parcel of a larger question – what is the *Mishkan* for? Since the altar is apparently the finale of *Mishkan* creation, left for last, it is necessary now, in light of the completion of the altar, to explain what is the *Mishkan*'s purpose. The answer – to bring a daily sacrifice. And what is the purpose of a daily sacrifice?

> A continual burnt-offering for your generations, at the entrance to the Tent of Meeting before God, where I shall meet with you there, to speak to you there.
>
> I shall meet there with the children of Israel, and it shall be sanctified with My Glory.
>
> And I shall sanctify the Tent of Meeting and the altar, and Aaron and his sons shall I sanctify to serve Me.
>
> *And I shall dwell within the children of Israel,* and shall be their God.
>
> *And they shall know that I am HaShem their God,* who has taken them out of Egypt in order to dwell in their midst, I am HaShem their God. (29:42–46)

In other words, the altar, and more specifically the presence of the sacrifice on it, is the basis for the presence of God in the *Mishkan*, whereby He "meets" (*"no'ad"*) the Jewish people and therefore "dwells in their midst." The first verse makes the connection between the sacrifice and the *"no'adeti"* clear. *"Olat tamid"* – where? – At the entrance to the tent where God meets with you (plural) and speaks to you (singular; i.e., Moses).

Hence the section of the *tamid* is not out of place. We expect a concluding section to the construction that will define the goals and purpose of the *Mishkan*. The *tamid* is part of that section, or perhaps, more precisely, the bridge between the two sections. The physical *Mishkan* results in the presence of God through the fulfillment of its permanent, *tamid*, purpose, exemplified by the *korban tamid* on the altar.

That is, in my opinion, the explanation of the word *"tamid."* As we know, the *tamid* is actually continual, all the time. It is brought twice a day. The commentators explain that *"tamid"* can mean daily. This is undoubtedly true, but the question remains why the Torah calls this state of twice daily sacrifices *"tamid."* The answer is that practically, it is done twice daily, but the effect is to make the altar a permanent base of service of God. The altar is defined as the altar with a permanent (*tamid*) state of sacrifice. Since the presence of God in their midst is meant to be permanent (He *dwells* in their midst, not visits on special occasions), and the altar is the basis for this presence, it must be in a permanent state of binding between the Jews and God.

III. THE *TAMID* AND THE EIGHTH DAY

Why, when this ceremony was carried out, is the *tamid* not mentioned, but rather a totally new ceremony of the "eighth day"? This question was discussed by Rav Chanoch Waxman who answered that our *parasha* reflects what should have been; the actual ceremony in *Tzav* and *Shemini* reflect what had to be done after the sin of the golden calf.[1] The eighth day ceremonies are extremely similar to the ritual for Yom Kippur. Although the *Mishkan* has been constructed as instructed, the Presence of God does not fill it because of the sin, and special purification ceremonies must be performed to atone. The difference is not merely technical – it is the difference between "*tamid*," a permanent day-by-day presence of God as part of our lives, and a special, Yom Kippur-like, descent of the Holy Presence as an extraordinary experience. Our section stresses that God meets with *all* the Jewish people at the entrance to the tent, even if He only speaks with Moses. The story of *Shemini*, of course, stresses how dangerous it is to meet with God without special protection – the sons of Aaron are consumed for bringing a "strange fire."

IV. MOUNT SINAI

The Torah in *Parashat Pinhas* is not describing the *Mishkan* as the meeting place between the Jews and the Presence of God. In fact, the *Mishkan* is not mentioned there at all. The idea of "*olat tamid*," however, still applies. Here it receives a different meaning. The *parasha* presents the *tamid* as part of a larger picture, the *tamid* together with the additional sacrifices for each special day (the *Musaf*). From the very beginning of that *parasha*, the sacrifices are described as "*re'ah niho'ah*" and "*isheh laShem*." The focus is not on the meeting with God but the service of

---

1. Available online at *http://www.vbm-torah.org/parsha.59/20tetzav.htm*.

God. "My sacrifices, the bread of My fire-offerings, My sweet savour, observe to sacrifice to Me *in their due times*." The emphasis is on duties to God. We are commanded to sacrifice *His* sacrifice, *His re'aḥ niḥo'aḥ*, at the proper times. The *tamid* element here defines not a state of the altar but a state of the Jew. He is in a permanent state of service of God. Hence, the defining verse – "A continual burnt-offering, which was made on Mount Sinai, for a sweet savour, a fire-offering to God." If the Jew turns himself into a permanent servant of God, he returns himself not to the Tent of Meeting, a place of rapturous communion, but to Mount Sinai, the scene where the Jews accepted God's law. The sacrifices make the moment of Sinai into a permanent one, a continual one.

The Miluim

Rav Nathaniel Helfgot

Careful comparison of the presentation of the command and its execution in various sections of the Torah often yields significant insight. This technique can be particularly helpful in our search for a proper understanding of the *Miluim*, the seven-day consecration ritual, and its place in the scheme of the book of Exodus.

The *Miluim* passage, with its elaborate ceremony, is presented in full detail in chapter 29 of Exodus as a command to Moses, and is carried out with the same measure of concern for details in chapter 8 of Leviticus (*Parashat Tzav*), whereupon it is followed in chapter 9 by the events of the eighth day, the *Yom HaShemini*, at the beginning of *Parashat Shemini*. In comparing the two texts, one notes many minor differences, such as small discrepancies in the sequence of events; for example, when the kohanim were anointed with oil, the precise order of the wearing of each vestment, etc.[1] I would like to deal, however, with just a few of the more significant discrepancies that may shed light on some fundamental issues in our narrative.

---

1. See especially the Malbim (commentary to Leviticus ad. loc.), who cites and attempts to explain many of these differences.

I. BETWEEN EXODUS AND LEVITICUS

Let us first outline the sacrifices of the *Miluim* section as they are presented and described in Exodus and Leviticus. The following sacrifices were brought every day of the seven-day period of consecration according to Exodus and Leviticus respectively:

EXODUS 29:

1. *"Par eḥad ben bakar"*– A bull (v. 1): the animal is subsequently referred to as *"par"* without any other appellation (v. 3, 10, 11, 14), and the procedures of the classical *korban ḥatat* (sin offering), are performed on it. In verse 14, a major deviation takes place: The meat and fats and inner organs are burnt *"miḥutz lamaḥaneh"* – outside the camp. This is anomalous as the meat and fats of the standard *ḥatat* are always burned within the *Mishkan*, on the altar outside the *Ohel Moed*. The only sin offerings that are burned outside the camp are ones in which the sprinkling of the blood takes place inside the *Ohel Moed*, such as the *Par HaKohen haMashiaḥ* (Lev. 4:12) or the service on Yom Kippur (Lev. 16:27). This leads Rashi (on v. 14) to note that this is the only *ḥatat* that is burned outside of the camp. In addition, it is only here, in verse 14, that the term *ḥatat* is used (*"ḥatat hi"*) to describe this sacrifice;
2. A ram which is brought as an *olah* (burnt offering; v. 16–19);
3. A second ram which is brought as a *shelamim* (peace offering; v. 19–23), later termed the *"eil haMiluim"*;
4. A *korban minḥa* (flour offering) consisting of the elements of matzot, regular loaves, and *rekikei matzot* mixed with oil, etc.

In effect, then, the *Miluim* consist of a representative sample of the classical sacrifices: *olah, minḥa, shelamim,* and some type of *ḥatat.*[2]

---

2. Why does the period of *Miluim* not include a *"korban asham"*? There are two possible answers. First, the *"korban asham"* may not be a separate type of offering, but simply a subset of a *"korban ḥatat."* Second, Ramban points out that in contrast to all other offerings, which appear in both personal and communal contexts, a *"korban asham"* is never brought in a communal context. Instead, it is brought only in the very specific personal situations mentioned in chapter 5 of Leviticus – *asham*

This can be seen as a sample collection of the sacrifices that the kohanim will deal with in the daily running of the *Mishkan* and *Mikdash*.

After this presentation, the Torah tells us that these sacrifices, along with other parts of the consecration ceremony, are to be repeated daily for seven straight days (v. 35). This is then followed by verse 36 which states "And each day you shall prepare a bull offering (*par ḥatat*) for atonement (*al hakippurim*); you shall purge the altar by performing atonement, and you shall anoint it to consecrate it."

The commentators debate as to the nature of this apparently additional sacrifice. Some explain that it is identical with that mentioned in the beginning of the section, and is simply being repeated here to emphasize its purificatory role as well as the Torah's insistence that it also be repeated for seven days. Others insist that this *par ḥatat* is a new sacrifice, to be brought in addition to the other sacrifices, as would appear from the simple reading of the text.[3]

Interestingly, the Torah continues by introducing the laws of the daily sacrifice, the *tamid*, (though the laws of all other sacrifices are left for the book of Leviticus), concluding this section with the very beautiful verses:

> A regular burnt offering throughout the generations, at the entrance of the Tent of Meeting (*petaḥ Ohel Moed*), for there I will meet you (*e'eva'ed shama*), and there I will meet with the Israelites, and it shall be sanctified in My Presence (*venikdash beKhvodi*). I will sanctify the Tent of Meeting and the altar, and I will consecrate Aaron and his sons to serve Me as priests. I will then abide amongst the Jewish people (*veshakhanti betokh Benei Yisrael*), and I will be their God. (v. 42–44)

---

gezeilot, me'ilot etc. Therefore, there is no communal dimension to it and therefore it is not included in the *Miluim* ritual.

3. Abarbanel adopts this position. It is also interesting to note that the Temple Scroll found at Qumran explicitly describes the *Miluim* as consisting of two separate sacrifices. See further 11QT 15–17 in Yigael Yadin, *The Temple Scroll* (Jerusalem, 1983), pp. 61–75.

LEVITICUS 8–9:

1. The chapter begins with God telling Moses to take Aaron and his sons, the priestly vestments and the oil, the *"par ḥatat"* (the sin offering) and the other animals and basket of matzot (Lev. 8:1–2). The *par* is termed a *ḥatat* from the very outset of the passage. The altar is anointed with oil to sanctify it (v. 10); the term is then used repeatedly throughout the section. Moses then immediately engages in purifying the altar. No further mention is made of any other *par* or purification ceremony of the altar.

2. The *"eil ha'olah"* is brought (v. 18–21).

3. The second ram, the *"eil haMiluim"* (*shelamim*) is brought (v. 22–25).

4. The *minḥa* is brought together with the *shelamim* (v. 22–31).

5. Aaron and his sons are instructed not to leave the area of the entrance of the Tent of Meeting – *petaḥ Ohel Moed* – for the entire seven-day consecration period, "day and night," in order to bring atonement upon themselves – *lekhaper aleikhem* (v. 34–35).

6. On the eighth day Aaron is commanded to bring a calf (*egel ben bakar*) as a sin offering, and a ram as an *olah* (Lev. 9:2).

7. The Jewish people are requested to bring a goat (*se'ir*) as a sin offering, and a calf (*egel*) and a sheep for an *olah*, together with an ox and a ram for *shelamim* and a *minḥa* sacrifice, for "on this day God will appear to you" (v. 3–4) and God's "Glory will appear upon you" (v. 5).

8. The text then describes an elaborate atonement ceremony with the word '*kapara*' repeated numerous times, and sets up the model, as Ramban and others point out, for what is later expanded into the yearly ritual of Yom Kippur.

9. The text then continues to describe the appearance of God's Glory, followed by the tragedy of the deaths of Nadav and Avihu at the hand of God.

Five striking distinctions emerge from carefully comparing these two texts:

1. While in Exodus the *par* is never called *"par haḥatat,"* and only once, in Exodus 29:14, is it even associated with the term *"ḥatat,"* in Leviticus it is immediately and always termed as such.

2. Related to this point: while in Exodus the impression one gets is of two *parim*, one to consecrate the kohen and one at the end to serve an expiatory role for the altar, in Leviticus the presentation speaks of only one *par haḥatat* which serves both functions.

3. In Exodus, no command is given to the kohanim to remain at the *Ohel Moed* for seven days and seven nights in constant presence, as appears in Leviticus (8:33). (Note carefully the language the Torah uses to describe this new directive, in contrast to all of the other parts of the consecration ceremony mentioned earlier in the chapter. Regarding these other elements, elements that are in effect fulfillments of the commands in Exodus, such as the wearing of the vestments, the sacrifice of the various *korbanot* etc., the Torah repeatedly writes that they were done *"ka'asher tziva HaShem et Moshe"* – "as God commanded Moses" (v. 9, 13, 17, 21, 29.) In describing the command not to leave the front of the *Ohel Moed* the Torah shifts terminology, with Moses admonishing the kohanim to fulfill this command *"Ki khen tzuveti"* – "for thus have I been commanded" (v. 35).

4. Neither the *tamid* nor the *ketoret* section is incorporated into the story in Leviticus, unlike in Exodus.

5. Finally and possibly the key to our entire question: in Exodus, there is no mention whatsoever of the need for an eighth day, the *Yom HaShemini*, with its elaborate Yom Kippur type ritual to bring about the process of divine revelation. In Leviticus, of course, this is a central, if not *the* central, facet of the consecration story, and is described in great detail.

II. BEFORE AND AFTER

The solution to these clearly distinct presentations lies in the chronological context in which they appear; namely Exodus being before *"ḥet ha'egel,"* the sin of the golden calf, and *Parashot Tzav* and *Shemini* being after it.

Before the sin of the golden calf, the *Miluim* ceremony is a consecration ritual in which the basic types of sacrifices, including a *ḥatat* (a sin offering), are exemplified. In truth, however, there is no actual sin for which the *par* will atone; it is not really a *par ḥatat* in the true sense (and is thus not termed as such), but rather a sacrifice that is treated with the status of a *ḥatat*, "*ḥatat hi*." In Leviticus, however, we are after the cataclysm of the *ḥet ha'egel* that almost destroyed the relationship between God and the Jewish people, as well as, due to Aaron's involvement in the sin, the position of Aaron and the kohanim in the divine scheme. In *Shemini*, the offering has now been transformed into a "*par haḥatat*," as it helps to bring atonement for Aaron and his family as they seek to re-establish contact with God.[4] The *par* of atonement, which in *Tetzaveh* only appears at the end of the section in relation to atoning for the altar – *shivat yamim tekhaper al hamizbe'aḥ* (Ex. 29:37) (implying that there were two separate offerings as we noted above), is transformed in *Shemini* into one *par, par haḥatat*, playing a dual role from the very outset of the ritual, bringing atonement for the altar (Lev. 8:15) and for the kohanim. Indeed it is striking to note that in our passage here the Torah tells us that the kohanim should engage in this ritual for seven days ("*temaleh yadam*," Ex. 29:35) and concludes that the ritual of the *par ḥatat* for the altar shall be done seven days to atone for the altar. In sharp contrast, in *Shemini* the entire procedure of the *Miluim* is presented as being for the atonement of the kohanim as well. It is thus they who must remain in front of the sanctuary – *petaḥ Ohel Moed* – for seven days – *to atone for themselves* (*lekhaper aleikhem* – 8:34), a term and concept wholly absent from the Exodus passage.

Taking this a step further, it would appear that had the sin of the golden calf not occurred, there would have been no ceremony of the *eighth day*, as the seven days alone would have been sufficient in their own right (See Ramban on Lev. 9:3). The manifestation of God's Presence would have automatically begun with daily worship in the *Mishkan*, with the daily *tamid* and *ketoret*, as is indicated by the juxtaposition and language of the text in chapter 29 of Exodus. Instead of the eighth day with its *special* ritual, there would have been an immediate commencement of the *daily* ritual, the daily sacrifice and daily incense. Once the altar was purified, that which was to be constant (*tamid*) – both in the morning and evening – was the bringing of certain regular sacrifices. It

---

4. See also Rav Kasher's reading of the Sifrei cited above, in *Torah Shelema – Parashat Tetzaveh*, pg. 200, note 19.

was these acts, the Torah very suggestively tells us, which were to be done constantly "at the door of the Tent of Meeting before the Lord, where I will meet you…. And there I will meet with the children of Israel, and it shall be sanctified by My Glory…. And I will dwell among the children of Israel "(Ex. 29:42–45).

Unfortunately this was not to be, as Jewish history went awry, transforming the *Miluim*, along with other elements in God's relationship with the Jewish people. By *Parashat Shemini*, the *Miluim* change from a unit in which the consecration itself takes place, into one of preparation for an eighth day; it is no longer a seven-day unit followed organically by the regular patterns of religious existence, i.e., the *tamid* and *ketoret*. At this point, that alone will not suffice to heal the rupture between God and his servants. The *Miluim* becomes a preparatory seven-day period paving the way for the climax of an eighth day. What in *Tetzaveh* is associated with the *korbanot tamid* and *ketoret*, namely their constantly being performed day and night – *petaḥ Ohel Moed* – is now transformed into a commandment for the kohanim themselves to sit constantly, day and night – *petaḥ Ohel Moed*! (Lev. 8:35). And of course, now the need for the eighth day, for the ritual of atonement with its *korbanot* of *"egel,"* so suggestive of the sin of the golden calf, together with the other elements of the Yom Kippur ritual, falls into place. God's revelation at this juncture of Jewish history will not occur with the implementation of the regular *Miluim* and the flow into the regular pattern of *Avodat haKorbanot* (i.e., *Tetzaveh*). Things are not simply as they were, and the need to re-establish contact with God and delineate the new boundaries and contours of that relationship are necessary. Now it is only in the aftermath of the ritual of the eighth day, the mini Yom Kippur of Aaron and his sons, that God's Presence will be manifest. The natural process was interrupted, and repairing the damage, literally restoring the loving relationship between the estranged couple, between *Benei Yisrael* and God, requires that much more work.

The Complementary Verses of the Command Concerning the Mishkan

Rav Yehuda Rock

The four complementary verses that conclude the commands concerning the *Mishkan* map out the important milestones in the narrative of the Torah, from the time of the forefathers up until the book of Numbers. To examine the above assertion, let us first clarify what it is that we are referring to as the "complement to the command concerning the *Mishkan*."

The command to build the *Mishkan* occupies two entire *parashot* – *Teruma* and *Tetzaveh* – as well as five more sections in *Parashat Ki Tisa* (30:11–31:11). The structure of the *parashot* clearly indicates that these latter five sections, along with the last section in *Parashat Tetzaveh* (on the subject of the incense altar, 30:1–10) are appendices, as it were, that are attached to the body of the command. The command to build the *Mishkan*, as set out in chapters 25 to 29, follows a fairly clear structure, moving from the inner parts of the *Mishkan* outward. *Parashat Teruma* starts with the fashioning of the vessels that are located in the *Mishkan*'s inner part: the Ark, the table for showbread, and the Menora. This is followed by a list of the components that make up the structure of the *Mishkan* itself – the curtains, covering, boards, sockets and bars, and the veil. This is followed by a description of the altar, and then the courtyard of the *Mishkan* with its hangings, pillars, and screen. The command concludes with all the laws concerning the kohanim and their garments, and the procedure for the sanctification of the kohanim and of the *Mishkan* (during the seven days of consecration).

In Exodus 29:38 we find the details of the daily sacrifice, which is manifestly meant as the conclusion of the command concerning the *Mishkan*. The daily sacrifice is presented as the central service performed upon the altar, facing the Tent of Meeting, and as the service that allows the Divine Presence to dwell there – which is cited at the outset of the command concerning the *Mishkan* as being its objective. While verses 38–41 address the offering of the daily sacrifice, verse 42 characterizes this daily service in two respects. Firstly, it is a continual service, for all generations. Secondly, it is a sacrifice made to God. What defines it as such is the fact that the altar is at the "entrance to the Tent of Meeting," with the "Tent of Meeting" representing – as its name testifies – a place of meeting between God and *Benei Yisrael*. The practical expression of this meeting is that God speaks to Moses as he stands in the Tent of Meeting (as described in Numbers 7:89 – "And when Moses came to the Tent of Meeting to speak with Him").

Verses 43–46 describe the results of the continual, daily offering in the *Mishkan* with a series of seven verbs in the future tense. By virtue of the daily sacrificial service, "I shall meet … it will be sanctified … I shall sanctify … I shall sanctify … I shall dwell … I shall be … they will know …." It is clear that these objectives are not the purpose of the daily sacrifice alone; they are the purpose of the *Mishkan* as a whole, which achieves its completion in the daily sacrifice. This is highlighted especially in the fifth verb – "I shall dwell amongst *Benei Yisrael*" – which clearly parallels the purpose of the *Mishkan* as set out at the beginning of *Parashat Teruma* (Ex. 25:8), "Let them make Me a Sanctuary, that I may dwell in their midst."

However, it is not only this fifth verb that has appeared previously in the text as a goal which is fulfilled by means of the *Mishkan*. As we shall see, all seven are either explicitly stated or hinted to in other places in the Torah. Let us review them in order of their appearance:

"And I shall meet there with *Benei Yisrael*, and it shall be sanctified with My Glory" (Ex. 29:43) – As stated, this concept of "meeting" is hinted at earlier, in verse 42, as the factor that defines the location of the altar as being "before God." Thus, the "meeting" is both a *condition* for the daily service (*in order* that this service will be "before God," as described in verse 42) and its *result* (as described in verse 43).

This meeting, together with its practical expression, has already appeared previously as a central purpose of the *Mishkan*. The section on the Ark, at the beginning of *Parashat Teruma* (25:10–22), ends with a description of the role of the Ark and the *keruvim* (v. 22): "And I shall meet with you there, and I shall speak with you from above the covering, from between the two *keruvim* that are upon the Ark of Testimony – all that I shall command you [to pass on] to *Benei Yisrael*." The essence of the purpose of the Ark and the *keruvim*, then, is to be the place of emanation for God's meeting with Moses, where He will speak with him from above the Ark, from between the *keruvim*. From the verses in our *parasha* it becomes clear that the meeting is not with Moses alone, but with *Benei Yisrael* ("And I shall meet there with *Benei Yisrael*"), and that the meeting and the speech are not two separate events or manifestations; rather, the speech is the practical expression of the meeting ("where I shall meet with you to speak with you there"). It also becomes clear that the sacrificial service, which completes the *Mishkan*, facilitates and brings about the meeting and the speech.

"And it shall be sanctified with My Glory" – The goal of sanctifying the Tent of Meeting has not been explicitly stated until now, but it is hinted to. At the end of *Parashat Mishpatim*, we find a description of God's revelation upon Mount Sinai in anticipation of Moses' ascent (during which he will be commanded concerning the *Mishkan*):

> And Moses ascended the mountain, and the cloud covered the mountain. And *God's Glory* rested upon Mount Sinai. And the appearance of God's Glory was like a consuming fire at the top of the mountain, before the eyes of *Benei Yisrael*. (24:15–17)

When our verse refers to "My Glory," it is the same "God's Glory" referred to at the end of *Mishpatim*. A further allusion is the use of the word "rested" (*vayishkon*), which hints to the *Mishkan*. The same revelation that was perceived by Moses, in preparation for the command to build the *Mishkan*, will come to the Tent of Meeting in the wake of the completion of the *Mishkan*: "And it will be sanctified with My Glory."

"And I shall sanctify the Tent of Meeting and the altar" – The sanctification of the Tent of Meeting is referred to already in the previous verse, since the Tent of Meeting is the subject of the clause "And *it* will be sanctified with My Glory." The new element that is introduced in verse 44 is that with the sanctification of the Tent of Meeting – and perhaps as a result of it – God will also sanctify the altar. The sanctification of the altar has been mentioned already in our chapter, in the command concerning the seven days of consecration:

> And you shall offer a bull on each day for a sin offering for atonement, and you shall cleanse the altar when you have made atonement for it, and you shall anoint it to sanctify it. For seven days you shall make atonement for the altar and sanctify it, and the altar shall be most holy; anyone who touches the altar shall be holy. (29:36–37)

These verses are talking about sanctification of the altar by Moses, by means of anointment, while in our verse it is God who sanctifies the altar. Nevertheless, these appear to be two stages in the same process that is aimed towards the same goal. First, man (Moses) sanctifies and consecrates the altar for the sacrificial service – a sanctification that is expressed through the act of anointing – and then God confirms the sanctification and accepts the altar and the sacrifices as His own.

"And I shall sanctify Aaron and his sons to minister to Me" – The sanctification of Aaron and his sons for priesthood is repeated several times in *Parashat Tetzaveh* (chapters 28–29):

> As for you – bring to you Aaron your brother and his sons with him from among *Benei Yisrael*, to minister to Me. (28:1)

> And they shall make Aaron's garments, to sanctify him that he may minister to Me. (v. 3)

And you shall dress Aaron your brother in them, and his sons
with him, and you shall anoint them and consecrate them and
sanctify them, that they may minister to Me. (v. 41)

And this is what you shall do with them, to sanctify them to minister to Me. (29:1)

He shall be sanctified, and his garments, and his sons, and his
sons garments with him. (v. 21)

And they shall eat those things with which atonement was made
to consecrate them and to sanctify them. (v. 33)

The above verses show that in essence, the purpose of making
the priestly garments and of consecrating Aaron and his sons is to sanctify them for priesthood. Here too, as in the case of the altar, there are
two stages of the same process that leads to the same goal: first Moses
sanctifies and consecrates Aaron and his sons for divine service, and
then God confirms this sanctification and accepts the kohanim as His
servants, who are close to and minister to Him.

"And I shall dwell in the midst of *Benei Yisrael*" (v. 45) – We have
already discussed this phrase as conveying the crux of the purpose of
the *Mishkan*, as stated at the beginning of *Parashat Teruma*: "Let them
make Me a Sanctuary, that I may dwell in their midst."

"And I shall be their God" – We will examine this objective
together with the next one.

"And they will know that I am the Lord their God who took them
out of the land of Egypt, to make My dwelling among them" (v. 46) – These
expressions appeared in almost identical form at the beginning of *Parashat
Va'era*, when God tells Moses about the plan for the exodus from Egypt:

Therefore, say to *Benei Yisrael*: "I am the Lord. And I shall take
you out from under the burdens of Egypt … and I shall take you
to be My nation … and I shall be your God … and you will know
that I am the Lord your God who brings you out from under the
burdens of Egypt." (6:6–7)

This goal of HaShem being our God was set forth already at Abraham's circumcision:

> And I shall establish My covenant between Me and you, and your descendants after you, for their generations, as an eternal covenant, to be your God – and to your descendants after you.... And I shall be their God. (Gen. 17:7–8)

From all the way back to the time of Abraham's circumcision, then, the purpose of the forging of the covenant had been clear, with the primary substance of the covenant being the forging of a relationship between the nation and God. In *Parashat Va'era* we are told that the aim of the exodus from Egypt is the realization of this aim. The purpose is not just the creation of this relationship, but also the inculcation of an awareness of the relationship amongst *Benei Yisrael*, through the memory of the exodus from Egypt. In our verses there is the added element of "to make My dwelling (*l'shokhni*) in their midst." This tells us that the purpose of the exodus – "And I shall take you as My nation"– will be realized with the completion of the *Mishkan* and the commencement of the divine service within it. We shall not elaborate here on the way in which the *Mishkan* serves to inculcate not only the consciousness of this relationship, but specifically the consciousness of the exodus. Suffice it to say that at the heart of the *Mishkan* are the tablets inscribed with the Ten Commandments, starting with the words, "I am the Lord your God who took you out of the land of Egypt."

Thus, these verses, describing the purpose of the completion of the *Mishkan* and the commencement of the divine service that is performed in it, actually describe the realization of God's long-term plans that were expressed long before, starting with the covenant with the forefathers, continuing through the plans for the exodus from Egypt and God's revelation to convey the command concerning the *Mishkan*, and ending with the purposes of the *Mishkan* in general, and of each of its constituent parts: the Ark and the *keruvim*, the consecration of Aaron and his sons for priesthood, and the sanctification of the altar.

The next stage of our study will examine how the completion of the *Mishkan* and the commencement of the divine service actually bring the aforementioned objectives to realization. If we follow the continuation of the story, we see the milestones on the path of realizing these objectives.

The completion of the job of building the *Mishkan*, with all of its vessels, occurs towards the end of *Parashat Pekudei*: "and Moses completed the work" (Ex. 40:33). Immediately afterwards, we read:

> And *the cloud covered* the Tent of Meeting,
> And *God's Glory* filled the *Mishkan*.
> And Moses was not able to come to the Tent of Meeting, for the *cloud rested upon it, and God's Glory* filled the *Mishkan*. (40:34–35)

> *And He called to Moses*, and God spoke with him from the Tent of Meeting, saying…. (Lev. 1:1)

These verses are a perfect parallel to the revelation discussed above, at the end of *Parashat Mishpatim*, just prior to the command concerning the *Mishkan*:

> And Moses ascended the mountain,
> And *the cloud covered* the mountain.
> And *God's Glory rested* upon Mount Sinai,
> And the cloud covered it for six days,
> And *He called to Moses* on the seventh day from within the cloud.
> And the appearance of *God's Glory* was like a consuming fire at the top of the mountain, before the eyes of *Benei Yisrael*. (Ex. 24:15–17)

In other words, the same revelation that God showed to Moses and to *Benei Yisrael* prior to the command concerning the *Mishkan*, and which God promised would be recreated in the Tent of Meeting once it was completed – "and it shall be sanctified with My Glory" – is what now fills the *Mishkan*.

However, there seems to be a problem: the promise of "it shall be sanctified with My Glory" is uttered in connection with the daily sacrifice, as a description of what is going to happen in the wake of the commencement of the divine service in the *Mishkan*. In practice, however, it appears that the promise is realized immediately upon the completion of the building of the *Mishkan*, without any mention of the sacrificial service taking place in it!

There is a well-known dispute among the commentators concerning the order of events at the end of *Parashat Pekudei* and in the first part of Leviticus. The view of Ibn Ezra would seem to make the most sense. He maintains that the text does in fact follow the chronological order of the events: God's Glory filling the *Mishkan*, described in *Parashat Pekudei*, took place at the beginning of the month of Nisan, immediately upon completion of its building. Thereafter, following the command concerning the sacrifices, came the seven days of consecration, as described in the second part of *Parashat Tzav* (Lev. 8). Then, on the eighth day of consecration – which apparently was on the eighth of Nisan – we are told:

> And it was, on the eighth day....
>
> For on this day God will appear to you....
>
> And Moses said: "This is the matter that God commanded that you do, *in order that God's Glory will appear for you....*"
>
> And Aaron came close to the altar, and he slaughtered the calf of the sin offering which was for himself....
>
> And he slaughtered the burnt offering... and he brought the offering of the people... and he sacrificed the burnt offering... and he sacrificed the meal offering... besides the burnt sacrifice of the morning....
>
> And he came down from offering the sin offering and the burnt offering and the peace offerings. And Moses and Aaron came to the Tent of Meeting.... And *God's Glory appeared* to all of the people.
>
> And a *fire* came out from before God, and it *consumed* upon the altar the burnt offering and the fats. And all the people saw, and they shouted, and they fell upon their faces. (Lev. 9)

Once again in *Parashat Shemini*, then, there is a description of a revelation of "God's Glory," in the form of a "consuming fire." Here it does indeed follow the commencement of the sacrificial service: the sacrifices are no longer being offered only to sanctify and consecrate the altar, and to inaugurate the kohanim (as during the seven days of consecration), but rather as an expansion of the daily sacrifice, an inauguration of the altar with its regular service – albeit in expanded form, to mark the beginning. This event seems better suited as a fulfillment of the promise "And it shall be sanctified with My Glory," and includes not only the Tent of Meeting, but "I shall sanctify the Tent of Meeting and the altar." Why, then, does God's Glory fill the *Mishkan* even before the commencement of the service in it, on Rosh Ḥodesh Nisan?

It seems that the answer to this question is quite simple. Concerning the daily sacrifice, our *parasha* tells us "a daily burnt sacrifice for your generations, at the entrance to the Tent of Meeting, where I shall meet with you, to speak with you there." Having the Tent of Meeting as a place of meeting and dialogue is a condition for the daily sacrifice to be considered as being offered "before God." These conditions are circular: the Divine Presence must be the result of the service, but the service cannot be carried out "before God" so long as the Divine Presence is absent!

For this reason the Divine Presence descended to the *Mishkan* at first in concealed form, and only afterwards was revealed. At the end of *Parashat Pekudei* we are told that God's Glory filled the *Mishkan*, but the cloud covered the *Mishkan* and God's Glory could not be seen; even Moses himself was unable to enter the Tent of Meeting because of the cloud. God speaks from inside the Tent of Meeting to Moses, who stands outside (in contrast to the opinion of the commentators, who maintain that God's call to Moses at the beginning of Leviticus facilitated his entry). This continues throughout the seven days of consecration, as well as during the sacrificial service of the eighth day. Thus, the Tent of Meeting indeed became the place "where I shall meet with you, to speak with you there," and the service took place "before God." It was only after the sacrifices of the eighth day that Moses and Aaron entered the Tent of Meeting for the first time, and then God's Glory appeared openly to the people, when the fire – the same consuming fire that is the appearance of God's Glory, as explained at the end of *Mishpatim* – emerged from the Tent of Meeting and consumed the sacrifices upon the altar. Only now was the Tent of Meeting truly sanctified with God's Glory, such that God truly met with *Benei Yisrael* there, and together with the Tent of Meeting God also sanctified the altar, by accepting the sacrifices through the revelation of the consuming fire upon the altar.

Not all of the expressions from our *parasha* appear here. Most conspicuous is the omission of the sanctification of Aaron and his sons for priesthood. From our verse it would seem that this was meant to happen together with the sanctification of the altar. From a thematic point of view, too, we would have expected it to occur close to their inauguration during the seven days of consecration.

Apparently, the sanctification of the kohanim by God was indeed meant to happen on the eighth day, and would have happened then had it not been for an unexpected hitch – the sin of Nadav and Avihu (10:1). Instead of "and I shall sanctify Aaron and his sons," there is an episode following which we are told, "I shall be sanctified among those who are near Me." Instead of God's Glory appearing as a consuming fire, sanctifying Aaron and his sons, it ends up consuming his sons. It is not clear how exactly the sanctification of Aaron and his sons would have been expressed had it not been for the sin (perhaps fire would have emerged from the Tent of Meeting and consumed the incense on their censers), but the sin of Nadav and Avihu disrupted the course of events from their planned progression.

Parashat Ki Tissa

The Half-Shekel

Rabbanit Sharon Rimon

I. INTRODUCTION

Parashat Ki Tissa opens with the subject of the half-shekel:

> God spoke to Moses, saying:
> "When you count the members of *Benei Yisrael* by their number, then each man shall give his soul's ransom to God when you count them, that there be no plague among them when you count them. This they shall give, every one that passes among those who are counted: *a half-shekel* of the shekel of the Sanctuary – twenty gera to a shekel – a half-shekel offering to God. Every one that passes among those who are counted, from the age of twenty years upwards, shall give the offering to God. The rich shall not give more, nor shall the poor give less than a half-shekel, when giving the offering to God, to make atonement for your souls. You shall take the atonement money of *Benei Yisrael* and set it aside for the service of the Tent of Meeting, that it may be a memorial to *Benei Yisrael* before God, to make atonement for your souls." (Ex. 30:11–16)

What are *Benei Yisrael* being commanded to do here? What is the purpose of giving a half-shekel?

The *parasha* opens with the subject of the census: "When you count the members of *Benei Yisrael* by their number (*lifkudeihem*)." Further on, the root *p-k-d* (פ.ק.ד. – to count) appears another four times:

> then each man shall give his soul's ransom to God *when you count* them ....
>
> that there be no plague among them *when you count them*.
>
> This they shall give, every one that passes among those *who are counted* ....
>
> Every one that passes among *those who are counted*, from the age of twenty years ....

Clearly, the issue of counting is central to this unit. But is there actually a command to hold a census? If there is a command here, then somewhere it must be fulfilled. In fact, in *Parashat Pekudei* we find that the Torah records a census taking place (38:25–27). In these verses we are told that a census was held, that the total number of men counted was 603,550 and, accordingly, that the amount of silver collected in the census was one-hundred talents and 1,775 shekels.[1] This silver was used for making the sockets and hooks. Apparently, Moses carried out the census by means of the half-shekel, just as described and commanded in *Parashat Ki Tissa*.

But the formulation of the verses in *Ki Tissa* does not follow the regular pattern of a command: "*When* (*ki*) you count the members of *Benei Yisrael*." In this verse, the word "*ki*" means when, or if. This is not the usual language of a command; rather, the census is a description of the condition to which the command refers later on. What the verse means, then, is: "When you count *Benei Yisrael*, every one shall give a ransom for himself."[2]

---

1. One talent equals three-thousand shekels; the total amount collected was 301,775 shekels. Since each person gave one half-shekel, the total number of people was 603,550.

2. There are many commandments that are introduced with the word "*ki*," in the sense of "when" or "if," and all include the description of a situation, followed by the command as to how to proceed in that instance. For example, Leviticus 25:25: "If your

The differences between the language in *Ki Tissa* and the language of the instruction to carry out a census at the beginning of the book of Numbers are striking:

> *Take a census* of all the congregation of *Benei Yisrael*.... From twenty years and upwards, all those who are fit to go out to war in Israel *you shall count them* by their hosts, you and Aaron. (Num. 1:2–3)

The language in Numbers is in the imperative: "Take"; "You shall count." Comparing the two, it becomes immediately clear that the language in *Ki Tissa* is not meant as a command.[3] The Malbim explains:

> The wording in *Ki Tissa* indicates something that is voluntary – "If you wish to count." It is not uttered in the imperative.... This was only a notification for the future – "If you need to do so, then."

What, then, is the command in this *parasha*? The command concerns the manner of conducting a census among *Benei Yisrael*. If we want or need to conduct a census, a ransom must be given.

---

brother becomes poor and he sells some of his possession, then his nearest kinsman shall come and redeem that which his brother sold." The text is certainly not commanding anyone to be poor, nor stipulating that a poor man must sell some of his possessions! The command, of course, concerns the redemption of that which was sold. If someone sells his possession, then his kinsmen are commanded to redeem. The same applies in the case of Deuteronomy 24, which discusses divorce. There is no commandment to hate one's wife, or to divorce her; rather, the command concerns the manner in which the divorce is carried out, along with a prohibition to remarry a wife that one divorced if she has been married to someone else. There are many other such examples.

3. If there is no command, why is this census carried out by Moses in *Parashat Pekudei*? We may explain that Moses himself wished to conduct the census, for whatever reason, and he did so in the manner commanded by God. In Ramban's view, the command is not to conduct a census right now, but rather a general command meaning that whenever *Benei Yisrael* are counted, a ransom of a half-shekel should be given. Moses understood, on the basis of this command, that he should also arrange a census right then.

II. A ONE-TIME COMMANDMENT?

Does this command to bring a half shekel apply to every census, or is it specific to certain censuses? According to most of the commentators, this is a permanent condition for any census. Rashi explains:

> If you wish to obtain the sum of their number, to know how many they are, do not count heads; rather, each should give a half-shekel, then you count the shekels and you know their number. "That there be no plague among them" – for a counting is susceptible to the evil eye, and then a plague will come upon them – as we find in the days of King David.

According to Rashi, the command is a fixed one. In every census, *Benei Yisrael* are to be counted by means of half-shekels. What is the reason for this command? Why must a half-shekel be given in every census? The reason is presented in the verses themselves, and heavily emphasized:

> Each man shall give *a ransom for his soul* ... that there not be among them *a plague* when you count them.

Twice more we find the expression "*to make atonement for your souls*," and the money itself is called "*money of atonement*." The text indicates that a census is problematic – it may cause a plague, and in order to prevent that a ransom must be given.

Towards the end of King David's life (II Sam. 24) the text describes a census that he conducted, in the wake of which a plague struck the nation. This story reinforces our perception of a census as being problematic.

What is the problem with a census? Rashi's view, as quoted above, is that the evil eye presides over a count. Therefore, people must not be counted directly, but by means of some device: an object is to be taken from every person, and then the objects are counted, rather than the people themselves. In this way the evil eye does not come to control the people being counted.

In Tanach we find evidence of counting by means of other devices.

In the war against Amalek, we read: "Saul gathered the people and counted them with lambs (*"tela'im"*): 200,000 foot-soldiers and 10,000 men of Judah" (1 Sam. 15:4). Saul counted the people by means of lambs: each gave a lamb, and then these were counted.

Similarly, when Saul wages war against Naḥash, King of Ammon, we read: "He counted them *in Bezek*, and *Benei Yisrael* were 300,000, and the men of Judah – 30,000" (1 Sam. 11:8). Some commentators understand *"Bezek"* as the name of the place, but Rashi explains:

> "He counted them in Bezek" – Our sages taught: with shards of pottery, or with stones – i.e., he took a stone from each of them and counted them, as in "He counted them with lambs" [1 Sam. 15:4], where he took a lamb from each and counted them, *just as they used to be counted using half-shekels.*

[handwritten margin note: EVIL EYE]

According to these sources, the problem is a direct counting of people. A direct count causes the evil eye to preside over them, and thus a plague is brought about. The half-shekel is a means of indirect counting, which prevents this problem. Since the people are counted using half-shekels – or pottery shards, or lambs – the evil eye is kept away.

However, others emphasize that the aim of the half-shekel is a ransom for the individual, "to atone for yourselves." It would seem that the purpose is to atone for some sin.[4] The counting itself is problematic, and therefore atonement is required when the nation is counted. Hence, it makes no difference whether we count heads or some representative device; *it is the actual counting of the nation that is problematic.*

[handwritten margin note: Atone]

---

4.   "Ransom" (*kofer*) is money that is given to redeem a person from the punishment of death, as we learn from the verses in Numbers 35:31–32: "You shall not take a ransom for the life of a murderer, who is guilty of death, for he shall surely be put to death." Likewise in Exodus 21:30.

   The expression "to atone" (*lekhaper* – the same root as *kofer*) means to remove sin, as we learn from a great number of sources (particularly in Leviticus). For example, Leviticus 4:20 – "The kohen shall make atonement for them and they shall be forgiven." Ramban, commenting on Exodus 21:30, connects the two concepts: "'If a ransom be placed upon him' – because the ransom (*kofer*) is an atonement (*kapara*), in the same manner as the sacrifices."

What is the problem with counting? The Malbim proposes three different reasons for the plague that arises from counting. One of these reasons is:

> So long as the nation is united and they are all like a single man, the merit of the collective is very great. But when they are numbered, such that each person is regarded individually, and their deeds are scrutinized, then the plague falls on them.

According to this explanation, the problem with counting is that people are separated, so that each stands alone and is judged according to his own actions, without having collective merit protecting him. Thus, they end up guilty according to strict justice, and are punished. The half-shekel therefore atones for the sins that would otherwise bring punishment.

This explanation gives rise to two questions. First, is it possible that the majority of people would emerge guilty by law, and that only collective merit protects them? Second, why is the census perceived as separating people? The point of counting would seem to be quite the opposite – it joins all of them into a single entity that numbers such-and-such. The counting does not highlight the unique status or situation of each individual, but does precisely the opposite: it joins them all together on a common basis.

We may explain the problematic nature of the census in a different way. Rabbenu Baḥya writes:

> Blessing is found not in that which has been measured, nor in that which has been counted, but rather only in that which is hidden from the eye.... For hidden miracles happen every day, in things which are not counted and measured. For if blessing came upon that which was counted, it would not be a hidden miracle but rather a revealed one, and not every person is worthy of experiencing revealed miracles.... And for this reason the Torah commands that Israel not be counted by head, but rather using shekels, in order that blessing rest upon them with the

increase of their children through hidden miracles, and that the evil eye not control them, for it rules over that which is counted.[5]

The problem with numbering is that when the nation is counted, their sum is fixed and publicized, as it were, at a certain total, and this prevents blessing from resting upon them. There is no room, as it were, for the showering of God's abundance.

According to all of these commentators, *Parashat Ki Tissa* conveys a commandment for all generations: every time the nation is counted, they are to be numbered using shekels, because direct counting is problematic. Do we find that *Benei Yisrael* were indeed always counted by means of a half-shekel? In the census recorded at the beginning of the book of Numbers, no mention whatsoever is made of the half-shekel. Similarly, in the census at the beginning of *Parashat Pinḥas* and in other censuses in Tanach, there is similarly no hint of the matter.

Rashi, in his commentary here and on Numbers, addresses this question. He suggests that God commanded in *Parashat Ki Tissa* that a census always be conducted using a half-shekel, and there is no need to mention it over again each time. When, in the days of King David, the nation was counted without the shekels – they were punished.

However, other commentators maintain that no mention is made of the half-shekel in the other censuses because the command in our *parasha* was a *one-time* requirement, only for a specific census, and not for all future generations.

Abarbanel proposes a compromise. He accepts that the evil eye

---

5. The same idea appears in the commentaries of Ḥizkuni and the Malbim, and is based upon the teaching of Ḥazal in *Ta'anit* 8b: "Rabbi Yitzḥak said: Blessing is found only in that which is hidden from the eye, as it is written: 'God will command the blessing upon you in your barns.' The Rabbis taught: One who comes in to measure [the produce of] his threshing floor says, 'May it be Your will, Lord our God, that You send a blessing upon the work of our hands.' Once he starts measuring, he says; 'Blessed is He who sends blessing upon this heap.' One who measures and then afterwards recites a blessing – this is a blessing uttered in vain. Because blessing is found not in something that is already weighed, nor something already measured, nor in something already counted, but only in that which is hidden from the eye."

does prevail over a count, therefore necessitating a ransom during the census in order to prevent harm. This applies, however, only to an instance where the nation is counted without any divine command to do so. When God commands that the nation be counted, no harm ensues, and therefore there is no need for atonement. Therefore, in the censuses conducted in the book of Numbers, no half-shekel ransom was taken, and for that reason this command is not included in the list of 613 commandments.

Taking another look at the verses, we noted that the roots *p-k-d* and *k-p-r* feature prominently. Further examination of the verses, though, reveals that this unit contains another expression that is repeated – "offering (*teruma*) to God." Three times, in verses 13–15, the Torah repeats and emphasizes that the half-shekel is given as an offering to God. And in verse 16, which summarizes the unit, we read that the money is given "for the service of the Tent of Meeting."

The first time that the half-shekel is mentioned is in verse 13, where we read: "This they shall give, every one that passes among those who are counted: a half-shekel of the shekel of the Sanctuary – a shekel is twenty gera; a half-shekel offering to God." In other words, the first time that the half-shekel is mentioned, we are not told that it is "to atone for yourselves," or a "ransom for himself," but rather that it is an offering to God. So is the half-shekel meant as atonement for the census, or is it an offering to God? The expression "offering to God" is repeated three times, and in addition we are told that the money is given for the service of the Tent of Meeting. This *parasha* is located in the midst of all the commandments concerning the building of the *Mishkan*, which serves to reinforce our impression that this unit, too, is principally about a contribution to the *Mishkan*. In chapter 38, in the description of the actual performance of the census, there is no description of the census itself. Rather, in the midst of the sum total of all the contributions to the *Mishkan*, we also find the amount of silver collected from the census. The census is mentioned only in passing. Finally, the list of commandments does not include a command to count *Benei Yisrael* by means of a half-shekel, but it does include a command to contribute a half-shekel to the Sanctuary every year: "It is a positive command from the Torah for every man of Israel to give a half-shekel each year." (Rambam, *Laws of Shekels*, 1:1).

Thus, our *parasha* has two aspects to it: an offering to God and a census.

III. DONATION OR COUNTING?

If the crux of the matter is that an offering should be given to God – a contribution to the *Mishkan*/Temple – then why is it presented as an offering that arises from the census? If the major issue is the census, what is the census doing here, in the middle of the sections dealing with the *Mishkan*?

The Netziv and Rav Samson Raphael Hirsch both propose that these are two separate subjects. They demonstrate that the text is talking about a contribution for two different purposes: One is "an offering to God," a contribution for the requirements of the Sanctuary, with no connection to census and atonement. The other is "money of atonement," which comes to atone for the census. These commentators base their interpretation on the strong impression that the text here incorporates two matters of equal weight: an offering to God, and a census. The Torah combines these two aspects of the half-shekel to the extent that we do not even realize that the text is talking about two separate matters.

Are these two purposes in any way connected to one another? The Netziv maintains that the two are not necessarily connected. The offering to God is a fixed matter – it is given every year, while the donation of the money of atonement – from which the sockets of the *Mishkan* were fashioned – was a one-time offering in the wake of the census conducted at that time.

However, most commentators view our text not as a one-time event, but rather a permanent command for all generations, arising from the fundamental problem of conducting a census. If so, the connection between the atonement for the census and the offering is an inherent one. What is this connection? Let us return to Abarbanel, who posits that the problem arises specifically in the context of a census initiated by man, but not in a census conducted at God's command.

Why do people conduct censuses? In general, the purpose of a census is organizational. In order to run a country properly, it is necessary to obtain population statistics – in order to divide the tax burden, to provide optimal organization of services to the citizenry, etc. The censuses most prevalent in Tanach are *military censuses*, conducted just prior to going out to war, and there seems to be no problem with these.

The story of the census at the end of David's life describes a different situation. Here the nation is not going out to war; there is no need for any special organization. David simply wants to number the people. Yoav senses the problem immediately when David asks him to carry out the census: "Yoav said to the king: 'May the Lord God multiply the people a hundred times over, and may my master, the king, see it – why does my master the king desire this thing?'" (II Sam. 24:3). David, it turns out, has no special reason for numbering the people. He wants to count them because he believes that they are many, and he wants to enjoy the sense of ruling over a large nation. This is the source of the problem. Abarbanel explains: "'David's heart reproached him' [24:10] ... when he perceived his sin *in becoming proud* concerning his nation and his inheritance, and his heart had turned from God, who was his true help."

Counting the nation conveys a sense of power and pride. When going out to war and counting the soldiers for this purpose, there is a similar danger of creating a sense of reliance upon human strength – the number of soldiers – instead of relying upon God. Even when we have no choice – sometimes a census must be conducted – there is a danger that the census will imbue the nation with improper pride, and it is this that causes the plague. Therefore it is specifically when we conduct a census that we must remember who it is that gives us the "strength to perform this valor."

How is a census to be performed properly, to avoid a sense of "My strength and the power of my hand"? God teaches us the proper manner of conducting the census: it must be conducted along with an offering to God, reminding us who made us numerous, who gave us the power to succeed. In *Parashat Ki Tissa*, among all the commands concerning the building of the *Mishkan*, God commands us to number the people by means of giving an offering to God in order to remind us – specifically during the census – the place of the Divine Presence amongst Israel, the dependence upon God, the need to turn to Him. And Moses demonstrates how such a census is performed, by combining the counting of the nation with the building of the *Mishkan*.

In the book of Numbers there is a census, but no mention is made of the half-shekel. Why? Because in the book of Numbers it is God who commands the census, hence there is no danger. Why not? According to what we have said above, we may explain that *Am Yisrael* will not be harmed because there is nothing wrong with such a census. It does not arise from a human desire to discover how powerful the nation is; rather, it is a response to divine command, and this can never be a problem. Moreover, the census in Numbers concerns the organization of the camp of Israel and the establishment of the area of the Divine Presence in its midst. Once again: when there is a strong connection between the census of the nation and the place of the Divine Presence within their camp, the census is not problematic in any way.

In the time of King David, as we have seen, the census was taken without any organizational need, without any divine command, and without the donation of the half-shekel, which would remind the nation of God during the course of the census. Such a counting, which amplifies the sense of human pride, is problematic, and therefore it ends in a plague.

What was the rectification for the census, what stopped the plague? The plague stopped when David purchased the future site of the Temple and built an altar to God. This is the connection between the offering made to God's Sanctuary and the solution to the problem of the census. This connection is no accident. An offering to God – an approach to God via the Sanctuary – shows that a person understands that in truth there is no significance to the numerical number; the power to perform valor lies with God. Within an atmosphere such as this, there is no problem with a census, and the plague is stayed.

Therefore, the giving of the half-shekel is not merely an external atonement for a problem that is created by the census. Rather, it is given as an offering to God that repairs the fundamental problem arising from the census. The offering turns the census from an expression or harbinger of the sense of "my power and the strength of my hand" into an act expressing recognition of the centrality of God.

The Jewelry and the Tent

Rav Chanoch Waxman

I. INTRODUCTION

In studying *Parashat Ki Tissa*, we are naturally drawn to the dramatic events of chapter 32. The sin of the golden calf, Moses' prayer, the tumultuous and bloody aftermath at the bottom of the mountain, and Moses' second prayer, including the offer of his own life on behalf of the children of Israel, almost never fail to grab our interest. Alternatively, we are captured by the pathos of Moses' third prayer during his dialogue with God, and the revelation of God's attributes of mercy in chapter 34. Sandwiched in between all the action and the passion lie the obscure and often neglected events of the beginning of chapter 33; what may be termed "The Jewelry and the Tent." What happens in this section? More importantly, how do these events affect our understanding of the action-packed portions of *Parashat Ki Tissa*?

Let us focus on the first part of chapter 33, and on the prominent roles of Moses' tent and of what the Torah terms "*ed*" (jewelry, ornaments or finery).

At the beginning of the chapter, God informs Moses that an angel (rather than God Himself) will lead the nation into the Promised Land, due to the people's stiff-necked nature and the consequent danger of their being consumed by God's Presence (33:1–3). In response to the bad news that God will not accompany them directly, "The people mourned and no man put on his ornaments (*edyo*)" (v. 4). At this juncture, God reiterates His claim that the children of Israel are a stiff-necked people and orders that the people remove their ornaments (*"hored edyekha"*) and then "I may know what to do with you" (v. 5). The Torah mentions jewelry and ornaments for the third time in recounting the people's fulfillment of God's command. "And the children of Israel stripped (*vayitnatzelu*) themselves of their ornaments (*edyam*) from Mount Horev" (v. 6). At this point, the narrative shifts focus and "the tent" emerges as the central topic. The Torah reports Moses' removal of "the tent" outside of the camp, the naming of the tent as "the Tent of Meeting" (*"Ohel Mo'ed"*), the details of Moses' journey to the tent, and the conference of God and Moses inside it (v. 7–11).

This brief sketch of the narrative raises many obvious questions. We note four.

1. Why do *Benei Yisrael* respond to the bad news that they will not be led directly by God by removing their ornamentation?

2. Next, God affirms the people's decision not to wear their finery, commanding them, "Remove your finery," and adding, "[Then] I may know what to do with you" (33:5). What is it about the removal of the finery that causes God to reconsider His relationship with the people?

3. In addition to the above, the Torah draws a connection between the ornaments and Mount Horev (33:6). What is the meaning of this connection to Sinai?

4. Finally, what constitutes the thematic relationship between the narrative of the ornaments and the story of Moses' removal of the tent outside of the camp? What explains the Torah's juxtaposition of the two events?

II. *"EDYAM MEHAR ḤOREV"*

Let us first turn our attention to the third question raised above, the issue of the connection between the finery and Sinai, the meaning of the phrase "*edyam meHar Ḥorev*" (33:5). This phrase might be interpreted as meaning something like "at *Har Ḥorev*" or "from *Har Ḥorev*." If so, the

Torah simply describes the location at which the Israelites removed their finery, or the chronological point at which the event took place. However, Rashi (on 33:3, based on *Shabbat* 88a) claims that "*edyam*" refers to the "crowns that the Israelites were given at Sinai when they proclaimed, '*na'aseh venishma*' (We will do and we will listen)." Accordingly, the phrase "*edyam meHar Ḥorev*" should be interpreted as meaning "of *Har Ḥorev*."

Rashi and the Midrash provide both an explanation of the textual meaning of the phrase "*edyam meHar Ḥorev*" and a conceptual explanation of the ornamentation. "*Edyam*" consists of the "crowns" received at Sinai. However, on the simple "*peshat*" level of the text, what exactly are the ornamentations of Ḥorev?

III. ARRIVING AT SINAI

The Torah first details the arrival of *Benei Yisrael* at Sinai in Exodus nineteen. As a preface to "*Ma'amad Har Sinai*," Moses ascends and descends the mountain, conducting a kind of shuttle diplomacy between God and the Israelites (19:3–9). The language of this section is unusually intimate. God refers to the fact that, "I bore you on eagle's wings and brought you to Myself" (v. 4). Similarly, God requests the keeping of His covenant and promises in exchange to keep the children of Israel as "My own treasure from among all peoples" (v. 5). Finally, picking up on the image of "bringing and coming," God states: "Behold, I come to you in a thick cloud." The images fit the content. God and *Benei Yisrael* are negotiating the terms of a meeting. However, this is not just any meeting. It is a meeting to contract and consummate the intimate covenantal relationship between God and Israel.

Immediately following the section of negotiations (19:1–9), the topic switches to preparations for the meeting (19:10–15). The primary preparation for the meeting consists of the command to Israel to "sanctify today and tomorrow.... Wash [your] clothes and be ready for the third day" (19:10–11). No doubt in accord with the sanctity and intimacy of the looming meeting with God, *Benei Yisrael* clothe themselves in their finest garments. But as a recently redeemed rabble of former slaves, from whence might they procure appropriate clothes and adornment for so grand an occasion?

The answer lies back in the redemption narrative. As per His promise to Abraham (Gen. 15:14), God ensures that the children of Israel leave Egypt with great wealth. Just before the Israelites leave Egypt, they request from the Egyptians "jewels of silver, jewels of gold and garments" (Ex. 12:35). God causes the Egyptians to view the Israelite's request favorably, and consequently, "They stripped (*vayinatzelu*) the Egyptians" (v. 36).

To put some of these disparate points together, the chronological and textual flow runs as follows: As part of His covenantal promise to Abraham, God arranges for the children of Israel to leave Egypt with great wealth in the form of jewels and finery. God then arranges a meeting between Himself and the newly redeemed people, through the intermediary of Moses, at a mountain in the desert. The purpose of this meeting is to contract another covenant, an intimate relationship between Himself and His people. The people agree and are told to prepare and dress for the occasion. By this point, the explanation of the phrase "*edyam meHar Ḥorev*," the jewels, ornaments and finery of *Har Ḥorev*, should readily be apparent. Certainly, the people bedeck themselves in their finest apparel, the gifts they have recently acquired as part of their historical relationship with God, the presents they received from their once and future partner in an intimate covenantal relationship. They stand at *Har Sinai* clothed in His gifts, awaiting His arrival.

IV. CHAPTER 24 – DOUBLING THE COVENANT

The role of the jewelry, ornaments, and finery as part and parcel of the first post-redemption covenant narrative are reported in chapter 19. However, in order to achieve a comprehensive understanding of the role of the ornaments in the aftermath of the sin of the golden calf, we must turn our attention to another post-redemption covenant narrative, the events reported in chapter 24.

Chapter 24 constitutes a complex and multi-layered structure. For the purpose of our analysis, we note a few key points:

1. Moses descends from the mountain and receives the agreement of the people to the commands (*divrei*) and rules (*mishpatim*) of God (v. 3).

2. Moses writes down all the commands of the covenant (*divrei*

haberit), gets up the next morning (*vayashkem baboker*) and builds an altar and twelve monuments, representing the twelve tribes, at the foot of the mountain (*taḥat hahar*) (v. 4).

3. After the offering of sacrifices, Moses sprinkles half of the blood on the altar, receives the agreement of the Israelites to the contents of the Book of the Covenant (*Sefer haBerit*), and sprinkles the remaining half of the blood on the people (v. 5–8).

4. Finally, Moses and the leadership ascend the mountain, receive a vision of the God of Israel and partake in food and drink (*vayokhlu vayishtu*) to celebrate the occasion (v. 9–11).

As is appropriate to a covenant ceremony, a deal contracted between two parties, everything comes in pairs. There are two sets of structures, the altar of God and the monuments of the Israelites, and two sprinklings of blood, one on God's altar and one on the people. In fact, there are even two copies of the treaty document. In parallel to the "*Sefer haBerit*" consisting of the commands (*divrei*) and rules (*mishpatim*) which Moses writes and the people accept, God tells Moses to ascend the mountain and receive "the tablets of stone (*luḥot*), the Torah and the commandments which I have written" (24:12). The "*luḥot*," Torah and commands constitute the divine side of the "*Sefer haBerit*," the physical record, symbol and contents of the covenant. Since they are God's copy of the treaty, they are to be kept in the divine "abode" (the *Kodesh Kodashim* – Holy of Holies) underneath the divine "throne."

V. THE COUNTER-COVENANT

Strikingly, after a lengthy digression commanding the building of the *Mishkan* (25:1–31:17), the Torah returns to the topic of the "*luḥot*" as a preface to the narrative of the sin of the golden calf (31:18). This is not just to remind the reader of the nature of the object that Moses drops and breaks in chapter 31. Rather, an integral connection exists between the events of chapter 24 (the second covenant narrative) and the events of chapter 32 (the sin of the golden calf). Let us work through the key verses that depict the reaction of the Israelites to the creation of the golden calf (32:4–6).

The first reaction of the people is to claim, "This is your God, O

Israel, who brought you out of the land of Egypt" (32:4). But, of course, HaShem personally redeemed Israel from Egypt, not any sort of idol or intermediary (see 12:12–13). This God had been "seen" by the elders of Israel at Sinai (24:10). Now the children of Israel look upon a golden calf and proclaim it their God and redeemer. This claim represents complete betrayal of the relationship between God and Israel and an explicit negation of the leadership's vision in chapter 24.

In addition to this first parallel, the Torah informs us that, just as during the covenant ceremony of chapter 24 Moses had gotten up the next day, built an altar and offered sacrifices (24:4–5), so too the people get up the next day and offer sacrifices (32:6) in front of the golden calf. Just as Moses and the elders had eaten and drunk as part of the covenant ceremony, so too the people eat and drink in front of the golden calf. In fact, the events of the sin of the golden calf constitute a kind of counter-covenant or anti-covenant ceremony. Consequently, when arriving upon the scene, Moses throws down the *luḥot* "*taḥat hahar,*" at the foot of the mountain (32:19). At the exact same location where the people had stood with the altar of God and contracted a covenant, now they stand, sacrifice and celebrate to an idol. The record of the covenant, the tangible symbol and contents of the God-Israel relation, lies broken on the ground, emptied of content by the people's act of betrayal.

This interpretation of the sin of the golden calf as the anti-covenant, the negation of the God-Israel relationship, receives further support from some of the other images in chapter 32. The Torah reports that the people got up to celebrate, "*vayakumu letzaḥek*" (32:6). However, the stem *tz-ḥ-k* (.ק.ח.צ) is not only associated with laughter and happiness, but also with infidelity. Potiphar's wife accuses Joseph of attempting to "mock her" (*letzaḥek bi*), of attempting to force her into illicit relations (Gen. 39:17). Furthermore, Moses grinds up the golden calf and forces the Israelites to drink waters containing its dust (Ex. 32:20), a ceremony reminiscent of the ordeal of the "*isha sota,*" a woman who stands accused of infidelity to her husband (Num. 5:18–24). When Israel sins with the golden calf, they not only dissolve and smash the covenant with God but also betray their intimate tie with God, their love relationship.

The last piece of the puzzle brings us full circle to the people's jewelry. By what means do the people construct their anti-covenantal object, sunder the relation between God and Israel and commit infidelity? Through their golden rings which they willingly donate to the cause. The jewelry that they received as a present from God and that they wore to the covenantal consummation ceremony at Sinai, becomes in their hands a tool and symbol not of the covenant and the intimate relation with God, but rather a tool and symbol of the anti-covenant and infidelity.

VI. A PEOPLE IN MOURNING

Let us return to some of the questions we posed above. Previously, the stripping of the people's ornamentation in response to God's decision to lead them indirectly had appeared rather opaque. Let us carefully reconsider the text. The Torah states "when the people heard these evil tidings, they mourned and no man put on his ornaments" (33:4). We may be inclined to interpret the dressing down as no more than an act of mourning. However, in light of our analysis, the removal of the finery appears to constitute much more. The finery constitutes the gifts received from God, the clothing of the covenant ceremony, and symbolizes the intimate relation between God and Israel consummated at Sinai. When the people hear the evil tidings that God will not lead them directly, they recognize that the finery has become no more than frivolous accoutrements. The relationship and covenant they symbolize no longer exist. Consequently, the people take them off.

On a deeper level, the mourning of the people consists of the realization that they are no longer deserving of the gifts of God, that they have sinned gravely and destroyed their intimate connection with God. Finally, the shedding of the jewelry represents an understanding that they have utilized some of those very gifts to betray God, to construct and create the anti-covenant. In sum, the removal of the finery reflects the beginnings of recognition of guilt, the seeds of shouldering responsibility and the incipient yearning that things be different. It represents the stirring of repentance for the sin of the golden calf (see Ibn Ezra and Ramban).

In this light, we need not be troubled by God's reaction to the Israelites' removal of their finery. God's mercy is immediate. He affirms the people's decision to remove their ornamentation and opens the door to reversing His decision: "Put off your ornaments and I will know what to do with you" (33:5). Although God does not change His mind arbitrarily, the gates of repentance stand open to the people.

VII. OUTSIDE THE CAMP

Let us turn our attention to the last question, the problem of the thematic relationship between the narrative of the ornaments and the story of Moses' removal of the tent outside of the camp. What connects the people's removal of their finery and Moses' removal of the tent?

As pointed out, the narrative of "The Tent" (33:7–11), describes more than just Moses' removal of the tent. It also details his renaming of the tent as "*Ohel Mo'ed*," the Tent of Meeting (33:7). Furthermore, it describes Moses' journey to the tent now located outside of the camp and the people's observation of the journey (33:8). Finally, the section also includes a description of the meeting of God and Moses in the tent and the people's reaction to the meeting (33:9–11).

The key to understanding the placement of this section lies not just in the events it describes but also in the terminology and imagery the text utilizes in presenting the events. The Torah emphasizes from the start the placement of the tent outside of the camp. The phrase "*miḥutz lamaḥaneh*" (outside the camp) appears twice in the opening verse (33:7), along with the parallel phrase, "*harḥek min hamaḥaneh*" (far from the camp). The tent is not just outside of the camp, but far from it. The result of the Tent of Meeting (*Ohel Mo'ed*) and Moses being outside of the camp is that "everyone who sought the Lord went…outside of the camp" (33:7). God cannot be found in the camp of Israel, but rather only outside of it. In the aftermath of the sin of the golden calf, the sundering of the covenant and intimate relationship between God and Israel, God has decided to lead the people indirectly rather than through direct contact. Consequently, He cannot be found in the camp. Moses, and those who seek him, must relocate to outside of the camp.

In addition, the Torah twice describes the meeting of Moses and God in the Tent of Meeting as involving the descent of a cloud ("*anan*") at the door of the tent ("*petaḥ ha'ohel*") so that God may speak ("*diber*") with Moses (33:8–9). This imagery clearly echoes the imagery the Torah often utilizes to describe the *Mishkan*. In *Parashat Tetzaveh*, after commanding the regimen of daily sacrifices, the Torah states that the sacrifices will take place "at the door (*petaḥ*) of the Tent of Meeting (*Ohel Mo'ed*), where I will meet you to speak (*ledaber*) with you" (29:42). Of course, God's Presence in the meeting at the door of the "*Ohel Mo'ed*" will be symbolized, as always, by a cloud (see Ex. 40:34 and Lev. 9:15–23). The meaning and spiritual significance of the meeting can be found a few verses later: "I will dwell (*veshakhanti*) among the children of Israel and will be their God" (29:45). Apparently, as a result of the sin of the golden calf, the betrayal of the covenant and the disruption of the God-Israel relationship, the people no longer deserve the gift of the Tent of Meeting. The vision of the *Mishkan* as the place where God would dwell amongst the people, meet with them (25:8, 22) and be their God (29:42–46), has apparently been cancelled. Now the Tent of Meeting and God's Presence reside outside of the camp. Now only Moses is privy to interaction and communication with the Divine Presence (33:6, 11). The national Tent of Meeting of God and Israel has been transformed into the private tent of meeting of God and Moses.

VIII. THE PEOPLE'S AWAKENING

The people's reaction to the removal of the tent outside of the camp and the alienation from God that it symbolizes constitutes the final piece of the puzzle. The Torah states that "whenever Moses went out to the tent, all the people would rise and stand, each at the door of *his* tent (*petaḥ ohalo*), and gaze after Moses until he had entered the tent" (33:8). When the pillar of cloud descended and God arrived to speak to Moses at the door of *the tent* (*petaḥ ha'ohel*), then "all the people would rise and bow low each at the door of *his* tent (*petaḥ ohalo*)." At first glance, the Torah seems to be playing some sort of word game. Just as the meeting of Moses and the pillar of cloud is twice described as taking place at "*petaḥ ha'ohel*," the door of *the* tent (33:9–10), so too the people, each and every individual, are twice described as located at "*petaḥ ohalo*," the door of *his own* tent (33:8–10). However, this is much more than a word game. The effect is to link the events at the "*Ohel Mo'ed*" and the events at the individual Israelite's tent.

The people gaze wistfully after Moses when he leaves their camp for the Tent of Meeting, and bow and worship when God's Presence arrives. From their perspective, there is little they can do. God has decreed that they will be led by an angel and has removed Himself from their encampment. The *luḥot*, the symbol of their covenant with God, lie smashed, and the Tent of Meeting, designed to house the *luḥot*, has been rendered a thing of the past. They can do no more than watch from afar and worship from a distance. Ironically, however, these very acts constitute the foundations of a new beginning.

Like the removal of their finery, the act of watching and yearning serves as an act of mourning. The people envy Moses and mourn for the loss of their direct relationship with God (Rashi on 33:8). At the very least, even if we do not wish to claim that they actively mourn, as they stand and watch they certainly are conscious of what they have lost. The first stage of return stirs in the hearts of the people. The act of bowing moves the repentance from the realm of the heart to the realm of the body. In informing Moses of the sin of the golden calf, God tells Moses that the people "have made a molten calf and *have bowed* to it" (32:8). Whereas before the people bowed to an idol, now they bow to the Divine Presence. In sum, like the story of the jewelry, the story of the tent describes the beginnings of repentance, mourning for what has happened and yearning for things to be different, which are the necessary conditions for God's mercy.

IX. WHO BRINGS FORGIVENESS?

To conclude, in thinking about the aftermath of the sin of the golden calf and God's eventual forgiving of the sin, we often focus exclusively on Moses and his power of prayer. Moses invokes the merit of the forefathers and the honor of God, and places his own life on the line and demands atonement from God. Finally, Moses speaks face to face with God, begs for guidance and revelation, and eventually prompts God's unilateral declaration of the Thirteen Attributes of Mercy. I have tried to argue that there is in fact nothing at all unilateral about God's mercy and the revelation of the Thirteen Attributes of Mercy. Buried in between Moses' second and third prayers, as a preface to the revelation of the attributes of mercy, lies the seldom noticed section of "The Jewelry and the Tent" (33:1–12), the story of the people's mourning and repentance. God is merciful and God forgives. Moses' prayers are fervent and powerful. But it is the people who have sinned, and the people who must begin to mend, rebuild and repair their relationship with God.

God's People or Moses'?

Rav Meir Spiegelman

I f we were to choose the gravest sins committed by *Benei Yisrael*, the episode of the golden calf would certainly feature in either first or second place on the list (the alternative being the sin of the spies in Numbers 13). This is the only sin where God promises Moses that the punishment will be felt for all generations. As a result of this sin, the Tablets are shattered, and they are lost – in that original format – forever. We shall examine here a further result of the sin of the golden calf – a result that is often overlooked, owing to the other serious ramifications.

I. *AM YISRAEL*: GOD'S NATION OR MOSES' NATION?

Moses becomes aware of the sin of the golden calf while still atop Mount Sinai. God tells him, "Go, descend, for *your nation* which you brought up from the land of Egypt has become corrupt" (32:7). God refers here to Israel as Moses' nation, thereby introducing the question of to whom, in fact, *Am Yisrael* (the Nation of Israel) belong. Moses, for his part, obviously thinks of the nation as belonging to God: "Why, O God, are You angry at *Your nation*, whom You brought out of the land of Egypt?" (32:11). This debate is quite surprising. How can we understand that

Am Yisrael belong to Moses, when it is abundantly clear that God was responsible for taking the nation out of Egypt?

In fact, this debate is not concluded on Mount Sinai. Following Moses' prayer on behalf of the nation, we are told, "God yielded concerning the evil which He had declared that He would do to *His people*" (32:14), but further on God again defines *Am Yisrael* as Moses' nation: "Go, arise from here – you and the nation *which you brought up* from the land of Egypt" (33:1).[1] This attitude on God's part also finds expression in the decision that He will not enter the land together with the nation, lest He consume them: "For I shall not ascend among you – for you are a stiff-necked nation – lest I consume you on the way" (33:3). Further on, again, God asserts that he will help Moses specifically; only later on does it become clear that He will be helping all of *Am Yisrael*. All of this creates the impression that *Am Yisrael* is not in direct contact with God. Rather, *Am Yisrael* is Moses' nation, and God assists Moses in his leadership role as an external partner, as it were. His help is only the help that He extends to Moses as the leader of the nation, rather than to *Am Yisrael* as His chosen nation.

This rupture between *Am Yisrael* and God was not always present. In the confrontation between God and Pharaoh, God declares several times that *Am Yisrael* is His nation. On the very first occasion where Moses and Aaron present themselves before Pharaoh, they convey God's instruction: "Let My people go" (5:1). Later, God addresses *Am Yisrael* in the first person, promising: "And I shall take you unto Myself as a nation" (6:7). As the story of the exodus progresses, this form of address is used less and less. In the warning that precedes the death of the Egyptian firstborn, this title does not appear (in contrast to the warning that precedes the plague of hail). Likewise we find in the *parasha* commanding the marking of the new month, God says, "I shall take out your hosts" (12:17), rather than "My hosts,"[2] as we find in the promise of redemption given to Moses at the beginning of *Parashat Va'era* (7:4).

1. See also further on, where Moses says: "For I have found favor in Your eyes – I and Your nation" (33:16), but in His answer God again insists, "Before all your nation I shall perform wonders" (34:10).
2. Although we read, further on, "On this very day all of God's hosts left the land of

We may suggest a process in which, starting at the time of the exodus, the selection of *Am Yisrael* is partially replaced by a selection of the firstborn. It is thus that the place of the section "Sanctify to Me every firstborn" (13:2), should be understood – against the background of the fact that in the verses following the exodus, the expression "My nation" is almost completely absent. In several places such an expression would seem appropriate, but there is no mention of it. At the splitting of the Red Sea, for instance, the Torah speaks of "*Benei Yisrael*" rather than "God's nation": "Speak to *Benei Yisrael* … and *Benei Yisrael* came" (14:15–16).

The epitome of this phenomenon is to be found on the occasion of the giving of the Torah, where – once again – no mention is made of the connection, although it would seem essential. In fact, the last time that the Torah defines *Benei Yisrael* as God's nation is in *Parashat Mishpatim*, which follows the giving of the Torah: "If you lend money to anyone of My people, to the poor among you" (22:24). The climax of this theme is the "argument" that takes place between Moses and God, where God insistently refuses to define *Am Yisrael* as His nation. The sin of the calf, then, represents the climax – or, more accurately, the final blow – in the process of *Am Yisrael* ceasing to be God's nation.

From this gloomy assessment we could, God forbid, conclude that *Am Yisrael* is indeed no longer God's nation. After all, God Himself refuses to accept Moses' definition of them as His nation, and thereafter – throughout the remainder of the Torah – there are very few instances of the nation being defined as such. One could claim that, following the catastrophic sin of the golden calf, the connection between them and God was severed. The obligation to observe the mitzvot still exists – and perhaps even the covenant between *Am Yisrael* and God is still valid – but the definition of *Am Yisrael* as God's nation is lost forever. Indeed, it is precisely this claim that Christianity has historically maintained, and from the Torah text it would appear, as it were, that there is substance to

___

Egypt," we must differentiate between an instance of God addressing Israel directly, and a description in the Torah of events as they happened. In the story of the golden calf, too, the Torah describes God as relenting of the evil that He had spoken about bringing upon His nation, but God does not relate to *Am Yisrael* in this way when He speaks to them or to Moses. In any event, even expressions such as these are no longer found after the golden calf.

this claim. It should be emphasized that two questions arise here. The first is the fundamental question of whether *Am Yisrael* ceased to be God's nation. The second question is exegetical: how can God assign the nation to Moses – when it is quite clear that it was God who initiated the idea of the exodus and also carried it out?

II. MOSES: AGENT OF THE NATION OR GOD'S AGENT?

An essential point should be added here, which may lessen the problem even if it cannot solve it entirely. Is Moses the representative of Israel before God, or is the essence of his task to serve as God's emissary to *Am Yisrael*? It would seem that the answer changes with different periods in the course of his leadership. While at the time of the giving of the Torah we relate to Moses as Israel's representative to speak with God, later his status changes and he becomes God's "partner," as it were.

Expressions of this transition may be detected in several places. The first Tablets are fashioned by God, while the second are made by Moses, and appear also to have been written (engraved) by him (see 34:27). Thus Moses becomes God's partner in creating the Torah and handing it over – which leads, thereafter, to the light emanating from his face, which makes *Am Yisrael* fearful to approach him, just as they feared to approach Mount Sinai. This also serves to explain the fact that, when God distances Himself from *Am Yisrael*, Moses also moves the tent (*Ohel*) outside the camp; it is as if Moses' dwelling, too, cannot reside amidst the nation.

This transition in Moses' role finds expression in the midrashic assertion that Moses' face shone because of a drop of ink that was placed upon his forehead. This teaching symbolizes the fact that Moses in fact turned into part of God's Torah, such that he may be perceived as God's partner in creating the Torah, rather than a partner of *Am Yisrael* receiving it. This leads us to understand, in a somewhat gentler light, the change that takes place in the relations between *Am Yisrael* and God. When Moses becomes God's agent, this change is accompanied by the fact that *Am Yisrael* now stands before Moses, rather than directly before God. Admittedly, even if we accept this interpretation for the breach that has been created between *Am Yisrael* and God, it does not solve the difficulty that such a breach creates.

I wish to propose a completely different interpretation of the discussion between God and Moses following the sin of the golden calf. This interpretation solves at least the first problem – the exegetical issue of God's claim as to the "ownership" of the nation.

III. TZIPORA AS THE BEGINNING OF ASSIMILATION

Moses' marriage to Tzipora, the daughter of the priest of Midian, is an issue that arises on several occasions in the Torah, starting with the marriage itself and concluding with the story of the complaint that Aaron and Miriam voice concerning the "*Kushite* woman" that Moses married. The Torah gives no indication of why this subject is of such great significance. Another question concerns the role played by Tzipora in Moses' return to Egypt following God's revelation at the burning bush. In chapter 4 it seems that Tzipora was accompanying him, but in chapter 18, Yitro visits the Israelite camp together with his daughter, Tzipora, "*after she had been sent away*" – proving that she had not joined him when he went to Egypt. The rabbis posit that somewhere in the course of the journey Moses sent her back to her father's house.

A further question arises with respect to the story of the encounter with the angel on the way to Egypt. Why does God want to put Moses to death? How does Tzipora's act of circumcising their son save him?

I believe that these questions should be addressed within the context of a discussion about the Egyptian "*asafsuf*" ("hangers-on"), a group noted in the Torah as having left Egypt together with Israel at the time of the exodus. The identity of this group could be either of the following:

1. The first possibility is a group of people who had no connection whatsoever with *Am Yisrael*, and who simply jumped on the bandwagon at the time of the exodus, grabbing the opportunity to escape from the country. If so, it is reasonable to assume that these people did not accompany *Benei Yisrael* all the way until they entered the Land. After achieving some distance from Egypt, they could go wherever they wanted to, and most of them probably did so.

2. The second possibility seems more probable: These were people who were not Jewish, but were connected to *Am Yisrael* through

family ties. If we adopt this explanation, this group would be similar to the people who returned from the Babylonian exile at the time of Ezra. Indeed, at that time too these "extras" caused many problems for the Jews who were returning to *Eretz Yisrael*, and a rigorous filtering process was necessary in order to separate them from *Am Yisrael*.

The phenomenon of the "hangers-on" – assuming that we accept the second possibility – is directly related to the story of Moses' marriage to Yitro's daughter. When Moses takes Tzipora with him to Egypt, he is thereby giving legitimacy to the phenomenon of the "*asafsuf*." He will no longer be able to criticize mixed marriages, for everyone will accuse him of hypocrisy. It is Moses who chooses to bring Tzipora with him to Egypt, without being commanded to do so, and as a result the angel awaits him and seeks to kill him, for by his actions Moses is endangering the future of *Am Yisrael*. It is only Tzipora's wholehearted readiness to be part of *Am Yisrael* – expressed in her circumcising her son – that allows God to forgive Moses, for thus the problem – at least on his private level – has found a solution.

However, even Tzipora's desire to join *Am Yisrael* does not solve the problem of legitimization. Since it is impossible to know the real intentions of each and every person seeking to become part of the nation, this will still open the door to a large influx of outsiders with a negative influence. Therefore, Moses decides to send Tzipora back, although she herself has already accepted the Israelite law. But despite the fact that Tzipora is sent back to Midian, the impression of Moses' marriage to her remains etched in the consciousness of *Benei Yisrael*. She therefore ends up exerting a real influence on their assimilation later on, and the creation of the *asafsuf*. Needless to say, the *asafsuf* bear considerable responsibility for leading *Benei Yisrael* astray and into sin in the desert – including, inter alia, the episode of the golden calf.

This, then, is the background to the argument between God and Moses. God insists that it is Moses' nation that has come out of Egypt. God is referring here to the *asafsuf*, whose creation and integration was facilitated by Moses. Moses, on the other hand, asks God to ignore the *asafsuf* – although these people are the source of the problem – and to relate instead to the great majority of those who left Egypt and who are, indeed, God's people.

IV. "MOSES AND AARON WITH HIS KOHANIM, AND SAMUEL WITH THOSE WHO CALL HIS NAME"

The above hypothesis applies only in the framework of our discussion of the exegetical question. The more fundamental problem is the other question presented above: did God indeed give up *Am Yisrael*, such that from now they are no longer His nation? In order to evaluate this question, we must locate the point where *Am Yisrael* is once again called God's nation. Obviously, in the books of the prophets we find many expressions identifying the nation of Israel with God, but – in contrast to Moses' prophecies – these are spoken in the personal style of each individual prophet, such that they may not be used as any type of proof. In any case, it is quite possible that *Am Yisrael* is referred to as God's nation by the prophets without this title actually being awarded by God. Therefore, we must find the place where God Himself calls *Am Yisrael* His nation.

The occasion that we seek awaits us in the book of Samuel. When God informs Samuel that he must anoint Saul as king, he tells him:

> You shall anoint him as ruler of My people Israel, and he shall deliver My people from the hand of the Philistines, for I have seen My people, for their cry has come to Me. (1 Sam. 9:16)

Here God calls *Am Yisrael* His nation, for the first time since the sin of the golden calf. The expression "My people" does not merely appear here, but is specially emphasized. Until now God has avoided all use of it, while here it appears no less than three times in a single verse. Likewise, we note that there is a stylistic parallel between this verse and the verses preceding the exodus: the words "for their cry has come to Me" are reminiscent of the verse at the end of chapter 2 of Exodus, "and their cry rose unto God…and God knew" (2:24–25).

Hence, we may say that Saul's coronation by Samuel represents, in a way, a closing of the circle that opened with the exodus. God took His nation out of Egypt, but in the wake of Israel's sin this endeavor failed, and God distanced Himself from *Am Yisrael*. *Am Yisrael* became

God's nation once again during the period of Samuel and Saul. It is no coincidence, then, that the rabbis assert – "Moses and Aaron with His *Kohanim*, and Samuel with those who call His name" (Psalms 99:6) – that Samuel was considered equal to Moses and Aaron together. During his time, the breach between *Am Yisrael* and their Father in heaven, which developed during the period of Moses and Aaron, was healed.

V. ROYALTY AND LEGISLATURE, PROPHECY AND PRIESTHOOD

Why is it specifically during Samuel's lifetime that God's relationship with *Am Yisrael* is renewed? What is it about that period that facilitated the return of the Divine Presence? The answer seems to lie in the lineup of all the key positions of national leadership, for the first time since the time of Moses and Aaron.

Moses and Aaron in fact fulfilled four different roles, which together represent the entire leadership body of *Am Yisrael*: kingship, priesthood, prophets, and legislators. Moses, as *Ḥazal* emphasize, serves as king, in addition to his role as legislator (insofar as it is he who is responsible for conveying the Torah to *Am Yisrael*). Prophecy, of course, is also Moses' role. Aaron fulfills the fourth aspect of the leadership spectrum with his role as kohen.

This situation, where all leadership functions in *Am Yisrael* are being fulfilled, did not exist again until the time of Samuel. During the period of the judges, obviously, there was no king or centralized leadership for the entire nation: "Each person did what was right in his eyes" (Judges 17:6). Only in Samuel's lifetime were these roles fully revived. Samuel himself served as prophet and legislator. The crown of priesthood was also given to him, as we may deduce from the fact that he slept in the Sanctuary of the *Mishkan* – which would have been unthinkable had he not been a kohen. He also temporarily fulfilled the role of national leader, but the institution of kingship returned to Israel with the coronation of Saul. It was this restoration of kingship that made it possible for the Divine Presence to reside once again amongst the nation, as we may learn from the obligation to appoint a king before the Temple is to be built.

In general, the leadership roles in Israel flow directly from God, and from there they pass down throughout the generations. Thus, the crown of priesthood is given to Aaron at the time of the revelation at Sinai, and from then on it is passed on dynastically. Similarly, the authority to legislate was given to Moses at Sinai and was then passed down through *semikha* (ordination). Prophecy was also given to Moses, while all the other prophets who followed, appointed by God, actually continued his prophecy – as Moses himself taught: "A prophet from among you, from your brethren, *like me*, shall the Lord your God raise up; you shall listen to him" (18:15).

The Israelite royalty was also meant to be passed on successively from Moses. But in the wake of the sin of *Mei Meriva*, it was decided that Moses would not enter the land – which led to a severing of the chain of leadership. God Himself had to choose a new king for Israel – and this development was fully realized only in Samuel's time. The rupture that prevailed between God and His people continued until that time. It was healed with the appointment of Saul as king of Israel:

> And you shall anoint him as a ruler over My people Israel, and he shall deliver My people from the hand of the Philistines, for I have seen My people, for their cry has come to Me. (1 Sam. 9:16)

The Commandments of the Covenant

Rav Tamir Granot

I. INTRODUCTION

After God is revealed to Moses for the second time on Mount Sinai, He reveals His attributes of mercy and tells Moses that He has forgiven the nation of Israel. God informs Moses that He is renewing His covenant with them, and adds a list of commandments – some related to the prohibition of idolatry, others related to Shabbat and the pilgrim festivals and all that they entail (such as, for instance, the prohibition of mixing meat and milk). We may refer to these collectively as "ritual" commandments. Part of this list looks very similar to *Parashat Mishpatim*, where the lengthy collection of "judgments" (*mishpatim*) is followed by an appendix of "ritual" laws, including Shabbat, pilgrim festivals, meat and milk, etc. The resemblance between these two *parashot* extends beyond their content; they are also similar in their style and language.

As we know, there are many commandments that appear twice or even three times in the Torah. In most cases, it is in Deuteronomy that we find repetitions of mitzvot that were transmitted previously. Indeed, this phenomenon is characteristic of Deuteronomy, which is also called *"Mishneh Torah"* (repetition of the Torah). In Exodus, Leviticus and Numbers, repetitions occur far less frequently. However, the almost word-for-word reiteration of an entire body of mitzvot is unique

447

to our *parasha*: Exodus 34:18–26 (the body of ritual laws which we shall refer to as the unit from *Ki Tissa*) is a repetition of Exodus 23:14–19 (henceforth, the unit from *Parashat Mishpatim*).

Moreover, the repetition here occurs within the same book, in close proximity of time and subject. In both cases, the commandments in question are conveyed by God to Moses at Mount Sinai: the first time – within the framework of the forging of the first covenant; the second time – when Moses ascends the mountain the second time, as part of God's assurance that the covenant has been renewed.

Hence, we need to understand why God repeats an entire body of mitzvot that has already been conveyed – and recently, too. Furthermore, what is the significance of the slight differences between the two versions?

II. COMPARING THE TWO UNITS

Let us start by comparing the two units. Our examination will include the verses that precede the ritual laws, with a view to clarifying the context. We shall also highlight the differences between the two units.

Topic	PARASHAT MISHPATIM	PARASHAT KI TISSA
Introduction	You shall not pervert the justice of your poor in his cause. Keep far from a false matter, and do not slay the innocent and the righteous, for I shall not justify the wicked. And do not take a bribe, for bribery blinds the wise and distorts the words of the righteous. And do not oppress a stranger, for you know the heart of a stranger, since you were strangers in the land of Egypt. (23:6–9)	He said: "Behold, I make a covenant before all of your nation; I shall perform wonders such as have not been conceived in all the land, nor among all the nations…. Watch yourself lest you forge a covenant with the inhabitants of the land to which you come, lest it become a snare in your midst. Rather, you shall smash their altars and break their statues and cut down their *asherim*. For you shall not worship any other god, for the Lord – Jealous is His name – is a jealous God.

Topic	PARASHAT MISHPATIM	PARASHAT KI TISSA
		Lest you make a covenant with the inhabitants of the land, and go astray after their gods, and sacrifice to their gods, and [they] call you, and you eat of [their] sacrifice. And take of their daughters for your sons, and their daughters will go astray after their gods, and they shall draw your sons astray after their gods. You shall make yourself no molten gods." (34:10–17)
The *Shemitta* Year	Six years you shall sow your land and gather its produce. But in the seventh you shall let it rest and lie fallow, that the poor of your nation may eat, and what they leave shall be eaten by the beasts of the field; so shall you with your vineyard and your olive grove. (23:10–11)	- omitted -
Shabbat	Six days shall you perform your activities, but on the seventh day you shall rest, in order that your ox and your donkey may rest, and the son of your handmaid and the stranger may be refreshed. (23:12)	(appears later, with a different emphasis)
Exhortation to perform the commandments	And concerning all that I have said to you – be mindful, and do not make mention of the name of other gods; let it not be heard from your mouth. (23:13)	- omitted -

Topic	PARASHAT MISHPATIM	PARASHAT KI TISSA
Introduction to pilgrim festivals	Three times you shall observe a festival for Me in the year. (23:14)	- omitted -
Festival of Matzot	You shall observe the Festival of Matzot: seven days shall you eat matzot, as I have commanded you, at the appointed time – the month of spring, for then you left Egypt; and *you shall not appear before Me empty-handed.* (23:15)	You shall observe the Festival of Matzot: for seven days shall you eat matzot, as I have commanded you, at the appointed time – the month of spring, for in the month of spring you left Egypt. (34:18)
A Firstborn Donkey	- omitted -	All that opens the womb is Mine, and every male firstling among your livestock, whether ox or sheep. But the firstling of a donkey you shall redeem with a lamb; if you do not redeem it then you shall break its neck. All the firstborn of your sons you shall redeem, and *you shall not appear before Me empty-handed.* (34:19–20)
Shabbat	(appeared previously, with social emphasis)	Six days shall you work, but on the seventh day you shall rest; in plowing and in harvest you shall rest. (34:21)
Festival of the Harvest and the Festival of the Ingathering	And the Festival of the Harvest, the first fruits of your labors which you have sown in the field, and the Festival of the Ingathering, at the end of the year, when you gather in your labors from the field. (23:16)	And you shall celebrate the Festival of Weeks, the first fruits of the wheat harvest, and the Festival of the Ingathering, at the year's end. (34:22)

Topic	*PARASHAT MISHPATIM*	*PARASHAT KI TISSA*
Obligation of pilgrimage to the Temple	Three times in the year all your males shall present themselves before the Lord God. (23:17)	Three times in the year all your males shall present themselves to the Lord God, God of Israel. (34:23)
Assurance concerning pilgrimage	- omitted -	For I shall cast out nations before you, and I shall expand your borders, and no man shall covet your land when you go up to present yourself before the Lord your God, three times in the year. (34:24)
Prohibitions against leftovers and leaven	You shall not *offer* the blood of My sacrifice with leaven, nor shall *the fat of My festive offering* remain until the morning. (23:18)	You shall not *slaughter* the blood of My sacrifice with leaven, nor shall the *sacrifice of the Pesaḥ feast* remain for the morning. (34:25)
First fruits and mixture of milk and meat	You shall bring the earliest of the first fruits of your land to the House of the Lord your God; you shall not cook a kid in its mother's milk. (23:19)	You shall bring the earliest of the first fruits of your land to the House of the Lord your God; you shall not cook a kid in its mother's milk. (34:26)
Conclusion	Behold, I send an angel before you, to watch over you on the way and to bring you to the place which I have prepared. Be mindful of him and obey his voice; do not provoke him, for he will not pardon your sins, for My name is in him.	The Lord said to Moses: "Write for yourself these things, for in accordance with these words I have forged a covenant with you, and with Israel." And he was there with the Lord for forty days and forty nights; he did not eat bread, nor did he drink water, and he wrote upon the tablets the words of the covenant – the Ten Utterances. (34:27–28)

Topic	PARASHAT MISHPATIM	PARASHAT KI TISSA
	But if you indeed obey him and do all that I say, then I shall be the enemy of your enemies, and the adversary of your adversaries. For My angel shall go before you and bring you to the Emorites and the Hittites and the Perizites and the Canaanites, the Hivites and the Jebusites, and I shall cut them off. (23:20–23)	.

Let us set out the information that arises from the above comparison, in order of its appearance.

A. The introduction: In *Parashat Mishpatim*, the body of ritual laws is preceded by some laws dealing with the obligation of ensuring justice and protection for the weak, and provides a general summary of the subjects addressed in *Parashat Mishpatim*. We began our comparison from the commandment not to distort justice for the poor, since this represents the beginning of a "closed" unit (*parasha setuma*), and because the mitzvot preceding it are still formulated in causal style ("If ... then ..."), whereas here we have three absolute, general commandments, which appear to be a general conclusion/introduction: "You shall not distort," "Keep yourself far," "Do not slay," etc. The introduction to the unit in *Ki Tissa*, however, deals with the obligation of keeping distant from the nations of the land, to avoid creating treaties with them, and to refrain from copying their behavior and their idolatry. This introduction appears to arise from the renewal of the covenant previously recorded between God and Moses – at the mountain. In summary, it is a prohibition against forging any other covenant, which would be a form of betrayal of God.

B. In *Parashat Mishpatim*, the unit includes the commandment of *Shemitta*, whereas in *Ki Tissa* it is omitted. The discussion of *Shemitta* is also presented from a moral, social perspective, its aim being "that the poor of your people may eat." Thus, it connects with the preceding body of laws, in that it deals with protection for the weak and improving their situation. It is therefore logical for the commandment of *Shemitta* to appear here, prior to the commandments concerning the pilgrim festivals, since on the one hand it is a time-dependent commandment; on the other hand, it is a social commandment, like those that conclude the "judgments" that precede it.

c. In *Parashat Mishpatim*, the commandment of Shabbat appears here, for three good reasons:

    I. It is similar in spirit and in its time-structure to the commandment of *Shemitta*, which precedes it.

    II. It serves as a basis for the sanctity of time and the holy days, and is indeed followed by the laws of the pilgrim festivals.

    III. The emphasis, in the commandment of Shabbat as it appears in *Parashat Mishpatim*, is once again social: "In order that your ox... may rest, and the son of your handmaid and the stranger be refreshed." This social emphasis links Shabbat with *Shemitta* as well as with the series of preceding commandments that addressed matters of justice and society, and particularly with the law, "You shall not oppress *a stranger.*"

Why, then, is there no parallel commandment of Shabbat in *Ki Tissa*? The answer would seem to arise from the perspective described above – the social context is altogether absent from *Ki Tissa*, there is no *Shemitta*, and therefore no room for a "social" Shabbat (see also below).

D. At this point in *Parashat Mishpatim* there is a warning that serves as a sort of summary as well as introduction: "Concerning all that I have told you – be mindful" – this applies to the preceding prohibitions. "And make no mention of other gods" – this introduces the unit of ritual laws; it is indeed appropriate that these be introduced with an exhortation that religious worship be directed to God alone. This warning and summary is unnecessary in *Ki Tissa*, since the context there is not one that follows immediately after a lengthy unit of laws, and the prohibitions of idolatry are set out at length in the preceding introduction, such that there is no need for another warning.

E. Heading for the festivals: The heading appears only in *Mishpatim* – apparently because what follows there is really only the commandments of the festivals, whereas in *Ki Tissa* there are also some additional laws, including the redemption of the firstborn and Shabbat, and therefore an introduction to the festivals exclusively would not be appropriate.

F. Identical commandment concerning the Festival of Matzot. In *Parashat Ki Tissa* the commandment "You shall not appear empty-handed" is postponed until after the commandment concerning the firstling of the donkey (which is absent from *Mishpatim*) since it includes both the pilgrimage and the firstling of the donkey.

G. Firstling of the donkey and the redemption of the firstborn: Here, for the first time, we encounter a commandment that appears in *Ki Tissa*, but not in *Mishpatim*. The commandments concerning the firstling of the donkey and the redemption of the firstborn are directly linked to the commandment of Pesaḥ, since they are meant as a reminder of the exodus (specifically, the slaying of the Egyptian firstborn). The commandment of the firstling/firstborn is essentially "ritual" (religious as opposed to moral, social etc.) and therefore it has a place in this group of ritual laws. This apparently defines the nature of the unit in *Ki Tissa* (see below). In *Parashat Mishpatim*, the emphasis thus far has been social; in this context the commandments concerning the firstling of a donkey and the firstborn son are irrelevant, and it is for this reason, it seems, that they do not appear here.

H. Shabbat: This is where the commandment of Shabbat appears in *Ki Tissa* (i.e. following the commandments of Pesaḥ and the firstling/firstborn). No social aspect is mentioned here; there is only the prohibition against labor. In *Mishpatim*, as we have seen, the emphasis was on social justice, and therefore it is juxtaposed with *Shemitta*, prior to any mention of the pilgrim festivals.

In *Ki Tissa* the command of Shabbat appears after the Festival of Matzot: the exodus from Egypt and the Festival of Matzot that commemorates it are the source of the covenant that serves as the basis for this unit. Therefore, the commandment of Pesaḥ comes first, followed by Shabbat – which is another expression of the covenant ("To perform the Shabbat throughout their generations; an eternal covenant") and a commemoration of the exodus from Egypt. The social aspect of Shabbat is irrelevant here.

I. The commandments of the Harvest Festival and the Festival of the Ingathering appear in very similar language; there seems to be no essential difference between the two units. The formulation in *Mishpatim* is longer ("When you gather your labor"), and this is logical, since the same command in *Ki Tissa* is a repetition. The "Festival of the Harvest" is referred to in *Ki Tissa* as "the Festival of Weeks"; there may be some significance to this point, since the name "Weeks" links this festival to the *Omer* and to Pesaḥ, which – as noted – represents the basis of the covenant (the exodus from Egypt). *Parashat Mishpatim* speaks of three set times of festivals during the year; therefore the festival is referred to as the "Festival of the Harvest," as a seasonal reference, with no specific connection to Pesaḥ.

J. The obligation of pilgrimage appears in similar form in the two sources. *Ki Tissa* uses the words, "Before the Lord God, God of Israel," and also *"et penei"* instead of *"el penei"* as in *Mishpatim*. The first difference appears to express the need, in *Ki Tissa*, for exact specification of whom it is that we are to address, in light of the episode of the golden calf, and the concern lest there be any deviation from the covenant, as expressed in the preceding list of prohibitions related to idolatry. The second difference may have broader significance: *"el penei"* means "towards," "before," "in the place of" – but not actually "facing." *"Et penei"* means actually standing in front of the object. It is perhaps only after the commandment concerning the *Mishkan*, and God's promise that He will accompany the nation, in their midst – "My countenance will go" – that this is possible.

K. The promise of protection during pilgrimage is mentioned only in *Ki Tissa*, and the reason for this seems simple. In *Parashat Ki Tissa*, we have already been told that God will lead the nation to the land and drive out the seven nations. On the basis of the end of *Parashat Mishpatim*, we may also include the promise to expand the nation's borders: "And I shall set your borders from the Red Sea to the Sea of the Philistines." Thus, the problem arises – what will happen to the land during the pilgrimage festivals? In *Ki Tissa*, God promises a solution to the problem. In *Parashat Mishpatim*, however, the unit of ritual laws appears before this promise is mentioned – indeed, prior to any promise concerning the conquest of the land in its entirety, and therefore there is no need to raise a problem that does not yet exist.

L. The prohibitions of leaven in sacrifices and allowing the sacrifices to remain until morning look very similar, but careful examination shows that the two sources are actually talking about different commandments. Some opinions interpret the unit in *Mishpatim* in light of that which is stated explicitly in *Ki Tissa* – i.e., that only the Pesaḥ sacrifice is involved. This seems unlikely, since if one source elaborates at greater length while the other is brief, it is more logical that it is the first source that should be longer, not the second – as noted above, in our discussion of the commandment concerning *Shavuot* and *Sukkot*. It would seem that the unit in *Mishpatim* represents a general instruction concerning the sacrifice of peace offerings and *ḥagiga* sacrifices, while the unit in *Ki Tissa* speaks only – or principally – about Pesaḥ. In *Parashat Mishpatim*, this is a complement to the general instructions concerning divine worship; the prohibition against leaven is not a law related to Pesaḥ, but rather a general law applicable to every type of sacrifice. The prohibition of allowing the sacrifice to remain until the morning concerns the fats of the *ḥagiga* offering, and hence is of ritual significance. In *Ki Tissa*, on the other hand, this law is a complement to the laws of Pesaḥ, which – as noted above – occupies a central place in this *parasha*. In fact, the *parasha* both starts and ends with laws of Pesaḥ. The prohibition against leaven appears here to be related to the laws of this festival, and it is possible that the expression "you shall not slaughter," instead of "you shall not offer," hints at the fact that this refers to the Pesaḥ sacrifice, which is not altogether an "offering" (*zevaḥ*).

M. The obligation concerning first fruits and the prohibition of mixing meat and milk appear in identical form in both sources. Apparently, the first context in which the prohibition against mixing meat and milk appears is ritual in nature, in keeping with the theme of the *parasha* as a whole. In other words, the Torah is prohibiting the cooking of a *ḥagiga* or peace offering in milk, or offering it in a manner reminiscent of the pagans etc., as Rambam, Ibn Ezra and others explain.

N. Following this collection of ritual laws in *Parashat Mishpatim*, God gives a promise concerning the conquest of *Eretz Yisrael*. Here we find laws prohibiting idolatry, adopting the practices of the nations, etc. All of this is connected to the entry into the land, and is similar to the laws that precede the unit in *Ki Tissa* ("Do not worship," "Do not adopt their practices," etc.).

III. THE PRINCIPAL DIFFERENCES BETWEEN THE TWO UNITS

Having examined the details of the differences between the two units and attempted to explain them, we may now point to some fundamental characteristics of each, which may help us to answer our original questions.

A. The unit in *Parashat Mishpatim* has a clearly social emphasis. This is prominently expressed in the social commandment of *Shemitta*, in the social justification for the commandment of Shabbat, in the link to the preceding social commandments, and perhaps also in other aspects, which we shall discuss below. The unit in *Parashat Ki Tissa* bears the stamp of the renewed covenant which precedes it, and it seeks mainly to highlight the ritual aspects of the commandments that were transmitted in *Parashat Mishpatim* – especially the worship of God and avoidance of any desecration of His covenant. This orientation is reflected in the omission of the social commandments and justifications, in the introduction of ritual laws such as redemption of the firstborn son and of the firstling of the donkey, in the significance attached to the festival of Pesaḥ, and to the link to the list of prohibitions related to idolatry that precedes this unit.

B. *Mishpatim* precedes the renewal of the covenant at Sinai, the promise concerning the entry into the land, the building of the *Mishkan*, and – certainly – the sin of the golden calf. Hence, there are elements that are related to this unit of laws that cannot appear in *Parashat Mishpatim* – or that would be irrelevant there – and that are added in *Ki Tissa*. Examples include the promise concerning property during the pilgrimages, following the expansion of the borders of the land, the emphasis on the "God of Israel," etc.

C. The crux of both of these units is the commandment of pilgrimage and the three pilgrim festivals. In other words, the essence of the unit is preserved, and it is here that the repetition is manifest. In the other aspects there are substantial differences, additions or omissions.

IV. THE ROLE OF THE "RITUAL" UNIT
IN *PARASHAT MISHPATIM*

Our conclusion thus far is that these two units, sharing the same halakhic core, emphasize different purposes. What is the role of this "ritual" unit in *Parashat Mishpatim*? Seemingly, this is not the natural place for such a unit, since the main theme of *Parashat Mishpatim* is justice and righteousness. In truth, however, a general view of God's command to Moses following the Ten Commandments reveals that this *parasha* fills a void; without it the covenant at Mount Sinai could not be complete. Let us review the order of the commandments, starting from right after the Ten Commandments:

A. Prohibitions of idolatrous worship ("You shall not make with Me gods of silver and gods of gold")

B. The order of proper worship – Freewill offering of the individual ("An earthen altar shall you make for Me, and offer upon it")

C. Judgments (*mishpatim*)

B1. The order of proper worship – Obligatory offerings of the congregation (the "ritual" unit with the three pilgrim festivals at its core)

A1. Prohibitions of idolatrous worship in *Eretz Yisrael* ("You shall not worship them, nor shall you serve them, nor shall you follow their actions")

This entire body of commandments is the "*Sefer haBerit* – the Book of the Covenant," concerning which we read, in chapter 24: "He placed before them all the words of God, and all the judgments" – this is the substance of the covenant. We conclude that the content of the covenant has a chiastic structure – with the beginning and end defining the nature of divine service, and the middle describing a social existence of justice and righteousness. The difference between the "ritual" beginning and the conclusion is the same difference that exists between the individual, voluntary aspect of the obligations and prohibitions of divine worship, and the obligatory, communal aspects, as expressed principally in the pilgrimage and the celebration of the holidays at their set times during the year. *Parashat Mishpatim*, which sets down the guidelines for proper social existence, facilitates the transition from the existence of individuals who serve God, to a national, public existence in the service of God, with fixed times and practices. The observance of all of this together makes it possible for God to realize the promise of the inheritance of the land, which follows the Book of the Covenant, and also allows the forging of a covenant with God. The centrality of the chapters of judgment and righteousness, in terms of location as well as quantity and content, shows that the metamorphosis of Israel into a nation worthy of entering into a covenant with God is dependent principally on social factors – i.e., the performance of justice and righteousness. Hence, even divine worship itself does not appear here as an independent subject; rather, it appears as part of the entire organization of a society that is righteous in the eyes of God. *Shemitta*, Shabbat, and – indirectly – even the pilgrim festivals, as stated explicitly in Deuteronomy 16, complete the charitable aspect of the social obligations.

V. ROLE OF THE "RITUAL" UNIT IN *KI TISSA*

In order to understand the reason for the repetition of a body of laws that the Torah has already commanded, we must consider what is omitted from this repetition, and what is added. We have already noted that the social aspects of the laws, as they appeared in the unit in *Mishpatim*, are entirely absent here; the social commandments themselves are also omitted here. The reason for this is simple: the social imperative itself was the principal message of the unit as it appeared in *Mishpatim*, and there is no reason for a repetition of the unit from that same perspective. What is added to the unit in *Ki Tissa*, which had not previously appeared in *Mishpatim*? An emphasis on ritual, and warnings. Why? After the sin of the golden calf, God promised that He would cause His Presence to rest in the midst of the nation. For this reason, the ritual laws must address this aspect of divine service. This was not yet applicable in *Parashat Mishpatim*, since in the meantime, the nation of Israel had sinned with the golden calf, betraying God and violating His covenant. When God renews that covenant, He completes His promise and the occasion of the covenant itself by means of laws that have a dual purpose: on the one hand, God warns against deviating from the covenant, since it has already become apparent that such a possibility exists. Moreover, the promise that Israel will enter *Eretz Yisrael* gives rise to major concerns as to possible deviations. Therefore, "You shall not marry among them," "You shall cut down their *asherim*," and – especially – "You shall make yourself no molten gods." On the other hand, God declares that following the renewal of the covenant, He may be served again as before; indeed, He may now be "beheld." This is not an obvious assumption; on the contrary, it was precisely for this reason that the nation mourned – even after God had been appeased by Moses' prayer and had decided against their annihilation. Now, when God promises, "Behold, I forge a covenant with you," He goes back to the ritual core of the first unit – as though renewing the invitation to "behold Him." As mentioned, there is no need here for any social exhortation; what is needed is the addition of emphases arising from the conditions that have changed in the meantime, in view of the renewal of the covenant. The crux of the message is, you (*Benei Yisrael*) are once again invited to My House: "Three times in the year, all of your males shall present themselves before the Lord God, God of Israel."

Two Sins, Two Covenants

Rav Menachem Leibtag

I. INTRODUCTION

No matter how one explains the sin of the golden calf, we encounter a problem. If we understand that *Benei Yisrael* truly believed that it was this "golden calf" (*Egel haZahav*) who took them out of Egypt – then it is simply hard to fathom how an entire nation would reach such a senseless conclusion. However, if we claim (as many commentators do) that Aaron had good intentions, for he only intended for the *egel* to be a physical representation of God (who took them out of Egypt) – why is God so angered to the point that he wants to destroy the entire nation? As such, we must look for the middle road as we attempt to find a logical explanation for the events as they unfold, based on our understanding of the overall themes of Exodus.

II. THE CAUSE OF THE SIN

According to the midrash quoted by Rashi (on Ex. 32:1), *Benei Yisrael's* miscalculation of Moses' return by one day led to the calamity. However, when one examines the details of this story, a very different picture emerges that provides a more logical explanation for the people's request. We shall examine the events as they unfold in *Parashat Ki Tissa* in light of the events that transpired at the end of *Parashat Mishpatim*. In the Torah's description of Moses' original ascent to Mount Sinai for forty days, Moses never provides the people with an exact date of his expected return:

> And God told Moses, "Come up to Me on the mountain...." Then Moses ascended God's mountain. To the elders he said: "Wait here for us, until we return to you. Behold, Aaron and Ḥur are with you, whoever has a problem, let him go to them." (24:12–14)

Even though several verses later the Torah tells us that Moses remained on the mountain for forty days, the text indicates that the people have no idea how long Moses would be gone – and most likely, neither did Moses or Aaron!

Considering this was not the first time that Moses had ascended Mount Sinai to speak to God (see 19:3, 20; 24:1, 2) – and in each previous ascent Moses had never been gone for more than a day or two – *Benei Yisrael* had ample reason to assume that this time he would not be gone much longer. How long could it possibly take to receive the "*luḥot*, Torah, and mitzva" (see 24:12) – a few days, a couple of weeks?

Days pass; weeks pass; yet Moses does not return. Add to this the fact that the last time that *Benei Yisrael* saw Moses, he had entered a cloud-covered mountain consumed in fire (see 24:17–18), and the people's conclusion that Moses has been taken away is quite logical. After all, how much longer can they wait?

Assuming that Moses is not returning, *Benei Yisrael* must do something. What are their options? Either to remain stranded in the desert, to return to Egypt, or to continue their journey to *Eretz Canaan*. Clearly the latter option was preferable – was this not the purpose of *Yetziat Mitzrayim* (see 3:8, 17; 6:8)? Furthermore, that is precisely what God had promised them numerous times.

This helps us understand why *Benei Yisrael* approached Aaron, whom Moses had left in charge (see 24:13–15), and why their opening complaint focused on their desire for new leadership – to replace Moses. Let's take a careful look now at the Torah's description of this event:

When the people saw that Moses was delayed in coming down from the mountain, the people gathered on Aaron and said to him: "Come make us an *elohim that will lead us* [towards the Promised Land] because Moses, who took us out of the land of Egypt [and promised to take us to *Eretz Canaan*], we do not know what has happened to him." (32:1)

Note the phrase "*elohim asher yelkhu lefanenu.*" The people do not request a new god, but rather an *elohim* that that will "walk in front," i.e., that will lead them to the Promised Land.

To understand how logical this request was, we need only conduct a quick comparison between this verse and God's earlier promise that He would send a *malakh* to lead them and help them conquer the Land: "Behold, I am sending a *malakh lefanekha* [before you] – to guard you and bring you to the place that I have made ready" (23:20). Two verses later, God continues this promise: "*ki yelekh malakhi lefanekha* – For My angel will go before you, and bring you to the Land" (23:23).

This was the last promise that they had heard before Moses ascended Mount Sinai. When *Benei Yisrael* first heard this promise, they most probably assumed that this *malakh* would be none other than Moses himself. (The *malakh* must be someone who commands them, leads them, while God's name is in his midst – see 23:21–22, compare 19:9.)

Now that Moses is presumed dead, the people simply demand that Aaron provide them with a replacement for (or possibly a symbol of) this *malakh*, in order that they can continue their journey to the Promised Land. In fact, from a simple reading of the text, it appears as though Aaron actually agrees to this request:

And Aaron said to them: "Take off your gold … and bring them to me … ." He took it from them and cast in a mold and made it into a molten calf. (32:2–4)

If our interpretation thus far is correct, then the people's statement (upon seeing this golden calf): "This is your god O Israel – who brought you out of the land of Egypt" (32:4), does not need to imply that this golden calf actually took them out of Egypt. (After all, they had already stated in 32:1 that Moses had taken them out of Egypt.) Rather, the people are simply stating their own perception – that this calf represents the God who had taken them out of Egypt, and will hopefully now act as His *malakh* who will lead them on their journey to *Eretz Canaan.*[1]

This also explains Aaron's ensuing actions: To assure that the *egel* is properly understood as a representation of God, Aaron calls for a celebration: "And Aaron saw, and he built a *mizbeah* in front of it, and Aaron called out and said: A celebration for HaShem [note: not *elohim*] tomorrow" (32:5).

Furthermore, this celebration parallels the almost identical ceremony that took place at Mount Sinai forty days earlier – when *Benei Yisrael* declared "*naaseh venishma.*" To verify this, we'll compare the Torah's description of these two ceremonies:

Parashat Mishpatim – Chapter 24	*Parashat Ki Tissa* – Chapter 32
And they *woke up early in the morning*, and they built a *mizbeah* at the foot of the mountain, and twelve monuments for the twelve tribes of Israel ... and they offered *olot* and sacrificed *shelamim.* (24:4–5)	And they *woke up early in the morning* [after Aaron had built a *mizbeah* in front of it in 32:5], and they offered *olot* and sacrificed *shelamim.* (32:6)

III. WHY AN 'EGEL'?

Even though our interpretation thus far has shown how the *egel* can be understood as a symbol of God's presence, we have yet to explain why specifically an *egel* (a calf) is chosen as that representation. Hizkuni offers an ingenious explanation, based on yet another parallel to *Maamad Har Sinai* (the Revelation at Sinai). At the conclusion of the ceremony at Mount Sinai (24:1–11), Aaron, Nadav, Avihu, and the seventy elders are permitted to 'see' God: "And they saw *Elokei Yisrael* and under His feet (*tahat raglav*) was like a shining sapphire" (24:10).

Obviously, God does not have feet! However, this description

---

1. See a similar explanation by Rav Yehuda HaLevi in the *Kuzari* 1:77, and the Ibn Ezra and Ramban on 32:1.

reflects a certain spiritual level. Moses, for example, achieved the highest level – "*panim bepanim*" – face to face. In contrast, the seventy elders perceived God's feet, reflecting a lower spiritual level.

Although it is very difficult for us to comprehend the description of God in such physical terms, Ḥizkuni (on 32:4) notes that we find a very similar description of the chariot of the *Shekhina* in Ezekiel:

And their feet were straight, and the bottom of their feet were similar to the feet of an *egel*. (Ezek. 1:7)

Alternately, one could suggest that an *egel* was chosen to represent the *parim* (oxen) which were offered on Mount Sinai during the ceremony when God informed them about the *malakh* (24:5 – note that an *egel* is a young *par*).

So if the people's original request was indeed legitimate, and Aaron's solution a sincere attempt to make a representation of God, why does God become so angered? Why does He threaten to destroy the entire nation?

To answer this question, we must once again return to our parallel with *Parashat Mishpatim*.

IV. THEY AROSE "*LETZAḤEK*"

Despite the many parallels noted above, we find one additional phrase that is unique to the story of *ḥet ha'egel*, and creates what may be called a contrasting parallel. Note the final phrase of each narrative:

Parashat Mishpatim – Chapter 24	Parashat Ki Tissa – Chapter 32
And they beheld God and they ate and drank. (24:11)	They sat to eat and drink and they rose *letzaḥek*. (32:6)

It is not by chance that many commentators find in this word the key to understanding *Benei Yisrael*'s sin. Even though the simple translation of '*letzaḥek*' is laughing or frivolous behavior, Rashi raises the possibility that it may refer to licentiousness (or even murder, see Rashi 32:7). To Aaron's dismay, what began as a quiet ceremony turned into a wild party. The celebration seems to have gotten out of hand.

To support this understanding of "*letzaḥek*," let's go to the Torah's account of Moses' descent from Mount Sinai (when he breaks the *luḥot*), noting what Moses and Joshua hear from the mountain:

> And Joshua heard the sound of the people (*berei'o*) screaming loudly, and said to Moses: "There are sounds of war in the camp." But Moses answered: "These are not the sounds of triumph, nor are they the groans of defeat, they are simply sounds that I hear." (32:17–18)

The noise from this "wild party" was so loud that it sounded to Joshua like a war was going on!

We also note what provoked Moses to actually break the tablets: "And he saw the *egel* and the dancing circles (*vayar et ha'egel umeḥolot*) and became enraged" (32:19). Moses was upset no less by the dancing than by the *egel* itself.

With this in mind, let's return now to study the Torah's account of God's anger with the *ḥet ha'egel*, as recorded earlier. First, God only becomes angry on the day *after* Aaron made the *egel*. Now if *Benei Yisrael's* primary sin was making the *egel*, God should have told Moses to go down on that very same day. The fact that God only tells him to go down on the next day, after we are told that "*vayakumu letzaḥek*," supports our interpretation that this phrase describes the primary sin of *ḥet ha'egel*.

IV. BACK TO OLD HABITS

What led to this calamity? What was this noise and wild party all about? Even though it is based on circumstantial evidence, one could suggest the following: Even though the celebration around the *egel* initiated by Aaron began with good intentions (see 32:5 – "*Ḥag laShem*"), for some reason, *Benei Yisrael's* behavior at this party quickly became wild and out of control. Apparently, once the drinking, dancing, and music began, the nation impulsively reverted back to their old ways, regressing back to their Egyptian culture.

To understand why, let us examine *Benei Yisrael's* spiritual level in Egypt, based on Ezekiel chapter 20. Before the exodus, *Benei Yisrael* were so immersed in Egyptian culture that God found it necessary to demand that they "change their ways" in order to prepare for their redemption (Ezek. 20:5–9). Even though they did not heed this plea, God took them out of Egypt in the hope that the miracles of the exodus, and their experiences on the way to Mount Sinai would create a "change of heart." When they arrived at Mount Sinai, *Benei Yisrael's* proclamation of *na'aseh venishma* showed God that they were finally ready to become God's special nation.

Unfortunately, the events at *ḥet ha'egel* forced God to change this perception. *Benei Yisrael's* inexcusable behavior at this celebration reflected the sad fact that despite His numerous miracles, deep down, nothing had really changed. God became more than angered; He became utterly disappointed. All of God's efforts to train His nation seemed to have been in vain.

V. THE DIVINE REACTION

In summary, we have suggested that there were two stages in *Benei Yisrael's* sin at *ḥet ha'egel*. The first – making a physical representation of God – although improper, was understandable. The second – the frivolous behavior after the eating and drinking at the conclusion of the ceremony – was inexcusable. We will now show how these two stages are reflected in God's "double statement" to Moses (32:7–10) in the aftermath of this sin:[2]

God's first statement: 32:7–8	God's second statement: 32:9–10
And God spoke to Moses: "Hurry down, for your people have corrupted (*ki shiḥet amekha*) …. They have turned astray from the way that I commanded them – they made an *egel masekha* [a representation of Me]."	And God spoke to Moses: "I see this nation, behold it is a stiff necked people (*am kesheh oref*). Now, allow Me, and I will kindle My anger against them and I will destroy them and I will make you a great nation [instead]."

God's first statement describes the act that began with good intentions but was nonetheless forbidden [see Exodus 20:20: "*lo ta'asun iti elohei*

---

2. Note, that "*vayomer HaShem el Moshe*" is repeated twice, even though Moses does not speak in between.

kesef"]. Although this sin requires rebuke and forgiveness (see 32:30), it was not severe enough to warrant the destruction of the entire nation. God's second statement is in reaction to *"vayakumu letzaḥek"*; i.e., their frivolous behavior. Because of this regression to Egyptian culture, God concludes that they are indeed a "stiff-necked people" – unable to change their ways. Therefore, God concludes that He must destroy *Benei Yisrael*, choosing Moses to become His special nation instead.

Similarly, these two stages are found in the conversation between Moses and Aaron in the aftermath of this event:

> And Moses said to Aaron: "What did this people do to you that caused you to bring upon them such a terrible sin?".... Aaron answered: "You know this people – their ways are evil (*ki ve'ra hu*)." (32:21–22)

One could suggest that Aaron's conclusion is based on his previous experiences with *Benei Yisrael*. It is clear, however, that Moses understands that Aaron had no intention that this situation would get out of hand. After all, Aaron himself is not punished. In fact, he later is appointed the High Priest.

Once Aaron had explained to Moses what transpired (32:22–24) in the first stage, Moses already understood what happened in the second stage:

> And Moses saw the people that they were *wild (ki parua hu)* [out of control], for Aaron had caused them to become wild [to the point of] their demise, when they *got up (bekameihem)* [to dance]. (32:25)

Finally, the two levels that we later find in *Benei Yisrael's* actual punishment may also reflect these two stages. First, the three thousand "instigators" who incited this licentious behavior (stage two) are killed. For that rebellious group, there is no room for forgiveness (32:26–29). However, on the second day, Moses approaches God to beg forgiveness for the rest of the nation (see 32:30–32). Even though they had sinned,

Moses hopes to secure them a pardon – because their actions began with good intentions (stage one).

Ultimately, Moses will receive this pardon – but it won't be simple.

VI. DELAYED PUNISHMENT OR FORGIVENESS

Even though God had originally agreed to Moses' first request not to totally destroy His nation (see 32:11–14, *"vayeḥal Moshe…vayinaḥem HaShem al hara'a"*), his next request for forgiveness (in 32:31–32) clearly indicates that the execution of the three thousand instigators did not absolve the rest of the nation.

To our surprise, Moses' second prayer (32:30–32) does not achieve forgiveness. Let us take a careful look at God's response to Moses' second prayer:

> And God told Moses: "He who has sinned to Me shall be punished. Now go lead the people to [the place] that I said, 'behold My angel will accompany you,' and on the day of My accounting, I will make My account with them for their sin." (32:34)

Note that God instructs Moses to lead Israel to the Promised Land, but He still plans to later punish them for *ḥet ha'egel*, at the time that He finds fit. Even though God will fulfill his covenant with the forefathers (*berit avot*), the covenant with the people (*berit Sinai*) remains broken. To prove this, note how the opening of chapter 33 explains what God told Moses in 32:34:

> And God said to Moses, "Set out from here, you and the people that you have brought out of Egypt to the Land that I swore to Abraham, Isaac, and Jacob [*berit avot*] …. But *I will not go in your midst* for you are a stiff necked people, lest I destroy you on the journey." (33:1–3)

In contrast to God's original promise that He will send a *malakh* with His name in his midst (*"Shemi bekirbo"* – 23:20–23), now He emphatically states that He will no longer be with them – *"ki lo a'aleh bekirbekha*" (33:3). Due to *het ha'egel, Benei Yisrael* are no longer worthy of the special relationship of *berit Sinai*.

This downgrade is reflected in God's next commandment that *Benei Yisrael* remove "their jewelry" that they received on Mount Sinai, undoubtedly the symbol of the high level they reached at *Matan Torah* (see 33:5–6). Furthermore, Moses must now move his own tent away from the camp, in order that God can remain in contact with him (see 33:7).

VII. WHERE DO WE GO FROM HERE?

A very strange predicament has arisen. Even though *Benei Yisrael* will not be destroyed (thanks to *berit avot*), God instructs Moses to continue on to *Eretz Canaan* without *berit Sinai*.

As unthinkable as this sounds, God's decision is very logical. Considering His conclusion that *Benei Yisrael* are an "*am kesheh oref,*" a stiff-necked people, and hence will not change their ways, there appears to be no other solution. Should He keep His Presence in their midst, *Benei Yisrael* will not survive.

Fortunately, Moses is not willing to accept God's decision:

And Moses beseeched God: "Look, you have instructed me to lead this people.... But recognize that this nation is Your people." God answered: "I will lead *you.*" But Moses insisted: "Unless Your Presence will go, do not make us leave this place (*Im ein Panekha holekhim, al ta'alenu mizeh*). For how should it be known that Your people have gained Your favor unless You go with us." (33:12–16)

Note how Moses demands that God keep His Presence (*Shekhina*) with them, threatening a 'sit down strike' should God refuse. Most powerful is Moses' demand that God recognize that they are *His* people: "*ure'eh ki amekha hagoy hazeh*" (33:13). God now faces a most difficult predicament. On the one hand, He cannot allow His Presence to return, for according to the terms of Sinai, the people could not survive His anger, and would eventually be killed. On the other hand, He cannot leave them in the desert (as Moses now threatens), for the *berit avot* must be fulfilled. However, He cannot take them to the land, for Moses is not willing to lead them unless He returns His *Shekhina*.

It is precisely here, in the resolution of this dilemma, where the thirteen *Midot HaRaḥamim* (Attributes of Mercy) appear.

VIII. A NEW COVENANT

Let's take a look now at God's response to Moses' request. This is the first time where God introduces the concept of divine mercy:

> And God said to Moses, "I will also do this thing that you request...."
>
> Then God answered, "I will pass all My goodness before you, and I will proclaim My name before you, and I will pardon he whom I will pardon, and I will have mercy on he to whom I give mercy." (33:17–22)

In contrast to His original threat of immediate punishment should they sin (if God is in their midst), God now agrees to allow *Benei Yisrael* a second chance. This divine promise sets the stage for the forging of a new covenant though which *berit Sinai* can be re-established, for it allows the *Shekhina* to return without the necessity of immediate severe punishment.

Therefore, God instructs Moses to ascend Mount Sinai one more time, in a manner parallel to his first ascent to Mount Sinai, to receive the second *luḥot*. As we expect, the laws remain the same. However, their terms are now modified by God's Attributes of Mercy. When Moses now ascends Mount Sinai, it is not necessary for God to repeat the commandments – instead, God will proclaim an amendment to how He will act in this relationship – i.e., His Attributes of Mercy.

As God had promised in 33:19, a new covenant, reflecting this enhanced relationship, is now forged:

> And God came down in a cloud...and proclaimed: "HaShem, HaShem *Kel Raḥum veḤanun, Erekh Apayim verav ḥesed veEmet, notzer ḥesed laAlafim.*" (34:5–8)

IX. BETWEEN THE ATTRIBUTES OF JUSTICE AND MERCY

With this background, we can now better appreciate the words that God chose to describe the new attributes. Recall that the Ten Commandments included not only laws, but also described how God will reward (or punish) those who obey (or disobey) His commandments. Let's review these original attributes:

> I am the Lord your God....
> You shall have no other gods besides Me....
> Do not bow down to them or worship them, for I the Lord am zealous God (*Kel kana*),
> Who remembers the sin of parents upon their children (*pokked avon avot al banim*) for those who reject Me (*lesonai*), but shows kindness (*oseh ḥesed*) for those who love me and follow my laws (*leohavai uleshomrei mitzvotai*).
> Do not bear in vain the name of God, for God will not forgive (*ki lo yenakeh HaShem*) he who bears His name in vain. (20:2–7)

Most of these attributes appear to be quite harsh. Even the trait of *oseh ḥesed* – divine kindness, does not necessarily imply mercy. Carefully note that God promises this kindness only for those who love Him and follow Him, and hence not for any others. Most definitely, all four of these attributes are quite the opposite of mercy; they are *midot hadin* – attributes of justice, exacting retribution.

Although these *midot* have a negative side, for they threaten immediate punishment for those who transgress (*lesonai*), they also express a positive side, for they assure immediate reward for those who obey (*leohavai*). In other words, they describe a very intense relationship, quite similar [and not by chance] to God's relationship with man in *Gan Eden* (see Gen. 2:16–17).

Yet another example of this intense relationship, and another attribute as well, is found at the conclusion of the unit of laws in *Parashat Mishpatim*. Recall that immediately after the Ten Commandments, Moses was summoned to Mount Sinai to receive a special set of commandment to relay to *Benei Yisrael* (Ex. 20:15–19). At the conclusion of those laws, God makes the following promise:

Behold, I am sending an angel before you to guard you on the way and help bring you into the Promised Land. Be careful of him and obey him, Do not defy him – for he shall not pardon your sins (*ki lo yisa lefishakhem*), since My name is with him. (23:20–24)

Once again, we find that God will exact punishment should *Benei Yisrael* not follow His mitzvot, and reward (i.e., assist in conquering the Land) should they obey Him.

Finally, after the sin of the golden calf, we find that God intends to act precisely according to these attributes of *midat hadin*:

And God told Moses, "Go down from the mountain for your people has sinned…they made a golden image…. And now allow Me, and I will kindle My anger against them that I may destroy them." (32:7–10)

Here we find yet another divine attribute – God's instant anger (*haron af*).

How do these six examples of *midat hadin* – unforgiving justice – relate to the new attributes that God now declares?

The *Midot HaDin* (Attributes of Justice) – the original covenant at Sinai:	The "new" *Midot HaRahamim* (Attributes of Mercy) – the revised covenant after the golden calf:
Kel kana	*Kel rahum vehanun*
Pokked avon…lesonai	*Pokked avon avot al banim*
Oseh hesed la'alafim…leohavai	*Rav hesed ve'emet…notzer hesed la'alafim*
Lo yenakeh	*Venakeh, lo yenakeh*
Lo yisa lefishekhem	*Nosei avon vafesha*
Haron af	*Erekh apayim*

Each attribute from the original covenant switches from *Midat HaDin* (justice) to *Midat HaRahamim* (mercy). Examining each change we see:

A. *HaShem Kel kana – HaShem Kel rahum vehanun*: The zealous God has become a merciful God.

B. *Haron af – Erekh apayim*: God is now slow to anger instead of angering instantly.

C. *Oseh hesed leohavai – Rav hesed ve'emet*: God will now demonstrate abounding kindness for all, potentially even for the wicked, as opposed to limiting kindness exclusively to those who obey Him. [Note that the new attributes must now include the *mida* of *emet* – truth, for this abounding kindness for all must be complemented by the attribute of truth to assure ultimate justice.]

  Oseh hesed... leohavai – Notzer hesed la'alafim: He stores His kindness, so that even if it is not rewarded immediately, it is stored to be given at a later time, in contrast to immediate kindness and reward for those who follow Him.

D. *Lo yisa lefishekhem – Nosei avon vafesha*: HaShem is now forgiving of sin.

E. *Lo yenakeh – Venakeh, lo yenakeh*: In contrast to never forgiving, now sometimes He will forgive, sometimes He may not (see Rashi who suggests that HaShem forgives those who repent).

F. *Pokked avon lesonai – Pokked avon avot al banim*: He now withholds punishment for up to four generations, in contrast to extending punishment for up to four generations.

These striking parallels demonstrate that each of the thirteen *Midot HaRahamim* lies in direct contrast to the *midot* of the original covenant at Mount Sinai.

This background can help us appreciate Moses' immediate reaction to God's proclamation of these *midot*:

> And Moses hastened to bow down and said: "If I have indeed gained favor in Your eyes – let HaShem go in our midst, for [*ki*; even though] *they are a stiff necked people*, and you shall pardon our sin." (34:8–9)

God's proclamation that He will now act in a less strict manner enables Moses to request that God now return His *Shekhina* to the people even though they are stubborn. This request stands in direct contrast to God's original threat that "He will not go up with them for they are a stiff necked people, less He smite them on their journey" (compare 33:3 with 34:9).

These divine attributes of mercy now allow the *Shekhina* to dwell within *Am Yisrael* even though they may not be worthy.

From a certain perspective, this entire sequence is quite understandable. On the one hand, to be worthy of God's presence, man must behave perfectly. However, man is still human. Although he may strive to perfection, he may often err and at times even sin. How then can man ever come close to God? To allow mortal man the potential to continue a relationship with God, a new set of rules is necessary – one that includes the *Midot HaRaḥamim*. The original terms of *berit Sinai*, although ideal, are not practical. In this manner, *Midot HaRaḥamim* allow *berit Sinai* to become achievable. They reflect God's kindness that allows man to approach Him and develop a closer relationship without the necessity of immediate punishment for any transgression.

Parashot Vayak'hel-Pekudei

The Value of Labor

Rav Avraham Walfish

After the dramatic events of *Parashat Ki Tissa*, the *Parashot* of *Vayak'hel* and *Pekudei* appear rather anti-climactic. Last week's reading described the golden calf and its aftermath; now nearly 250 verses describe in excruciating and repetitive detail how the *Mishkan* was constructed. Undoubtedly, it is important to know that the *Mishkan* was, indeed, constructed – Ramban explains that the climax of the book is in its last verses, which describe how the Glory of HaShem fills the newly-consecrated sanctuary:

> The exile is not concluded until they return to their place and to the spiritual level of their fathers, and when they left Egypt, even though they departed from the house of bondage, they were still considered exiled, because they were in a foreign land wandering in the desert. When they came to Mount Sinai and built a sanctuary and the Holy One, be He blessed, returned His Presence to dwell among them, then they returned to the level of their fathers…and then they were considered redeemed, and this is why the book closes with the construction of the sanctuary filled

continuously with the Glory of HaShem. (Ramban's Introduction to Exodus)

Nevertheless, it is still not clear why the Torah has to detail the construction process at such length. As Ramban remarks:

> It would have been sufficient for the entire matter to say: "And Moses told the whole congregation of Israel all the work which HaShem had commanded him," and "The Israelites executed everything as God had commanded Moses." (Ramban on Ex. 36:8)

Some commentators have attempted to find a more general message in the Torah's apparent verbosity. Ramban finds the loving attention that the Torah lavishes on the construction process a reflection of the great love that HaShem has for the *Mishkan*. Other commentators, such as Rav Samson Raphael Hirsch, focus on the symbolic meanings of each of the *Mishkan*'s parts, and suggest that the Torah's focus on the details indicates that the workers who performed the construction needed to have a profound understanding of the significance of each detail in order to endow the structure with its symbolic meaning. Nechama Leibowitz approvingly cites Moses Mendelssohn's explanation:

> Just as God commanded his people to consecrate their firstborn and their first fruits to His name, and the sages have remarked: "there is nothing whose beginning is not sanctified to Heaven," so too He wanted them to dedicate to Him the first fruits of their thinking and all other talents pertaining to establishing a society, and to consecrate them to His service. (Commentary to Exodus [Hebrew], pp. 458–461)

According to Mendelssohn, the Torah concentrates on the labor performed in the construction of the *Mishkan*, because the labor is significant in itself, not only as a means to the goal of producing the sanctuary. Since all "secular" endeavors are given spiritual meaning by consecrating their "first fruits" to God, the Torah indicates the spiritual value of all constructive and creative professions necessary for the functioning of a society by describing in detail how the Israelites devoted their first major constructive project to the service of HaShem.

We may arrive at a deeper understanding of the meaning of the Torah's laboriously detailed description of the construction of the *Mishkan* by noting the background to our *parasha*. Between the commandment to construct the *Mishkan* (*Parashot Teruma* and *Tetzaveh*) and the actual construction in our *parasha* are the fateful events surrounding the golden calf. Following *Benei Yisrael's* betrayal of the Second Commandment by worshipping the golden calf, God announces He will not go up in their midst (33:3). In contrast to the promise that He will meet ("*veno'adeti*" – 25:22) with Moses in the Tent of Meeting (28:43, 29:4, etc.: "*Mo'ed*"), Moses establishes a Tent of Meeting ("*Mo'ed*") outside the camp of Israel. Only Moses' intensive negotiations with God (33:12 etc.; also 34:9) succeed in persuading Him to go forward with the project of constructing the *Mishkan*.

The shadow of the golden calf falls over the entire discussion of the construction of the *Mishkan*. This is indicated already by the first word of the *parasha*: "*Vayak'hel*." This word echoes the opening of the golden calf episode (32:1): "*Vayikahel ha'am al Aaron*." The contrast between the two similar words, both translated as "congregating," could not be starker. In the golden calf episode, the Torah employs "*vayikahel... al*," indicating a rowdy and quarrelsome congregating (Ibn Ezra, Ḥizkuni). Our *parasha's* opening describes Moses convening the entire community ("*kol adat Benei Yisrael*") in an orderly and respectful convocation.

The full meaning of this wordplay emerges clearly from a careful reading of the golden calf episode. Commentators such as Rabbi Yehuda HaLevi (*Kuzari* 1:97) and Ramban have observed that the golden calf was not designed to serve as a substitute for God, but rather for Moses. This is, nonetheless, a violation of the Second Commandment, which forbids use of forms or images for worship of God. However, the sin of the golden calf was not merely a technical violation of a formal commandment, but rather a case study of the features which characterize idolatrous worship.

The golden calf episode is framed by the word "arise" (*kum* – 32:1, 6). The first use of this word indicates the sense of urgency felt by the people, who demand of Aaron that he arouse himself and hasten to assuage the people's anxieties by replacing their lost leader Moses with a visible symbol of the Divine Presence. The second use of the word "*kum*" represents the culmination of the sin – "*vayakumu letzaḥek.*" This is the point where the narration of the sin breaks off and God commands Moses to go down from the mountain. It seems that until this point the people have not passed the point of no return. What is the terrible sin of "*vayakumu letzaḥek*," which makes it the climax of the golden calf? Midrashim find many sinister overtones associated with the verb "*letzaḥek*," but the simple meaning seems clear: after sitting down to eat and drink, the people are in a mood of joyous and boisterous levity. This is why, when Moses descends from the mountain, he discerns – unlike his disciple Joshua – that the cries emanating from the encampment of Israel are not war cries but rather cries of boisterousness.

The Torah regards the levity indicated by "*vayakumu letzaḥek*" with grave seriousness. Until this stage, Aaron still has a measure of control over the people. He can still attempt to steer their spiritual needs and yearnings towards proper worship of and belief in God, despite their apparent need for pagan-like modes of representing God. The rowdy revelry fueled by "eating and drinking" (32:6) is both thoroughly pagan and uncontrollable. Perhaps we should reformulate this – thoroughly pagan *because* uncontrollable. God desires the worship of people who are in control of their faculties and can observe the boundaries and proprieties associated with nearness to the Divine Presence. Once the people have reached the point of rowdiness, they have gone completely beyond those bounds. Where God can recognize the golden calf as a form of His worship, albeit illegitimate, He now can regard their behavior only as idolatrous.

The use of the verb "*kum*" at the beginning and at the climax of the sin of the golden calf focuses our attention on the underlying spiritual problem associated with this story – the people have "lost it." The profound anxiety with which they urge Aaron to "arise" culminates in the orgiastic abandon with which they "arise" from their eating and drinking at the end of the narrative. At the beginning of the story, they are distraught because they fear they have lost their leader. At the end of the story, they have gone beyond the bounds where their replacement leader can have any influence upon them. The Torah sums up Moses' understanding of the sin and its consequences with the following words (32:25): "And Moses saw the people that they were out of control ["*parua*"– wild], for Aaron had let it get out of hand." The "*hikahel… al*" which opens the golden calf episode also symbolizes its underlying meaning. The pagan behavior of the people is rooted in their inability to act coherently as a society and results in their careering completely out of control. Only drastic and decisive action on the part of Moses, breaking the *luḥot* and sending the Levites on a mission of mass executions, is able to restore the people to a sense of sobriety and an awareness of their true station.

Against this backdrop we can understand the purpose of Moses' convening (*"Vayak'hel"*) the people at the beginning of our *parasha*. Moses wants the entire people to congregate in an orderly and purposeful fashion in order to counteract the *"vayikahel ha'am al Aaron,"* which initiates and symbolizes the golden calf. The people's response to Moses' instructions regarding the building of the *Mishkan* is highly gratifying. Indeed one might legitimately term the *Mishkan* project the most successful building drive in history. As described in 35:21–36:7, there is a tremendous outpouring of desire to contribute to the *Mishkan* and participate in its construction. Note the appearance of various sectors of the population: men and women, artisans and skilled women, princes. Especially noteworthy in these verses are the frequent repetition of the word "all" (*"kol"* – fourteen times in 35:21–29 alone), and the repeated stress that all contributions, whether of labor or of material, were made out of a voluntary desire to contribute: *nesiut lev* (35:21, 26; 36:2), *nedivut lev* (35:22, 29; compare 35:21: *"nadvah ruḥo"*). Clearly the Torah wants us to appreciate how deeply motivated the people are to contribute.

So deeply do the people feel the need to contribute that the workmen in charge of the building come to Moses to complain (36:5), "The people are bringing too much," and the command is issued to stop bringing contributions. The enormity of the people's desire to contribute bears comparison with the depth of the people's need for the golden calf in the previous *parasha*. There is a midrash which notes the comparison. When the people are told to contribute to the golden calf, they do so, and when they are told to contribute to the *Mishkan*, they do so. The import of the Midrash is ironic – the people seem to be so eager for a palpable representation of God's presence that they will readily give to any project, legitimate or illegitimate, done for that purpose.

However, the comparison between the giving to the golden calf and to the *Mishkan* may be seen in a different light – the latter serves to atone for the former. In order to support this way of understanding the relationship between the two projects, we may note that there are significant differences between the way in which the people express their desire for the golden calf and for the *Mishkan*. The actual building of the golden calf is a one-man affair, done by Aaron alone. The people, while they feel an overwhelming need to have this physical symbol, are confined to a one-time gift of golden earrings. The Torah does not stress the quantity of the gift, its encompassing the entire social spectrum, or the outpouring of volunteer spirit that motivates it, as our *parasha* does. This suggests that one of the differences between the golden calf and the *Mishkan* is that the power of the golden calf lies entirely in the *form* itself, whereas the power of the *Mishkan* is rooted – at least partially – in the *process* by means of which it is constructed. Only a sanctuary produced, in response to God's express command, by the willing participation of the entire people can serve as a vehicle for the Divine Presence.

We may further suggest that the profundity of the people's desire to contribute to the *Mishkan* may stem, in part, from their sense of guilt and shame at having worshipped the golden calf. After having experienced the removal of God's Presence from their encampment, they are eager to atone for their sin, and for God to show His reconciliation with them by restoring His Presence. The universality and eagerness of their participation in the construction reflects the depth of their shame and of their need for atonement. Given the depth of their need to participate in the building of the *Mishkan*, we may now understand some puzzling details in the narration of *Parashat Vayak'hel*.

A. Why does Moses change the position of the laws of Shabbat? In God's instructions to Moses, the laws of Shabbat come at the conclusion of the instructions regarding the *Mishkan*, whereas Moses places the laws of Shabbat at the beginning, before instructing the people about the *Mishkan*.

B. Why does Moses single out the *melakha* of kindling fire for special mention (35:3)?

C. What is the significance of Moses' command (36:6) to stop bringing gifts, and of the people's compliance?

Rabbi Zvi Dov Kanatopsky (*A Night of Watching*, p. 143 ff.), following a suggestion by Rav Joseph B. Soloveitchik, has suggested that the key to questions A and B is to be found in the golden calf episode. The golden calf was forged in fire, as Aaron stresses: "and I threw it in the fire and this calf emerged" (32:24). Fire may be seen here both as a representation of man's technological mastery (Kanatopsky, p. 145) and as a symbol of man's emotional drives. Shabbat represents man's ability to curb his limitless desire for mastery of his environment. As Rabbi Kanatopsky notes, "If he learns that his power and mastery are limited, the door to idolatry is, to a great extent, closed."

After the experience of the golden calf, Moses wants to stress at the very outset that volunteer spirit is not enough to sanctify the *Mishkan*. The people must also know how to control and to channel their desires and emotions. This is why the Torah stresses that the people ceased bringing their contributions when Moses commanded them to. Their overwhelming desire and need to be part of the process of constructing the *Mishkan* had been demonstrated. Now the people needed to exhibit the ability to withdraw, to demonstrate that they are not "out of control." This ability is an essential component of worshipping God and sanctifying His name. The proper balance between the eager drive to create a sanctuary and the ability to curb and channel one's creative drives is essential in producing a personality, as well as a society, in which the Divine Presence can dwell.

The overwhelming urges and anxieties revealed in the golden calf episode, even if some of them stem from worthwhile desires, can only lead to the disintegration of the society and of the spiritual personality. The *Mishkan* serves as atonement for the golden calf, inasmuch as it reflects the proper balance, within the society as well as the personality, between admirable desires and a controlling will capable of channeling these desires in positive directions.

Shabbat of Sinai, Shabbat of the Mishkan

Rav Yonatan Grossman

The first three verses of the *parasha* deal with the observance of Shabbat. Whereas God, in His presentation to Moses, discussed Shabbat at the very end of the instructions *vis-à-vis* the *Mishkan* (Ex. 31:12–17), Moses opens his set of guidelines regarding the *Mishkan* with the mitzva of Shabbat.

For two reasons, this switch should come as no surprise:

1. On the literary level, the verses dealing with Shabbat serve to return the narrative to the flow of events which had been disrupted by the golden calf. The mitzva of Shabbat immediately reminds the reader of God's discussion of Shabbat which occurred just prior to the sin of the golden calf (31:12–17), thus restoring the narrative flow.

2. On the logical level, it made sense for God to have left this detail until the end. First He described the essence of the task (building the *Mishkan* and its utensils), and only then did He relate to technical details, such as who is to build it and when. Moses, on the other hand, was giving the people practical instructions in order to carry out this major operation. Thus, he begins his

remarks with the basic limitations on the construction, when the work may be performed and when not.

Although these answers may suffice to resolve the change of order, they do not explain the actual need for this lengthy treatment of Shabbat in the first place. Granted, God and Moses need to warn the workers that the construction of the *Mishkan* would not override the prohibitions of Shabbat. But this reminder could have been expressed in just a few words. Why invest so much text to the laws of Shabbat observance? The people had already been instructed with regard to Shabbat observance both in the context of the manna and again at Mount Sinai. Despite this, God spends six verses telling Moses about Shabbat at the conclusion of His remarks regarding the construction of the *Mishkan*. Why?

Upon closely examining the commandment of Shabbat presented in conjunction with the *Mishkan*, we will discover new dimensions of Shabbat, qualities fundamentally connected to the function and conceptual underpinnings of the *Mishkan*. In order to fully appreciate the unique contribution of this account of the mitzva of Shabbat, let us recapitulate the six appearances of Shabbat in the book of Exodus, pointing out the special characteristics of each:

1. In the Tzin desert, the Jews were instructed not to collect manna on Shabbat. Instead, they were to stay at home and take advantage of the double portion given on Friday.
2. In the Ten Commandments, the mitzva of Shabbat appears in a clear chiastic structure, which enables the reader to easily detect the character and function of Shabbat (Ex. 20:8–11):
   A. Remember the *Shabbat day* and *make it holy*.
      B. *Six days* you shall labor and do (Hebrew: *make*) *all* your work, but the *seventh day* is a Shabbat of God your God.
         C. You shall not do any work – you, your son or daughter, your male or female servant, or your cattle, or the stranger who is within your settlements.
      B1. For in *Six days* God *made* heaven and earth and sea, and *all* that is in them, and He rested on the *seventh day*.
   A1. Therefore, God blessed the *Shabbat day* and *made it holy*.

One must sanctify the day of Shabbat, just as the Creator did (A). This sanctification is effectuated by halting work on the seventh day, following the pattern established by the Almighty at Creation (B). The centerpiece of the commandment transmits the fundamental precept of Shabbat – that no labor be performed, neither by the individual himself nor by those who generally work for him.

The structure of the Fourth Commandment clearly associates the individual's observance of Shabbat with that of the Almighty. At Mount Sinai, God stresses man's obligation to follow God's lead and sanctify the day of Shabbat.

3–4. The Torah refers to the mitzva of Shabbat once again towards the end of *Parashat Mishpatim* (23:12) and, correspondingly, in the renewal of the covenant in the aftermath of the sin of the golden calf (*Parashat Ki Tissa*, Ex. 34). However, there is a totally different reason for the mitzva: "Six days you shall do your work, but on the seventh day you shall cease from labor, in order that your ox and donkey may rest, and that your bondman and the stranger may be refreshed." Here, Shabbat is characterized by the societal interest in allowing the workers an opportunity to rest. Employers are bidden to allow their employees a weekly vacation.[1]

5–6. The two final references to the mitzva of Shabbat appear in the context of the building of the *Mishkan*, as we noted above. In these final two references, two significant and heretofore unseen pieces of information appear: "He who desecrates it shall be put to death; whoever does work on it, that person shall be cut off from among his kin" (31:14). For the first time, we encounter a punishment for the violation of Shabbat – "*karet.*" Secondly, we discover in these verses the concept of "*ḥillul,*" desecration. One who fails to observe the Shabbat has not only *violated* a commandment, but has *desecrated* the Shabbat. The Shabbat

---

1. This reason appears once again in Moses' recounting of the Ten Commandments in Deuteronomy. This relates to the general question of the complex relationship between the Ten Commandments as presented in Exodus and as presented in Deuteronomy, a topic beyond the scope of our discussion.

is to be viewed as a sacred entity, and thus neglect of its laws results in a desecration of its sacred quality. This concept – the inherent sanctity of Shabbat – appears for the first time in this context, in association with the *Mishkan*. Although the Ten Commandments require the individual to "sanctify the Shabbat," that obligation relates to the person's refraining from work. Here, one who neglects the Shabbat not only fails to sanctify the day, but he desecrates and profanes it.

The unique contribution of this *parasha* to our understanding of Shabbat becomes clearer upon a closer literary analysis of God's presentation of the mitzva to Moses, which Moses himself paraphrases in his own presentation to the people (31:12–17):

A. Nevertheless, you must keep My Shabbatot.
  B. For this is a sign between Me and you throughout the ages
    C. that you may know that I, God, have sanctified you.
      D. *You shall keep the Shabbat,* for it is holy for you
        E. he who desecrates it *shall be put to death*; whoever does work on it, that person shall be cut off from among his kin.
          F. Six days may work be done, but on the seventh day there shall be a Shabbat of complete rest, holy to God
        E1. whoever does work on the Shabbat day *shall be put to death.*
      D1. The Israelite people shall keep the Shabbat
    C1. observing the Shabbat throughout the ages as a covenant for all time.
  B1. It shall be a sign for all time between Me and the people of Israel
A1. for in six days God made heaven and earth, and on the seventh day He ceased from work, and was refreshed.

Here, too, the chiastic structure cannot be overlooked. The central feature (F) stresses the basic command; one must refrain from work on the seventh day. Were the final verse (A1) placed immediately following this basic command, then this treatment of Shabbat would parallel that of the Ten Commandments. However, this section features several other elements: the death penalty for violators (E), emphasis on the requirement to observe (D), the unique relationship between the Almighty and *Benei Yisrael* as expressed by the institution of Shabbat ("I have sanctified you," "observing the Shabbat as a covenant" – (C) and the quality of Shabbat as an "*ot*" – an eternal sign between God and His people (B). Thus, although the basic command (F) as well as the opening and ending (A) correspond to the commandment of Shabbat at Mount Sinai, this framework underscores the added information contained here.

Significantly, there exist two differences between the section's two halves (A–E, E1–A1). In the first half God refers to the nation in second person, in the second half the third person form is employed. As opposed to "for this is a sign between Me and you throughout the ages" in the first half, the second half reads "it shall be a sign for all time between Me and the people of Israel." Similarly, while the first half orders the people directly, "You shall keep the Shabbat," the second half states, "The Israelite people shall keep the Shabbat," and so on.

This distinction between the two halves relates to another clear difference between them. The first section consistently focuses on the element of *kedusha* (holiness) as the underlying motif of Shabbat, a component omitted from the second half. The *kedusha* of Shabbat is manifest in three ways:

A. God sanctifies *Benei Yisrael*: "for I am God who sanctified you."
B. *Benei Yisrael* sanctify the Shabbat: "You shall keep the Shabbat, for it is holy for you."
C. God Himself sanctifies the Shabbat: "a Shabbat of complete rest, holy to God."

Thus, Shabbat is holy both for God and the Jewish people, and, consequently, *Benei Yisrael* become a sacred people in the eyes of God. In other words, God, in order to sanctify the people, presents them with His unique gift, an item of ultimate sanctity to Him. The moment they, too, sanctify the Shabbat, they become sacred before the One who had sanctified the Shabbat in the first place – God. Through the Shabbat, which is sanctified to both God and *Benei Yisrael*, *Benei Yisrael* become a holy nation before the Almighty.

In *Parashat Vayak'hel*, as Moses recounts God's commandment regarding the Shabbat, he includes both elements of the sanctification of the Shabbat: "On six days work may be done, but the seventh day shall be holy for you, a Shabbat of complete rest to God; whoever does any work on it shall be put to death" (35:2). The seventh day will be "holy for you," for it is a "day of complete rest to God." Based on the lengthier commandment he heard from God, Moses incorporates both sources of the sanctity of Shabbat in his monologue to the people.

This "romantic" quality of Shabbat uniting God and Israel, captured by Rabbi Shlomo Alkabetz's *"Lekha Dodi"* prayer, has never appeared earlier in the Torah. The previous references to Shabbat involve the individual's cessation of work on the seventh day, thereby testifying to God's having brought into existence the entirety of creation. Here, for the first time, *Benei Yisrael* stand before the Almighty and are elevated to a unique stature of *kedusha*.

The second half of the *parasha* in *Ki Tisa* seems to reflect the earlier aspect of Shabbat, the one expressed by the Ten Commandments. In this sense, Shabbat involves not *Benei Yisrael's* position *vis-à-vis* the Almighty, but rather "For in six days God made heaven and earth, and on the seventh day He ceased from work and was refreshed." Thus, God's discussion of Shabbat, with which He concludes His guidelines regarding the *Mishkan*, combines the two different functions of Shabbat – the testimony to God's having created the world, and the more "intimate" quality of Shabbat – the unique, sacred relationship between the Almighty and His people.

For this reason, specifically in the first half of this section, God refers to the nation in second person, as if He converses with *Benei Yisrael*. In the first half, the people stand directly before the Almighty as they become sanctified to Him. In the second half, by contrast, *Benei Yisrael* are referred to in third person. Here they stand not before God, but before creation, testifying to its having emerged by the divine word.

Since the element of *kedusha* emerges here as a central theme of Shabbat for the first time, it now becomes clear why the concept of "desecration" of Shabbat first appears in this presentation of Shabbat. One who violates the Shabbat undermines its sacred quality, and is guilty of not only violating God's commandment but of desecrating His holy day.

The final issue to be addressed is why does this concept of the sanctity of Shabbat first appear here, in the context of the construction of the *Mishkan*? It would seem that the answer lies in another form of *kedusha*, that of the *Mishkan* itself. After the people learn of the proverbial "House of God," after hearing about the *Mishkan*, which represents the concept of ontological sanctity of place, they are now prepared to appreciate the concept of sanctity of time. If there can be a specific location that is elevated to a superior level of *kedusha*, then there can exist as well one timeframe exalted over other periods of time. God thus introduces the concept of the sanctity of Shabbat, a status capable of desecration, whose violators are thus liable for the punishment of "*karet.*"

When delineating the specific forbidden activities that warrant capital punishment on Shabbat, *Ḥazal* based themselves on this association between the *Mishkan* and Shabbat. Specifically from here one can derive the concept of "*ḥillul*" (desecration) and, consequently, specifically here one can speak of capital punishment. Indeed, the sanctity of Shabbat, the prominent theme in this specific context, warrants severe punishment for its desecration.

The Efod

Rabbanit Sharon Rimon

I. INTRODUCTION

The *Parashot* of *Vayak'hel-Pekudei* describe the construction of the *Mishkan*, concerning which *Benei Yisrael* were commanded in detail in the *Parashot* of *Teruma-Tetzaveh*. *Vayak'hel* describes the construction of the actual *Mishkan* and its vessels, while *Pekudei* describes the fashioning of the priestly garments, and the establishment of the *Mishkan*. Is there any logic underlying the order of the garments as presented in the Torah?

The first garment mentioned in *Pekudei* is the *efod*:

> And from the blue and purple and scarlet they made the uniforms with which to serve in the holy place, and the fashioned the holy garments belonging to Aaron, as God had commanded Moses. *And he made the efod.* (Ex. 39:1–2)

In *Parashat Tetzaveh*, the breastplate (*ḥoshen*) is the first garment mentioned in the command concerning the garments; this apparently reflects its importance.[1] However, in the detailed command concerning

---

1. In the opening verse of the command concerning the priestly garments, the first garment to be mentioned is the breastplate. Like the Ark, which is mentioned first

the fashioning of each garment, the breastplate does not appear first. Rather, the *efod* comes first, and the breastplate follows. Why is this so? If the breastplate is indeed the most important of all the garments, why does it not appear here first? (In contrast, the detailed command concerning the Ark does come before all the other vessels of the *Mishkan*.)

Ibn Ezra, in his long commentary, explains that "The reason for the *efod* [being mentioned first] is that it is larger than the breastplate, and it must not move from the girdle." In his view, the command to make the *efod* comes first not because it is more important than the breastplate, but simply because the breastplate is attached to the *efod*, and therefore it is necessary first to make the *efod* and only afterwards to make the breastplate and attach it. This is a logical enough explanation, but it is more appropriate as an explanation of the order in *Parashat Pekudei*, which describes order in which the garments were made.

Another place where we find the *efod* and breastplate mentioned together is where the Torah describes the precious stones required for the *Mishkan*: "Shoham stones and stones to be inlaid in the *efod* and the breastplate" (25:7). The exact same words appear again in 35:9, and again in verse 27, where the Torah describes the contributions being brought. It is interesting to note that in the context of the contributions, too, the *efod* is mentioned before the breastplate in all three places. Why is this so?

Is the *efod* mentioned first for purely technical reasons, since the breastplate rested on and was fastened to the *efod*, and therefore the *efod* had to be made first? Perhaps the *efod* is nothing more than the basis for the breastplate, devoid of any independent importance, such that

---

out of all the vessels of the *Mishkan* because of its centrality and importance, so the breastplate appears first out of all the priestly garments because of its importance. The Ark and the breastplate are both artifacts that express the special connection between God and Israel. The breastplate is composed of two elements, each of which has its own important function: one is a display of the names of the tribes of Israel, meant to serve as a perpetual "reminder" of Israel before God, and to show that the *Kohen Gadol*, in approaching the Holy of Holies, is the representative of all of Israel. The other important element is the *Urim veTumim*, which facilitate the presentation of inquiries to God. God's answer is transmitted specifically through the letters comprising the names of the tribes; this symbolizes the idea that Israel stand before God, and turn to Him for guidance.

its creation is the first stage in the fashioning of the breastplate, and it is for this reason that it is mentioned only in relation to the breastplate.

Alternatively, it may be that the *efod* is mentioned first for exactly the opposite reason – to emphasize its own importance. Perhaps, in a certain sense, the *efod* is more important than the breastplate.

II. MAKING THE *EFOD*

What is the *efod*? In what way does its function differ from that of the breastplate? In order to attain a better understanding of why the *efod* is mentioned first, and the relationship between it and the breastplate, let us review the fashioning of the *efod* as described in *Parashat Tetzaveh*:

> They shall make the *efod* with gold, blue and purple, scarlet, and fine twined linen; an artistic creation. (28:6)

The *efod* was made from fabric that was woven from five different types of thread that were spun together into a single fiber. The Torah provides no description as to how the *efod* itself looked; it tells us only how the shoulder-pieces and the girdle should look:

> It shall have two shoulder-pieces joined to its two edges, and it shall be joined. And the finely wrought girdle of the *efod*, which is upon it, shall be of the same, in accordance with its fashioning: gold, blue and purple, and scarlet, and fine twined linen. (28:7–8)

Rashi, commenting on the *efod* in 28:4, notes:[2]

> I have neither heard nor found in any source an explanation of its form. I imagine that it was worn at the back and was as wide as the girth of a man's back, like a sort of apron that noblemen wear when they ride upon horses. So was its fashioning from below.

---

2. There is some controversy as to how the *efod* looked. We have chosen to follow Rashi's approach, and where there is debate, we note the other opinions in the footnotes.

Since neither the Torah nor any rabbinic sources describe how the *efod* looked, Rashi is forced to imagine its appearance, based on existing forms of clothing. To his view, the *efod* is a sort of long apron that is worn at the back, open at the front, and tied in front. The Torah makes no mention of this part of the *efod*. It addresses only the shoulder pieces and the girdle. Rashi raises the question why he includes a part that is not mentioned in the Torah, and answers as follows:

> We cannot say that it possessed only a girdle, for it is written, "He put upon him the *efod*" [Lev. 8:7] – and then afterwards, "And girded him with the wrought girdle of the *efod*".... Thus, we conclude that the "artistically wrought girdle" is a belt, while the *efod* is an independent article of decoration.
>
> Nor can we say that what is referred to as the *efod* is the two shoulder pieces, for the Torah states, "The two shoulder-pieces of the *efod*" [Ex. 28:27]. Thus, we conclude that there is an *efod*, there are shoulder-pieces, and there is a girdle.
>
> Therefore I conclude that the name *efod* refers to the apron [that hangs] down, since he [the kohen] is bound and decorated by means of it, as it is written, "And he bound him with it" [Lev. 8:7]. The girdle is the belt at the top of it, and the shoulder pieces are attached to it.

The Torah describes the shoulder pieces and the girdle as being joined to the *efod*; hence, they themselves cannot be the *efod*. The *efod* itself, then, is not described in the Torah.[3] According to Rashi, it is sort of long apron that is worn at the back and tied in front.

How are the shoulder-pieces meant to look? The description in the text is not altogether clear, and there is some controversy in this regard. To Rashi's view (commentary on verse 6), the shoulder pieces

---

3. Why is the fashioning of the *efod* itself not described? Is it because it was clear how it was supposed to look, or is there some special hidden matter that should not be revealed?

were attached to the *efod* from behind, and then came up to hook over the kohen's shoulders.[4]

The "wrought girdle" is the belt by means of which the *efod* is tied. What are the Shoham stones? The Torah states:

And you shall take two Shoham stones, and engrave upon them the names of the children of Israel.

Six of their names on one stone, and the names of the six others on the other stone, according to their birth.

With the work of an engraver in stone, like the engravings of a signet, shall you engrave the two stones with the names of the children of Israel; you shall place them in settings of gold.

And you shall place the two stones upon the shoulder pieces of the *efod*. (Ex. 28:9–12)

On the shoulder pieces of the *efod*, upon the kohen's shoulders, there were two gold settings, one on each side; each of them held a Shoham stone. The Shoham stones were engraved with the names of the tribes of Israel – six names on each stone.

There are differences of opinion as to the order in which the names were written on the stones. According to Rashi, they were written in order of their birth.[5]

The second part of verse 12 describes the function of these stones set in the shoulder pieces worn by the kohen "as stones of *memorial* for

---

4. According to Tiferet Yisrael, they were joined in the front, too. Rashbam, commenting on verse 7, posits that they were not two separate straps, but rather joined together and covering the entire back. Ḥizkuni and Rambam (*Laws of the Temple Vessels*, 9:11)say that the *efod* was a short garment worn on the top part of the body, down to the hips (like a modern jacket). For illustrations, see "*Bigdei HaKodesh, Bigdei HaKehuna*" by S.D. Steinberg.
5. Other opinions appear in Rambam (*Laws of the Temple Vessels*, chapter 9) and in the Gemara (*Sota* 36a). See *Mishkan HaShem* by S. Shapiatzky, pp. 140–141. There is also debate as to the color of the Shoham stones. The author of *Shiltei Giborim* maintains that they were green. Rav Sa'adia Gaon (commenting on verse 9) suggests that they were a translucent white. Ibn Ezra (on verse 9) also mentions white. According to Rabbenu Baḥya (commenting on Numbers 2:2) the stones were black.

the children of Israel; and *Aaron shall bear their names before God*, upon his two shoulders, *as a memorial.*"

The purpose of the Shoham stones on the shoulder pieces of the *efod* is reminiscent of the function of the stones set in the breastplate. In verse 29 we read, concerning the stones of the breastplate: "*Aaron shall bear the names* of the children of Israel ... *as a memorial before God* at all times."

Aaron's bearing of the names of the children of Israel, as a remembrance, before God, includes all three elements that were also mentioned in relation to both the breastplate and the *efod*. On the basis of the similarity between the function of the breastplate (mentioned in verse 29) and the function of the *efod* (mentioned in verse 12), it would seem that the *efod* and the breastplate share the same function.

III. IS SOMETHING HERE SUPERFLUOUS?

Is there indeed no difference between the *efod* and the breastplate? Do they share the same function of bearing the names of the children of Israel as a remembrance before God? If we conclude that both share the same function, then we could explain why the *efod* appears before the breastplate. The Torah seeks to teach us that the *efod* itself (independently of the breastplate) plays a role in the "bearing of the names of the children of Israel as a memorial before God." However, if we adopted this view, we would have to ask: what need is there for two garments that both share exactly the same function? Isn't one of them redundant?

Obviously, the breastplate cannot be redundant, since it also has another function. It is not only a set of stones bearing the names of *Benei Yisrael* before God. It also contains the *Urim veTumim*, by virtue of which the breastplate becomes the "breastplate of judgment," facilitating inquiries of God. This other function of the breastplate is mentioned in verse 30, and there is no parallel function in the case of the *efod*. If the breastplate has an additional function that does not exist in the case of the *efod*, then clearly the breastplate cannot be redundant.

This leads us to consider the possibility that the *efod* is redundant. If the breastplate alone also fulfills the function of bearing the names of *Benei Yisrael* before God, then what need is there for the *efod*?

In verses 29 and 30, which describe the function of the breastplate, emphasis is placed on the expression, "before God." Likewise, in Numbers 27:21, describing the function of the breastplate, the expression "before God" appears.

In contrast, when it comes to the *efod*, it is the matter of "memorial" or "memory" that is emphasized. In verse 12, describing the role of the *efod*, the word *"zikaron"* (memorial) appears twice – at the beginning of the description of the role of the *efod*, and at the end, such that a framework is created that highlights the "memory":

> stones of *memorial for the children of Israel*; and Aaron shall bear their names before God, upon his two shoulders, *as a memorial.* (Ex. 28:12)

In *Parashat Pekudei*, the function of the *efod* is described very briefly. When the function of the *efod* is compressed in this way, the crux of it stands out clearly: the essence of the *efod* is the matter of "remembrance."

> He put them on the shoulders of the efod – stones of *memorial for Benei Yisrael.* (39:7)

In contrast, with regard to the breastplate, the Torah teaches:

> Aaron shall bear the names of *Benei Yisrael*... as a *memorial before God,* at all times. And you shall place upon the breastplate of judgment the *Urim* and the *Tumim,* and they shall be upon Aaron's heart when he comes in *before God,* and Aaron shall bear the judgment of *Benei Yisrael* upon his heart, *before God,* at all times. (29–30)

The crux of the role of the *efod* is to serve as a memorial for *Benei Yisrael.* The breastplate, on the other hand, is meant mainly to be "before God." Admittedly, the breastplate is also "a memorial," and the matter of "before God" is mentioned in connection with the *efod,* too, but these are not the most central, defining symbols of these garments.

IV. WHAT IS THE SIGNIFICANCE OF THE "MEMORIAL"?

What is a "memorial"? Obviously, the implication is not that God forgets, and therefore needs reminding. Rather, the "memorial" invokes God's providence, His guidance of people's lives. The *efod* symbolizes God's special providence towards *Benei Yisrael*. When the *efod* is worn for the divine service, *Benei Yisrael* must remember the special relationship between them and God, with the special guidance that He gives.

The breastplate emphasizes the aspect of *Benei Yisrael* standing before God. Aaron's approach of the holy place, before God, represents all of Israel standing before God.

These two elements are strongly interdependent, and for this reason the *efod* and the breastplate are attached to one another. For the same reason there are also parallels in the description of their functions – to the extent that we have the impression of them sharing the same function. Nevertheless, the *efod* has its own importance and significance, and the fact that it is described prior to the breastplate, separately from it, demands that we pay attention to its uniqueness.

Only after the Torah notes the fashioning of the *efod*, and its function, does it go on to describe the fastening of the breastplate to the *efod*:

> And you shall make fittings of gold. And you shall make them two chains of pure gold at the ends, of braided work, and you shall attach the braided chains to the fittings. (28:13–14)

V. THE MISSING BREASTPLATE

If we review the biblical narratives that describe the use of the *efod* and the breastplate, we discover an interesting phenomenon. The *breastplate* is never mentioned as a vessel used for inquiring of God. In fact, the breastplate is mentioned nowhere in the whole of Tanach, except in the *parashot* dealing with the construction of the *Mishkan* and its vessels!

The *Urim veTumim*, whose function is to facilitate inquiring of God, are mentioned only twice in this context. The first occasion concerns the appointment of Joshua:

> He shall stand before Elazar the Kohen, and he shall seek the judgment of the *urim* for him, before God. (Num. 27:21)

The second occasion is during Saul's last battle, when he attempts to inquire of God, via the *urim*, and God does not answer him:

> Saul inquired of God, but God did not answer him – neither in dreams, nor through the *urim*, nor by means of the prophets. (1 Sam. 28:6)

There is no other mention of inquiring via the *urim* anywhere else in Tanach.

However, we find that there are several instances of Israel inquiring of God before going out to war (as well as in certain other situations). We assume that the inquiry was made via the *Urim veTumim*, which are meant to serve as the channel for such communication. Nevertheless, it is interesting that no explicit mention is made of the fact that the *Urim veTumim* were involved.

The *efod*, in contrast, appears in several places. It, too, is mentioned as a vessel used for inquiring of God (which is most surprising, as nowhere in the Torah is there any indication that this is part of its function). The impression arising from this is that the *efod* is a vessel (or garment) of great importance.

VI. THE *EFOD* IN TANACH

Let us examine some sources that make mention of the *efod*:

1. The creation of an *efod* for purposes of divine service: Two narratives include the fashioning of an *efod* (i.e., an item is made, apparently similar in form to the *efod* of the *Mishkan*, but not as a garment to be worn by priests; rather, it is apparently made of gold) that is used for divine service:

> Gideon made it into an *efod* and he displayed it in his city, in Ofra, and all of Israel went astray there after it, and it became a snare to Gideon and to his household. (Judges 8:27)

> The man, Micah, had a shrine, and he made an *efod* and *terafim*, and he consecrated one of his sons, who became his priest. (Judges 17:5)

Obviously, in these narratives the use that is being made of the *efod* is unlawful, but what we learn from this is that the *efod* itself was significant, and therefore there was good reason to reproduce it.

2. In a number of places, mention is made of kohanim wearing a linen *efod*:

> Samuel ministered before God, as a child, girded with a linen *efod*. (I Sam. 2:18)

> Doeg the Edomite turned and he smote the kohanim, and there died on that day eighty-five men, wearers of the linen *efod*. (I Sam. 22:18)

> David leaped about with all his might before God, and David wore a linen *efod*. (II Sam. 6:14)

In all of the above instances, it is clear that the reference is not to the *efod* that Moses was commanded to make, to which the breastplate was attached. There was only one such *efod*, and this garment was worn only by the *Kohen Gadol*. As Ibn Ezra explains, in his long commentary on verse 6:

> The linen *efod* was made of some sort of linen. The *efod* of Moses was not made of [linen] fabric, but rather [was woven from] gold, blue, purple, scarlet, and fine twined linen all together. And it was not only of the breastplate of judgment that they inquired.

Nevertheless, we learn from here that the *efod* was a garment that signified either priesthood or some other important status.

3. Description of the Kohen as wearing an *efod*:
In God's revelation to Eli, He says:

> I chose him out of all the tribes of Israel to minister to Me, to offer sacrifice upon My altar, to offer incense, to wear the *efod* before Me. (I Sam. 2:28)

God mentions specifically the *efod* as a symbol of the importance of the priesthood.

4. The *efod* appears several times as a means of inquiring of God:

   A. In the battle waged by Saul and Jonathan against the Philistines, mention is made of the kohen wearing the *efod*:

      > Aḥiya, son of Aḥituv, brother of Ikhavod son of Pinḥas, the son of Eli, was God's priest at Shilo, wearing an *efod*. (1 Sam. 14:3)

      Further on in the story, we read of an attempt to inquire of God; no mention is made of the breastplate, but the account features the Ark:

      > Saul said to Aḥiya: "Bring the Ark of God," for the Ark of God was, at that time, with *Benei Yisrael*. And it was, while Saul was speaking to the priest, that the tumult in the camp of the Philistines grew increasingly great, and Saul said to the priest, "Withdraw your hand." (1 Sam. 14:18–19)

      In these verses we find the *efod* and the Ark mentioned as being connected to the inquiry of God, but the breastplate is entirely absent.

   B. In David's battle against Ke'ila, we read that David inquired of God by means of the *efod*:

      > David inquired of God, saying: "Shall I go and smite these Philistines".... And it was, when Evyatar, son of Aḥimelekh, fled to David at Ke'ila, that he came down with an *efod* in his hand .... David knew that Saul had devised this evil against him, and he said to Evyatar the priest: "Bring the *efod*." (1 Sam. 23:2, 6, 9)

   C. David's battle against Amalek in Tziklag:

      > David said to Evyatar, the priest..."Please bring the *efod* to me." So Evyatar brought the *efod* to David. And David

inquired of God, saying: "Shall I pursue this legion? Shall I catch them?" And God said to him: "Pursue, for you shall surely catch them, and you shall surely save." (I Sam. 30:7–8)

A review of all of the above verses gives rise to a difficulty. According to the Torah, inquiry of God is performed using the breastplate, by means of the *Urim veTumim*. Why does the text in these places refer only to the *efod* and not the breastplate?

One possibility is that these verses are meant to imply that it was the breastplate that was consulted, but since it is attached to the *efod*, the combined vessel is referred to as an *efod*. Thus, the combined garment is called an *efod*, even though technically the inquiry of God is performed by means of the breastplate, which is attached to the *efod*.

However, if the breastplate is really the most important part of this combination, why is the garment in its entirety not referred to as the "breastplate" – at least in those instances where it is used for inquiring of God, since this is achieved solely through using the breastplate? Why is the *efod* awarded such an important place?

Ibn Ezra (in his long commentary) provides a surprising explanation. To his view, while the breastplate is the vessel that is meant to be used for inquiring of God, it was also possible to inquire by means of the actual *efod*, without involving the breastplate:

> There were many *efodim* among the kohanim, and they all had girdles; all that they lacked were a breastplate and *urim*. In the same way that the *Urim veTumim* that were upon the breastplate of judgment could be used, so a questioner could obtain his answer purely through the likeness of the *efod*, but not at all times.

Ibn Ezra expounds at length in his description of the "secret essence" of the *efod* and the breastplate, and explains the connection between the form of the *efod* and breastplate and the possibility of inquiring of God by means of them. We shall not attempt here to delve into these secrets; suffice it to summarize from Ibn Ezra's words that there was one special *efod* to which the special breastplate fashioned by Moses was attached, and via this it was possible at all times to inquire and to receive a clear, absolute response. In addition, there were other *efodim* – linen *efod*s – to which no breastplate or *urim* were attached.[6]

It was possible to inquire by means of an *efod* that did not contain *Urim veTumim*, but this was an inferior option;[7] the answer to the inquiry was not accessible "at all times," and was also less clear. Only someone who was experienced in the communications of the breastplate might be able to decode it. The answer provided by the *Urim veTumim* was far more absolute, leaving no room for doubt.

Ibn Ezra's thesis does explain the fact that it is always the *efod* that is mentioned, rather than the breastplate. According to his view, it is the *efod* that is mentioned because it was possible to inquire of an *efod*, without a breastplate. The *efod* itself served as a vessel for inquiring of God.

We conclude, then, that the *efod* is mentioned often because it is significant in its own right. It is not simply the "basis" for the breastplate, but may be used independently to inquire of God. At the same time, though, it is specifically the fact that the *efod* is mentioned so often, while the breastplate is absent, that testifies that there was only one breastplate, special and sanctified, that was fashioned by Moses, while the *efod* was of a lower level and was therefore more common. A number of *efodim* existed, they were more accessible, and a question could be posed by means of them without having to involve the *Kohen Gadol* himself.

---

6. From where does Ibn Ezra deduce the existence of several *efodim*? He bases his opinion on the fact that there was an *efod* in the possession of Evyatar the Kohen, who accompanied David in his wanderings in the Judean desert, and which David used to inquire of God (as recounted in 1 Sam. 23 and 30), while at the same time there was an *efod* in the possession of the kohen who was with Saul, such that Saul was able to inquire of the *Urim veTumim* (as narrated in 1 Sam. 28, concerning his final battle). How was this possible? Ibn Ezra (as well as Ramban) maintains that the original *efod* was in the hands of Saul, but there was another in the possession of Evyatar; this was a linen *efod* that could similarly be used to inquire of God.

7. Ramban agrees with Ibn Ezra that additional *efod*s existed, and that they could be used to inquire of God, on a lower level than that afforded by the *efod* and breastplate of Moses. According to his view, however, these other *efod*s also had breastplates attached to them and featured *Urim veTumim*.

VII. FORTUNE-TELLING OR PERFORMING
THE WILL OF GOD?

The Torah describes the breastplate as a vessel used for inquiring of God, while assigning the *efod* a different function – the "memorial" of *Benei Yisrael* before God. Perhaps the *efod* represents the basic level of connection between Israel and God. Upon the kohen's shoulders sit the Shoham stones, with the names of the tribes of Israel. The breastplate, with the *Urim veTumim* and God's Ineffable Name, represents a higher level of that connection – a level whose source is the name of God, and whose essence is "before God."

The *efod* appears first – not because of the order of importance, nor for merely technical reasons (the order in which the garments are donned); rather, for a substantial reason: the *efod* testifies to the basic level of connection between Israel and God, and the measure of God's divine providence towards Israel.

Having established this level of connection, the next stage is the breastplate, with the Name of Forty-two Letters, from which the names of *Benei Yisrael* arise. This is no normal connection; it is a connection whose source and roots lie in the divine realm.

The basis of the connection between Israel and God is what facilitates the inquiry and clarification of the future. It is the basis of God's providence in the world that allows mortals to seek knowledge of what is going to happen in the future.

Accordingly, we can understand that there is a fundamental difference between clarification of the future in the light of the *efod*, and clarification of the future in the light of the breastplate.

Inquiring of the *efod* is based on the fundamental connection between God and the nation of Israel. This type of questioning may be interpreted as divining or fortune-telling, as a device used by man to make decisions on the basis of the data that he obtains. The *efod*, then, becomes a provider of information, a fortune-telling device, facilitating more propitious decision-making.

The use of the breastplate, on the other hand, is open to no such misinterpretation. Here, the whole picture arises from "standing before God." God's name, located in the center of the breastplate, symbolizes total commitment to performing the will of God. Here, there is no impression of man standing in front of a device that provides information; rather, man stands in front of his Creator, seeking to know God's will in the world. This is not fortune-telling or divining; there is no hint of using the vessels of the *Mishkan* as a device for serving ourselves. We stand before God with commitment, and with the goal of performing His will.

It is possible that *Benei Yisrael*'s need to know the future was very strong, and therefore additional *efodim* were used to inquire of God. It is for this reason that there are so many instances in which an *efod* is mentioned. This phenomenon, taken to an extreme, at times led to the *efod* turning into a religious symbol, and even actual idolatry (as in the case of Gideon, and of Micah).

This may explain the words of the prophet Hosea:

> I said to her: "For many days you shall remain with me; you shall not play the harlot, nor shall you belong to another man, and so I will be towards you. Since for many days *Benei Yisrael* will remain with no king, and no prince, nor any sacrifice, nor pillar, nor '*efod*,' nor *terafim*. Thereafter, the children of Israel will return, and they shall seek the Lord their God." (Hosea 3:3–5)

Ibn Ezra explains that the reference here is not to an *efod* fashioned for the sake of idolatry, but rather to an *efod* used for inquiring of God. But what is evil about an *efod* used for inquiring of God?

Apparently, *Benei Yisrael* turned the technique of inquiring of God via the *efod* into an external form of worship, like fortune-telling. Only after they would separate themselves from this approach "for many days" would they be able to return to God in the proper manner.

This problem of turning the *Mikdash* into an external form of worship arises from several sources in the books of the prophets, with reference to both the sacrifices and the Ark.[8] The prophets expect *Benei*

---

8. The "ritualistic" view of the *Mikdash*, devoid of understanding of its inner significance, is improper, and therefore the prophets convey the message that God has no desire for sacrifices performed in this manner. In many places the prophets cry out that God is not interested in burnt offerings and sacrifices; what He desires is

Yisrael to understand the inner meaning of the *Mikdash*: its significance not as a center for worship rituals, similar to those used by the idolaters, but rather the connection between Israel and God, and Israel's commitment to stand before God, to represent His path in the world, and to perform His will.

---

that people will listen to His words (as Samuel reprimands Saul in 1 Sam. 15:22). For instance, Jeremiah (chapter 7) states: "So says the Lord of Hosts, God of Israel: Add your burnt offerings to your sacrifices, and eat their meat. For I did not speak with your forefathers, nor did I command them, on the day when I took them out of the land of Egypt, concerning burnt offerings and sacrifices. Rather, this thing I commanded them, saying: 'Listen to Me, and I shall be your God, and you shall be My nation, and walk in all the ways that I have commanded you.'" And likewise in many other sources.

The same idea arises from the words of Hosea concerning the *efod* (quoted above), as well as in the words of Jeremiah (chapter 3) concerning the Ark: "In those days, promises God, people shall no longer say, 'The Ark of God's Covenant,' nor shall it be recalled to their heart, nor will they remember it, nor visit it, nor will they make it again." From these verses we conclude that in the time to come, perhaps the *efod* and the Ark will no longer be used, since they were turned into vessels of external ritual.

The most important vessels of the *Mikdash* – the Ark, the *efod* and the breast-plate – are meant to express the special connection between Israel and God, and the Divine Presence that rests amongst Israel; God's special providence towards Israel, and Israel's commitment to stand before God and to obey Him.

It is specifically these vessels which, according to these prophets, will be done away with in the time to come, because *Benei Yisrael* apparently used them in the wrong way. But perhaps, in the time to come, *Benei Yisrael* will know how to attribute the proper significance to these vessels, and then they will be worthy of using them.

Two Curtains: Parokhet HaKodesh and Parokhet HaMasakh

Rav Amnon Bazak

I. THE CONTRADICTION

After describing the construction of the *Mishkan* in the *Parashot* of *Teruma* and *Tetzaveh*, the Torah reiterates the *Mishkan* and its furnishings once again in the *Parashot* of *Vayak'hel* and *Pekudei*, with significant distinctions between them. Our analysis will deal with the differences between the two *parashot* regarding the *parokhet*, the curtain which separates between the *Kodesh* (the "Holy," i.e., the Sanctuary) and the *Kodesh haKodashim* (the "Holy of Holies," containing the *Aron*, the Ark).

There is an apparent contradiction in the sequence of events required to set up the *Mishkan*: is the *Aron* to be brought first into the *Kodesh haKodashim* and after that the *parokhet* hung outside, or is the *parokhet* first unfurled and afterwards the *Aron* brought into the *Kodesh haKodashim*?

In *Parashat Teruma*, the Torah states:

> And you shall make a curtain of blue, dark red and crimson worm, and twined linen.... And you shall bring the curtain under the clasps, and you shall bring therein, inside the curtain, the Ark of

the Testimony; and the curtain shall divide for you between the Holy and the Holy of Holies. And you shall put the cover upon the Ark of the Testimony in the Holy of Holies. And you shall set the table outside the curtain, and the candelabrum over against the table on the side of the tabernacle toward the south; and you shall put the table on the north side. (26:31, 33–35)

First, the Israelites are to hang the *parokhet*, then bring the Ark of the Testimony into the *Kodesh haKodashim* ("inside the curtain"), and afterwards they are to put the cover on the *Aron*.

However, in the actual fulfillment of the command, we find the opposite order. The command of the erecting the *Mishkan* reads:

On the first day of the first month you shall set up the tabernacle of the Tent of Meeting. And you shall place therein the Ark of the Testimony, and you shall screen the Ark with the curtain. (40:2–3)

Here it appears that Moses has to first put the *Aron* inside and only afterwards drape the *parokhet* in front of it. Subsequently, this is how the Torah describes the actual execution:

And he took and put the testimony into the Ark, and he placed the poles in the Ark, and he put the cover above upon the Ark. And he brought the Ark into the tabernacle, and he placed the screen curtain, and he screened the Ark of the Testimony, as God commanded Moses. (40:20–21)

It appears that Moses first puts the cover on the *Aron* and then brings the *Aron* to its place, and only afterwards does he hang the *parokhet*.

How may we resolve this contradiction? Ramban suggests that the verses in *Parashat Teruma* ("And the curtain shall divide for you between the Holy and the Holy of Holies") do not come to determine the sequence of actions, but only to explain the role of the *parokhet*:

He does not command him now to do it in this order.... Rather, the idea is that the verse commands him to put the *parokhet* under the clasps, so that the *Aron* will be there inside the curtain, and the *parokhet* will divide between the *Kodesh* and the *Kodesh haKodashim*. (Ramban on Ex. 40:21)

Still, why does it appear that the verse intends to give the sequence of actions?

II. THE *PAROKHET*'S TWO FUNCTIONS

Possibly, the variations reflect two different functions of the *Parokhet*. In *Parashat Teruma*, the role of the *parokhet* is as follows: "And the curtain shall divide for you between the Holy and the Holy of Holies." Rashbam writes (on 26:31): "According to its function, this is a term of division and partition between one room and another." The *parokhet* symbolizes the boundary between the two parts of God's house – just like the clasps, below which it is hung, mark this border on the roof of the *Mishkan*. According to this, it is understood why hanging the *parokhet* must be done before the *Aron* is brought in – as long as the *Kodesh haKodashim* is not defined by the *parokhet*, it is impossible to bring the *Aron* there, because the place designed for it has not yet been demarcated.[1]

In *Parashat Pekudei*, on the other hand, the function of the *parokhet* is expressed in the following way: "He screened the Ark of the Testimony" – a unique shield for the *Aron*. Rashi comments: "'And you shall screen the ark with the curtain' [40:3] – a term of protection,

---

1. This aspect of the *parokhet* – delineating the place of the *Kodesh haKodashim* – is particularly prominent in the Yom Kippur service: "And God said to Moses: 'Speak to Aaron your brother, that he not come at all times into the Holy, inside the curtain, before the cover which is upon the Ark; so that he may not die; for I appear in the cloud upon the cover…. And he shall take a censer full of fiery coals from off the altar before God, and his hands full of fine spice incense, and bring it inside the curtain…. Then he shall kill the goat of the sin-offering that is for the people, and he shall bring its blood inside the curtain.'" Similarly, we find this definition of the priestly watch in *Parashat Korah* (Numbers 18:7): "And you and your sons with you shall keep your priesthood in everything that pertains to the altar and to that which is inside the curtain, and you shall serve; I give you the priesthood as a service of gift; and the foreigner who draws close must die." None of these verses mention the *Kodesh haKodashim* by name – they only refer to the area that is "inside the curtain."

because it is a partition." According to this, there is no significance to unfurling the *parokhet* before the arrival of the *Aron* which it protects.

These two functions of the *parokhet* are expressed in two names. In our portion, it is called *"parokhet hamasakh,"* "the *screen* curtain," corresponding with "And you shall screen the Ark with the curtain." However, the *parokhet* is also called *"the holy curtain"* (Lev. 4:6), and this reflects its function in *Parashat Teruma*: "And the curtain shall divide for you between the Holy and the Holy of Holies." The role of the *parokhet* as the shield of the *Aron* finds a unique expression in Numbers 4:5: "Aaron and his sons will come when the camp will journey, and they will take down the screen curtain, and they will cover the Ark of Testimony with this." When travelling, the *Aron* is actually wrapped up in the *parokhet*, and it is not surprising that the latter is described there as *"parokhet hamasakh."*

This explains why in *Parashat Teruma*, it would have been proper to hang the *parokhet* first and only afterwards to bring the *Aron* to its place. However, in practice, things are done according to the conceptualization of *Parashat Pekudei*. So that the *parokhet* can serve as a *parokhet hamasakh*, the *Aron* is brought in first. Why does the *parokhet hamasakh* aspect overpower the *parokhet hakodesh* facet?

Apparently, while the *parokhet hakodesh* separates between the *Kodesh* and the *Kodesh haKodashim*, this function is already filled by a different element of the *Mishkan*: "And you shall bring the curtain under the clasps." The clasps separate the two sets of lower sheets, marking this separation by their actual location.[2] Possibly, the place of the *Kodesh haKodashim* is already delineated and defined by the clasps, and the *parokhet* only strengthens and emphasizes this demarcation. Therefore,

---

2. The lower sheets are referred to as the *"mishkan"* (the same term as the tabernacle overall, but here having a much narrower definition). There are ten sheets, each 28 by 4 cubits. They are divided into two sets, five sheets in every set, making a set of 28 by 20 cubits – and the two sets together, joined by the clasps, measure 28 by 40 cubits. The *mishkan* is thirty cubits long, ten wide and ten high. With the sheets above it, one set would cover from the *Mishkan*'s entrance to the clasps, the twenty cubits of the *Kodesh*, and the sheets of the second set would cover the ten cubits of the *Kodesh haKodashim* and the ten cubits of the height of the boards behind them. Thus, the clasps stand exactly over the line dividing the *Kodesh* from the *Kodesh haKodashim*, twenty cubits from the *Mishkan*'s entrance.

when the two roles of the *parokhet* contradict, the *parokhet hamasakh* identity has the advantage; at the critical moment, the Torah gives up on the symbolic meaning of the *parokhet hakodesh*, which is accomplished regardless by the clasps, and expresses the *parokhet hamasakh* aspect, which can be achieved only when the *Aron* is already in its place.[3]

An interesting ramification of the expression of the double function of the *parokhet* may in fact be found in the Mishna (*Yoma* 5:1) about the High Priest's entrance into the *Kodesh haKodashim* on Yom Kippur:

> He would walk in the Sanctuary until he reached the two curtains separating between the *Kodesh* and the *Kodesh haKodashim*, and there was a cubit between them.
>
> Rabbi Yossi says: "There was only one curtain there, as it says, 'And the curtain shall divide for you between the Holy and the Holy of Holies.'"

The Mishna brings the Tannaitic dispute as to whether there was one curtain in the Temple or two. The Gemara (*Yoma* 51b) challenges the view of the sages: "Rabbi Yossi has responded well to the Rabbis!" It then answers:

> The Rabbis will say to you that this is true of the *Mishkan*. However, in the Second Temple, there was no *amma teraksin*, while in the First Temple there was. Thus, the rabbis had a doubt about its sanctity, whether it should be the same as the inside or as the outside, and so they made two curtains.[4]

---

3. Accordingly, one may add that the two aspects of the *parokhet* are also expressed in the lower sheets themselves. On the one hand, the lower sheets must be a "*mishkan*" – a roof for the structure in which the God's Presence (*Shekhina*) rests: just as the *parokhet hamasakh* covers the *Aron* from the side, so the sheets covers the *Aron* from above. On the other hand, dividing the sheets into two sets then connected by clasps symbolizes the boundary between the *Kodesh* and the *Kodesh haKodashim* (see the previous note); this is the idea of the *parokhet hakodesh*, which separates between the *Kodesh* and the *Kodesh haKodashim*. Indeed, the *parokhet* and the lower sheets are all made of linen and dyed wool: "twined linen, and blue, dark red and crimson worm, *keruvim*" (36:8; see v. 35 concerning the *parokhet*).

4. In the First Temple, there was a cubit-thick wall between the *Kodesh* and the *Kodesh*

According to this, in the Temple there were indeed two curtains! However, the Gemara gives a technical reason – the doubt in terms of the status of that cubit dividing between the *Kodesh* and the *Kodesh haKodashim*. Nevertheless, it may be that in fact the two curtains represent the two aspects of the *parokhet*; one serves as *parokhet hamasakh*, while its companion serves as the *parokhet hakodesh*.[5]

III. CREATIVITY IN MAKING THE *PAROKHET*

The function of the *Parokhet* according to *Parashat Teruma* has an additional expression. *Parashat Teruma* describes the structure of *Mishkan* in three essential sections: first comes the command of the vessels of the *Mishkan* – the *Aron*, *Shulḥan* (table) and *Menora* (25:10–40); then the infrastructure – the sheets and the boards (26:1–30); and finally the command about the Outer Altar (27:1–8). *Parashat Teruma* concludes with the structure of the *ḥatzer* (courtyard) (27:9–19). There is an important distinction between the three sections of the *Mishkan* and the *ḥatzer*. At the beginning of the portion, God orders Moses to make the *Mishkan* and its vessels. "According to all that I show you, the likeness of the tabernacle, and the likeness of all its utensils, so shall you make it" (25:9) – as Rashbam explains: "All the forms of the utensils and the structures, God actually showed them to Moses." Therefore, the first three sections conclude accordingly. At the end of the first part with the vessels, the Torah states, "See and make according to their likeness, *as you are shown on the mountain*" (25:40); after the description of the curtains and the boards, it says, "You shall set up the tabernacle, accord-

---

haKodashim (known as the "*amma teraksin*"). The Second Temple had a much higher ceiling than the First, and it was impossible to make a wall so high with the thickness of one cubit; for this reason, they made two curtains one cubit apart, but the status of that cubit – whether it had the sanctity of the *Kodesh* or that of the *Kodesh haKodashim* – was questionable (see Rashi ad loc.).

5. Perhaps we may offer a bolder proposal. Based on the simple meaning of the text, the sages could respond to Rabbi Yossi that there is another verse: "And you shall place therein the Ark of the Testimony, and screen the Ark with the curtain." From this, one may conclude that also in the *Mishkan* there was another, additional, *parokhet*. According to this proposal, the Tannaitic dispute touches on the *Mishkan* as well, not merely the Temple.

ing to its rule, *as you were shown on the mountain*" (26:30); and at the end of the command to make the Outer Altar, it says once again, "*As He showed you on the mountain, so shall they do*" (27:8). In the *ḥatzer*, however, this conclusion is not mentioned. The idea that these things should be done exactly as Moses saw on Sinai applies only to the *Mishkan* and its furnishings, not the *ḥatzer*.

However, we skipped over one passage in the survey above, that of the *parokhet* (26:31–37), which appears between the command about the *Mishkan's* structure and the command about the Outer Altar. Apparently, the *parokhet* is part of the structure of the *Mishkan*. However, as we have said, the verse which summarizes the description of the *Mishkan's* structure – "You shall set up the tabernacle, according to its rule, as you were shown on the mountain" (26:30) – appears at the end of the command about the sheets and the boards, and the passage of the *parokhet* is not included. This implies that the law of the *parokhet* is equivalent to the law of the *ḥatzer*, and its manufacture is not limited to a specific blueprint shown by God to Moses on Mount Sinai. What is the reason for the distinction between the *parokhet* and the other components of the *Mishkan*?

It appears that this distinction springs from the prominent difference between the *parokhet* and the other components of the *Mishkan*. At the beginning of the *Parashat Teruma*, God says to Moses: "Speak to the *Benei Yisrael* and they shall take a contribution for me" (25:2), and the aim of this contribution is as follows (25:8): "And they shall make a Temple for me, and I will reside among them." The *Mishkan* is designed to be the place for God's Presence to reside, and therefore one must stress that everything about it must be done according to the exact plan commanded by God, without any human improvisation. Only one part of the *Mishkan* is not designed for God, the *parokhet*, the role of which is, according to *Parashat Teruma*, (26:33) as follows: "And the curtain shall divide *for you* between the Holy and the Holy of Holies." The *parokhet* is designed for the Israelites, separating different domains. Because of this, there is a place for human creativity in its manufacture, and only its general likeness is dictated by the Torah.

However, in the summation of the work of the *Mishkan* in our portion, the Torah says:

As everything which God commanded Moses, thus the Israelites did all of the work. And Moses saw all of the labor, and behold they made it; just as God commanded, so they did, and Moses blessed them. (39:42–43)

From this we may conclude that the *parokhet* – the role of which in these portions is to be *parokhet hamasakh,* and not only as something to separate domains for the Israelites – is made like all of the other utensils. (Indeed, the *parokhet hamasakh* is mentioned in the list of all of the components of the *Mishkan,* preceding these summarizing verses.)

This leads to the following conclusion: in making the *parokhet hakodesh* there is a place for human creativity, but the *parokhet hamasakh* is done precisely as God commanded Moses.

Of Parts and Pieces: The Instructions and Assembly of the Mishkan

Rav Chanoch Waxman

I. INTRODUCTION

Exodus closes with the assembly of the *Mishkan*. After God commands Moses to set up the *Mishkan* and instructs him with regard to the order of its assembly (40:1–16), the Torah reports that Moses accomplished the divine command.

> And it was in the first month in the second year, on the first day of the month, the *Mishkan* was erected. (Ex. 40:17)

In apparent emphasis of Moses' faithful accomplishment of God's instructions, the Torah continues to detail his carrying out of God's instructions. Following the verse above, it presents eight mini-*parashot*, each detailing the assembly by Moses of some part of the *Mishkan* mentioned in the original instructions section (40:1–16), and each bracketed by Masoretic text breaks known as "*setumot*" (40:17–33). Each of the first seven sections ends with the refrain, "just as God had commanded Moses," and the eighth ends with the claim that "Moses finished the work" (40:33). The point cannot be missed. Moses, ever the faithful servant, has fulfilled God's word to the last iota, and not missed a step.

At this point, after the "instructions" and "performance" sections of the narrative, we arrive at what might be thought of as the third stage in the process of assembling the *Mishkan*, the divine aspect – the descent of God's Presence onto the *Mishkan*:

> Then a cloud covered the *Mishkan* and the Glory of the Lord filled the *Mishkan*. And Moses was not able to enter the Tent of Meeting, because the cloud rested upon it, and the Glory of the Lord filled the *Mishkan*. And when the cloud rose from upon the *Mishkan*, the children of Israel went onward in their journeys: but if the cloud did not rise, they did not set out until the day it rose. For the cloud of the Lord was upon the *Mishkan* by day, and fire by night, in the view of all the house of Israel throughout their journeys. (40:34–38)

As Rashbam points out (on 40:35), God descends to inaugurate and sanctify the newly built *Mishkan* with His very Presence.

If so, we might think of the penultimate chapter of Exodus, the story of the assembly of the *Mishkan*, as possessing a simple linear structure. This can be mapped as follows:

> Section One (40:1–16) – the instructions
> Section Two (40:17–33) – the performance
> Section Three (40:34–38) – the public descent of the Divine Presence, and divine sanctification of the newly completed *Mishkan*

However, things are not as simple as they appear.

II. MISSING SECTIONS

The "command-execution" relationship outlined above – "instructions" (40:1–16) and "performance" (40:17–33) – leads to a very simple expectation. Everything that happens in the "instructions" should happen again in the "performance." This expectation gains strength from some of the phrases and literary devices utilized in the "performance" section, such as the reference to Moses "finishing the work" and the seven-fold refrain of "just as God had commanded him."

Moreover, the eight mini-*parashot*, each describing the assembly of a particular vessel or structure in the *Mishkan*, parallel in number, content and order the eight verses that command the assembly of the vessels and structures of the *Mishkan* (40:1–8). Finally, the overall "instructions" section closes with a forward-looking verse that serves as a transition to the upcoming "accomplishment" section.

> And Moses did in accord with *all* that the Lord had commanded him, so he did. (40:16)

This brings us to the nub of the matter. For those who have been following the numbers, the "instructions" section contains seven verses (40:9–15) that find no parallel in the "accomplishment" section. A quick glance at the text yields the following: After God commands Moses about assembling the structure and vessels of the *Mishkan* (40:1–8), He commands him to anoint the various parts of the *Mishkan* and thereby sanctify them (40:9–11). At this point, God commands Moses regarding the preparation of the priests, including bringing them to the door of the Tent of Meeting, washing them, dressing them and anointing them for divine service (40:12–15). None of this is mentioned in the "accomplishment" section! The following chart should illustrate the problem:

Moses' Task	Instructions	Performance
Assembly of structure and vessels.	40:1–8	40:17–33
Anointing and sanctification.	40:9–11	?
Preparation, anointing and sanctification of priests.	40:12–15	?

While much space is given to the physical arranging of the *Mishkan*, no mention is made of the procedures necessary for its actual operation. This leads to the following dilemma: If Moses did not carry out the commands of sanctification and priest-preparation at this point, why does the Torah emphasize that Moses did "according to all that God commanded him" (40:16)? Alternatively, if he did carry out the sanctification and priest preparation at this point, why does the Torah omit them from the "performance" narrative of chapter 40?

The mystery of the missing sanctification and priest-preparation accomplishment sections should help us uncover another problem with the structure and story line of chapter 40. Let us take a look at the first time that the Torah mentions priest preparation and arrangements for the daily functioning of the *Mishkan*.

Back in *Parashat Tetzaveh* the Torah detailed the process of *"miluim,"* the ordaining or consecration of Aaron and his sons. Besides involving various sacrifices over a seven-day period, the process of sanctification also involves Moses preparing Aaron and his sons in a very particular way (see 29:1). God commands Moses to bring them to the door of the Tent of Meeting, wash them, dress them and anoint them (29:4–9). In other words, here we have the identical instructions once again given in chapter 40 and omitted from the "accomplishment" section at the end of the book.

The lengthy instructions in chapter 29 – regarding the *miluim* process, the process of priest-preparation, sanctification and transition to daily operation of the *Mishkan* – end with the orders for daily sacrifices at the door of the Tent of Meeting and the following proclamation by God:

> This shall be a regular burnt offering throughout the generations, at the entrance of the Tent of Meeting before the Lord.... And there I will meet with the children of Israel, and it shall be sanctified by My Glory. And I will sanctify the Tent of Meeting, and the altar, and *Aaron* and his sons I will sanctify to serve Me. And I will dwell among the Israelites and I will be their God. And they shall know that I am the Lord their God who brought them out of Egypt, that I may dwell among them. (29:42–46)

Apparently, the presence of God in His house, the "dwelling of the Glory of God" in the Tent of Meeting, depends upon the daily functioning of the *Mishkan*. As a consequence of priestly activity and sacrifices, God's "Glory" appears at the entrance to the Tent of Meeting, sanctifies the tent, "meets" with the children of Israel and dwells amongst them. This constitutes the message of chapter 29.

In fact, chapters 8 and 9 of Leviticus, which recount the eventual accomplishment of *parashat miluim*, confirm this point. Chapter 8 describes the bringing of Aaron and his sons to the Tent of Meeting and the other details of priest-preparation and sanctuary sanctification (see 8:1–13). In completing the story, chapter 9 concludes with the appearance of the "Glory of God" in front of all the people at the entrance to the Tent of Meeting and God's fiery consumption of a sacrifice (9:23–24).

All of this should lead us to question our assumptions about the end of Exodus. Previously, it seemed obvious that section three of chapter 40, the filling of the newly erected *Mishkan* by the Glory of God (40:34–38), constituted the natural consequence and culmination of setting up the *Mishkan*. God's purpose in commanding the building of the *Mishkan* was to dwell amongst the Israelites (see 25:8). Alternatively, the event comprised an act of divine sanctification of the newly constructed sanctuary (Rashbam). However, as of now, all of this seems difficult. The meeting between God and Israel at the Tent of Meeting should take place at its entrance. The resting of His Glory upon the *Mishkan*, His revelation to the children of Israel and His sanctification of the *Mishkan* should take place in the context of priests and the transition to the daily functioning of the *Mishkan*. These are exactly the details omitted from the "accomplishment" section of chapter 40.

In other words, what is the purpose of the public divine revelation at the end of Exodus? If it is not about fulfilling the expectations of *parashat miluim* and the transition from preparation to operation, what is it about? If the theophany is not for the purpose of sanctifying and inaugurating the Tent of Meeting, what is the purpose of this unusual public revelation?

III. CONNECTING TO LEVITICUS AND NUMBERS

The solution to our dual problem, the problem of the missing priest-preparation and sanctification "performance" sections, and the problem of the nature of the divine revelation that closes Exodus, may lie in a close analysis of the literary structure of the third section of chapter 40. Previously, we defined this section as the public descent of the Divine Presence, and divine sanctification of the newly completed *Mishkan*.

The second half of this definition clearly needs some work. Let us return to the text.

> Then a cloud covered the *Mishkan* and the Glory of the Lord filled the *Mishkan*. And Moses was not able to enter the Tent of Meeting, because the cloud rested upon it, and the Glory of the Lord filled the *Mishkan*. And when the cloud rose from upon the *Mishkan*, the children of Israel went onward in their journeys; but if the cloud did not rise they did not set out until the day it rose. For the cloud of the Lord was upon the *Mishkan* by day, and fire by night, in the view of all the house of Israel throughout their journeys. (40:34–38)

As argued above, no mention is made of divine sanctification of the *Mishkan*. Moreover, in place of this "expected" sentence, we are informed of the strange fact that Moses could not enter the tent, an altogether unexpected situation (40:35).

To add to the perplexity, the Torah terminates its discussion of Moses, the *Mishkan* and the cloud situation on the day that the *Mishkan* was set up. In a radical shift of place, time and theme, the Torah digresses to another *Mishkan*-cloud context. It elaborates on the travel arrangements of the children of Israel during their wanderings in the desert. God signaled them to journey onwards by raising the cloud, which appeared to the eyes of Israel by day as cloud and by night as fire (see 40:36–38).

Realizing that these last three closing verses of Exodus are more appropriate for the story of "travel arrangements," the story of Numbers 9:15–23 that prefaces the Israelites' first journey from Sinai should highlight this point:

> And on the day the *Mishkan* was erected, the cloud covered the *Mishkan*, the Tent of the Testimony, and at evening there was upon the *Mishkan* the appearance of fire, until the morning. So it was always; the cloud covered it by day, and the appearance of fire by night. And when the cloud rose from upon the *Mishkan*, then the children of Israel journeyed, and in the place where the cloud

dwelled (*yishkon he'anan*), there the children of Israel encamped. (Num. 9:15–17)

Just as at the end of Exodus a cloud covered the *Mishkan* on the day it was erected (40:17, 34), so too according to Numbers 9:15, a cloud covered the *Mishkan* on the day it was erected. However, in Numbers, a story concerned with traveling, the ensuing discussion of the cloud and fire seen by the Israelites and the rising cloud signal constitutes a natural continuation of the reference to the cloud of the first day. By contrast, in Exodus, the cloud, fire and signal passages seem a strange digression, an inexplicable foreshadowing of a passage and journey that will not take place until deep into the book of Numbers.

Finally, a quick glance at the beginning of Leviticus should complement the argument above. Leviticus opens with God calling Moses:

And the Lord called to Moses, and spoke to him from the Tent of Meeting. (Lev. 1:1)

As pointed out by most commentaries (see Ibn Ezra and Seforno 1:1), God's unusual act of summoning Moses picks up on the fact that Moses was prevented from entering the Tent of Meeting at the very end of Exodus (40:35). Consequently, God summons Moses and invites him in (Ibn Ezra). If so, the last three verses of Exodus, the story of the cloud signal and vision of cloud and fire, constitute not just a shift in time and space, a foreshadowing of later events, but a parenthetical comment, a deliberate disruption in the flow of the text. What are we to make of this? Is the Torah attempting a literary flourish, a high note on which to finish the book?

In fact, this deliberate digression creates an intricate parallel between the end of Exodus and an earlier part of the book. Let us consider another ending in Exodus, the last verses in the story of Sinai.

And Moses went up onto the mountain and the cloud covered the mountain. And the Glory of the Lord dwelled upon Mount Sinai and the cloud covered it for six days; on the seventh day He called to Moses from the midst of the cloud. And the sight of the Glory of the Lord was like a devouring fire on the top of the mountain before the eyes of the children of Israel. And Moses went up onto the mountain, and Moses was on the mountain forty days and forty nights. (Ex. 24:15–18)

This last Sinai scene, Moses' ascent to receive "the tablets of stone, the Torah and commandments" (24:12), may be thought of as consisting of the following five elements:

1. Moses acts alone (see 24:12–15).
2. God's Glory embodied in a cloud covers the mountain and dwells upon it.
3. Moses is held back. He cannot enter and must await the divine summons.
4. God calls Moses, and Moses enters to be with God.
5. The children of Israel witness Sinai enveloped in cloud and fire.

The point should be relatively clear. These are the five elements present in our story, the seam between Exodus and Leviticus. Just as Moses acted alone at Sinai, so too he assembles the *Mishkan* seemingly unaided (see 40:17–33). Just as the cloud of God's Glory covered and dwelled upon the mountain, so too the cloud of God's Glory covered and dwelled in the *Mishkan* (40:34–35). Just as Moses was held back at Sinai, and only entered when called by God, so too here he cannot enter the area of God's Glory until summoned by God (40:38, Lev. 1:1). Finally, by virtue of the "digression" foreshadowing their travels, the children of Israel are depicted as seeing the *Mishkan* enveloped in cloud and fire, just as at Sinai.

All our questions about the structure and story line of the third section of chapter 40 should be answered. Moses' inability to enter the *Mishkan* should no longer surprise us, and the shift of the last three verses should no longer shock us. The Torah arranges the events and verses to remind us of Sinai. The book ends not with a mere literary flourish, but with a reminder of Sinai, a deliberate echoing of Moses' ascent to receive the stone tablets, Torah and commandments.

IV. THE *MISHKAN* AND SINAI

To close the circle, let us return to the questions raised earlier: the problem of the missing priest-preparation and sanctification "performance" sections, and the problem of the nature of the divine revelation that seals Exodus.

Hopefully, our analysis has uncovered the fact that the "dwelling" of the Divine Presence in the Tent of Meeting constitutes a complex and multifaceted phenomenon. On the one hand, it constitutes a means of immanent connection to God. Through the service of the priests, the sacrifices, the consumption of the sacrifices by signs of the Divine Presence, and the overall structure of the House of God, the *Mishkan* provides an almost material meeting between God and Israel. However, this is just one aspect. The "dwelling" of God's Glory and Presence in the *Mishkan*, or above the *Mishkan*, also constitutes a recreation of the experience at Sinai. As God "descended" to teach Torah and contract a covenant with Israel at Sinai, so too He "descends" to continue in an on-going fashion the teaching of Torah and the covenantal relationship. On both the psychological and metaphysical planes, the *Mishkan* provides a "portable" Sinai, an on-going experience and reminder of Sinai.

All of this should help us resolve our outstanding problems. Quite simply, the end of Exodus is concerned with *Mishkan* as Sinai rather than *Mishkan* as a place of meeting (entailing priests and sacrifices). As such, the end of Exodus is carefully structured to emphasize the Sinai-*Mishkan* parallel. Therefore, the last chapter of Exodus fails to mention the inauguration of the priests, the sanctification of the sanctuary and the transition to standard functioning. This is left for the book of Leviticus.

To close, I would argue that the emphasis on *Mishkan*-as-Sinai, i.e., communication and covenant, as opposed to *Mishkan*-as-sanctuary, i.e., a religious mechanism for meeting with God, comprised of priests, cult and atonement, constitutes a fitting end for Exodus. As Ramban famously emphasizes, the overarching theme of Exodus is redemption. However, redemption constitutes more than just a physical state. Not until the Israelites stood at Sinai, heard God's word and entered into a covenant with Him, were they both physically and spiritually redeemed. Hence, the end of Exodus, the Book of Redemption, harks back to Sinai and reminds us that the spiritual redemption of Sinai was not an isolated moment in time for the children of Israel. It was captured and continued in the *Mishkan*, the portable Sinai.

Contributors

Rav **Amnon Bazak** serves as a *Ram* in Yeshivat Har Etzion and teaches Tanach at Herzog College and at the SKA Beit Midrash for Women in Migdal Oz. He authored the two-volume *Nekudat Petiḥa* – short studies in *peshuto shel mikra*, and *Makbilot Nifgashot*, on literary parallels in the book of Samuel.

Rav **Yaakov Beasley** graduated Yeshiva University with a degree in Tanach and Jewish Education. He has taught Tanach in schools and programs in and around Jerusalem for the past fifteen years.

Rav **Ezra Bick** teaches Talmud and Jewish philosophy at Yeshivat Har Etzion, and is the Director of the Israel Koschitzky Virtual Beit Midrash. He is the author of *In His Mercy: Understanding the Thirteen Midot*.

Rav **Yoel Bin-Nun** studied at Yeshivat Merkaz HaRav and Yeshivat Har Etzion, where he was among the founders. He was Rosh Yeshiva of Yeshivat HaKibbutz HaDati, and currently teaches Bible and Jewish Philosophy in Herzog College.

Rav Mordechai Breuer *zt"l* taught at Yeshivat Har Etzion for over thirty years, where he trained a generation of younger scholars. He was the originator of the method of biblical interpretation known as *"shitat habehinot."* He authored two volumes of *Pirkei Moadot* (1986). Two volumes of his articles on Genesis (*Pirkei Bereshit*) appeared after his death, as well as a volume on the book of Isaiah.

Rav Yonatan Grossman studied in Yeshivat Har Etzion and received a doctorate in Bible from Bar-Ilan University. He has taught at the Yeshivat Har Etzion since 1998 and currently teaches Bible at Bar-Ilan University and Herzog College.

Rav Tamir Granot studied at Yeshivat Har Etzion and earned a doctorate in Jewish Philosophy from Bar-Ilan University. He teaches Talmud and Jewish Philosophy at Herzog College, and is the author of a VBM series on Jewish thought and the Holocaust.

Rav Nathaniel Helfgot is chair of the Tanach and Jewish Thought departments Yeshivat Chovevei Torah, and Rabbi of Congregation Netivot Shalom in Teaneck, NJ. He edited *Community, Covenant, and Committment: Selected Letters and Communications of Rabbi Joseph B. Soloveitchik.*

Rav Alex Israel has been teaching Tanach in Jerusalem *Yeshivot* and *Midrashot* for the past twenty years. He teaches at Yeshivat Eretz Hatzvi and is Director of Community education at the Pardes Institute. His book, *1 Kings: Torn in Two*, based on his VBM *shiurim*, is slated to be published in 2012.

Rav Yair Kahn is head of the Overseas Students Program and has been a *Ram* at Yeshivat Har Etzion since 1987. Rav Kahn is the editor of the *Shiurei HaGrid* series.

Rav Menachem Leibtag headed the Overseas Program at Yeshivat Har Etzion for over a decade. He initiated the Tanach Study Center, a comprehensive program for the study of Tanach on the Internet. He teaches Tanach at Yeshivat Har Etzion, Midreshet Lindenbaum and Yeshivat Sha'alvim.

Rav Aharon Lichtenstein is senior Rosh Yeshiva of Yeshivat Har Etzion, and the author of numerous works on Jewish Philosophy and Talmud.

Rav Mosheh Lichtenstein is Rosh Yeshiva of Yeshivat Har Etzion. He holds a degree in English Literature from Hebrew University, and is the author of *Moses: Envoy of God, Envoy of His People.*

Rav Yaakov Medan is Rosh Yeshiva at Yeshivat Har Etzion and teaches Tanach and Jewish Thought at Herzog College.

Rabbanit Sharon Rimon holds a master's degree in Bible from Matan Institute and Baltimore University. She teaches Tanach at the Women's Beit Midrash in Efrat.

Rav Yehuda Rock received his *semikha* from Rav Aharon Lichtenstein. He has taught in the Otniel *Hesder* Yeshiva, and was Rosh Kollel at the Boca Raton Community Kollel. He is the author of *Eved HaMelekh* on *Tzitzit* and *Tekhelet.*

Rav Mordechai Sabato studied at Yeshivat Har Etzion. He received his B.A. in Bible and Ph.D. from the Department of Talmud of the Hebrew University of Jerusalem. Dr. Sabato is presently a senior lecturer in the Department of Talmud at Bar-Ilan University and teaches Bible at Matan Jerusalem.

Rav Elchanan Samet has taught at Yeshivat Birkat Moshe (Maale Adumim) and currently is a senior lecturer at the Herzog Teacher's College. He is the author of two series of studies in *parashat hashavua* as well as *Pirkei Eliyahu, Pirkei Elisha,* and *Yad LaRambam.*

Rav Meir Spiegelman studied in Yeshivat Har Etzion. He has been teaching there for more than twenty-five years and has authored numerous articles on Tanach and Talmud.

Rav Moshe Taragin has been a *Ram* at Yeshivat Har Etzion since 1994. He has *semikha* from the Rabbi Isaac Elchanan Theological Seminary and an M.A. in English Literature from City University.

Rav Avraham Walfish received his B.A. from Yeshiva University, and his Ph.D. in Talmudic Literature from Hebrew University. He received *semikha* from Rav Zalman Neḥemiah Goldberg. Currently he teaches at Herzog College, at the *Hesder* yeshiva in Tekoah, and heads the M.Ed. program in Talmud and Jewish Thought at Jerusalem College for Women.

Rav Chanoch Waxman received *semikha* from Yeshiva University and holds Master's degrees in Jewish and General Philosophy. He has taught at Matan in Jerusalem and been the Rosh Kollel of the Torah Mitzion Kollel in Chicago. He currently teaches at Yeshivat HaMivtar.

Rav Zev Weitman studied in Yeshivat Har Etzion and Michlelet Herzog. He was the Rabbi of Kibbutz Kfar Etzion, and today serves as the Rav of the Tnuva Company. He is the author of *Likrat Shemitta Mamlakhtit BiMedinat Yisrael*.

The fonts used in this book are from the Arno family

*Other works in the Torah MiEtzion series
available from Maggid Books:*

Bereshit

Forthcoming books in the series:

Vayikra

Bemidbar

Devarim

*Maggid Books
The best of contemporary Jewish thought from
Koren Publishers Jerusalem*